Artificial Intelligence

Policy Perspectives and Global Impacts

New York

Computer Science, Technology and Applications Series

Big Data, Big Impact: Navigating Competition, Privacy, and Reform
Jessica Andrews (Editor)
ISBN: 979-8-89530-538-6
eBook ISBN: 979-8-89530-565-2

Blockchain Technology for Healthcare Applications: Challenges, Privacy, and Securing of Data
Ahmed J. Obaid, PhD,
Vinod Kumar Shukla, PhD,
Soumi Dutta, PhD,
Abhishek Bhattacharya, PhD,
and Satyajit Chakraborti, PhD
ISBN: 979-8-89530-132-6
eBook ISBN: 979-8-89530-359-7

Cognitive Connections: Unleashing the Potential of Interactive Technologies
Yogesh Kumar Rathore, PhD,
Shweta Bansal, PhD,
Suman Kumar Swarnkar, PhD,
Vishal Sharma, PhD,
and Saroj Pandey, PhD
ISBN: 979-8-89530-157-9
eBook ISBN: 979-8-89530-310-8

Thinking Machine
Ping Zhu
ISBN: 979-8-89530-203-3
eBook ISBN: 979-8-89530-274-3

Accessible Technology for People with Disabilities, Older Americans, and Veterans
Willis S. Roland (Editor)
ISBN: 979-8-89530-232-3
eBook ISBN: 979-8-89530-254-5

Cybersecurity: Improvements Needed, National Strategy, and Operational Technology
Sander T. Karlsen (Editor)
ISBN: 979-8-89530-101-2
eBook ISBN: 979-8-89530-201-9

Ensemble Machine Learning: Advances in Research and Applications
M. A. Jabbar, PhD,
Loveleen Gaur, PhD,
and Abdelkrim Haqiq, PhD
ISBN: 979-8-89530-004-6
eBook ISBN: 979-8-89530-088-6

More information about this series can be found at
https://novapublishers.com/product-category/series/computer-science-technology-and-applications/

Sonja Buckley
Editor

Artificial Intelligence

Policy Perspectives and Global Impacts

snova
New York

Library of Congress Cataloging-in-Publication Data

ISBN: 979-8-89530-859-2 (Hardcover)
ISBN: 979-8-89530-960-5 (eBook)

Published by Nova Science Publishers, Inc. † New York

Contents

Preface

Artificial intelligence (AI)—a term generally thought of as computerized systems that work and react in ways commonly thought to require intelligence—can encompass a range of technologies, methodologies, and application areas, such as natural language processing, facial recognition, and robotics. The concept of AI has existed for decades, with the term first being coined in the 1950s, followed by alternating periods of much development and lulls in activity and progress. A notable area of recent advancement has been in generative AI (GenAI), which refers to machine learning (ML) models developed through training on large volumes of data in order to generate content.

This book provides a brief background on AI technologies and recent advances, including in generative AI (GenAI); benefits and risks of AI tools; current federal laws addressing AI; and perspectives on regulating AI, It also provides an overview of AI in selected sectors.

Chapter 1

Artificial Intelligence: Overview, Recent Advances, and Considerations for the 118th Congress[*]

Laurie A. Harris

Abstract

Artificial intelligence (AI)—a term generally thought of as computerized systems that work and react in ways commonly thought to require intelligence—can encompass a range of technologies, methodologies, and application areas, such as natural language processing, facial recognition, and robotics. The concept of AI has existed for decades, with the term first being coined in the 1950s, followed by alternating periods of much development and lulls in activity and progress.

A notable area of recent advancement has been in generative AI (GenAI), which refers to machine learning (ML) models developed through training on large volumes of data in order to generate content. Technological advancements in the underlying models since 2017, combined with the open availability of these tools to the public in late 2022, have led to widespread use. The underlying models for GenAI tools have been described as "general-purpose AI," meaning they can be adapted to a wide range of downstream tasks. Such advancements, and the wide variety of applications for AI technologies, have renewed debates over appropriate uses and guardrails, including in the areas of health care, education, and national security.

AI technologies, including GenAI tools, have many potential benefits, such as accelerating and providing insights into data processing,

---

[*] This is an edited, reformatted and augmented version of Congressional Research Service, Publication No. R47644, dated August 4, 2023.

In: Artificial Intelligence
Editor: Sonja Buckley
ISBN: 979-8-89530-859-2

augmenting human decisionmaking, and optimizing performance for complex systems and tasks. GenAI tools, for example, are increasingly capable of performing a broad range of tasks, such as text analysis, image generation, and speech recognition. However, AI systems may perpetuate or amplify biases in the datasets on which they are trained; may not yet be able to fully explain their decisionmaking; and often depend on such vast amounts of data and other resources that they are not widely accessible for research, development, and commercialization beyond a handful of technology companies.

Numerous federal laws on AI have been enacted over the past few Congresses, either as standalone legislation or as AI-focused provisions in broader acts. These include the expansive National Artificial Intelligence Initiative Act of 2020 (Division E of P.L. 116-283), which included the establishment of an American AI Initiative and direction for AI research, development, and evaluation activities at federal science agencies. Additional acts have directed certain agencies to undertake activities to guide AI programs and policies across the federal government (e.g., the AI in Government Act of 2020, P.L. 116-260; and the Advancing American AI Act, Subtitle B of P.L. 117-263). In the 117th Congress, at least 75 bills were introduced that either focused on AI and ML or had AI/ML-focused provisions. Six of those were enacted.

In the 118th Congress, as of June 2023, at least 40 bills had been introduced that either focused on AI/ML or contained AI/ML-focused provisions, and none has been enacted. Collectively, bills in the 118th Congress address a range of topics, including federal government oversight of AI; training for federal employees; disclosure of AI use; export controls; use-specific prohibitions; and support for the use of AI in particular sectors, such as cybersecurity, weather modeling, wildfire detection, precision agriculture, and airport safety.

A primary consideration under debate in the United States and internationally is whether and how to regulate AI technologies. The European Union's draft Artificial Intelligence Act would broadly take a risk-based approach to regulatory requirements and prohibitions for certain uses. In the United States, previously introduced legislation has sought to require impact assessments and reporting for automated decision systems—including but not limited to AI systems—in critical areas (e.g., health care, employment, and criminal justice). Other perspectives on AI regulation have suggested a sector-specific approach with interagency coordination. A general concern for Congress might be how to approach AI regulatory efforts in a way that balances support for innovation and beneficial uses while minimizing current and future harms.

Additional considerations for the 118th Congress might include whether the current federal government mechanisms are sufficient for AI oversight and policymaking, the role of the federal government in supporting AI research and development, the potential impact of AI technologies on the workforce, disclosure of AI use, testing and validation of AI systems, and potential ways to support the development of trustworthy and responsible AI.

Introduction

As the use of artificial intelligence (AI) has grown across a wide range of sectors, so too have strategies to influence the growth of AI and mitigate potential risks. This report provides a brief background on AI technologies and recent advances, including in generative AI (GenAI); benefits and risks of AI tools; current federal laws addressing AI; perspectives on regulating AI; and selected other considerations for the 118th Congress. This report also provides an overview of AI in selected sectors; however, it does not attempt to address all applications of AI. Information on the application of AI technologies in additional sectors can be found in separate CRS products.[1]

Artificial Intelligence Background and History

AI can generally be thought of as computerized systems that work and react in ways commonly thought to require intelligence, such as the ability to learn, solve problems, and achieve goals under uncertain and varying conditions, with varying levels of autonomy. AI is not one thing; rather, AI systems can encompass a range of methodologies and application areas, such as natural language processing, robotics, and facial recognition.

Common terms used in the field of AI include machine learning (ML), deep learning (DL), and neural networks. ML, often referred to as a subfield of AI, examines how to build computer programs that automatically improve their performance at some task, through experience, without relying on explicit rules-based programming to do so.[2] One of the goals of ML is to teach

---

[1] For example, additional products cover AI in consumer lending, defense, and copyright law. See CRS In Focus IF12399, *Automation, Artificial Intelligence, and Machine Learning in Consumer Lending*, by Cheryl R. Cooper; CRS Report R46458, *Emerging Military Technologies: Background and Issues for Congress*, by Kelley M. Sayler; and CRS Legal Sidebar LSB10922, *Generative Artificial Intelligence and Copyright Law*, by Christopher T. Zirpoli.

[2] Adapted from Erik Brynjolfsson, Tom Mitchell, and Daniel Rock, "What Can Machines Learn, and What Does It Mean for Occupations and the Economy?," *AEA Papers and*

algorithms to successfully interpret data that have not previously been encountered. DL systems learn from large amounts of data to subsequently recognize and classify related, but previously unobserved, data. Neural networks, a type of DL often described as being loosely modeled after the human brain, consist of thousands or millions of processing nodes (i.e., computational units). DL approaches have been used in systems across many areas of AI research, from autonomous vehicles to voice recognition technologies.[3]

Historically, there has been debate over which technologies should be classified as AI. For example, robotic process automation (RPA) has been described as the use of rules-based software to automate highly repetitive, routine tasks normally performed by knowledge workers.[4] Because it automates activities performed by humans, it is often described as an AI technology. However, some argue that RPA is not AI because it does not include a learning component. Others discuss RPA as a basic tool that can be combined with AI to create complex process automation, or intelligent process automation, along an "intelligent automation continuum."[5]

The term *artificial intelligence* was coined at the Dartmouth Summer Research Project on Artificial Intelligence, a conference proposed in 1955 and held the following year.[6] Since that time, the field of AI has gone through what some have termed summers and winters—periods of much research and advancement followed by lulls in activity and progress. The reasons for the AI winters have included a focus on theory over practical applications, research problems being more difficult than anticipated, and limitations of the technologies of the time. Much of the current progress and research in AI, which began around 2010, has been attributed to the availability of large

---

Proceedings, vol. 108 (May 1, 2018), pp. 43-47, https://dspace.mit.edu/bitstream/handle/1721.1/120302/pandp.20181019.pdf.

[3] Larry Hardesty, "Explained: Neural Networks," *Massachusetts Institute of Technology (MIT) News*, April 14, 2017, http://news.mit.edu/2017/explained-neural-networks-deep-learning-0414.

[4] For more information, see IBM, "What Is Robotic Process Automation (RPA)?," https://www.ibm.com/topics/rpa.

[5] IBM Global Business Services, "Using Artificial Intelligence to Optimize the Value of Robotic Process Automation," September 2017, at https://www.ibm.com/downloads/cas/KDKAAK29.

[6] See J. McCarthy et al., "A Proposal for the Dartmouth Summer Research Project on Artificial Intelligence," August 31, 1955, http://www-formal.stanford.edu/jmc/history/dartmouth/dartmouth.html.

datasets (i.e., big data), improved ML approaches and algorithms, and more powerful computers.[7]

Recent Artificial Intelligence Advances

One of the most notable areas of advancement in AI has been in GenAI models and applications, such as ChatGPT.[8] *GenAI* refers to ML models developed through training on large volumes of data in order to generate content. ChatGPT is an AI chatbot[9] from a company called OpenAI, underpinned by a type of AI called a large language model (LLM).[10] LLMs are trained on massive amounts of data, largely collected from public internet sites. When a user provides a prompt, usually a text prompt, the model can generate words or paragraphs with human-like quality. Other models can create different types of outputs from text prompts, such as images, music, videos, and computer code. GenAI models work to match the style and appearance of the underlying data, and they have shown what has been called "capability overhang," meaning hidden capabilities of AI systems that researchers have not uncovered or thought to test for yet. While GenAI tools are not new, recent advances—particularly since the introduction of the transformer architecture[11] in 2017 and improvements in "generative pre-trained transformer" (GPT) models since 2019—combined with the open availability to the public of these tools (2022) have led to widespread use.

---

[7] Executive Office of the President, National Science and Technology Council, Committee on Technology, *Preparing for the Future of Artificial Intelligence*, October 2016, pp. 5-6. For additional information on these factors and a short history of AI, see also the appendix of Peter Stone et al., "Artificial Intelligence and Life in 2030," *One Hundred Year Study on Artificial Intelligence: Report of the 2015-2016 Study Panel*, Stanford University, September 2016, http://ai100.stanford.edu/2016-report.

[8] For more information on GenAI, see CRS In Focus IF12426, *Generative Artificial Intelligence: Overview, Issues, and Questions for Congress*, by Laurie A. Harris.

[9] An AI chatbot is a computer program that uses AI to interpret user questions and generate automated responses.

[10] AI chatbots from other companies include Bard from Google and Claude from Anthropic.

[11] Transformer models process a sequence of whole sentences (rather than analyzing word by word), which helps them to "remember" past information. They use mathematical techniques called *attention* or *self-attention* to detect how data elements, even when far away sequentially, influence and depend on each other. These methods make GPT models faster to train, more efficient in understanding context, and highly scalable. See Ashish Vaswani et al., "Attention Is All You Need," 31st Conference on Neural Information Processing Systems, Long Beach, CA, 2017, https://papers.nips.cc/paper/2017/file/3f5ee243547dee91fbd053c1c4a845aa-Paper.pdf.

Various measures may be used to assess the state of development and impacts of AI technologies, such as research and development (R&D) activities, technical performance of AI systems against established benchmarks, education and employment of AI experts, adoption of AI tools by public and private sector entities, and the development of AI policies and governance models in the United States and other countries. The annual AI Index report, led by a steering committee at Stanford University, is a prominent example of an attempt to quantify and collate such measures. The 2023 AI Index report, released in April 2023, noted that "AI continued to post state-of-the-art results, but year-over-year improvement on many benchmarks continues to be marginal" while also highlighting that "AI models are starting to rapidly accelerate scientific progress," being used in 2022, for example, to aid hydrogen fusion work and generate new antibodies for use in medical therapies.[12]

Benefits and Potential Risks of Artificial Intelligence Technologies

AI technologies and services hold the potential to both be beneficial in a number of sectors and pose a number of societal risks. Broadly, AI technologies can accelerate and provide insights into data processing, augment human decisionmaking, optimize performance for complex tasks and systems, and improve safety for people in dangerous occupations. In medicine, for example, AI technologies that can rapidly and accurately predict protein structures, such as AlphaFold from DeepMind and ESMFold from Meta, can aid researchers in understanding how diseases work and creating new drugs to treat them.[13] Large-scale GenAI models are capable of an increasingly broad range of tasks, from text manipulation and analysis, to image generation, to unprecedentedly good speech recognition. These systems demonstrate capabilities in question answering and the generation of text, image, and code

[12] Nestor Maslej et al., *The AI Index 2023 Annual Report*, AI Index Steering Committee, Institute for Human-Centered AI, Stanford University, April 2023, p. 73, https://aiindex.stanford.edu/wp-content/uploads/2023/04/HAI_AI-Index-Report_2023.pdf.

[13] Melissa Heikkila and Will Douglas Heaven, "What's Next for AI," *MIT Technology Review*, December 23, 2022, https://www.technologyreview.com/2022/12/23/1065852/whats-next-for-ai/.

unimagined a decade ago, and they outperform the state of the art on many benchmarks, old and new.[14]

However, AI systems may perpetuate or amplify biases contained in the datasets that they are trained on, may not yet be fully able to explain their decisionmaking, and often depend on vast datasets that are not widely accessible to facilitate R&D. Together, such challenges can lead to an inability to fully assess and understand the operations and outputs of AI systems—sometimes referred to as the "black box" problem. Large-scale models are prone to generating false content—sometimes called "hallucinating"—and are routinely biased, as they are largely trained on data scraped from the internet and therefore reflect the human biases expressed there.

Stakeholders have questioned the adequacy of current laws and regulations for dealing with societal and ethical issues that may arise with the continued development and broad application of AI.[15] Further, stakeholders have raised concerns about potential job losses from AI automation and questioned the adequacy of human capital in both the public and private sectors to develop and work with AI.[16]

Artificial Intelligence Technologies in Selected Sectors

AI technologies have potential applications across a wide range of sectors. A selection of broad, crosscutting issues with application-specific examples of ongoing congressional interest are discussed in the CRS report *Artificial Intelligence: Background, Selected Issues, and Policy Considerations*.[17] Those issues and examples include implications for the U.S. workforce, international competition and federal investment in AI R&D, standards

[14] Maslej et al., *The AI Index 2023 Annual Report*, "Introduction to the AI Index Report 2023," p. 2.

[15] See, for example, Anton Korinek, "Why We Need a New Agency to Regulate Advanced Artificial Intelligence: Lessons on AI Control from the Facebook Files," Brookings Institution, December 8, 2021, https://www.brookings.edu/research/why-we-need-a-new-agency-to-regulate-advanced-artificial-intelligence-lessons-on-ai-control-from-the-facebook-files/.

[16] See, for example, European Commission and the U.S. Council of Economic Advisors, *The Impact of Artificial Intelligence on the Future of Workforces in the European Union and the United States of America*, December 5, 2022, https://www.whitehouse.gov/wp-content/uploads/2022/12/TTC-EC-CEA-AI-Report-12052022-1.pdf.

[17] CRS Report R46795, *Artificial Intelligence: Background, Selected Issues, and Policy Considerations*, by Laurie A. Harris.

development, and ethical AI—including questions about bias, fairness, and algorithm transparency (for example, in criminal justice applications).

In addition to those issues and applications, three areas of potential use that may be of growing interest to Congress—particularly in light of the advances in, and widespread availability of, GenAI tools—are health care, education, and national security. In other parts of the federal government, experts have asserted a need to understand the impacts and future directions of AI applications in these areas. For example, the chief AI officer at the Department of Health and Human Services, Greg Singleton, at a June 2023 Health Innovation Summit discussed "the role that AI will play in health care, as well as the importance of regulations."[18] A May 2023 Department of Education report, *Artificial Intelligence and the Future of Teaching and Learning*, describes the rising interest in AI in education and highlights reasons to address AI in education now.[19] And the 2023 *Annual Threat Assessment of the U.S. Intelligence Community* states, "New technologies—particularly in the fields of AI and biotechnology—are being developed and are proliferating faster than companies and governments can shape norms, protect privacy, and prevent dangerous outcomes."[20] This section will discuss some of the potential benefits and concerns with the use of AI technologies in these sectors.

Health Care

Numerous companies and researchers have been developing and testing AI technologies for use in health care—for example, to improve the drug development process by increasing efficiency and decreasing time and cost,[21]

---

[18] Jose Rascon, "HHS CAIO: AI's Impact on Healthcare Sector Still to Be Determined," *Meritalk*, June 8, 2023, https://meritalk.com/articles/hhs-caio-ais-impact-on-healthcare-sector-still-to-be-determined/.

[19] Department of Education, Office of Educational Technology, *Artificial Intelligence and the Future of Teaching and Learning: Insights and Recommendations*, May 2023, pp. 1-3, https://tech.ed.gov/files/2023/05/ai-future-of-teaching-and-learning-report.pdf.

[20] Office of the Director of National Intelligence (ODNI), *Annual Threat Assessment of the U.S. Intelligence Community*, February 6, 2023, p. 26, https://www.odni.gov/files/ODNI/documents/assessments/ATA-2023-Unclassified-Report.pdf.

[21] U.S. Government Accountability Office (GAO), *Artificial Intelligence in Health Care: Benefits and Challenges of Machine Learning in Drug Development*, GAO-20-215, January 31, 2020, https://www.gao.gov/products/gao-20-215sp.

to detect diseases earlier, and to more consistently analyze medical data.[22] A 2022 report by the Government Accountability Office identified a variety of ML-based technologies to assist with the diagnostic processes for five selected diseases—certain cancers, diabetic retinopathy (an eye condition that can cause blindness in diabetic patients), Alzheimer's disease, heart disease, and COVID-19—though these ML technologies have generally not been widely adopted.[23] Some hospitals have also experimented with using voice recognition, and associated ML and natural language processing technology, to assist doctors and patients.[24]

While there are many encouraging developments for using AI technologies in health care, stakeholders have remarked on the slow progress in using AI broadly within health care settings, and various challenges remain. Researchers and clinicians have raised questions about the accuracy, security, and privacy of these technologies; the availability of sufficient health data on which to train systems; medical liability in the event of adverse outcomes; the adequacy of current user consent processes; and patient access and receptivity.[25] These questions reflect the potential risks from using AI systems. For example, a poorly designed system might lead to misdiagnosis; systems trained on biased data can reflect or amplify those biases in their outputs; and if a flawed AI system is adopted widely, it might result in widespread injury to patients.[26]

---

[22] GAO, *Artificial Intelligence in Healthcare: Benefits and Challenges of Machine Learning Technologies for Medical Diagnostics*, GAO-22-104629, September 29, 2022, https://www.gao.gov/products/gao-22-104629.

[23] Ibid.

[24] Ruth Hailu, "5 Burning Questions About Deploying Voice Recognition Technology in Health Care," *STAT News*, July 10, 2019, https://www.statnews.com/2019/07/10/5-questions-voice-recognition-technology/.

[25] Hailu, "5 Burning Questions;" and Lauren Joseph, "5 Burning Questions About Using Artificial Intelligence to Prevent Blindness," *STAT News*, July 17, 2019, https://www.statnews.com/2019/07/17/artificial-intelligence-to-prevent-blindness/.

[26] Alvin Powell, "AI Revolution in Medicine," *Harvard Gazette*, November 11, 2020, https://news.harvard.edu/gazette/ story/2020/11/risks-and-benefits-of-an-ai-revolution-in-medicine/; and W. Nicholson Price, "Risks and Remedies for Artificial Intelligence in Health Care," Brookings Institution, November 14, 2019, https://www.brookings.edu/articles/risks-and-remedies-for-artificial-intelligence-in-health-care/.

Education

According to the U.S. Department of Education, AI, ML, and related technologies "will have powerful impacts on learning, not only through direct supports for students, but also by empowering educators to be more adaptive to learner needs and less consumed by routine, repetitive tasks."[27] The report also notes that AI in education presents risks, including apprehension from parents and educators and the potential for AI algorithms to be biased, possibly leading to unfair decisions about what or how a student should learn.[28]

The rapid development of AI chatbots and the public release of ChatGPT in November 2022 have spurred debate among teachers and education administrators. Some teachers have begun using these AI tools in their classrooms, highlighting benefits such as making lessons more interactive, aiding the development of critical thinking skills, teaching students media literacy, generating personalized lesson plans, saving teachers time on administration, and aiding students whose first language is not English.[29] Others have raised concerns about students using the systems to cheat on assignments by writing essays and taking tests for them, with some school systems banning the use of chatbots on their networks.[30] Numerous researchers and companies have been developing and deploying detection tools to identify text generated by AI, though there remain issues with the accuracy of these tools.[31] Stakeholders have also raised concerns about data privacy risks, including, for example, whether information shared or stored in AI-enabled systems is used for further product training without gaining explicit user consent and, more broadly, whether such systems are subject to federal or state privacy laws, such as the Family Educational Rights and Privacy Act.[32]

---

[27] Department of Education, Office of Educational Technology, "Artificial Intelligence," https://tech.ed.gov/ai/.

[28] Ibid.

[29] Will Douglas Heaven, "ChatGPT Is Going to Change Education, Not Destroy It," *MIT Technology Review*, April 6, 2023, https://www.technologyreview.com/2023/04/06/1071059/chatgpt-change-not-destroy-education-openai/.

[30] Dan Rosenzweig-Ziff, "New York City Blocks Use of the ChatGPT Bot in Its Schools," *Washington Post*, January 5, 2023, https://www.washingtonpost.com/education/2023/01/05/nyc-schools-ban-chatgpt/.

[31] Geoffrey A. Fowler, "We Tested a New ChatGPT-Detector for Teachers. It Flagged an Innocent Student," *Washington Post*, April 3, 2023, https://www.washingtonpost.com/technology/2023/04/01/chatgpt-cheating-detection-turnitin/.

[32] See, for example, Department of Education, Office of Educational Technology, *Artificial Intelligence and the Future of Teaching and Learning*, pp. 32-33.

National Security

AI technologies have a wide range of national security applications, including intelligence, surveillance, and reconnaissance; logistics; cyber operations; command and control; semi-autonomous and autonomous vehicles; and weapons systems.[33] Since at least 2017, the U.S. military has begun integrating AI systems into combat systems and discussing AI as a key technology to ensure future warfighting capabilities.[34] At the same time, other countries, including China and Russia, have released national plans and statements of intent to lead in the development of AI technologies.[35]

The Department of Defense's (DOD's) unclassified investments in AI have grown from just over $600 million in FY2016 to approximately $1.1 billion in FY2023, with DOD maintaining over 685 active AI projects.[36] DOD has an AI strategy, which outlines the following aims: delivering AI-enabled capabilities for key missions; partnering with leading private sector technology companies, academia, and global allies; cultivating a leading AI workforce; and leading in military ethics and AI safety.[37] The intelligence community (IC) has also released a strategy for using AI—the AIM

---

[33] For more information on AI and national security considerations for Congress, see CRS Report R45178, *Artificial Intelligence and National Security*, by Kelley M. Sayler; and CRS Report R46458, *Emerging Military Technologies: Background and Issues for Congress*, by Kelley M. Sayler.

[34] Department of Defense, *Summary of the 2018 National Defense Strategy*, p. 3, https://dod.defense.gov/Portals/1/Documents/pubs/2018-National-Defense-Strategy-Summary.pdf; and Marcus Weisgerber, "The Pentagon's New Algorithmic Warfare Cell Gets Its First Mission: Hunt ISIS," *Defense One*, May 14, 2017, http://www.defenseone.com/technology/2017/05/pentagons-new-algorithmic-warfare-cell-gets-its-first-mission-hunt-isis/137833/.

[35] China State Council, "A Next Generation Artificial Intelligence Development Plan," July 20, 2017, translated by New America, https://www.newamerica.org/documents/1959/translation-fulltext-8.1.17.pdf; and Tom Simonite, "For Superpowers, Artificial Intelligence Fuels New Global Arms Race," *Wired*, August 8, 2017, https://www.wired.com/story/for-superpowers-artificial-intelligence-fuels-new-global-arms-race.

[36] The amount listed as the FY2023 investment reflects DOD's FY2023 unclassified budget request for AI. DOD's actual investments in AI in FY2023 may be higher. Office of the Under Secretary of Defense (Comptroller)/Chief Financial Officer, *Defense Budget Overview: United States Department of Defense Fiscal Year 2023 Budget Request*, April 2022, p. 4-7, https://comptroller.defense.gov/Portals/45/Documents/defbudget/FY2023/FY2023_Budget_Request_Overview_Book.pdf; and GAO, *Artificial Intelligence: Status of Developing and Acquiring Capabilities for Weapon Systems*, GAO-22-104965, February 2022, https://www.gao.gov/assets/gao-22-104765.pdf.

[37] DOD, *Summary of the 2018 Department of Defense Artificial Intelligence Strategy*, 2018, https://media.defense.gov/2019/Feb/12/2002088963/-1/-1/1/SUMMARY-OF-DOD-AI-STRATEGY.PDF.

Initiative—as well as AI ethics principles and an AI ethics framework for the IC.[38] While AI holds to potential to assist the IC in its work, AI systems also "pose grave security challenges for which [the United States is] currently unprepared, including the development of novel cyber weapons, large-scale disinformation attacks, and the design of advanced biological weapons."[39]

Artificial Intelligence Laws and Legislation

Current Federal Laws Addressing Artificial Intelligence

Federal laws addressing AI or including AI-focused provisions have been enacted over the past few Congresses. Arguably the most expansive law was the National Artificial Intelligence Initiative (NAII) Act of 2020 (Division E of the William M. (Mac) Thornberry National Defense Authorization Act [NDAA] of FY2021, P.L. 116-283). The NAII Act included sections

- codifying the establishment of an American AI Initiative,
- establishing a National Artificial Intelligence Initiative Office to support federal AI activities,
- establishing an interagency committee at the Office of Science and Technology Policy to coordinate federal programs and activities in support of the NAII, and
- establishing a National AI Advisory Committee.

The NAII Act further directed AI activities at the National Science Foundation (NSF), National Institute of Standards and Technology (NIST),[40]

---

[38] ODNI, *The AIM Initiative: a Strategy for Augmenting Intelligence Using Machines* , January 16, 2019, https://www.dni.gov/files/ODNI/documents/AIM-Strategy.pdf; ODNI, *Principles of Artificial Intelligence Ethics for the Intelligence Community*, https://www.intelligence.gov/principles-of-artificial-intelligence-ethics-for-the-intelligence-community; and ODNI, *Artificial Intelligence Ethics Framework for the Intelligence Community*, June 2020, https://www.intelligence.gov/artificial-intelligence-ethics-framework-for-the-intelligence-community.

[39] Written testimony of Jason Matheny, President and CEO, RAND Corporation, in Senate Committee on Homeland Security and Governmental Affairs, *Artificial Intelligence: Risks and Opportunities*, hearing, March 8, 2023, https://www.hsgac.senate.gov/hearings/artificial-intelligence-risks-and-opportunities/testimony-matheny-2023-03-08/.

[40] Included in the direction to NIST was development of a risk management framework for trustworthy AI systems, which was released in January 2023. See NIST, *AI Risk*

National Oceanic and Atmospheric Administration, and Department of Energy. Specific provisions include mandating (1) NSF support for a network of National AI Research Institutes; (2) a National Academies of Sciences, Engineering, and Medicine study on the current and future impact of AI on the U.S. workforce across sectors;[41] and (3) a task force to investigate the feasibility of, and plan for, a National AI Research Resource.[42]

Individual agencies—including the General Services Administration (GSA), the Office of Management and Budget (OMB), and the Office of Personnel Management (OPM)—have also been statutorily directed to undertake activities to support the use of AI across the federal government:

- *GSA*. The AI in Government Act of 2020 (AGA, Division U, Title I, of the Consolidated Appropriations Act, 2021, P.L. 116-260) created within GSA an AI Center of Excellence to facilitate the adoption of AI technologies in the federal government and collect and publicly publish information regarding federal programs, pilots, and other initiatives.[43]
- *OMB*. The AGA required OMB to issue a memorandum to federal agencies regarding the development of AI policies; approaches for removing barriers to using AI technologies; and best practices for identifying, assessing, and mitigating any discriminatory impact or bias and any unintended consequences of using AI. The Advancing American AI Act (Subtitle B of the James M. Inhofe National Defense Authorization Act for Fiscal Year 2023, P.L. 117-263) required OMB to (1) incorporate additional considerations when developing guidance for the use of AI in the federal government; (2) develop an initial means to ensure that contracts for acquiring AI address privacy, civil rights and liberties, and the protection of government data and information; (3) require the head of each federal

---

Management Framework (AI RMF 1.0), January 26, 2023, https://doi.org/10.6028/NIST.AI.100-1.

[41] National Academies of Sciences, Engineering, and Medicine, "Automation and the U.S. Workforce: An Update," study overview, https://www.nationalacademies.org/our-work/automation-and-the-us-workforce-an-update. According to the project website, the study is currently ongoing, and the final report has not yet been released.

[42] The National AI Research Resource Task Force released its final report, *Strengthening and Democratizing the U.S. Artificial Intelligence Innovation Ecosystem: An Implementation Plan for a National Artificial Intelligence Research Resource*, in January 2023 at https://www.ai.gov/wp-content/uploads/2023/01/NAIRR-TF-Final-Report-2023.pdf.

[43] The act codified the GSA AI Center of Excellence that was launched in 2019. See https://www.ai.gov/legislation-and-executive-orders/.

agency (except DOD) to prepare and maintain an inventory of current and planned AI use cases; and (4) lead a pilot program to initiate four new AI use case applications to support interagency or intra-agency modernization initiatives. Additionally, the AI Training Act (P.L. 117-207) required OMB to establish an AI training program for the acquisition workforce of executive agencies.

- *OPM.* The AGA required OPM to establish or update an occupational job series to include positions with primary duties in AI and to estimate current and future numbers of federal employment positions related to AI at each agency.

NDAAs have also included provisions focused on AI in the defense, national security, and intelligence communities each year beginning with the FY2019 John S. McCain NDAA, which included the first definition of AI in federal statute.[44] These provisions have included a focus on AI development, acquisition, and policies; AI data repositories; recruiting and retaining personnel in AI; and implementation of recommendations from the 2021 final report of the National Security Commission on AI.[45]

Additionally, some enacted legislation has focused on AI R&D or the use of AI in particular federal programs. For example:

- The CHIPS and Science Act (P.L. 117-167) included numerous AI-related provisions directing the Department of Energy, NIST, and NSF to support AI and ML R&D activities and the development of technical standards and guidelines related to safe and trustworthy AI systems. NSF was further directed to (1) evaluate the establishment of an AI scholarship-for-service program to recruit and train AI professionals to support AI work in federal, state, local, and tribal governments; and (2) study AI research capacity at U.S. institutions of higher education.
- The Countering Human Trafficking Act of 2021 (P.L. 117-322) provided statutory authority for the Department of Homeland Security's (DHS's) Center for Countering Human Trafficking (CCHT) and required the CCHT director to develop a strategy and proposal to modify systems and processes throughout DHS that are

---

[44] P.L. 115-232, §238; 10 U.S.C. §2358 note.

[45] National Security Commission on AI, *Final Report*, 2021, https://www.nscai.gov/2021-final-report/.

related to CCHT's mission in order to, among other things, provide AI and ML to increase system capabilities and enhance data availability, reliability, comparability, and verifiability.

- The Identifying Outputs of Generative Adversarial Networks Act (P.L. 116-258) directed NSF and NIST to support research on generative adversarial networks (GANs), including research on manipulated or synthesized content and information authenticity and the development of measurements and standards necessary to accelerate the development of technical tools to examine the function and outputs of GANs.

Federal AI Legislation Introduced in the 117th and 118th Congresses

In addition to the enacted legislation, numerous bills for which AI or ML technologies were the main focus, or that had at least one provision focused on AI/ML, were introduced in the 117th Congress and have been introduced in the 118th Congress in both the Senate and the House of Representatives.[46]

In the 117th Congress, a search of Congress.gov for all the subject legislation resulted in 235 bills, six of which were enacted into law.[47] Of those, CRS identified 34 bills that have a main focus on AI/ML (six of which are identical bills). Additionally, CRS identified 41 pieces of legislation that include provisions related to AI/ML (19 of which were identical bills or had nearly identical AI/ML-related provisions). Collectively, the introduced and enacted legislation addressed many AI/ML-related topics, including federal planning and coordination; research and education investment; job displacement and workforce retraining; commercial technology use; ethics, bias, and algorithm accountability; government efficiency and cost savings; and health care, defense, national security, and intelligence applications and activities.

In the 118th Congress, a search of Congress.gov as of June 2023 resulted in 94 bills, none of which has been enacted.[48] Of those bills, CRS identified

---

[46] Legislation that only mentions the terms *artificial intelligence* or *machine learning* was also introduced, but those bills are not discussed in this report (e.g., if AI/ML is included in a broader list of technologies or research topics, or AI/ML is only mentioned in the bill's findings or sense of Congress).

[47] Based on search results of Congress.gov as of January 11, 2023.

[48] Based on search results of Congress.gov as of June 23, 2023. CRS searched Congress.gov for legislation in the 118th Congress that included the term *artificial intelligence*, *machine learning*, or *facial recognition* in the text or title.

22 pieces of legislation that have a main focus on AI/ML (of which six were identical bills) and 18 with provisions related to AI/ML (of which 12 were identical or have nearly identical relevant provisions). Collectively, the legislation addresses a range of topics, including

- oversight of the federal government's approach to AI governance and regulation;
- AI training for federal employees;
- requirements for federal agencies and the private sector to disclose the use of GenAI broadly and the use of AI in certain contexts, such as political advertisements;
- assessing export controls for national interest technologies, including AI, to the People's Republic of China;
- prohibiting the use of AI in certain contexts (e.g., decisionmaking for the use of nuclear weapons, biometric surveillance, and workplace surveillance); and
- support for the use of AI in various areas, including cybersecurity, classification and declassification systems, advanced weather modeling, wildfire detection, airport efficiency and safety, precision agriculture, and prescribing certain pharmaceuticals.

Perspectives on Regulating Artificial Intelligence

As the use of AI technologies has grown, so too have discussions of whether and how to regulate them. Internationally, the European Union has proposed the Artificial Intelligence Act (AIA),[49] which would create regulatory oversight for the development and use of a wide range of AI applications, with requirements varying by risk category, from banning systems with "unacceptable risk" to allowing free use of those with minimal or no risk.[50] In

---

Legislation that only briefly mentioned the terms was excluded (e.g., if one of the terms is included in a broader list of technologies or research topics or only mentioned in the bill's findings or sense of Congress).

[49] European Commission, *Proposal for a Regulation of the European Parliament and the Council Laying Down Harmonized Rules on Artificial Intelligence (Artificial Intelligence Act) and Amending Certain Union Legislative Acts*, April 21, 2021, https://eur-lex.europa.eu/resource.html?uri=cellar:e0649735-a372-11eb-9585-01aa75ed71a1.0001.02/DOC_1&format=PDF.

[50] See European Commission, "Regulatory Framework Proposal on Artificial Intelligence," https://digital-strategy.ec.europa.eu/en/policies/regulatory-framework-ai.

one recently passed version of the AIA, the European Parliament agreed to changes that included a ban on the use of AI in biometric surveillance and a requirement for GenAI systems to disclose that the outputs are AI-generated.[51] In the United States, legislation such as the Algorithmic Accountability Act of 2022 (H.R. 6850 and S. 3572, 117th Congress) would have directed the Federal Trade Commission to require certain organizations to perform impact assessments of automated decision systems—including those using ML and AI—and augmented critical decision processes. Some researchers have noted that these proposals "spring from widely different political contexts and legislative traditions."[52] The United States has yet to enact legislation to broadly regulate AI, and the AIA now enters a trilogue negotiation among representatives of the three main institutions of the EU (Parliament, Commission, and Council).[53] Depending on the final negotiated text of the AIA, the EU and United States might begin to align or diverge on AI regulation, as discussed by researchers.[54]

Rather than broad regulation of AI technologies that could be used across sectors, some stakeholders have suggested a more targeted approach, regulating the use of AI technologies in particular sectors. The federal government has taken steps over the past few years to evaluate AI regulation in this way. In November 2020, in response to Executive Order 13859, "Maintaining American Leadership in Artificial Intelligence," OMB released a memorandum to the heads of federal agencies providing guidance for regulatory and nonregulatory oversight of AI applications developed and deployed outside of the federal government.[55] The memorandum laid out 10

---

[51] Spencer Feingold, "The European Union's Artificial Intelligence Act—Explained," World Economic Forum, June 30, 2023, https://www.weforum.org/agenda/2023/06/european-union-ai-act-explained/.

[52] Jakob Mokander et al., "The US Algorithmic Accountability Act of 2022 vs. the EU Artificial Intelligence Act: What Can They Learn from Each Other?," *Minds and Machines*, vol. 32 (August 2022), pp. 751-758, https://link.springer.com/article/10.1007/s11023-022-09612-y.

[53] For more information on the EU structure, see CRS In Focus IF11211, *The European Parliament and U.S. Interests*, by Kristin Archick; and James McBride, "How Does the European Union Work?," Council on Foreign Relations, updated March 11, 2022, https://www.cfr.org/backgrounder/how-does-european-union-work.

[54] See for example Alex Engler, "The EU and U.S. Are Starting to Align on AI Regulation," Brookings Institution, February 1, 2022, https://www.brookings.edu/blog/techtank/2022/02/01/the-eu-and-u-s-are-starting-to-align-on-ai-regulation/; Alex Engler, "The EU and U.S. Diverge on AI Regulation: A Transatlantic Comparison and Steps to Alignment," Brookings Institution, April 25, 2023, https://www.brookings.edu/articles/the-eu-and-us-diverge-on-ai-regulation-a-transatlantic-comparison-and-steps-to-alignment/.

[55] Russell Vought, Director, OMB, "Guidance for Regulation of Artificial Intelligence Applications," November 17, 2020, https://www.whitehouse.gov/wp-content/uploads/2020/11/M-21-06.pdf.

principles for the stewardship of AI applications, including risk assessment, fairness and nondiscrimination, disclosure and transparency, and interagency coordination. It further touched on reducing barriers to the deployment and use of AI, including increasing access to government data, communicating benefits and risks to the public, engaging in the development and use of voluntary consensus standards, and engaging in international regulatory cooperation efforts.

Additionally, the memorandum directed federal agencies to provide plans to conform to the guidance, including any statutory authorities governing agency regulation of AI applications, regulatory barriers to AI applications, and any planned or considered regulatory actions on AI. So far, few agencies appear to have provided comprehensive, publicly available responses.[56]

Industry has echoed calls for regulation of AI technologies, with some companies putting forth recommendations.[57] However, some analysts have argued that the push for regulations from technology firms is intended to protect companies' interests and might not align with the priorities of other stakeholders.[58] Further, some argue that large technology companies continue to prioritize the speed of AI technology deployment ahead of concerns about safety and accuracy.[59] In March 2023, the U.S. Chamber of Commerce released a report calling for AI regulation, stating,

> Policy leaders must undertake initiatives to develop thoughtful laws and rules for the development of responsible AI and its ethical deployment. A failure to regulate AI will harm the economy, potentially diminish individual rights, and constrain the development and introduction of beneficial technologies.[60]

In July 2023, the Biden Administration convened representatives from seven AI companies— Amazon, Anthropic, Google, Inflection, Meta,

---

[56] For information on the memorandum, see https://www.whitehouse.gov/wp-content/uploads/2020/11/M-21-06.pdf.

[57] See, for example, Google, *Recommendations for Regulating AI*, https://ai.google/static/documents/recommendations-for-regulating-ai.pdf.

[58] Justin Sherman, "Oh Sure, Big Tech Wants Regulation—On Its Own Terms," *Wired*, January 28, 2020, https://www.wired.com/story/opinion-oh-sure-big-tech-wants-regulationon-its-own-terms/.

[59] Nico Grant and Karen Weise, "In A.I. Race, Microsoft and Google Choose Speed over Caution," *New York Times*, April 7, 2023, https://www.nytimes.com/2023/04/07/technology/ai-chatbots-google-microsoft.html.

[60] U.S. Chamber of Commerce, "Artificial Intelligence Commission Report," March 9, 2023, https://www.uschamber.com/technology/artificial-intelligence-commission-report.

Microsoft, and OpenAI—and announced voluntary commitments from each of them "to help move toward safe, secure, and transparent development of AI technology."[61] According to the Administration, the voluntary commitments "are consistent with existing laws and regulations," and "companies intend these voluntary commitments to remain in effect until regulations covering substantially the same issues come into force."[62] Additionally, the Administration reportedly consulted on the voluntary commitments with 20 other countries and has stated that it "will work with allies and partners to establish a strong international framework to govern the development and use of AI."[63]

Other Considerations for the 118th Congress

Interest in AI—including from the public, industry, and lawmakers—shows no signs of slowing in the near future, particularly in light of recent advances and widespread use of GenAI models since fall 2022 across a number of sectors. Just as the potential of these and other AI technologies is expanding, so too is recognition of potential harms and calls for congressional action. As debates among stakeholders continue, cross-cutting issues addressing AI for consideration during the 118th Congress might include

- How might Congress approach AI regulation in a way that supports innovation and beneficial uses of AI technologies while minimizing current harms and potential future negative outcomes? How might such approaches align with international efforts to regulate AI technologies or their uses?
- Are current mechanisms within the federal government sufficient for AI oversight and policymaking? How might broader efforts—such as

---

[61] White House Briefing Room, "Fact Sheet: Biden-Harris Administration Secures Voluntary Commitments from Leading Artificial Intelligence Companies to Manage the Risks Posed by AI," July 21, 2023, https://www.whitehouse.gov/briefing-room/statements-releases/2023/07/21/fact-sheet-biden-harris-administration-secures-voluntary-commitments-from-leading-artificial-intelligence-companies-to-manage-the-risks-posed-by-ai/.

[62] White House, "Ensuring Safe, Secure, and Trustworthy AI," July 21, 2023, https://www.whitehouse.gov/wp-content/uploads/2023/07/Ensuring-Safe-Secure-and-Trustworthy-AI.pdf.

[63] White House Briefing Room, "Fact Sheet: Biden-Harris Administration Secures Voluntary Commitments."

calls for the creation of a new agency focused on AI—fit with the current federal government approaches to AI?

- What is the role of the federal government in supporting AI R&D and addressing calls for the "democratization" of AI—for example, by making R&D resources more available to academic researchers and startup businesses?
- Additional areas of consideration include the potential impact of AI technologies on the workforce; disclosure of AI use; testing and validation of AI systems; and potential ways to support the development of trustworthy and responsible AI.

Disclaimer

Chapter 2

Artificial Intelligence: Background, Selected Issues, and Policy Considerations*

Laurie A. Harris

Abstract

The field of artificial intelligence (AI)—a term first used in the 1950s—has gone through multiple waves of advancement over the subsequent decades. Today, AI can broadly be thought of as computerized systems that work and react in ways commonly thought to require intelligence, such as the ability to learn, solve problems, and achieve goals under uncertain and varying conditions. The field encompasses a range of methodologies and application areas, including machine learning (ML), natural language processing, and robotics.

In the past decade or so, increased computing power, the accumulation of big data, and advances in AI techniques have led to rapid growth in AI research and applications. Given these developments and the increasing application of AI technologies across economic sectors, stakeholders from academia, industry, and civil society have called for the federal government to become more knowledgeable about AI technologies and more proactive in considering public policies around their use.

Federal activity addressing AI accelerated during the 115th and 116th Congresses. President Donald Trump issued two executive orders, establishing the American AI Initiative (E.O. 13859) and promoting the use of trustworthy AI in the federal government (E.O. 13960). Federal committees, working groups, and other entities have been formed to coordinate agency activities, help set priorities, and produce national

* This is an edited, reformatted and augmented version of Congressional Research Service, Publication No. R46795, dated May 19, 2021.

In: Artificial Intelligence
Editor: Sonja Buckley
ISBN: 979-8-89530-859-2

strategic plans and reports, including an updated *National AI Research and Development Strategic Plan* and a *Plan for Federal Engagement in Developing Technical Standards and Related Tools in AI*. In Congress, committees held numerous hearings, and Members introduced a wide variety of legislation to address federal AI investments and their coordination; AI-related issues such as algorithmic bias and workforce impacts; and AI technologies such as facial recognition and deepfakes. At least four laws enacted in the 116th Congress focused on AI or included
AI-focused provisions.

- The National Defense Authorization Act for FY2021 (P.L. 116-283) included provisions addressing various defense- and security-related AI activities, as well as the expansive National Artificial Intelligence Initiative Act of 2020 (Division E).
- The Consolidated Appropriations Act, 2021 (P.L. 116-260) included the AI in Government Act of 2020 (Division U, Title I), which directed the General Services Administration to create an AI Center of Excellence to facilitate the adoption of AI technologies in the federal government.
- The Identifying Outputs of Generative Adversarial Networks (IOGAN) Act (P.L. 116-258) supported research on Generative Adversarial Networks (GANs), the primary technology used to create deepfakes.
- P.L. 116-94 established a financial program related to exports in AI among other areas.

AI holds potential benefits and opportunities, but also challenges and pitfalls. For example, AI technologies can accelerate and provide insights into data processing; augment human decisionmaking; optimize performance for complex tasks and systems; and improve safety for people in dangerous occupations. On the other hand, AI systems may perpetuate or amplify bias, may not yet be fully able to explain their decisionmaking, and often depend on vast datasets that are not widely accessible to facilitate research and development (R&D). Further, stakeholders have questioned the adequacy of human capital in both the public and private sectors to develop and work with AI, as well as the adequacy of current laws and regulations for dealing with societal and ethical issues that may arise. Together, such challenges can lead to an inability to fully assess and understand the operations and outputs of AI systems—sometimes referred to as the "black box" problem.

Because of these questions and concerns, some stakeholders have advocated for slowing the pace of AI development and use until more research, policymaking, and preparation can occur. Others have countered that AI will make lives safer, healthier, and more productive, so the federal government should not attempt to slow it, but rather should give broad support to AI technologies and increase federal AI funding. In response to this debate, Congress has begun discussing issues such as the trustworthiness, potential bias, and ethical uses of AI; possible disruptive impacts to the U.S. workforce; the adequacy of U.S. expertise and training in AI; domestic and international efforts to set technological standards and testing benchmarks; and the level of U.S. federal investments in AI research and development and how that impacts U.S. international competitiveness. Congress is likely to continue grappling with these issues and working to craft policies that protect American citizens while maximizing U.S. innovation and leadership.

Introduction

Artificial intelligence (AI)—a term first used in the 1950s—can broadly be thought of as computerized systems that work and react in ways commonly thought to require intelligence, such as the ability to learn, solve problems, and achieve goals under uncertain and varying conditions.[1] In the past decade, increases in computing power, thc availability of large-scale datasets (i.e., big data), and advances in the methodologies underlying AI, have led to rapid growth in the field. AI technologies currently show promise for improving the safety, quality, and efficiency of work and for promoting innovation and economic growth. At the same time, the application of AI to complex problem solving in real-world situations raises concerns about trustworthiness, bias, and ethics and potential disruptive effects on the U.S. workforce. In addition, numerous policy questions are at issue, including those concerning the appropriate U.S. approach to international competition in AI research and development (R&D), technological standard setting, and the development of testing benchmarks.

Given the increasing use of AI technologies across economic sectors, stakeholders from academia, industry, and civil society have called for the federal government to become more knowledgeable about AI technologies and more proactive in considering public policies around their use. To assist Congress in its work on AI, this report provides an overview of AI technologies and their development, recent trends in AI, federal AI activity, and selected issues and policy considerations.

---

[1] Adapted from Office of Science and Technology Policy, *Preparing for the Future of Artificial Intelligence*, October 2016, p. 6.

This report does not attempt to address all applications of AI. Information on the application of AI technologies in transportation, national security, and education can be found in separate CRS products.[2]

What Is AI?

While there is no single, commonly agreed upon definition of AI, the National Institute of Standards and Technology (NIST) has described AI technologies and systems as comprising "software and/or hardware that can learn to solve complex problems, make predictions or undertake tasks that require human-like sensing (such as vision, speech, and touch), perception, cognition, planning, learning, communication, or physical action."[3] Definitions may vary according to the discipline in which AI is being discussed.[4] AI is often described as a field that encompasses a range of methodologies and application areas, such as machine learning (ML), natural language processing (NLP), and robotics.

Defining AI is not merely an academic exercise, particularly when drafting legislation. AI research and applications are evolving rapidly. Thus, congressional consideration of whether to include a definition for AI in a bill, and if so how to define the term or related terms, necessarily include attention to the scope of the legislation and the current and future applicability of the definition. Considerations in crafting a definition for use in legislation include whether it is expansive enough not to hinder the future applicability of a law as AI develops and evolves, while being narrow enough to provide clarity on the entities the law affects. Some stakeholders, recognizing the many challenges of defining AI, have attempted to define principles that might help

---

[2] See CRS Report R44940, *Issues in Autonomous Vehicle Deployment*, by Bill Canis; CRS In Focus IF10737, *Autonomous and Semi-autonomous Trucks*, by John Frittelli; CRS Report R45178, *Artificial Intelligence and National Security*, by Kelley M. Sayler; and CRS In Focus IF10937, *Artificial Intelligence (AI) and Education*, by Joyce J. Lu and Laurie A. Harris.

[3] National Institute of Standards and Technology, *U.S. Leadership in AI: A Plan for Federal Engagement in Developing Technical Standards and Related Tools*, August 9, 2019, pp. 7-8.

[4] See, for example, AI definitions in the categories of ordinary language, computational disciplines, engineering, economics and social sciences, ethics and philosophy, and international law and policy, in Sara Mattingly-Jordan et al., *Ethically Aligned Design: First Edition Glossary*, Institute of Electrical and Electronics Engineers (IEEE), January 2019, p. 8, at https://standards.ieee.org/content/dam/ieee-standards/standards/web/documents/other/ead1e_glossary.pdf.

guide policymakers. Research suggests that differences in definitions used to identify AI-related research may contribute to significantly different analyses and outcomes regarding AI competition, investments, technology transfer, and application forecasts.[5]

The John S. McCain National Defense Authorization Act for Fiscal Year 2019 (P.L. 115-232) included the first definition of AI in federal statute.[6] Like those in other previously introduced bills, the definition incorporated a commonly cited framework of four possible goals that AI systems may pursue: systems that think like humans (e.g., neural networks), act like humans (e.g., natural language processing), think rationally (e.g., logic solvers), or act rationally (e.g., intelligent software agents embodied in robots).[7] However, AI research and applications do not necessarily fall solely within any one of these four categories.

In December 2020, the National Artificial Intelligence Act of 2020, enacted as part of the William M. (Mac) Thornberry National Defense Authorization Act (NDAA) for Fiscal Year 2021 (P.L. 116-283), included the following definition:

> The term "artificial intelligence" means a machine-based system that can, for a given set of human-defined objectives, make predictions, recommendations or decisions influencing real or virtual environments. Artificial intelligence systems use machine and human-based inputs to—(A) perceive real and virtual environments; (B) abstract such perceptions into models through analysis in an automated manner; and (C) use model inference to formulate options for information or action.[8]

Current AI systems are considered to be *narrow AI*, meaning that they are tailored to particular, narrowly defined tasks. Example applications of AI in everyday life include email spam filtering, voice assistance (e.g., Siri, Alexa, Cortana), financial lending decisions, and search engine results. AI technologies are being integrated in a range of sectors, including transportation, health care, education, agriculture, manufacturing, and

---

[5] Dewey Murdick, James Dunham, and Jennifer Melot, *AI Definitions Affect Policymaking*, Center for Security and Emerging Technology, June 2020, at https://cset.georgetown.edu/wp-content/uploads/CSET-AI-Definitions-Affect-Policymaking.pdf.

[6] P.L. 115-232, Section 238; 10 U.S.C. §2358 note.

[7] Stuart Russell and Peter Norvig, *Artificial Intelligence: A Modern Approach*, 3rd ed. (Upper Saddle River, NJ: Prentice Hall, 2010), pp. 1-5.

[8] P.L. 116-283 (hereinafter referred to as the FY2021 NDAA); H.R. 6395, Division E, Section 5002(3).

defense. Some AI experts use the terms *augmented intelligence* or *human-centered AI* to capture the various AI applications in physical and connected systems, such as robotics and the Internet of Things,[9] and to emphasize the use of AI technologies to enhance human activities rather than to replace them.

Most analysts believe that *general AI*, meaning systems that demonstrate intelligent behavior across a range of cognitive tasks, is unlikely to occur for a decade or longer. Some AI researchers believe that general AI can be achieved through incremental development and refining of current AI and machine learning tools, while others believe it will require the discovery and development of a new breakthrough technique.

Just as there is debate over the definition of AI, there is debate over which technologies should be classified as AI. For example, robotic process automation (RPA) has been defined as "the use of software to automate highly repetitive, routine tasks normally performed by knowledge workers."[10] Because it automates activities performed by humans, it is often described as an AI technology. However, some argue that RPA is not AI because it does not include a learning component. Others discuss RPA as a basic tool that can be combined with AI to create complex process automation (CPA) or intelligent process automation (IPA), along an "intelligent automation continuum."[11]

AI Terminology

Some stakeholders, including industry, advocacy groups, and policymakers, have raised questions about whether specific AI technologies and techniques require tailored legislation. For example, legislation enacted in the 116th Congress focused on generative adversarial networks (GANs), described below, which are the main underlying AI technique used in generating deepfakes,[12] which are most commonly described as realistic audio, video, and

[9] For more information on the Internet of Things, see CRS In Focus IF11239, *The Internet of Things (IoT): An Overview*, by Patricia Moloney Figliola; and to identify additional CRS experts who work on IoT and related topics, see CRS Report R44225, *The Internet of Things: CRS Experts*, coordinated by Patricia Moloney Figliola.

[10] See IBM, "Automate Repetitive Tasks," at https://www.ibm.com/automation/rpa.

[11] IBM Global Business Services, "Using Artificial Intelligence to Optimize the Value of Robotic Process Automation," September 2017, at https://www.ibm.com/downloads/cas/KDKAAK29.

[12] The Identifying Outputs of Generative Adversarial Networks (IOGAN) Act (P.L. 116-258).

other forgeries created using AI techniques.[13] This section is meant to provide a broad understanding of a subset of common terms used in the field of AI and how they relate to one another. These include the subfield of machine learning (ML); ML techniques such as deep learning, neural networks, and GANs; and training methods such as supervised, unsupervised, and reinforcement learning. However, just as there are variations in how AI is defined, researchers and practitioners describe various AI-related terms in slightly different ways. Further, the following terms and techniques are not mutually exclusive; AI systems may employ more than one. For example, AlphaGo—the first AI program to beat a human master at the ancient Chinese game of Go—combined deep neural networks, supervised learning, and reinforcement learning.[14]

- *Machine learning (ML),* often referred to as a subfield of AI, examines how to build computer programs that automatically improve their performance at some task through experience without relying on explicit rules-based programming to do so.[15] One of the goals of ML is to teach algorithms to successfully interpret data that have not previously been encountered. ML is one of the most common AI techniques in use today, and most ML tasks are narrowly specified to optimize specific functions using particular datasets. Deep learning, neural networks, and GANs represent a few of the ML techniques frequently used today.
- *Deep learning (DL)* systems learn from large amounts of data to subsequently recognize and classify related, but previously unobserved, data. For example, *neural networks,* often described as being loosely modeled after the human brain, consist of thousands or millions of processing nodes generally organized into layers. The strength of the connections among nodes and layers are repeatedly

---

[13] For additional information on deepfakes, see CRS In Focus IF11333, *Deep Fakes and National Security*, by Kelley M. Sayler and Laurie A. Harris.

[14] Richard S. Sutton and Andrew G. Barto, *Reinforcement Learning: An Introduction*, 2nd ed. (Cambridge, MA: MIT Press, 2018), pp. 441-442.

[15] Adapted from Erik Brynjolfsson, Tom Mitchell, and Daniel Rock, "What Can Machines Learn, and What Does It Mean for Occupations and the Economy?," *AEA Papers and Proceedings*, vol. 108 (May 1, 2018), pp. 43-47, at http://www-cgi.cs.cmu.edu/~tom/pubs/AEA2018-WhatCanMachinesLearn.pdf. ML is defined in P.L. 116-293 to mean "an application of artificial intelligence that is characterized by providing systems the ability to automatically learn and improve on the basis of data or experience, without being explicitly programmed."

tuned—based on characteristics of the training data—to correspond to the correct output. Advances in hardware, such as the development of graphical processing units (GPUs), have allowed these networks to have many layers, which is what puts the "deep" in deep learning. DL approaches have been used in systems across many areas of AI research, from autonomous vehicles to voice recognition technologies.[16]

- *Generative adversarial networks (GANs)* consist of two competing neural networks—a generator network that tries to create fake outputs (such as pictures), and a discriminator network that tries to determine whether the outputs are real or fake. A major advantage of this structure is that GANs can learn from less data than other deep learning algorithms.[17] Adversarial ML systems can be used in other ways, as well; for example, they can try to improve fairness in financial service decisionmaking by having a second model try to guess the protected class of applicants based on models built by another model.[18]
- *Supervised learning* algorithms learn from a training set of data that is labeled with the correct description (e.g., the correct label for this picture is "cat"); the system subsequently learns which components of the data are useful for classifying it correctly and uses that information to correctly classify data it has never encountered before. In contrast, *unsupervised learning* algorithms search for underlying structures in unlabeled data.
- *Reinforcement learning (RL)* refers to giving computer programs the ability to learn from experience, providing them with minimal inputs and human interventions.[19] RL algorithms learn by trial and error, being rewarded for reaching specified objectives—both for immediate actions and long-term goals. The emphasis on simulated motivation and learning from direct interaction with the environment,

---

[16] Larry Hardesty, "Explained: Neural Networks," *Massachusetts Institute of Technology (MIT) News*, April 14, 2017, at http://news.mit.edu/2017/explained-neural-networks-deep-learning-0414.

[17] Jamie Beckett, "What's a Generative Adversarial Network? Leading Researcher Explains," *NVIDIA*, May 17, 2017, at https://blogs.nvidia.com/blog/2017/05/17/generative-adversarial-network/.

[18] Sally Ward-Foxton, "Reducing Bias in AI Models for Credit and Loan Decision," *EE Times*, April 30, 2019, at https://www.eetimes.com/reducing-bias-in-ai-models-for-credit-and-loan-decisions/#.

[19] Sean Garrish, *How Smart Machines Think* (Cambridge, MA: MIT Press, 2018), p. 91.

without requiring explicit examples and models, are among the characteristics that set RL apart from other ML approaches.[20]

Algorithms and AI

As interest in AI continues to grow, some analysts assert that general data analytics and specialized algorithms are increasingly being referred to, erroneously, as AI. It can be challenging to make such distinctions clearly, given the variability in definitions of AI and related terms and because these distinctions have arguably shifted over time. For example, an algorithm is basically a procedure or set of instructions designed to perform a specific task or solve a mathematical problem. Some early products of AI research, such as rule-based expert systems, are algorithms encoded with expert knowledge but lacking a learning component. Some feel that rule-based systems are a simple form of AI because they simulate intelligence, while others think that without a learning component a system should not be considered AI.[21] Generally, however, the goals of AI—automating or replicating intelligent behavior—have remained consistent.[22]

Historical Context of AI

The ideas underlying AI and its conceptual framework have been researched since at least the 1940s and initially formalized in the 1950s. Ideas about intelligent machines were discussed and popularized by scientists and authors such as Alan Turing and Isaac Asimov,[23] and the term "artificial intelligence"

---

[20] Adapted from Richard S. Sutton and Andrew G. Barto, *Reinforcement Learning: An Introduction*, 2nd ed. (Cambridge, MA: MIT Press, 2018).

[21] For a brief discussion see, for example, Tricentis, "AI Approaches Compared: Rule-Based Testing vs. Learning," at https://www.tricentis.com/artificial-intelligence-software-testing/ai-approaches-rule-based-testing-vs-learning/.

[22] Office of Science and Technology Policy, *Preparing for the Future of Artificial Intelligence*, October 2016, pp. 5-6.

[23] Alan M. Turing, "Computing Machinery and Intelligence," *Mind*, vol. 49 (1950), pp. 433-460, at https://www.csee.umbc.edu/courses/471/papers/turing.pdf; and Isaac Asimov, *I, Robot* (Garden City, NY: Doubleday, 1950).

was coined at the Dartmouth Summer Research Project on Artificial Intelligence, proposed in 1955 and held the following year.[24]

Since that time, the field of AI has gone through what have been termed by some as summers and winters—periods of much research and advancement, followed by lulls in activity and progress. The reasons for the AI winters have included a focus on theory over practical applications, research problems being more difficult than anticipated, and limitations of the technologies of the time. Much of the current progress and research in AI, which began around 2010, has been attributed to the availability of big data, improved ML approaches and algorithms, and more powerful computers.[25]

Waves of AI

The Defense Advanced Research Projects Agency (DARPA), which has funded AI R&D since the 1960s, has described the development of AI technologies in terms of three waves.[26] These waves are described by the varying abilities of technologies in each to *perceive* rich, complex, and subtle information; to *learn* within an environment; to *abstract* to create new meanings; and to *reason* in order to plan and reach decisions.[27]

First Wave: Handcrafted Knowledge

The first wave of AI technologies have abilities primarily to perceive and reason but no learning capability and poor handling of uncertainty. For such technologies, researchers and engineers create sets of rules to represent

---

[24] See J. McCarthy et al., "A Proposal for the Dartmouth Summer Research Project on Artificial Intelligence," August 31, 1955, at http://www-formal.stanford.edu/jmc/history/dartmouth/dartmouth.html.

[25] Executive Office of the President, National Science and Technology Council, Committee on Technology, *Preparing for the Future of Artificial Intelligence*, October 2016, pp. 5-6.; for additional information on these factors and a short history of AI, see also the appendix of Peter Stone et al., "Artificial Intelligence and Life in 2030," *One Hundred Year Study on Artificial Intelligence: Report of the 2015-2016 Study Panel*, Stanford University, Stanford, CA, September 2016, at http://ai100.stanford.edu/2016-report.

[26] See "DARPA Announces $2 Billion Campaign to Develop Next Wave of AI Technologies," September 7, 2018, at https://www.darpa.mil/news-events/2018-09-07.

[27] Arati Prabhakar, former Director of DARPA, "Powerful but Limited: A DARPA Perspective on AI," presentation at National Academies of Sciences, Engineering, and Medicine workshop, *Robotics and Artificial Intelligence: Policy Implications for the Next Decade*, December 12, 2016, at https://www.nationalacademies.org/event/12-12-2016/ robotics-and-artificial-intelligence-policy-implications-for-the-next-decade(hereinafter "Prabhakar, 2016").

knowledge in well-defined domains for narrowly defined problems. The TurboTax software, an expert system, is one example. Rules are built into the application, which then turns input information into tax form outputs, but it has only a rudimentary ability to perceive and no ability to learn (e.g., about a new tax law) or to abstract beyond what it is programmed to know.

Second Wave: Statistical Learning

Starting in the 1990s, a second wave of AI technologies were developed with more nuanced abilities to perceive and learn, with some ability to abstract, minimal reasoning ability, but no contextual ability. For these systems, engineers create statistical models for specific problem domains and train them on big data. Generally, while such systems are statistically powerful, they can be individually unreliable, especially in the presence of skewed training data (e.g., a face recognition system trained on a limited range of skin tones can be powerful for similar faces, but highly unreliable for individuals outside of the training spectrum). As noted by DARPA, these technologies are "dependent on large amounts of high quality training data, do not adapt to changing conditions, offer limited performance guarantees, and are unable to provide users with explanations of their results."[28] Additional examples of second wave AI technologies include voice recognition and text analysis.

Third Wave: Contextual Adaptation

The third wave of AI technologies is oriented toward making it possible for machines to adapt to changing situations (i.e., contextual adaptation). Engineers create systems that construct explanatory models of real world phenomena, and "AI systems learn and reason as they encounter new tasks and situations."[29] Examples of third wave technologies would include explainable AI (XAI), as described below.

Recent Growth in the Field of AI

There are many potential indicators of growth in the AI field. This section presents indicators of growth based on R&D activities and public and private investments in areas of frequent congressional interest. It also provides a brief

[28] See "DARPA Announces $2 Billion Campaign to Develop Next Wave of AI Technologies," September 7, 2108, at https://www.darpa.mil/news-events/2018-09-07.

[29] Prabhakar, 2016.

discussion of AI hype versus the reality of what AI technologies are capable of today. It can be challenging to obtain comprehensive and directly comparable data for the indicators discussed in this section, particularly for AI investments.

Therefore, such data should be evaluated carefully and treated as only indicative of trends.

AI Research and Development

One way to assess the growth in AI R&D is based on the publication of peer-reviewed papers, including both conference papers and journal articles. According to the AI Index group, between 2000 and 2019, the total number of peer-reviewed AI publications in Elsevier's Scopus database—the world's largest abstract and citation database—grew nearly 12-fold.[30] Authors based in the Europe Union (EU) published the most peer-reviewed AI publications as a percentage of the world total from 2000 to 2007 and again from 2012 to 2016, while authors based in China published the most from 2008 to 2011 and 2017 to 2019.[31] In 2020, the papers published by authors in China surpassed those of authors in the United States in the share of AI journal citations in the world for the first time. However, over the past decade, authors in the United States have consistently had more cited AI conference papers than authors based in China.[32] Further, the number of publications a researcher or country produces does not necessarily equate to scientific impact or research quality. As one researcher at the University of Oxford, UK, reportedly stated, "Just pumping out raw numbers of papers that don't have a lasting impact isn't really useful. It's more important to keep up with the technology frontier."[33] Such evaluations, however, do not discuss the finer points of which studies included teams of researchers from more than one country, raising the question of how to neatly attribute papers to regions, organizations, or funding sources.

In addition to published papers, many AI researchers in recent years have published preprint papers (submitted before peer review) to an online

---

[30] AI Index Steering Committee, *The AI Index 2021 Annual Report*, Human-Centered AI Institute, Stanford University, Stanford, CA, March 2021, p. 18 (hereinafter, "AI Index 2021"). The AI Index 2021 report authors provided this information only for the United States, China, and the Europe Union (EU), not individual countries within the EU.

[31] Ibid., p. 20.

[32] Ibid., p. 17.

[33] Neil Savage, "The Race to the Top Among the World's Leaders in Artificial Intelligence," *Nature Index*, December 9, 2020, at https://www.nature.com/articles/d41586-020-03409-8.

repository called arXiv (pronounced "archive"). As reported by the AI Index group, between 2015 and 2020, the total number of AI papers on arXiv increased over six-fold, with more growth in certain subcategories, providing a rough indication of areas of research activity across a range of AI subfields.[34] As of 2020, the most common subcategories of preprint papers were ML and computer vision (Figure 1).[35]

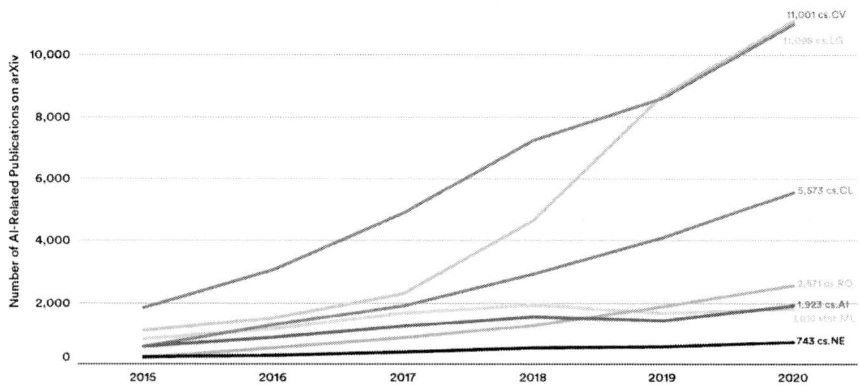

Source: AI Index Steering Committee, *The AI Index 2021 Annual Report*, Human-Centered AI Institute, Stanford University, Stanford, CA, December 2021, p. 34.

Notes: The arXiv is an online repository for pre-publication papers, which generally means they have not undergone prior peer review. The papers on arXiv listed here are grouped by field of study, including cs.CV (computer vision), cs.LG (machine learning in computer science), cs.CL (computation and language), cs.RO (robotics), cs.AI (artificial intelligence), stat.ML (machine learning in statistics), and cs.NE (neural and evolutionary computing).

Figure 1. Total Number of AI-Related Publications on arXiv, by Field of Study, 2015-2020.

Groups like the AI Index have also attempted to measure progress in AI and its fields of study, though critics have categorized such efforts as reporting "trends in data that are related to AI" rather than tracking progress.[36] Further, recent research has raised concerns about the accuracy of reported improvements. By some measures, such as training time and cost, areas such

---

[34] Ibid., p. 32.

[35] Ibid., p. 34.

[36] Jeffrey Funk and Gary Smith, "Stanford's AI Index Report: How Much Is BS?," *Mind Matters News*, March 3, 2020, at https://mindmatters.ai/2020/03/stanfords-ai-index-report-how-much-is-bs/.

as image classification have improved substantially.[37] By other measures, researchers assert that progress has come from tweaks, rather than core innovations, and some purported progress might not have taken place. For example, some researchers using meta-analyses of algorithms in various fields and applications—such as pruning algorithms used to make neural networks more efficient and information retrieval programs used in search engines—have found no clear evidence of performance improvements over the 10-year period from 2010 to 2019.[38]

Private and Public Funding

Since around 2015, private funding for AI has been increasing, both in the United States and globally. For example, according to the AI Index 2021 report, global corporate investment in AI—including private investment, public offerings, mergers and acquisitions, and minority stakes—increased from $12.8 billion raised in 2015 to over $67.8 billion in 2020.[39] Global AI startup funding also increased steadily from 2015 to 2020, though the number of companies funded has decreased for each year from 2017 through 2020.[40] The United States continues to lead the world in private AI investments, with $23.6 billion in funding in 2020, followed by China ($9.9 billion) and the European Union ($2.0 billion). The top area of private investment in AI in 2020 was "Drugs, Cancer, Molecular, Drug Discovery" with more than $13.8 billion, 4.5 times higher than in 2019.[41] This increased funding for this particular area in 2020 may have been in large part a response to the Coronavirus Disease 2019 (COVID-19) pandemic; among the additional areas that also saw substantial increases in funding from 2019 to 2020 were "Students, Courses, Edtech, English language" and "Speech Recognition, Computer interaction, Dialogue, and Machine translation."[42] According to a McKinsey 2020 survey of over 1,000 company respondents, over half reported

---

[37] AI Index 2021, pp. 48-49. Image classification broadly refers to the assigning of identification labels to images.

[38] Matthew Hutson, "Core Progress in AI Has Stalled in Some Fields," *Science*, vol. 368, no. 6494 (May 29, 2020), p. 927, at https://science.sciencemag.org/content/368/6494/927.

[39] AI Index 2021, p. 93.

[40] Ibid., p. 94.

[41] Ibid., p. 11.

[42] Ibid., p. 97.

no change in AI investments amid the coronavirus pandemic, and 25% increased their investment in AI.[43]

In FY2020, U.S. public funding for AI R&D was reported for the first time across non-defense federal agencies in a supplemental report to the President's FY2020 budget, submitted by the Networking and Information Technology Research and Development (NITRD) Program. The annual NITRD supplemental report includes funding information across Program Component Areas (PCAs), which are major subject areas of federal IT R&D and may change each year. For FY2021, AI is included as a stand-alone PCA, and the report includes FY2019 actual investments, FY2020 enacted investments, and FY2021 requested funding amounts. While AI is a stand-alone PCA, some other PCAs have AI as a component.[44] Total FY2021 requested funding for non-defense agency AI R&D under the AI PCA was $912 million (an increase from the FY2020 enacted and supplemental total amount of $660 million); for AI-related efforts reported in other PCAs, the request was $590 million (an increase from the FY2020 enacted and supplemental total amount of $466 million). Thus, the total requested federal FY2021 non-defense budget for AI across PCAs was $1.5 billion (an increase from the FY2020 enacted and supplemental total amount of $1.1 billion).[45] By agency, the largest proportions of the FY2021 non-defense AI PCA request were from the National Science Foundation (NSF, $457 million), the U.S. Department of Agriculture (USDA, $128 million), and the Department of Energy (DOE, $84 million).[46]

Although defense agencies did not report AI funding numbers as part of the NITRD supplemental report, Bloomberg Government reported that the Department of Defense (DOD) FY2020 enacted budget for AI R&D was $5.0 billion, equal to the estimated FY2021 request.[47] The FY2021 request estimate included $568 million at DARPA, $250 million for the Algorithmic Cross

[43] Tara Balakrishnan et al., *The State of AI in 2020*, McKinsey & Company, November 17, 2020, at https://www.mckinsey.com/Business-Functions/McKinsey-Analytics/Our-Insights/Global-survey-The-state-of-AI-in-2020. The survey and interviews with executives were conducted from May to August, 2020, and included 1,151 respondents from organizations that had adopted AI in at least one function out of a total of 2,395 participants.

[44] Examples of activities under the AI PCA include R&D that is primarily ML, and R&D focused on cybersecurity challenges unique to AI, and on computing architectures or chips optimized for neural networks. Examples of AI activities captured under other PCAs include R&D on robots that employ machine vision, R&D on the broad problem of human-machine interaction, and general research on neuromorphic computing. Ibid., pp. 11-12.

[45] Ibid., p. 11.

[46] Ibid., pp. 8-9; DOE NNSA is listed separately from DOE.

[47] As reported in AI Index 2021, p. 168.

Functional Team (also known as "Project Maven"), and $132 million for the Joint Artificial Intelligence Center (JAIC).[48]

Another measure of public investment in AI comes from data on government spending on AI contracts. According to analysis by Bloomberg Government using the Federal Procurement Data System (FPDS), in FY2018, U.S. federal agencies spent a total of $1.8 billion on unclassified AI-related contracts in FY2020, more than six times higher than the approximately $300 million spent in FY2015.[49] DOD accounts for the vast majority of FY2020 AI-related contract spending ($1.4 billion); after DOD, the National Aeronautics and Space Administration (NASA), the Department of Homeland Security (DHS), and the Department of Health and Human Services (HHS) have accounted for the largest share of spending on AI contracts among federal agencies since 2010.[50] FPDS data may be helpful in identifying broad trends and producing rough estimates, but as other analysts have noted, these data may not be reliable and decisionmakers should understand its limitations and be cautious in using the data to develop policy or draw conclusions.[51]

Important considerations in evaluating any of these numbers, and especially in attempting to compare them to funding amounts reported by other countries, are the various potential discrepancies in the numbers by year, investment type, and reporting entity. The AI Index group has previously asserted that there is no consensus on standard labeling for AI related investment activities, no existing measurement and accounting standards for public investment or expenditures in AI, and no consistently available data comparing public investments across countries.[52]

---

[48] Ibid. Project Maven was launched in April 2017 and charged with rapidly incorporating AI into existing DOD systems to demonstrate the technology's potential; Robert Work, Former Deputy Secretary of Defense, Memorandum, "Establishment of an Algorithmic Warfare Cross-Functional Team (Project Maven)," April 26, 2017, at https://www.govexec.com/media/gbc/docs/pdfs_edit/establishment_of_the_awcft_project_maven.pdf. The JAIC is tasked with coordinating the efforts of DOD to develop, mature, and transition AI technologies into operational use, per P.L. 115-232, Section 2, Division A, Title X, §1051. Details and analysis for the FY2022 request are not yet available.

[49] As reported in AI Index 2021, p. 169.

[50] Ibid.

[51] For additional discussions of FDPS data and how the FDPS system operates, see CRS Report R44010, *Defense Acquisitions: How and Where DOD Spends Its Contracting Dollars*, by John F. Sargent Jr. and Christopher T. Mann.

[52] AI Index Steering Committee, *The AI Index 2019 Annual Report*, Human-Centered AI Institute, Stanford University, Stanford, CA, December, 2019, p. 98.

AI Hype and Reality

The recent growth and advances in the field of AI have been impressive, and notable researchers have highlighted both the far-reaching potential benefits, as well as the constraints and potential pitfalls of current and future AI technologies. Sergey Brin, co-founder of Google, has called the period of advancements over the past decade or so a "new spring in artificial intelligence," stating that we are in a "technology renaissance" with monthly advances and "applications across nearly every segment of modern society," while also highlighting potential concerns that accompany these advances (e.g., effects on employment, fairness, transparency, and safety).[53] AI systems currently remain constrained to narrowly-defined tasks and can fail with small modifications to inputs. For example, deep learning systems that have excelled at recognizing facial images can be deceived by the introduction of simple image distortions, or "noise" in the data.[54] The introduction of imperceptible or seemingly irrelevant changes to inputs, such as images, text, or sound waves, by malevolent actors has raised concerns about unforeseen vulnerabilities of AI, particularly in applications in autonomous vehicles, medical technologies, and defense systems. One expert noted, "While some people are worried about 'superintelligent' A.I., the most dangerous aspect of A.I. systems is that we will trust them too much and give them too much autonomy while not being fully aware of their limitations."[55] Many researchers agree that continued progress in AI requires the development and refinement of new techniques, in addition to increased availability of data and improvements in computing capacity.[56]

Selected Research and Focus Areas

AI research currently spans a broad range of techniques and application areas. This section describes a selection of areas that have received attention in recent

---

[53] Sergey Brin, "2017 Founders' Letter," at https://abc.xyz/investor/founders-letters/2017/index.html.

[54] Gaurav Goswami et al., "Unravelling Robustness of Deep Learning Based Face Recognition Against Adversarial Attacks," *Association for the Advancement of Artificial Intelligence*, February 22, 2018, at https://arxiv.org/abs/ 1803.00401.

[55] Melanie Mitchell, "Artificial Intelligence Hits the Barrier of Meaning," *New York Times*, November 5, 2018, at https://www.nytimes.com/2018/11/05/opinion/artificial-intelligence-machine-learning.html.

[56] Tom Simonite, "Your Instagram #Dogs and #Cats Are Training Facebook's AI," *Wired*, May 2, 2018, at https://www.wired.com/story/your-instagram-dogs-and-cats-are-training-facebooks-ai/.

years and may be of particular interest to Congress, including an example of AI in healthcare; it is not meant to portray any area as more or less valuable than another to the overall progress of AI research. Some of these areas include explainable AI, data access and models that can learn from reduced amounts of data, and hardware to improve the speed of, and reduce the computing power required to run, AI algorithms.

Explainable AI

As mentioned above in the discussion of third wave AI technologies, explainable AI has been an active area of research in recent years. As described by experts at DARPA, XAI research aims to create AI applications that can explain their actions and decisions to human users to improve trust and collaboration between humans and AI systems (Figure 2). Such explanations could help people identify and correct errors that AI systems make when generalizing from training data.

This is of particular concern in high-stakes applications, such as classifying disease in medical images and classifying combatants and civilians in military surveillance images.[57]

Federal agencies and the White House have been working to define and guide federal development and use of understandable and explainable AI systems. In August 2020, NIST released a draft publication for public comment on "Four Principles of Explainable Artificial Intelligence" that presents principles, categories, and theories of XAI.[58] In December 2020, Executive Order 13960 included, as a principle guiding the use of AI in federal government, that AI should be understandable, specifically that agencies shall "ensure that the operations and outcomes of their AI applications are sufficiently understandable by subject matter experts, users, and others."[59]

---

[57] For a deeper discussion of XAI, see also Alejandro Barredo Arrieta et al., "Explainable Artificial Intelligence (XAI): Concepts, Taxonomies, Opportunities and Challenges Toward Responsible AI," *Information Fusion*, vol. 58 (June 2020), pp. 82-115, at https://www.sciencedirect.com/science/article/pii/S1566253519308103.

[58] National Institute of Standards and Technology, *Four Principles of Explainable Artificial Intelligence*, Draft NISTRIR 8312, August 2020, at https://www.nist.gov/document/four-principles-explainable-artificial-intelligence-nistir-8312.

[59] Executive Order 13960, "Promoting the Use of Trustworthy Artificial Intelligence in the Federal Government," 85 *Federal Register* 78939, December 3, 2020, at https://www.federalregister.gov/documents/2020/12/08/2020-27065/promoting-the-use-of-trustworthy-artificial-intelligence-in-the-federal-government.

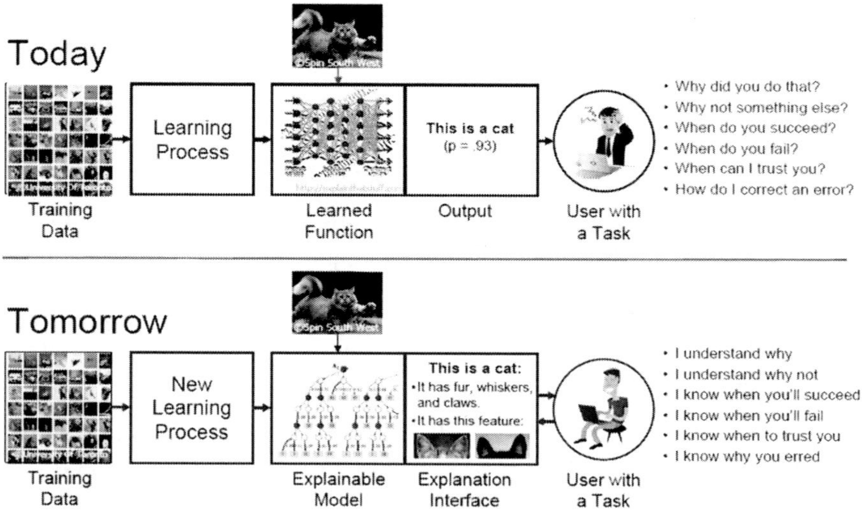

Source: David Gunning, DARPA, "Explainable Artificial Intelligence (XAI) Program Update," November 2017, at https://web.archive.org/web/20200501004458/https://www.darpa.mil/attachments/XAIProgramUpdate.pdf.

Figure 2. Examples of Non-Explainable and Explainable AI Systems.

Data Access

The availability of big data to train AI models enabled major advances in the field over the last decade. For example, the ImageNet project, which contains over 14 million publicly available labeled images, held competitions from 2010 through 2017 that led to improvements in AI visual recognition performance.[60] However, those developing AI technologies face barriers to using currently available datasets. In addition to the sheer amount of data available, researchers have noted the importance of using specific types of data of requisite quality for various applications of AI technologies, which can be expensive and time consuming to generate (e.g., data that have been digitally stored, cleaned, transformed, labeled, and optimized to be deployed in AI algorithms).[61] Associated data management infrastructure requirements can be extensive, including cloud technology, edge computing (computing done

[60] See "ImageNet Large Scale Visual Recognition Challenge," at http://www.image-net.org/challenges/LSVRC/.

[61] Husanjot Chahal, Ryan Fedasiuk, and Carrick Flynn, *Messier Than Oil: Assessing Data Advantage in Military AI*, Center for Security and Emerging Technology, July 2020.

closer to the source of the data), and labeling and annotation capacity (human capital).[62]

While big data sets continue to be instrumental in various AI advances, some have raised concerns that such datasets are increasingly held by private companies and argued for more publicly available datasets and incentives for technology companies to share proprietary datasets. One study asserted that "As long as large firms have both the computational resources and the access to proprietary datasets to combine with open data, they are likely to maintain a competitive advantage."[63] Concerns about private-sector competition and innovation constraints have been noted particularly for AI researchers and developers with limited access to data and testing and training resources, such as academic researchers, small businesses, and startups.

In response, the Select Committee on Artificial Intelligence of the National Science and Technology Council (NSTC) included "develop shared public datasets and environments for AI training and testing" as a priority area in its AI R&D Strategic Plan in 2016 and the 2019 update.[64] Additionally, the February 2019 Executive Order on *Maintaining American Leadership in Artificial Intelligence* directed the heads of all federal agencies to

> review their federal data and models to increase access and use by the greater non-federal AI research community in a manner that benefits that community, while protecting safety, security, privacy, and confidentiality. Specifically, agencies shall improve data and model inventory documentation to enable discovery and usability, and shall prioritize improvements to access and quality of AI data and models based on the AI research community's feedback.[65]

Since the national AI R&D strategic plan was first announced in 2016, numerous federal agencies have made varying degrees of progress toward collecting and sharing data. However, challenges remain, such as labeling and

---

[62] Ibid.

[63] T. Davies et al., (Eds.), "Algorithms and AI," in *State of Open Data: Histories and Horizons*, 2019, at https://www.stateofopendata.od4d.net/chapters/issues/artificial-intelligence.html.

[64] Select Committee on Artificial Intelligence, National Science and Technology Council, *The National Artificial Intelligence Research and Development Strategic Plan: 2019 Update*, June 2019, pp. 27-31 (hereinafter, "NSTC Select Committee on Artificial Intelligence 2019 AI R&D Strategic Plan"). See also below under "Federal Activity in AI."

[65] Executive Order 13859, "Maintaining American Leadership in Artificial Intelligence," 84 *Federal Register* 3967, February 11, 2019, at https://www.federalregister.gov/documents/2019/02/14/2019-02544/maintaining-american-leadership-in-artificial-intelligence.

curating datasets so that they are useful for AI research, working with AI stakeholders to ensure that datasets and models are fit for use and are maintained as standards and norms evolve, and developing tools to verify data provenance and oversee proper use policies.

The strategic plan notes that "data alone are of little use without the ability to bring computational resources to bear on large-scale public datasets."[66] Demonstrating the intensive training needed for some systems, Facebook has described an AI experiment using billions of Instagram photos that required hundreds of graphics chips across 42 servers for almost a month.[67] An analysis by the nonprofit OpenAI found that the amount of computing power used for training certain AI systems is now rising seven times faster than it did before about 2012 (doubling every approximately 3.4 months post-2012 versus approximately 2 years pre-2012).[68] The OpenAI group recommended that policymakers consider increasing funding for academic research, as some types of AI research are becoming more computationally intensive and expensive.[69]

Building on federal strategic planning and agency efforts to provide greater access to computational resources and high-quality data to support AI research, Congress directed the Director of the National Science Foundation in coordination with the Office of Science and Technology Policy to establish a National AI Research Resource Task Force through the National Artificial Intelligence Initiative Act of 2020.[70] The task force is to include four federal members, four members from academic institutions, and four private sector members. The task force is meant to investigate and report on the feasibility and advisability of establishing and sustaining a National Artificial Intelligence Research Resource, defined as "a system that provides researchers and students across scientific fields and disciplines with access to compute resources, co-located with publicly-available, artificial intelligence-ready

---

[66] NSTC Select Committee on Artificial Intelligence 2019 AI R&D Strategic Plan, p. 28.

[67] Tom Simonite, "Your Instagram #Dogs and #Cats Are Training Facebook's AI," *Wired*, May 2, 2018, at https://www.wired.com/story/your-instagram-dogs-and-cats-are-training-facebooks-ai/.

[68] As reported by Karen Hao, "The Computing Power Needed to Train AI is Now Rising Seven Times Faster than Ever Before," *MIT Technology Review*, November 11, 2019, at https://www.technologyreview.com/2019/11/11/132004/the-computing-power-needed-to-train-ai-is-now-rising-seven-times-faster-than-ever-before/.

[69] OpenAI, "AI and Compute: Addendum," *OpenAI Blog*, May 16, 2018, at https://openai.com/blog/ai-and-compute/ #addendum.

[70] P.L. 116-283, Division E, Section 5106.

government and non-government data sets and a research environment with appropriate educational tools and user support."[71]

AI Training with Small and Alternative Datasets

Some researchers have responded to the concern over limited access to big datasets for training by focusing on alternative ways to obtain or use data to reduce costs and computing power requirements. One method that has been explored is creating techniques and models that can learn from reduced amounts of data or fewer training iterations. For example, researchers at Google DeepMind created AI software that initially needs to analyze several hundred categories of images, but afterwards can learn to recognize new objects from just one picture—called "one-shot learning."[72]

Additional approaches include using alternative datasets and techniques. Some startups have reportedly created synthetic data to generate a large enough dataset for training AI models.[73] Others have demonstrated the promise of relatively unknown or novel AI techniques. For example, in recent years, some AI technologies developed by smaller AI groups have outperformed technologies from large companies such as Google and Intel in certain benchmark measures at Stanford University's DAWNBench challenge.[74] One report on this competition states

> these metrics [such as cost and algorithm speed] help us judge whether small teams can take on the tech giants. The results don't give a straightforward answer, but they suggest that raw computing power isn't the be-all and end-all for AI success. Ingenuity in how you design your algorithms counts for at least as much. While big tech companies like

---

[71] P.L. 116-283, Division E, Section 5106(g). According to information on AI.gov, information about members and meetings of the task force will be announced and posted once it is established; see https://www.ai.gov/nairrtf/ #MEMBERS.

[72] Will Knight, "Machines Can Now Recognize Something After Seeing It Once," *MIT Technology Review*, November 3, 2016, at https://www.technologyreview.com/2016/11/03/6485/machines-can-now-recognize-something-after-seeing-it-once/.

[73] Tom Simonite, "Some Startups Use Fake Data to Train AI," *Wired*, April, 25, 2018, at https://www.wired.com/story/ some-startups-use-fake-data-to-train-ai/.

[74] The DAWNbench challenge is an AI engineering competition in which teams and individuals from universities, governments, and industry compete to design the best algorithms, with Stanford's researchers acting as adjudicators. Each entry must meet basic accuracy standards (for example, recognizing 93% of dogs in a given dataset) and is judged on metrics training time and cost. See James Vincent, "An AI Speed Test Shows Clever Coders Can Still Beat Tech Giants Like Google and Intel," *The Verge*, May 7, 2018, at https://www.theverge.com/2018/5/7/17316010/fast-ai-speed-test-stanford-dawnbench-google-intel.

Google and Intel had predictably strong showings in a number of tasks, smaller teams (and even individuals) ranked highly by using unusual and little-known techniques."[75]

AI Hardware

Sector Example: AI in Healthcare

Numerous companies and researchers have been developing and testing AI technologies for use in healthcare, for example, to detect diabetic retinopathy (an eye condition that can cause blindness in diabetic patients) and skin cancer, and to mine large quantities of medical data to derive insights.[76] Some hospitals are also experimenting with using voice recognition, and associated ML and NLP technology, to assist doctors and patients.[77]

Growth in AI and its potential healthcare applications has led to the development of various partnerships among public and private sector groups. In 2019, for example, established pharmaceutical companies partnered with startups and researchers working on AI use for drug discovery and development.[78] Federal agencies have also begun assessing the potential for AI in certain settings, such as drug discovery and clinical trials,[79] and working with the private sector to evaluate the use of AI systems. For example, a partnership between the Department of Veterans

[75] James Vincent, "An AI Speed Test Shows Clever Coders Can Still Beat Tech Giants Like Google and Intel," *The Verge*, May 7, 2018, at https://www.theverge.com/2018/5/7/17316010/fast-ai-speed-test-stanford-dawnbench-google-intel.

[76] Google, "Seeing Potential: How a Team at Google Is Using AI to Help Doctors Prevent Blindness in Diabetics," at https://www.google.com/about/stories/seeingpotential/; Melanie Evans and Laura Stevens, "Big Tech Expands Footprint in Health," November 27, 2018, at https://www.wsj.com/articles/amazon-starts-selling-software-to-mine-patient-health-records-1543352136; and H.A. Haenssle et al., "Man Against Machine: Diagnostic Performance of a Deep Learning Convolutional Neural Network for Dermoscopic Melanoma Recognition in Comparison to 58 Dermatologists," *Annals of Oncology*, vol. 29, no. 8 (August 1, 2018), pp. 1836-1842.

[77] Ruth Hailu, "5 Burning Questions About Deploying Voice Recognition Technology in Health Care," *STAT News*, July 10, 2019, at https://www.statnews.com/2019/07/10/5-questions-voice-recognition-technology/.

[78] Robert Langreth, "AI Drug Hunters Could Give Big Pharma a Run for Its Money, *Bloomberg*, July 15, 2019, at https://www.bloomberg.com/news/features/2019-07-15/google-ai-could-challenge-big-pharma-in-drug-discovery.

[79] Government Accountability Office, *Artificial Intelligence in Health Care: Benefits and Challenges of Machine Learning in Drug Development*, GAO-20-215SP, January 21, 2020, at https://www.gao.gov/products/GAO-20-215SP.

Affairs and DeepMind has worked to identify risk factors for patient deterioration during hospitalization in an effort to develop early interventions and improve care.[80] Further, the Food and Drug Administration has been developing a framework for regulating AI- and ML-based software as a medical device and addressing subsequent modifications to such software.[81]

While there are many encouraging developments for using AI technologies in healthcare, stakeholders have remarked on the slow progress in using AI broadly within healthcare settings, and various challenges and questions remain. Researchers and clinicians have raised questions about the accuracy, security, and privacy of these technologies; the availability of sufficient health data on which to train systems; medical liability in the event of adverse outcomes; patient access and receptivity; and the adequacy of current user consent processes.[82] A 2019 literature review and meta-analysis of the performance of DL systems compared to medical professionals in detecting disease from medical imaging concluded that few of the 82 identified studies presented externally validated results and "poor reporting is prevalent in deep learning studies, which limits reliable interpretation of the reported diagnostic accuracy," concluding that new reporting standards could improve future studies.[83]

Hardware advances have played another key role in AI progress over the past decade, and hardware development—including AI chips and high performance computing (HPC) for AI applications—is an active research area. According to data from CB Insights, global equity funding for AI chip startups rose from just over $200 million from 13 deals in 2016 to approximately $700

[80] Department of Veterans Affairs, Office of Public and Intergovernmental Affairs, "VA Partners With DeepMind to Build Machine Learning Tools to Identify Health Risks for Veterans," February 21, 2018, at https://www.va.gov/opa/ pressrel/pressrelease.cfm?id=4013.

[81] See U.S. Food and Drug Administration, "Artificial Intelligence and Machine Learning in Software as a Medical Device," at https://www.fda.gov/medical-devices/software-medical-device-samd/artificial-intelligence-and-machine-learning-software-medical-device.

[82] Ruth Hailu, "5 Burning Questions About Deploying Voice Recognition Technology in Health Care," *STAT News*, July 10, 2019, at https://www.statnews.com/2019/07/10/5-questions-voice-recognition-technology/; and Lauren Joseph, "5 Burning Questions About Using Artificial Intelligence to Prevent Blindness," *STAT News*, July 17, 2019, at https://www.statnews.com/2019/07/17/artificial-intelligence-to-prevent-blindness/.

[83] Xiaoxuan Liu et al., "A Comparison of Deep Learning Performance Against Health-Care Professionals in Detecting Diseases from Medical Imaging: A Systematic Review and Meta-Analysis," *The Lancet*, vol. 1, no. 6 (October 1, 2019), pp. E271-E297.

million from 30 deals in 2018.[84] Companies including Nvidia, Google, Microsoft, and Facebook have been working on AI chip R&D, including developing chips designed for specialized tasks and designed to optimize energy efficiency for particular AI applications.[85]

One of the largest recent efforts in the United States to use HPC for AI applications comes from a partnership between the DOE's Oak Ridge National Laboratory (ORNL) and IBM to create the Summit supercomputer. Summit contains "AI-optimized" graphical processing units (GPUs) and has been described as "a supercomputer suited for AI."[86] The type and large number of chips allow it to run intensive ML techniques, such as DL.[87]

Federal Activity in AI

In recent years, the federal government—including the White House, federal agencies, and Congress—has increasingly supported and conducted AI R&D, invested in AI technologies, and worked to address issues with AI development and use. AI has been of interest to Congress since at least the 1980s and congressional AI activities, including legislation and oversight hearings, increased in the 115th and 116th Congresses.[88] This section of the report focuses on selected federal activities during the Administrations of Donald J. Trump and Barack Obama and in the 115th and 116th Congresses.

Executive Branch

The Trump and Obama Administrations took a variety of actions related to AI, by establishing initiatives through executive order, forming committees, and

---

[84] Data from CB Insights as reported in Richard Waters, "Facebook Joins Amazon and Google in AI Chip Race," *Financial Times*, February 18, 2019, at https://www.ft.com/content/1c2aab18-3337-11e9-bd3a-8b2a211d90d5.

[85] Ibid.

[86] Department of Energy, Oak Ridge National Laboratory, "Summit," at https://www.olcf.ornl.gov/summit/, and "ORNL Launches Summit Supercomputer," news release, June 8, 2018, at https://www.ornl.gov/news/ornl-launches-summit-supercomputer.

[87] Tom Simonite, "The US Again Has the World's Most Powerful Supercomputer," *Wired*, June 8, 2018, https://www.wired.com/story/the-us-again-has-worlds-most-powerful-supercomputer.

[88] For example, see U.S. Congress, Subcommittee on Investigations and Oversight, Committee on Science and Technology, U.S. House of Representatives, *Robotics*, 97th Congress, 2nd sess., June 2 and 23, 1982 (Washington, DC: GPO, 1983).

releasing reports. Further, in accordance with the National Artificial Intelligence Initiative Act of 2020 (P.L. 116-283, Division E, as described in the "Legislation" section), the Office of Science and Technology Policy (OSTP) launched the National AI Initiative Office (NAIIO) on January 12, 2021, to coordinate and support the National AI Initiative (the act is further described in the "Legislation" section).[89]

Executive Orders on AI

In February 2019, President Trump released an executive order establishing the American AI Initiative (E.O. 13859).[90] In addition to promoting AI R&D investment and coordination, objectives of the E.O. include making federal data, models, and computing resources available for AI development, reducing barriers to the use of AI technologies, developing technical and international standards around AI innovation, preparing an action plan around AI and national security concerns, and training the workforce to develop and use AI.

In December 2020, President Trump released an executive order promoting the use of trustworthy AI in the federal government (E.O. 13960).[91] The E.O. establishes a common set of principles for the design, development, acquisition, and use of AI in the federal government to foster public trust and confidence, and directs the Office of Management and Budget (OMB) to develop policy guidance for implementing the principles across agencies. The E.O. further includes direction to federal agencies (1) to provide annual, publicly-available inventories of nonclassified, nonsensitive use cases of AI, and (2) to undertake activities to expand the number of AI experts at federal agencies, including through creating an AI track within the Presidential Innovation Fellows program and by assessing potential expansion of federal rotational programs.

---

[89] See information provided by National Artificial Intelligence Initiative Office, "NAIIO—National Artificial Intelligence Initiative Office," at https://www.ai.gov/about/#NAIIO_National_Artificial_Intelligence_Initiative_Office. The "AI.gov" website was originally launched by the Trump Administration; a new version of the website was launched by the Biden Administration on May 5, 2021.

[90] Executive Order 13859, "Maintaining American Leadership in Artificial Intelligence," 84 *Federal Register* 3967, February 11, 2019.

[91] Executive Order 13960, "Promoting the Use of Trustworthy Artificial Intelligence in the Federal Government," 85 *Federal Register* 78939, December 8, 2020, at https://www.federalregister.gov/d/2020-27065.

National Science and Technology Council Committees

The National Science and Technology Council (NSTC) convenes federal science and technology leaders as a primary means within the executive branch to coordinate science and technology policies across federal agencies.[92] The Trump Administration established a new committee and expanded on committees and working groups established by the Obama Administration, with the following NSTC bodies coordinating cross-agency efforts in AI and ML:

- The Select Committee on Artificial Intelligence was established in May 2018 and rechartered on January 5, 2021 "in accordance with the National Artificial Intelligence Act of 2020 … with a broader scope and membership." The Committee is comprised of heads of agencies and advises the White House on interagency AI R&D priorities; provides a formal mechanism for interagency policy coordination and the development of federal AI activities; and addresses national and international AI policy matters.[93]
- The ML and AI (MLAI) Subcommittee is the operations and implementation arm of the Select Committee on Artificial Intelligence and includes federal employees with budgetary decisionmaking responsibilities to help focus priorities for AI investments through agency programs.

---

[92] For additional information on the NSTC, see CRS Report R43935, *Office of Science and Technology Policy (OSTP): History and Overview*, by John F. Sargent Jr. and Dana A. Shea.

[93] For additional information on the NSTC Select Committee on Artificial Intelligence, see the January 5, 2021 charter, at https://trumpwhitehouse.archives.gov/wp-content/uploads/2021/01/Charter-Select-Committee-on-AI-Jan-2021-posted.pdf.

- The AI Interagency Working Group is a community of practice,[94] taking on tasks that require deep expert knowledge and producing products such as the AI R&D Strategic Plan and its updates.[95]

Select AI Reports and Documents

As federal government interest and engagement in AI has grown, the executive branch has included a focus on AI in a variety of strategic plans, reports, and memoranda, including the following.

- The NSTC first released the *National AI Research and Development Strategic Plan* in 2016 with seven strategic priorities.[96] In September 2018, NITRD's National Coordination Office requested input from the public on whether and how the plan should be revised and improved.[97] In response, various industry groups requested more detail on federal priorities in AI R&D—including on specific challenges, applications, ways to incorporate private sector participation, and goals for investments from both technical and social impact perspectives. Some groups also asserted a need to align federal plans for enabling technologies such as 5G and quantum computing with the AI strategy.[98] In June 2019, NSTC released an updated plan with eight strategic priorities, the last of which was new: (1) make long-term investments in AI research; (2) develop effective methods for human-AI collaboration; (3) understand and address

---

[94] A community of practice is generally a group of professionals who are active in, or interested in, a particular craft or profession. For example, the General Service Administration (GSA) also leads an AI community of practice to "bring together federal employees who are active in, or interested in, AI policy technology, standards, and programs to facilitate the sharing of best practices, use cases, and lessons learned; and [to] advance and share tools, playbooks success stories with a community of interested professionals." Steven Babitch, "GSA Launches Artificial Intelligence Community of Practice," *GSA Blog*, November 5, 2019, at https://www.gsa.gov/blog/2019/11/05/gsa-launches-artificial-intelligence-community-of-practice.

[95] Overviews of the activities of each body include descriptions provided during a telephone conversation between CRS and Dr. Lynne Parker, Deputy Chief Technology Officer of the United States, March 2019.

[96] National Science and Technology Council, Networking and Information Technology Research and Development Subcommittee, *The National Artificial Intelligence Research and Development Strategic Plan*, October 2016.

[97] NITRD National Coordination Office, "Request for Information on Update to the 2016 National Artificial Intelligence Research and Development Strategic Plan," 83 *Federal Register* 48655, September 26, 2018.

[98] MeriTalk, "Industry Wants More Detail on AI R&D Plan," December 21, 2018, at https://www.meritalk.com/articles/industry-wants-more-detail-on-ai-rd-plan/.

ethical, legal, and societal implications of AI; (4) ensure the safety and security of AI systems; (5) develop shared public datasets and environments for AI training and testing; (6) measure and evaluate AI technologies through standards and benchmarks; (7) better understand the national AI R&D workforce needs; and (8) expand public-private partnerships to accelerate advances in AI.[99]

- In August 2019, in response to E.O. 13859, NIST released the *Plan for Federal Engagement in Developing Technical Standards and Related Tools in AI.* NIST noted that the plan was prepared with broad public and private sector input. It includes recommendations for federal government activities to engage in deep, long-term AI standards development "to speed the pace of reliable, robust, and trustworthy AI technology development."[100]
- In August 2020, OMB and OSTP provided their annual memorandum to the heads of federal R&D agencies laying out the Administration's R&D budget priorities for FY2022. The memorandum stated that industries of the future— including AI—remained a top R&D priority for the Administration, as in prior years.[101]
- In November 2020, OMB released a memorandum to the heads of federal agencies providing guidance for the regulation of AI. The purpose of the memo was to guide regulatory and nonregulatory oversight of AI applications developed and deployed outside of the federal government. It lays out 10 principles for the stewardship of AI applications, including topics such as risk assessment, fairness and nondiscrimination, disclosure and transparency, and interagency coordination. It further touches on reducing barriers to the deployment and use of AI, including increasing access to government data, communicating benefits and risks to the public, engaging in the development and use of voluntary consensus standards, and engaging in international regulatory cooperation efforts. Agency plans to conform to the memorandum are due on May 17, 2021, and must

---

[99] NSTC Select Committee on Artificial Intelligence 2019 AI R&D Strategic Plan.

[100] National Institute of Standards and Technology, *U.S. Leadership in AI: A Plan for Federal Engagement in Developing Technical Standards and Related Tools*, August 9, 2019, pp. 3-6.

[101] Office of Management and Budget and Office of Science and Technology Policy, "Memorandum for the Heads of Executive Departments and Agencies: Fiscal Year (FY) 2022 Administration Research and Development Budget Priorities and Cross-cutting Actions" August 14, 2020, at https://www.whitehouse.gov/wp-content/uploads/2020/08/M-20-29.pdf.

include any statutory authorities governing agency regulation of AI applications, information collections on AI from regulated entities, regulatory barriers to AI applications, and any planned or considered regulatory actions on AI.[102]

In addition to the initial National AI R&D Strategic Plan, two other background documents on AI were also prepared in 2016 by the NSTC and other offices in the Executive Office of the President. These reports were *Preparing for the Future of Artificial Intelligence*, and *Artificial Intelligence, Automation, and the Economy*.[103]

Federal Agency Activities

Engagement on AI varies across agencies and may include examining and adopting AI technologies for internal agency use, holding hearings to examine issues surrounding the development and use of AI,[104] conducting AI R&D in-house (intramural R&D), and funding AI R&D by outside groups (extramural R&D), including at institutions of higher education (IHEs), nonprofits, and industry. E.O. 18539 directed federal R&D agencies to "promote sustained investment in AI R&D in collaboration with industry, academia, international partners and allies, and other non-Federal entities" and the heads of those agencies to consider AI as an R&D priority when preparing their budget requests to Congress. E.O. 13960 highlighted a range of ways that federal agencies are already employing AI, including identifying information security threats, facilitating review of large datasets, streamlining processes for grant applications, modeling weather patterns, and facilitating predictive maintenance.

Although there are numerous examples of federal agencies using AI in-house, there is currently no comprehensive database of AI projects within agencies, though some recent efforts have attempted to better compile such

---

[102] Russell Vought, Director of the Office of Management and Budget, "Guidance for Regulation of Artificial Intelligence Applications," Memorandum for the heads of executive departments and agencies, November 17, 2020, at https://www.whitehouse.gov/wp-content/uploads/2020/11/M-21-06.pdf.

[103] Available at https://obamawhitehouse.archives.gov/sites/default/files/whitehouse_files/microsites/ostp/NSTC/preparing_for_the_future_of_ai.pdf; and https://obamawhitehouse.archives.gov/sites/whitehouse.gov/files/documents/Artificial-Intelligence-Automation-Economy.PDF.

[104] For example, the Federal Trade Commission (FTC) held a hearing in November 2018 focused on consumer welfare implications associated with the use of algorithmic decision tools, AI, and predictive analytics; see https://www.ftc.gov/ news-events/events-calendar/ftc-hearing-7-competition-consumer-protection-21st-century.

information.[105] The General Services Administration (GSA) has reportedly been working to catalogue some use cases of AI across the federal government.[106] Additionally, the Administrative Conference of the United States (ACUS) commissioned a study, completed in February 2020, "to map how federal agencies are currently using AI to make and support decisions."[107] Among 142 federal agencies, the study authors identified use cases— defined as "instance[s] in which an agency had considered using or had already deployed AI/ML technology to carry out a core function"—in 64 (45%) agencies, based on searches of publicly available information.[108] Of the 157 use cases, the authors noted that 84 (53%) were built in-house, rather than being procured through private contracting or noncommercial collaboration (e.g., with an academic laboratory or through a public-facing competition).[109] Building on this initial study, E.O. 13960 requires federal agencies to create publicly available inventories of use cases of AI, based on common criteria, format, and inventory mechanisms created by the Federal Chief Information Officers Council.

Some examples of federal agencies using AI in-house include the following:

- The Department of Health and Human Services used AI and NLP technologies to identify incorrect citations and outdated regulations in the Code of Federal Regulations as part of a "department-wide regulatory clean-up initiative."[110]
- NASA launched RPA pilot projects in accounts payable and receivable, IT spending, and human resources. The projects appeared to work well—in the human resources application, for example, 86%

---

[105] CRS communications with the Office of Science and Technology Policy, February 2020; and David Freeman Engstrom et al., *Government by Algorithm: Artificial Intelligence in Federal Administrative Agencies*, Report delivered to the Administrative Conference of the United States, February 2020.

[106] CRS communications with the Office of Science and Technology Policy, February 2020.

[107] See Administrative Conference of the United States, Office of the Chairman Projects, "Artificial Intelligence in Federal Agencies," February 2020, at https://www.acus.gov/research-projects/artificial-intelligence-federal-agencies (hereinafter, "ACUS report 2020").

[108] Ibid., pp. 15-18. The authors limited the included agencies to those with over 400 employees and excluded active military and intelligence-related organizations.

[109] Ibid. p. 18.

[110] Department of Health and Human Services, "HHS Launches First-of-Its-Kind Regulatory Clean-Up Initiative Utilizing AI," November 17, 2020, at https://www.hhs.gov/about/news/2020/11/17/hhs-launches-first-its-kind-regulatory-clean-up-initiative-utilizing-ai.html.

of transactions were completed without human intervention—and are being rolled out across the organization. NASA reportedly moved forward with implementing more RPA bots, some with higher levels of intelligence.[111]

- The National Oceanic and Atmospheric Administration (NOAA) has developed an AI strategy to "expand the application of [AI] in every NOAA mission area by improving the efficiency, effectiveness, and coordination of AI development and usage across the agency."[112]
- The Social Security Administration has used AI/ML in its adjudication work to address challenges from high caseloads and in ensuring accuracy and consistency of decisionmaking, which have reportedly persisted through decades of quality improvement efforts.[113]

Considerations for agency adoption of AI mirror private sector considerations—namely, how can AI be used as a tool to advance process automation, provide insight into data analyses, and improve services (i.e., improve timeliness and enhance citizen interactions with federal agencies, such as through the use of chatbots). Technology leaders in federal agencies, industry, and academia have argued that the initial implementation of AI technologies should be evaluated in terms of challenges and opportunities associated with an agency's current data collection, management, and analysis processes, rather than the capabilities of AI systems themselves.[114] Additional considerations include how to evaluate and acquire AI systems.

To further guide agencies, E.O. 13960 provides broad principles for federal design, development, acquisition, and use of AI, including that AI systems should be (1) lawful and respectful of the nation's values; (2) purposeful and performance-driven; (3) accurate, reliable, and effective; (4) safe, secure and resilient; (5) understandable; (6) responsible and traceable;

---

[111] Thomas H. Davenport and Rajeev Ronanki, "Artificial Intelligence for the Real World," *Harvard Business Review*, January-February 2018, pp. 108-116, at https://hbr.org/2018/01/artificial-intelligence-for-the-real-world.

[112] National Oceanic and Atmospheric Administration, *NOAA Artificial Intelligence Strategy: Analytics for Next-Generation Earth Science*, February 2020, at https://nrc.noaa.gov/LinkClick.aspx?fileticket=0I2p2-Gu3rA%3d&tabid= 91&portalid=0.

[113] Administrative Conference of the United States, "Artificial Intelligence in Federal Agencies," February 2020, pp. 38-39.

[114] See remarks by Stephen Dennis, Director of the Data Analytics Engine, Science and Technology Directorate, Department of Homeland Security at the FCW Workshop, "Artificial Intelligence: Moving from Vision to Implementation," March 13, 2018; and Davenport and Ronanki, 2018.

(7) regularly monitored; (8) transparent; and (9) accountable. Given that OMB is tasked with developing, by June 2021, a roadmap for policy guidance to better support federal government use of AI, more concrete plans and actions may be specified across agencies.

The National Science Foundation (NSF) has been a primary nondefense source of federal extramural support for AI R&D for decades and currently "supports fundamental research, education and workforce development, and advanced, scalable computing resources that collectively enhance fundamental research in AI."[115] Fundamental AI research areas include how computer systems represent knowledge; learn; process spoken and written language; and solve problems, as well as the impacts of AI on continuing education and adult retraining.[116] Additional federal agency activities in AI R&D include

- NIST engaged in national and international AI standards development activities;
- DARPA launched the AI Next campaign, focused on "improving the robustness and reliability of AI systems; enhancing the security and resiliency of machine learning and AI technologies; reducing power, data, and performance inefficiencies; and pioneering the next generation of AI algorithms and applications, such as 'explainability' and common sense reasoning";[117]
- DOE established the Artificial Intelligence and Technology Office to "accelerate the delivery of AI-enabled capabilities, scale the department-wide development and impact of AI, and synchronize AI activities to advance the agency's core missions, expand partnerships, and support American AI Leadership";[118]
- The Department of Veteran's Affairs (VA) established a National Artificial Intelligence Institute (NAII) to develop AI R&D capabilities in the VA;[119] and

---

[115] Information about NSF support for AI research and workforce programs and interagency work can be found at "Artificial Intelligence at NSF," at https://www.nsf.gov/cise/ai.jsp.

[116] NSF, "Statement on Artificial Intelligence for American Industry," press statement 18-005, May 10, 2018, at https://www.nsf.gov/news/news_summ.jsp?cntn_id=245418.

[117] DARPA, "DARPA Announces $2 Billion Campaign to Develop Next Wave of AI Technologies," September 7, 2018, at https://www.darpa.mil/news-events/2018-09-07.

[118] See U.S. Department of Energy, Artificial Intelligence and Technology Office, at https://www.energy.gov/science-innovation/artificial-intelligence-and-technology-office.

[119] See U.S. Department of Veterans Affairs, Office of Research and Development, "National Artificial Intelligence Institute (NAII)," at https://www.research.va.gov/naii/.

- The National Institute for Justice—the research wing of the Department of Justice—supported research on "crime-fighting AI" which "it believes could be used to fight human trafficking, illegal border crossings, drug trafficking, and child pornography" by helping investigators sort through data.[120]

Congress

The 115th and 116th Congresses focused on AI more frequently and explicitly than previous Congresses, in terms of enacted and introduced legislation and hearings. Additionally, bipartisan AI caucuses were launched in the House and the Senate.[121] The AI Index group used data from McKinsey & Company to assess mentions of AI in Congress based on the *Congressional Record*. The analysis found, after a maximum of 9 mentions in any year from 2011 through 2016, mentions increased each year throughout the 115th and 116th Congresses, with 129 mentions reported in 2020 (Figure 3).[122] This section of the report provides a brief summary of legislative activities in the 116th and 117th Congresses, including descriptions of laws and selected bills that focused on, or included specific provisions focused on AI and ML, as well as hearings from the 115th-117th Congresses (as of the date of this report).[123]

---

[120] Kate Conger, "Justice Department Drops $2 Million to Research Crime-Fighting AI," *Gizmodo*, February 27, 2018; and DOJ's solicitation for the program can be found at https://nij.gov/funding/Documents/solicitations/NIJ-2018-14000.pdf.

[121] The House Congressional AI Caucus was originally launched in 2015; see https://artificialintelligencecaucus-olson.house.gov/. The Senate AI Caucus was announced on March 13, 2019; see announcements from the caucus co-chairs at https://www.portman.senate.gov/public/index.cfm/2019/3/portman-heinrich-launch-bipartisan-artificial-intelligence-caucus, and https://www.heinrich.senate.gov/press-releases/heinrich-portman-launch-bipartisan-artificial-intelligence-caucus.

[122] AI Index 2021 Annual Report, p. 172.

[123] Additional bills mentioned AI or ML without including specific provisions related to the technologies. For example, the Developing Innovation and Growing the Internet of Things Act (S. 1611, 116th Congress) stated in the findings that "the Internet of things will … play a key role in developing artificial intelligence and advanced computing capabilities," but AI was not included anywhere else in the bill. Such bills are not discussed in this section.

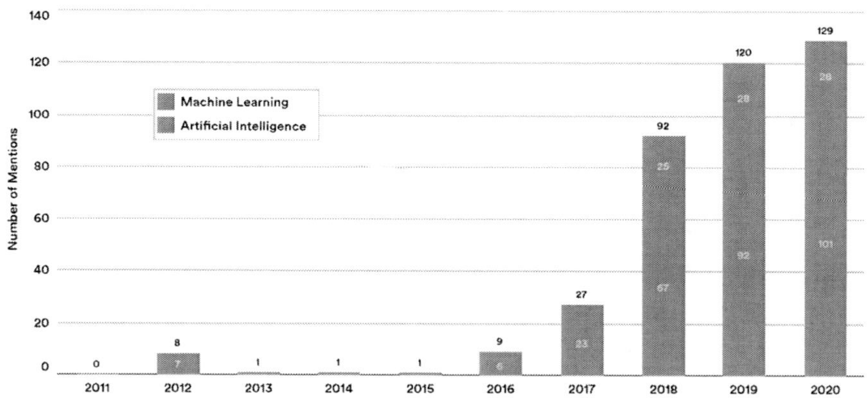

Source: AI Index Steering Committee, *The AI Index 2021 Annual Report*, Human-Centered AI Institute, Stanford University, Stanford, CA, March 2021, pp. 171-172; data from the McKinsey Global Institute, 2020.

Notes: Per the AI Index 2021 Annual Report, each count indicates that AI or ML was mentioned during a particular event contained in the *Congressional Record*, including the reading of a bill. If a speaker or member mentioned AI or ML multiple times within remarks, or multiple speakers mentioned AI or ML within the same event, it appears only once as a result. Counts for AI and ML are separate, as they were conducted in separate searches. Mentions of the abbreviations "AI" or "ML" are not included. Additional information about the search methodology is included in the AI Index 2021 Annual Report appendix, p. 216.

Figure 3. Mentions of Artificial Intelligence and Machine Learning in the Congressional Record, 2011-2020.

Legislation

As of the date of this report, multiple bills introduced in the 117th Congress have included language about AI, either as a focus of the bill or in a specific provision, though no legislation has been enacted. Some bills have included AI as one of multiple key technology areas important for U.S. competitiveness.[124] Other bills have focused on federal AI expertise; addressed potential bias in automated decision systems that may use AI; or included AI as a technology with potential applications in healthcare.[125]

---

[124] For the 117th Congress, see, for example, the Endless Frontier Act (S. 1260) and the Strategic Competition Act of 2021 (S. 1169), the STRATEGIC Act (S. 687), and the Democracy Technology Partnership Act (S. 604).

[125] For the 117th Congress, see, for example, "A bill to establish a Federal artificial intelligence scholarship-for-service program" (S. 1257), the Unemployment Insurance Technology

At least four laws enacted in the 116th Congress focused on AI or included AI-focused provisions. The FY2021 NDAA included multiple sections related to Department of Defense (DOD) AI activities in R&D, acquisitions, and workforce expansion and training. These sections built on prior direction in the FY2020 NDAA, which included provisions related to recruiting expertise at the DOD Joint Artificial Intelligence Center (JAIC); establishing DOD processes to update policies on emerging technologies, including AI; extending authorization for the National Security Commission on Artificial Intelligence; and requiring an analysis of major initiatives of the intelligence community in AI and ML.

Further, the FY2021 NDAA incorporated the expansive National Artificial Intelligence Act of 2020 (Division E), which included sections related to

- codifying the establishment of an American AI Initiative (Section 5101);
- establishing the National AI Initiative Office to support federal AI activities, including technical, programmatic, and administrative support for activities of the AI Initiative, as specified (Section 5102);
- establishing an Interagency Committee at OSTP to coordinate federal programs and activities in support of the AI Initiative, including developing periodic strategic plans for AI (Section 5103);[126]
- establishing a National AI Advisory Committee with representatives from academic institutions, companies, nonprofit and civil society entities, and federal laboratories to provide to the President and the AI Initiative Office "advice and information on science and technology research, development, ethics, standards, education, technology transfer, commercial application, security, and economic competitiveness" related to AI (Section 5104(a));
- establishing as part of the National AI Advisory Committee a Subcommittee on AI and Law Enforcement to provide advice on bias, data security, adoptability, and legal standards (Section 5104(e));
- directing NSF to contract with the National Academies of Sciences, Engineering, and Medicine to conduct a study on the current and

Modernization Act of 2021 (S. 490); the Black Maternal Health Momnibus Act of 2021 (S. 346 and H.R. 959); and the Tech to Save Moms Act (H.R. 937).

[126] This section effectively expanded on and codified the NSTC Select Committee on Artificial Intelligence that was established in the Trump Administration.

future impact of AI on the U.S. workforce across sectors (Section 5105);

- establishing a task force to investigate the feasibility of, and plan for, a National AI Research Resource, defined as "a system that provides researchers and students across scientific fields and disciplines with access to compute resources, co-located with publicly-available, AI-ready government and non-government data sets and a research environment with appropriate educational tools and user support" (Section 5106);
- directing NSF to establish a program to support a network of National AI Research Institutes, which shall be public-private partnerships that focus on a particular economic or social sector and associated ethical, societal, safety, and security implications, or a cross-cutting challenge for AI systems, with the potential to create or enhance innovation ecosystems and support interdisciplinary R&D, education, and workforce development in AI (Section 5201);[127]
- directing NIST to support AI standards development, develop a risk management framework for trustworthy AI systems, and develop best practices for documenting and sharing data sets used to train AI systems (Section 5301);
- directing the NOAA to establish a Center for AI (Section 5303);
- directing NSF to fund research and education activities in AI and related fields (Section 5401); and
- directing the DOE to carry out a cross-cutting R&D program to advance AI tools, systems, capabilities, and workforce needs and to improve the reliability of AI methods and solutions relevant to DOE's mission (Section 5501).

The Consolidated Appropriations Act, 2021 (P.L. 116-260) included the AI in Government Act of 2020 (Division U, Title I), which created within the General Services Administration (GSA) an AI Center of Excellence (CoE) to facilitate the adoption of AI technologies in the federal government.[128] The AI

---

[127] NSF began funding National AI Research Institutes in FY2020 in a joint effort with the U.S. Department of Agriculture National Institute of Food and Agriculture, the Department of Homeland Security Science and Technology Directorate, and the Department of Transportation Federal Highway Administration; see NSF's program description page at https://www.nsf.gov/funding/pgm_summ.jsp?pims_id=505686.

[128] The act codified the GSA AI Center of Excellence that was launched in 2019; see https://www.ai.gov/legislation-and-executive-orders/.

CoE is further required, among other activities, to collect, aggregate, and publish on a publicly available website information regarding federal programs, pilots, and other initiatives; and to advise federal agencies on the acquisition and use of AI through technical insight and expertise. The act required OMB to issue a memorandum to federal agencies regarding the development of AI policies, approaches for removing barriers to using AI technologies, and best practices for identifying, assessing, and mitigating any discriminatory impact or bias and any unintended consequences of using AI. Additionally, the act required the Office of Personnel Management to establish or update an occupational job series to include positions with primary duties in AI and to estimate current and future numbers of federal employment positions related to AI at each agency.

The Further Consolidated Appropriations Act, 2020 (P.L. 116-94) included a provision amending the Export-Import Bank Act of 1945 to establish a Program on China and Transformational Exports (Section 402). This program is directed to support the extension of loans, guarantees, and insurance that aim to "advance the comparative leadership of the United States with respect to the People's Republic of China, or support United States innovation, employment, and technological standards, through direct exports in" artificial intelligence, among other areas.

The Identifying Outputs of Generative Adversarial Networks Act (P.L. 116-258) directed NSF and NIST to support research on generative adversarial networks, including research on manipulated or synthesized content and information authenticity and the development of measurements and standards necessary to accelerate the development of technical tools to examine the function and outputs of GANs.

Multiple additional bills introduced in the 116th Congress address AI applications, such as facial recognition and deepfakes,[129] and areas in which AI is deployed, including law enforcement and criminal justice, healthcare, energy efficiency, natural resources, and defense and national security.[130]

---

[129] For the 116th Congress, see, for example, the Ethical Use of Facial Recognition Act (S. 3284); the Facial Recognition Technology Warrant Act of 2019 (S. 2878); the Facial, Analysis, Comparison, and Evaluation (FACE) Protection Act of 2019 (H.R. 4021); the Commercial Facial Recognition Privacy Act of 2019 (S. 847); the Deepfakes Report Act (H.R. 3600 and S. 2065); and the Deep Fake Detection Prize Competition Act (H.R. 5532).

[130] For the 116th Congress, see, for example, the Advancing Innovation to Assist Law Enforcement Act (H.R. 2613); the Black Maternal Health Momnibus Act of 2020 (S. 3424, H.R. 6142); the Department of Energy Veterans' Health Initiative Act (S. 143 and H.R. 617); the Securing American Leadership in Science and Technology Act of 2020 (H.R. 5685); and the BLUE GLOBE Act (H.R. 3548), in addition to the aforementioned

Some of these bills are focused on AI, while others include AI-specific provisions as part of a broader focus.

Hearings

Various committees in both the House of Representatives and the Senate held hearings focused on issues in AI and ML during the 115th, 116th, and 117th Congresses. Given its many, wide-ranging applications, the topic of AI has arisen as a consideration during numerous hearings. Hearing subjects with an explicit focus on AI and ML have ranged from broad considerations of AI and ML technologies and policies, including societal and ethical issues,[131] international research and competition,[132] and national security,[133] to more focused topics, such as use by the federal government,[134] potential impact to the U.S. workforce,[135] and consequences for human rights.[136] Hearings have also focused on specific AI applications, such as facial recognition and

---

provisions in the National Defense Authorization Acts in FY2019 (P.L. 115-232) and FY2020 (P.L. 116-92).

[131] U.S. Congress, House Committee on Science, Space, and Technology, *Artificial Intelligence: Societal and Ethical Implications*, 116th Cong., 1st sess., June 26, 2019.

[132] U.S. Congress, Joint U.S.-China Economic and Security Review Commission, *Hearing on Technology, Trade, and Military-Civil Fusion: China's Pursuit of Artificial Intelligence, New Materials, and New Energy*, 116th Cong., 1st sess., June 7, 2019.

[133] For example, U.S. Congress, Senate Committee on Armed Services, *Emerging Technologies and Their Impact on National Security*, 117th Cong., 1st sess., February 23, 2021, at https://www.armed-services.senate.gov/hearings/21-02-23-emerging-technologies-and-their-impact-on-national-security.

[134] For example, U.S. Congress, House Committee on Science, Space, and Technology, Subcommittee on Research and Technology and Subcommittee on Energy, *Artificial Intelligence: With Great Power Comes Great Responsibility*, 115th Cong., 2nd sess., June 26, 2018; and U.S. Congress, Senate Committee on Armed Services, Subcommittee on Emerging Threats and Capabilities, *Artificial Intelligence Initiatives Within the Department of Defense*, 116th Cong., 1st sess., March 12, 2019.

[135] U.S. Congress, House Committee on the Budget, *Machines, Artificial Intelligence, and the Workforce: Recovering and Readying Our Economy for the Future*, 116th Cong., 2nd sess., September 10, 2020; and U.S. Congress, House Committee on Science, Space, and Technology, Subcommittee on Research and Technology, *Artificial Intelligence and the Future of Work*, 116th Cong., 1st sess., September 24, 2019.

[136] U.S. Congress, House of Representatives, Tom Latos Human Rights Commission, *Artificial Intelligence: The Consequences for Human Rights*, 115th Cong., 2nd sess., May 22, 2018.

deepfakes,[137] and contact tracing for COVID-19 cases,[138] as well as use areas, such as financial services[139] and counterterrorism.[140]

Additionally, in the 115th Congress, the House Committee on Oversight and Government Reform held a series of three hearings focusing on AI: "Game Changers: Artificial Intelligence Part 1" on February 14, 2018; "Game Changers: Artificial Intelligence Part II, Artificial Intelligence and the Federal Government" on March 7, 2018; and "Game Changers: Artificial Intelligence and Public Policy" on April 18, 2018. Subsequently, the chairman and ranking member of the Subcommittee on Information Technology released a white paper summarizing lessons learned from the hearings and related oversight activities, as well as recommendations for the federal government in moving forward on AI. Broadly, the recommendations included increased engagement on AI by Congress and the Administration, including increased federal R&D funding; increased stakeholder engagement in developing strategies to improve worker education, training, and reskilling; agency reviews of federal privacy laws and regulatory frameworks; and assurance that AI systems are "accountable and inspectable" when agencies use them for decisionmaking about people.[141]

---

[137] U.S. Congress, House Permanent Select Committee on Intelligence, *National Security Challenges of Artificial Intelligence, Manipulated Media, and "Deepfakes,"* 116th Cong., 1st sess., June 13, 2019.

[138] U.S. Congress, House Committee on Financial Services, Task Force on Artificial Intelligence, *Virtual Hearing— Exposure Notification and Contact Tracing: How AI Helps Localities Reopen Safely and Researchers Find a Cure*, 116th Cong., 2nd sess., July 8, 2020, at https://financialservices.house.gov/calendar/eventsingle.aspx?EventID=406731.

[139] The House Committee on Financial Services established a Task Force on AI in May 2019, to examine issues including AI in financial services regulation, risk management, digital identification and combatting fraud, and reducing AI bias; see for example, U.S. Congress, House Committee on Financial Services, Task Force on AI, *Equitable Algorithms: Examining Ways to Reduce AI Bias in Financial Services*, 116th Cong., 2nd sess., Feb. 12, 2020, at https://financialservices.house.gov/calendar/eventsingle.aspx?EventID=406120; and U.S. Congress, House Committee on Financial Services, Task Force on AI, *Equitable Algorithms: How Human-Centered AI Can Address Systemic Racism and Racial Justice in Housing and Financial Services*, 117th Cong., 1st sess., May 7, 2021.

[140] U.S. Congress, House Committee on Homeland Security, Subcommittee on Intelligence and Counterterrorism, *Artificial Intelligence and Counterterrorism: Possibilities and Limitations*, 116th Cong., 1st sess., June 25, 2019.

[141] Rep. Will Hurd and Rep. Robin Kelly, "Rise of the Machines: Artificial Intelligence and Its Growing Impact on U.S. Policy," Subcommittee on Information Technology, Committee on Oversight and Government Reform, U.S. House of Representatives, September 2018.

Selected Issues for Congressional Consideration

Though specific AI technologies and application areas each have their own benefits, challenges, and policy issues, this section of the report will focus on some broad, crosscutting issues, with application-specific examples.

The broad potential benefits of AI technologies include opportunities for speed of data analysis and insights into big datasets, such as identification of patterns; augmentation of human decisionmaking; performance optimization for complex tasks and systems; and improved safety for people in dangerous occupations. For example, AI systems can improve facilities operations and efficiency, providing cost savings. In one application of such benefits, DeepMind reported applying ML to Google data centers to make recommendations to reduce the amount of energy used for cooling by up to 40%, subsequently moving to autonomous operations.[142]

At the same time, there are challenges and pitfalls associated with deployment and use of AI systems. For example, AI systems may perpetuate or amplify bias (as described in the "Ethics, Bias, Fairness, and Transparency" section) and may not yet be able to fully explain their decisionmaking (sometimes referred to as the "black box" problem), which can be particularly problematic in high-stakes situations, for example when they inform health and safety decisions. To train and evaluate complex AI systems, researchers and developers may need large datasets that are not widely accessible. Further, stakeholders have questioned the adequacy of public and private sector workforces to develop and work with AI, as well as the adequacy of current laws and regulations in dealing with societal and ethical issues that may arise.

In response to such overarching considerations, Congress might weigh the potential benefits of AI, such as increasing human safety, health, and productivity, with potential consequences, intended or otherwise, including job displacement and biases in algorithmic decisionmaking, when considering potential AI funding, policies, and regulation.

The passage of the National Artificial Intelligence Initiative Act of 2020 included provisions that directed federal government-wide activities and touched on many of the AI-associated issues raised in this report. Subsequently, Congress may decide that no additional legislative action is

---

[142] DeepMind, "DeepMind AI Reduces Google Data Centre Cooling Bill by 40%," July 20, 2016, at https://deepmind.com/blog/article/deepmind-ai-reduces-google-data-centre-cooling-bill-40; and Google, "Safety-First AI for Autonomous Data Center Cooling and Industrial Control," August 17, 2018, at https://www.blog.google/inside-google/infrastructure/safety-first-ai-autonomous-data-center-cooling-and-industrial-control/.

currently necessary, instead focusing in the near term on oversight of the implementation and effectiveness of the activities and programs directed by the act. This, along with activities begun in response to the aforementioned E.O.s, may provide better data and information for developing future legislation and congressional activities. Alternatively, given the rapid development of AI technologies and the wide range of sectors in which AI is deployed, Congress may decide that more actions are necessary to begin addressing issues surrounding AI use. Several major issues associated with the further development and use of AI and policy questions that Congress might consider are discussed below.

Implications for the U.S. Workforce

Concerns about job losses resulting from technological advances are not new.[143] Historically, advances in technology have had varied impacts on the labor market, with new technologies reducing demand for some skills and increasing demand for others.[144] The rapid advance of AI technologies and their application in multiple sectors of the economy have increased fears about possible job losses and spurred academic and government interest in studying potential impacts. Meanwhile, this has also led to concern that too few workers have AI expertise, both to work with AI in their jobs and to conduct AI R&D. Thus, discussions of AI and the U.S. workforce largely focus on two main issues: (1) the potential impact of AI and AI-driven automation on workers, including job displacement and job shifts; and (2) whether the United States has enough AI experts (people with advanced degrees in AI who work or teach in AI fields) for research, development, and application of AI across sectors, as well as teaching the next generation of AI experts.

Job Displacement and Skill Shifts

Economists and researchers are divided on possible answers to the question of how many jobs will be lost, gained, or changed, due partly or wholly to the development and application of AI technologies. Some analysts may argue

---

[143] For a historical perspective, see for example, David H. Autor, "Why Are There Still So Many Jobs? The History and Future of Workplace Automation," *Journal of Economic Perspectives*, vol. 29, no. 3 (Summer 2015), pp. 3-30.

[144] Executive Office of the President (EOP), *Artificial Intelligence, Automation, and the Economy*, December 2016, p. 11, at https://obamawhitehouse.archives.gov/sites/whitehouse.gov/files/documents/Artificial-Intelligence-Automation-Economy.PDF.

that AI-related technologies are unprecedented in their speed of development, their range of applications, and the number of jobs they threaten, while others may argue that technology has a long history of displacing labor yet simultaneously creating new jobs, any net loss would be negligible, and the factors affecting the pace and extent of automation and AI adoption have not changed.[145] However, newly created jobs may be quite different from those eliminated and subsequently burden workers with the need to invest time, money, and relocation efforts in order to train for or acquire new jobs. A 2019 McKinsey Global Institute report that examined the impact of automation technologies on local economies and demographic groups stated, "While there could be positive net job growth at the national level, new jobs may not appear in the same places, and the occupational mix is changing. The challenge will be in addressing local mismatches and helping workers gain new skills."[146]

The potential impacts of AI technologies on the number and types of jobs that are or will be available are challenging to measure and predict for a variety of reasons.

- First, definitions of AI and related technologies vary across industries, studies, and reports; further, potential job impacts from AI, computers, robots, and automation more generally are often conflated, making the specific workforce effects from AI technologies challenging to specify.
- Second, the numerous studies conducted to date vary in scope, including the labor sectors, populations, and countries assessed; the timeframes of predicted impacts; and the granularity of the datasets analyzed (e.g., whole occupations, specific tasks, or skillsets). One news article in 2018 attempted to compile all the available studies on how automation, AI, and robots could affect job losses or gains. The author summarized 19 studies that ranged in prediction dates (where specified) from 2016 to 2035, in jobs eliminated from 1.8 million to 1 billion, in jobs created from 1 million to 890 million, and in geographic focus from single countries (the United States or the

[145] For example, these perspectives are discussed in "Automation and Anxiety: Will Smarter Machines Cause Mass Unemployment," *The Economist*, June 23, 2016, at https://www.economist.com/special-report/2016/06/23/automation-and-anxiety.

[146] Susan Lund et al., *The Future of Work in America: People and Places, Today and Tomorrow*, McKinsey Global Institute, July 2019, available at https://www.mckinsey.com/featured-insights/future-of-work/the-future-of-work-in-america-people-and-places-today-and-tomorrow.

United Kingdom) to worldwide. The author concluded that "there are about as many predictions as there are experts."[147] Further, many studies have relied on case studies and subjective assessments by experts.[148]

- Third, AI technologies are rapidly evolving, and it is difficult to predict what specific tasks they might be used to automate in the future, even in the short term. Some experts have asserted that "there is no widely shared agreement on the tasks where ML systems excel, and thus little agreement on the specific expected impacts on the workforce and on the economy more broadly."[149] And while AI is predicted to have greater displacement effects on higher skill professional and technical workers than earlier waves of automation, robust measures of current and future effects are still in development.[150]

While many reports and news stories related to job automation focus on worker displacement, some companies report using AI-enabled automation to perform jobs that are "dirty, dull, and dangerous," such as sorting at recycling facilities,[151] or to make up for labor shortages in the tight labor market. For example, some agriculture companies report developing autonomous systems to help make up for a shortage of farm workers.[152] Other companies making use of automation still report a high demand for employees. For example, Amazon reportedly expanded its workforce by 300,000 people since acquiring robotics company Kiva and deploying its robots in 2012 in its distribution

---

147 Erin Winick, "Every Study We Could Find on What Automation Will Do to Jobs, in One Chart," *MIT Technology Review*, January 25, 2018, at https://www.technologyreview.com/s/610005/every-study-we-could-find-on-what-automation-will-do-to-jobs-in-one-chart/.

148 Mark Muro, Jacob Whiton, and Robert Maxim, *What Jobs Are Affected by AI? Better-Paid, Better-Educated Workers Face the Most Exposure*, Brookings, November 2019, at https://www.brookings.edu/wp-content/uploads/2019/11/2019.11.20_Brookings Metro_What-jobs-are-affected-by-AI_Report_Muro-Whiton-Maxim.pdf.

149 Erik Brynjolfsson and Tom Mitchell, "What Can Machine Learning Do? Workforce Implications," *Science*, vol. 358, no. 6370 (2017), pp. 1530-1534.

150 Michael Webb, "The Impact of Artificial Intelligence on the Labor Market," Stanford University Working Paper, July 2019.

151 Bryn Nelson, "How Robots Are Reshaping One of the Dirtiest, Most Dangerous Jobs," *NBC News*, April 17, 2018, at https://www.nbcnews.com/mach/science/how-robots-are-reshaping-one-dirtiest-most-dangerous-jobs-ncna866771.

152 Erin Winick, "New Autonomous Farm Wants to Produce Food Without Human Workers," *MIT Technology Review*, October 3, 2018, at https://www.technologyreview.com/s/612230/new-autonomous-farm-wants-to-produce-food-without-human-workers/.

centers. An employee overseeing robotics work at Amazon stated that "the biggest problem is not having enough people, and I don't think that is going to change."[153]

While many studies over the past few years have discussed AI as part of automation technologies more broadly, some have begun trying to assess the AI- and ML-specific portions of potential impacts. Prior analyses looking more broadly at automation of job skills have generally found that lower-wage, blue-collar workers will be more affected. However, one 2018 study concluded that although most occupations have some tasks that could be automated using ML, there are few, if any, where all tasks are suitable for automation.[154] A 2019 study looking at AI-specific technologies found that (1) higher-wage, white-collar occupations and some agriculture and manufacturing positions may be the most exposed to AI disruptions; (2) AI seems likely to affect men, prime-age workers, and white and Asian American workers; and (3) large metropolitan areas with a concentration of high-tech industries and communities heavily involved in manufacturing are likely to experience the most AI-related disruption.[155] The authors caveat their work by noting that studies examining employment effects with any nuance are preliminary and that "the onset of AI will introduce new riddles into speculation about the future of work."[156] In general, recent studies indicate that most if not all occupations will be impacted by the introduction of AI and AI-enabled technologies in some way.

A 2020 report from the MIT Task Force on the Work of the Future asserted that the "momentous impacts of technological change are unfolding gradually," and that while applications and impacts from AI and robotics applications are coming, "they are not as close as some would fear."[157] The report discusses a variety of factors informing these findings, including that

---

[153] Cade Metz, "FedEx Follows Amazon into the Robotic Future," *New York Times*, March 18, 2018, at https://www.nytimes.com/2018/03/18/technology/fedex-robots.html.

[154] Erik Brynjolfsson, Tom Mitchell, and Daniel Rock, "What Can Machines Learn and What Does It Mean for Occupations and the Economy?," *AEA Papers and Proceedings*, vol. 108 (May 2018), pp. 43-47, at https://pubs.aeaweb.org/doi/pdfplus/10.1257/pandp.20181019.

[155] Mark Muro, Jacob Whiton, and Robert Maxim, *What Jobs Are Affected by AI? Better-Paid, Better-Educated Workers Face the Most Exposure*, Brookings, November 2019, at https://www.brookings.edu/wp-content/uploads/2019/11/2019.11.20_BrookingsMetro_What-jobs-are-affected-by-AI_Report_Muro-Whiton-Maxim.pdf.

[156] Ibid., p. 22.

[157] David Autor, David Mindell, and Elisabeth Reynolds, *The Work of the Future: Building Better Jobs in an Age of Intelligent Machines*, Massachusetts Institute of Technology (MIT) Task Force on the Work of the Future, November 2020, pp. 5, 32-34, at https://workofthefuture.mit.edu/wp-content/uploads/2021/01/2020-Final-Report4.pdf.

AI systems are still narrow and that policies, organizational cultures, economic incentives, and management practices can shape "the rate and manner in which firms develop and adopt technologies" beyond what is technologically possible.[158]

AI Expert Workforce

Tied to considerations of U.S. competitiveness, policymakers and stakeholders in academia and technology companies have expressed concerns about a lack of adequate AI expertise, not only for AI R&D and education in industry and academia, but also in the federal and congressional workforces. A September 2019 report highlighted several indicators of a tight market for AI talent, though the authors caveated their findings, noting that there is broad consensus in the field that talent shortages are substantial, but the exact extent is difficult to measure, and different organizations may publish very different estimates:[159]

- Job site statistics show that demand for workers far exceeds supply. For example, based on data from Burning Glass Technologies, job listings for AI skills have "grown significantly" from 2013 to 2020, with the total number of AI jobs posted in the United States above 300,000 in 2019 and 2020.[160] And as reported in April 2019, the market intelligence firm Element AI estimated that, in the United States, there were around 144,000 AI-related job openings and only about 26,000 developers and specialists seeking work.[161]
- The private sector is paying high salaries for workers with AI skills. For example, a 2018 news report stated that "even newly-minted Ph.D.s in machine learning and data science can make more than $300,000" at technology companies such as Google, Facebook, and Apple.[162]

---

[158] Ibid.

[159] Remco Zwetsloot, Roxanne Heston, and Zachary Arnold, *Strengthening the U.S. AI Workforce*, Center for Security and Emerging Technology, Georgetown University, September 2019, pp. 9-10. See the callout box, "What is the 'AI workforce,' and who counts as an 'AI expert'?", p. 3, for additional discussions of measuring the AI expert workforce.

[160] AI Index 2021, p. 86.

[161] As reported in Roberta Kwok, "Junior AI Researchers Are in Demand by Universities and Industry," *Nature*, April 23, 2019, at https://www.nature.com/articles/d41586-019-01248-w.

[162] Jeremy Kahn, "Sky-High Salaries Are the Weapons in the AI Talent War," *Bloomberg*, February 13, 2018, at https://www.bloomberg.com/news/articles/2018-02-13/in-the-war-for-ai-talent-sky-high-salaries-are-the-weapons.

- Subjective assessments from employers align with the indicators. For example, among firms surveyed by the World Economic Forum in 2020, most of which reported a desire to invest in AI, "skills gaps" and "inability to attract specialized talent" ranked among the top two barriers to the adoption of new technologies, especially when hiring for "emerging roles," including AI and ML specialists.[163]

Perhaps for this reason, some companies such as Google, Amazon, and Facebook, are recruiting professors while allowing them to retain positions at universities.[164] However, the details of these arrangements are important, as Oren Etzioni of the Allen Institute for Artificial Intelligence notes in an example from Facebook: "What are the ethics of a major corporation suddenly going after the entire [natural language processing] faculty in a computer science department? I believe their original offers had the faculty members spending 80 percent of their time at Facebook, which would not allow them time to carry out their educational responsibilities at [the University of Washington]." Some have referred to this as *eating the seed corn*, which could lead to less capacity to train future AI experts. Facebook disputed the claim, noting that while the relationship between academia and industry may be changing, the company is trying to be careful about not draining universities.[165] However, in a March 2019 survey of 111 AI researchers and university administrators by *Times Higher Education* and Microsoft, 89% said that it was "difficult" or "very difficult" to hire and retain AI experts.[166]

Other companies are collaborating with universities, such as Google's partnership with Princeton University to open an AI laboratory that will engage faculty members, graduate and undergraduate students, recent graduates, and software engineers. One of the collaborating faculty members, who previously split time between Princeton and Google, noted that it was an

---

[163] World Economic Forum, Center for the New Economy and Society, *The Future of Jobs Report 2020*, October 2020, pp. 27 and 35, at http://www3.weforum.org/docs/WEF_Future_of_Jobs_2020.pdf.

[164] Daniela Hernandez and Rachael King, "Universities' AI Talent Poached by Tech Giants," *Wall Street Journal,* November 24, 2016, at https://www.wsj.com/articles/universities-ai-talent-poached-by-tech-giants-1479999601.

[165] Alan Boyle, "FAIR Competition? Facebook Creates Official AI Labs in Seattle and Pittsburgh, Vying for Top Talent," *GeekWire*, May 5, 2018, at https://www.geekwire.com/2018/fair-competition-facebook-raises-status-ai-research-labs-seattle-pittsburgh/.

[166] As reported in Roberta Kwok, "Junior AI Researchers Are in Demand By Universities and Industry," *Nature*, April 23, 2019, at https://www.nature.com/articles/d41586-019-01248-w.

opportunity for those at Princeton to "benefit from exposure to real-world computing problems, and for Google to benefit from long-term, unconstrained academic research that Google may incorporate into future products."[167]

Within the federal government, the *Government by Algorithm: Artificial Intelligence in Federal Administrative Agencies* report asserted that "if we expect agencies to make responsible and smart use of AI, technical capacity must come from within" and "in-house expertise promotes AI tools that are better tailored to complex governance tasks and more likely to be designed and implemented in lawful, policy-compliant, and accountable ways."[168] To gain such expertise, the report states that "fully leveraging agency use of AI will require significant public investment to draw needed human capital."[169] Further, E.O. 13960 states that "agencies shall provide appropriate training to all agency personnel responsible for the design, development, acquisition, and use of AI." However, the March 2021 final report of the National Security Commission on Artificial Intelligence (NSCAI) states, "The human talent deficit is the government's most conspicuous AI deficit and the single greatest inhibitor to buying, building, and fielding AI-enabled technologies for national security purposes."[170]

Policy Considerations

Studies that attempt to identify the workforce effects of AI and ML technologies specifically, rather than those that address automation generally, conclude that there has been insufficient data collection and analyses specific to AI technologies and job skills conducted to fully understand the issue and inform policy decisions. For example, one study identified barriers that inhibit researchers from measuring the labor effects of AI, including (1) lack of high-quality data about the nature of work; (2) lack of empirically informed models of key microlevel processes (e.g., skill substitution and human-machine complementarity); and (3) insufficient understanding of how cognitive technologies interact with broader economic dynamics and institutional

---

[167] Steven Schultz, "Google to Open Artificial Intelligence Lab in Princeton and Collaborate with University Researchers," Princeton University news communication, December 18, 2018, at https://www.princeton.edu/news/ 2018/12/18/google-open-artificial-intelligence-lab-princeton-and-collaborate-university.

[168] ACUS report 2020, p. 7.

[169] Ibid.

[170] National Security Commission on Artificial Intelligence, *Final Report*, March 2021, p. 3, at https://www.nscai.gov/wp-content/uploads/2021/03/Full-Report-Digital-1.pdf (hereinafter, "NSCAI 2021 Final Report").

mechanisms.[171] The study asserted that overcoming such barriers requires improvements in the longitudinal and spatial resolution of data and refinements to data on workplace skills.[172] Another study, commissioned by the Bureau of Labor Statistics (BLS) to identify constructs that would complement BLS's existing products to assess the impact of automation on labor outcomes, echoed these findings. The BLS-commissioned study by Gallup states that "the primary lesson learned from [the] report is that researchers and, by extension, policymakers lack the data necessary to fully understand how new technologies impact the labor market" and identified gaps in BLS data products, specifically with regards to the classification of skills, task performance, and the adoption of new technologies.[173]

Some experts emphasize training people for skills and jobs that will be in high demand even with implementation of AI technologies, such as skills needed in management and personal interactions, two areas for which AI is not well suited.[174] Stakeholders have also asserted that a focus on lifelong learning and programs to retrain and upskill workers will be important for addressing skill shifts related to deployment of AI technologies.[175] In one 2017 survey of 300 C-suite and senior executives about their AI strategies, 82% of leaders planned to implement AI in the next three years, but only 38% provided programs aimed at reskilling employees to work with the

---

[171] Morgan R. Frank et al., "Toward Understanding the Impact of Artificial Intelligence on Labor," *Proceedings of the National Academy of Sciences of the United States of America*, vol. 116, no. 14 (April 2, 2019), pp. 6531-6539.

[172] Ibid.

[173] Jenny Marler, Gallup Project Director, Assessing the Impact of New Technologies on the Labor Market: Key Constructs, Gaps, and Data Collection Strategies for the Bureau of Labor Statistics, Contract No: GS-00F-0078M, February 7, 2020, pp. 3, 25 (hereinafter referred to as the Gallup study), at https://www.bls.gov/bls/congressional-reports/assessing-the-impact-of-new-technologies-on-the-labor-market.pdf.

[174] David Rotman, "Obama Economist: We're Not Preparing Workers for Changing Jobs," *MIT Technology Review*, June 4, 2018, at https://www.technologyreview.com/s/611297/obama-economist-were-not-preparing-workers-for-changing-jobs/; video of Jason Furman's talk at the 2018 EmTech conference, covered in the article, can be found at https://events.technologyreview.com/video/watch/jason-furman-harvard-automation-future-work/.

[175] James Manyika et al., *A Future That Works: Automation, Employment, and Productivity*, McKinsey Global Institute, January 2017, available at https://www.mckinsey.com/featured-insights/digital-disruption/harnessing-automation-for-a-future-that-works; and Joseph E. Aoun, *Robot-Proof: Higher Education in the Age of Artificial Intelligence* (Cambridge, MA: MIT Press, 2017). Generally, reskilling refers to learning new skills for a different job or occupation, while upskilling refers to learning new skills for growth within an existing job or occupation.

technology.[176] Still other experts assert that "the concern should not be about the number of jobs, but whether those are jobs that can support a reasonable standard of living and what set of people have access to them."[177]

In response to these issues, some policy questions and considerations for Congress may include the following:

- What types of granular labor data are needed to better inform analyses and identify key skills for future jobs, and how might the federal government help gather and disseminate such information?
- In conjunction with efforts by employers and educators, what is the appropriate role of the federal government in supporting the reskilling or upskilling of employees for whom certain tasks or their entire jobs will be shifted or displaced? Are federal programs to assist workers sufficient to help address potential workforce shifts? How can federal direction of workforce support programs balance providing AI-specific legislative direction while allowing states and localities flexibility to meet their specific workforce needs?
- For those federal offices and agencies facing a shortage of technical expertise in AI, what are the best options to attract and retain talent? For example, former Secretary of Defense Robert Work has argued for the development of an AI training corps—similar to the CyberCorps program[178] (educational training in exchange for expert work for the federal government, but where workers could keep their regular jobs).[179]
- In addition to developing internal expertise, how might federal agencies and executive offices expand access to outside expertise, as from academia, industry, and nonprofit groups? For example, the

---

[176] Genpact, "Is Your Business AI-Ready?," 2017, at http://www.genpact.com/downloadable-content/insight/is-your-business-ai-ready.pdf.

[177] David Autor, "No, Robots Won't Take All the Jobs," *Brookings Creative Lab*, March 12, 2018, at https://www.youtube.com/watch?v=SrprBJf7Nd4 (video discussion of the paper, David Autor and Anna Salomons, "Is Automation Labor-Displacing? Productivity Growth, Employment, and the Labor Share," Brookings Papers on Economic Activity, Spring 2018, at https://www.brookings.edu/bpea-articles/is-automation-labor-displacing-productivity-growth-employment-and-the-labor-share/).

[178] See for example, the CyberCorps Scholarship for Service program at https://www.sfs.opm.gov/.

[179] David Ignatius, "China's Application of AI Should Be a Sputnik Moment for the U.S. but Will It Be?," *Washington Post*, November 6, 2018, at https://www.washingtonpost.com/opinions/chinas-application-of-ai-should-be-a-sputnik-moment-for-the-us-but-will-it-be/2018/11/06/69132de4-e204-11e8-b759-3d88a5ce9e19_story.html.

> NSCAI 2021 Final Report recommends establishing a civilian National Reserve Digital Corps modeled after the military reserve's commitment and incentive structure.[180]

In order to address the dearth of data on the potential impacts of AI on the workforce, Congress may consider various actions. The FY2021 NDAA calls for the commissioning of a study by the National Academies of Sciences, Engineering, and Medicine on the current and future impact of AI on the workforce of the United States across sectors, including addressing research gaps and data needed to better understand workforce impacts. The study may yield useful information to inform the debate and future policy options; the final report is due more than two years from enactment, which occurred in January 2021. During that time, Congress may hold hearings to obtain related information on new or updated data collection and research at federal agencies in response to prior studies. Further, Congress may direct federal agencies to begin collecting additional information to fill data gaps identified in prior research, such as in the Gallup study for BLS.

Should Congress decide to assist federal agencies in attracting outside expertise and developing internal expertise in AI, a variety of policy responses have been discussed by stakeholders. For example, Congress may consider directing federal agencies to develop or expand on scholarship-for-service (SFS) programs to attract new AI talent to federal service. However, simply expanding the number of offerings may not result in more students participating—such programs have been criticized for being difficult to find online, being spread across multiple and possibly outdated agency websites, and not supporting continued professional development once a student is employed in the federal government.[181] While SFS programs have had reportedly high placement rates for graduates—94% for CyberCorps graduates in 2016—some critics have expressed discomfort with the repayment requirements for students who enter the program but leave before completing their degree or federal service requirement.[182] Further challenges for growing a federal workforce in AI include higher salaries for comparable

---

[180] NSCAI 2021 Final Report, p. 125.

[181] Cindy Martinez, "Saving the Federal Cyber and AI Workforce from Obsolescence: How to Attract and Retain a New Generation," *FedScoop*, December 22, 2020, at https://www.fedscoop.com/saving-federal-cyber-ai-workforce-obsolescence-attract-retain-new-generation/.

[182] For additional discussions of SFS programs and the federal workforce in the context of cybersecurity, see CRS In Focus IF10654, *Challenges in Cybersecurity Education and Workforce Development*, by Boris Granovskiy.

jobs in the private sector and time-consuming and opaque hiring practices. Thus, Congress may consider directing agencies to take actions to improve the recruitment and retention of AI experts, including through the establishment or modification of federal programs such as SFS.

Developing internal expertise at agencies to not only develop, but use, understandable and transparent AI systems may have multiple benefits for agencies. For example, agency experts likely have a deeper, more nuanced understanding of the technical needs and challenges at their agency for which an AI system is developed or tailored. Further, by developing their own AI systems, agencies may be better able to create understandable, transparent, and accountable systems, in contrast to the estimated 33% of federal AI systems that are built by external contractors using proprietary software and obtained through the federal procurement process.[183]

Congress may consider ways to support or augment AI expertise within the existing federal workforce through the establishment of federal advisory committees and directing agencies to develop internal training programs.

International Competition and Federal Investment in AI R&D

According to the National Science Board's *Science and Engineering Indicators for 2020*, the United States and China lead in research and commercialization of AI technologies, though business adoption of AI is occurring across the world.[184] Numerous international governments have initiated activities focused on AI (e.g., task forces, research activities, discussion papers), and dozens have released national AI strategies, though these vary in scope.[185] Further, multiple countries are cooperating in international AI initiatives. For example, the United States and other Organisation for Economic Co-operation and Development (OECD) member countries committed to common AI principles in May 2019.[186] Building on

---

[183] Administrative Conference of the United States, Office of the Chairman Projects, "Artificial Intelligence in Federal Agencies," February 2020, p. 88-98.

[184] National Science Board, National Science Foundation, "Production and Trade of Knowledge- and Technology-Intensive Industries," *Science and Engineering Indicators 2020*, NSB-2020-5, p. 55, at https://ncses.nsf.gov/pubs/ nsb20205/.

[185] One of the most comprehensive efforts to compile information on AI initiatives across countries has been conducted through the Organisation for Economic Co-operation and Development's (OECD's) AI Policy Observatory, at https://oecd.ai/.

[186] OECD, *Recommendation of the Council on Artificial Intelligence*, adopted on May 21, 2019, at https://legalinstruments.oecd.org/en/instruments/OECD-LEGAL-0449.

the commitment to these principles, the United States and 14 other countries launched the Global Partnership on AI in June 2020 to bring together expertise from a range of stakeholders "with the goal of bridging the gap between the theory and practice of AI."[187] In September 2020, the United States and the United Kingdom signed a declaration of cooperation in AI R&D.[188]

Public investments in AI R&D vary widely by country. In the United States, as previously noted, FY2020 funding for AI activities at defense and non-defense agencies was approximately $4 billion and $1.1 billion, respectively. In comparison, a recent report from the Center for Security and Emerging Technology at Georgetown University estimated that Chinese government spending on AI R&D in 2018 was on the order of a few billion dollars.[189] Though a substantial amount, this is less than the estimate of tens of billions that others have suggested. The European Union previously communicated a commitment to increase investments from $500 million to $1.5 billion by the end of 2020. In 2018, Germany and France pledged €3 billion and €1.5 billion, respectively, for AI investments by the end of 2020, and Canada previously committed to spending $125 million over five years.[190]

Policy Considerations

The appropriate level for U.S. federal R&D support, the nature of the R&D investments, such as basic versus applied research, as well as the most effective additional mechanisms to support innovation, such as prize competition incentives and public-private partnerships, remain areas of discussion among lawmakers.

---

[187] National Artificial Intelligence Initiative Office, "Global Partnership on AI," at https://www.ai.gov/strategic-pillars/ international-cooperation/#Global-Partnership-on-AI. For additional information about the Global Partnership on Artificial Intelligence, see https://gpai.ai/.

[188] U.S. Department of State, "Declaration of the United States of America and the United Kingdom of Great Britain and Northern Ireland on Cooperation in Artificial Intelligence Research and Development: A Shared Vision for Driving Technological Breakthroughs in Artificial Intelligence," September 25, 2020, at https://www.state.gov/declaration-of-the-united-states-of-america-and-the-united-kingdom-of-great-britain-and-northern-ireland-on-cooperation-in-artificial-intelligence-research-and-development-a-shared-vision-for-driving/.

[189] Ashwin Acharya and Zachary Arnold, *Chinese Public AI R&D Spending: Provisional Findings*, Center for Security and Emerging Technology, Georgetown University, December 2019.

[190] Information on the status of these investments is unknown. As previously noted, it is important to keep in mind that reliable cross-country measures on public investments are difficult to obtain for a variety of reasons, including varying levels of reporting, and the range of measurements that countries could use to tally spending.

Historical considerations of international competition in science and technology have led to prior recommendations for increased federal funding of research, particularly in the physical sciences and engineering (PS&E).[191] For example, the America COMPETES Act (P.L. 110-69) in 2007 and the America COMPETES Reauthorization Act of 2010 (P.L. 111-358) were originally enacted to address concerns that the United States could lose its advantage in scientific and technological innovation. The COMPETES Acts included authorizations of appropriations in line with doubling research in PS&E, including doubling NSF's budget. Appropriations for the COMPETES Acts activities never reached authorized levels, and opposition to the efforts included various perspectives, including a preference for alternative federal approaches to support innovation, such as research tax credits or reducing regulatory costs, as well as a concern about the national debt.[192]

More recently, regarding federal funding and support for AI R&D, some stakeholders assert that the federal government should invest more money and direct structural or programmatic changes to certain R&D agencies to promote U.S. technological primacy, particularly in key areas of emerging technologies such as AI. For example, the President's Council of Advisors on Science and Technology (PCAST) released recommendations in June 2020 on strengthening U.S. American Leadership in industries of the future, which included growing federal investment in AI R&D by a factor of 10 over 10 years (e.g., increase nondefense R&D from $1 billion in FY2020 to $10 billion in FY2030).[193]

The National AI Initiative Act, passed in the FY2021 NDAA, authorized appropriations for AI activities at NSF, NIST, and DOE for FY2021-FY2025. In the 117th Congress, the Endless Frontier Act (S. 1260) would redesignate the NSF as the National Science and Technology Foundation, establishing a Directorate for Technology and authorizing appropriations of $100 billion

---

[191] National Academies of Sciences, Engineering, and Medicine, *Rising Above the Gathering Storm: Energizing and Employing America for a Brighter Economic Future*, 2007, at https://doi.org/10.17226/11463.

[192] For additional discussions of the America COMPETES Acts and efforts to double federal PS&E funding, see CRS Report R41951, *An Analysis of Efforts to Double Federal Funding for Physical Sciences and Engineering Research*, by John F. Sargent Jr.

[193] President's Council of Advisors on Science and Technology (PCAST), *Recommendations for Strengthening American Leadership in Industries of the Future*, June 2020, p. 6, at https://science.osti.gov/-/media/_/pdf/about/pcast/202006/PCAST_June_2020_Report.pdf?la=en&hash=019A4F17C79FDEE5005C51D3D6CAC81FB31E3ABC.

over five years for the new directorate.[194] The final report of the National Security Commission on AI recommends scaling and coordinating federal AI R&D funding, including through establishing a National Technology Foundation as a sister agency to the NSF "to provide the means to move science more aggressively into engineering and scale innovative ideas into reality"; funding AI R&D at compounding levels; and establishing additional National AI Research Institutes.[195] Congress considers the appropriations for these authorities as part of its annual discretionary appropriations process and enacted amounts may or may not match the authorized levels.

An additional consideration, given the R&D engagement in the private sector, is the extent to which the federal government might leverage private funding through expanding public-private partnerships. In the 2019 update to the *National AI R&D Strategic Plan*, expanding public-private partnerships to accelerate advances in AI was a new, additional strategy.

Standards Development

AI standards development became an area of increasing interest for the Trump Administration and the 116th Congress, for both domestic R&D and international competitiveness reasons. The 2019 *National AI R&D Strategic Plan* noted that "development and adoption of best practices and standards in documenting dataset and model provenance will enhance trustworthiness and responsible use of AI technologies."[196] E.O. 13859 aimed to "Ensure that technical standards … reflect Federal priorities for innovation, public trust, and public confidence in systems that use AI technologies … and develop international standards to promote and protect those priorities." In response, NIST produced the *Plan for Federal Engagement in Developing Technical Standards and Related Tools* (AI Standards Plan) in August 2019. The plan identifies nine areas of focus for AI standards: concepts and terminology; data and knowledge; human interactions; metrics; networking; performance testing and reporting methodology; safety; risk management; and trustworthiness.[197]

---

194 For comparison, FY2021 appropriations for NSF were approximately $8.5 billion total. The Endless Frontier Act was first introduced in the 116th Congress (S. 3832 and H.R. 6978).

195 NSCAI 2021 Final Report, p. 435.

196 NSTC Select Committee on Artificial Intelligence 2019 AI R&D Strategic Plan, p. 28.

197 National Institute of Standards and Technology, *U.S. Leadership in AI: A Plan for Federal Engagement in Developing Technical Standards and Related Tools*, August 9, 2019, pp. 3, 10-12. The plan further states that "Trustworthiness standards include guidance and

The standards development process in the United States is predominantly a voluntary, consensus-based effort, driven by the private sector, including through Standards Development Organizations (SDOs). NIST (with other federal agencies, as appropriate) is a participant and facilitator, providing agency requirements to standards projects and technical expertise to standards development, incorporating voluntary standards into policies and regulations, and citing standards in agency procurements.[198] Standards can be horizontal (i.e., used across many applications and industries), or vertical (i.e., developed for specific application areas such as healthcare or transportation). Further, nontechnical standards can be important to inform policy and human decisionmaking (e.g., standards for governance and privacy), and "standards should be complemented by an array of related tools," such as standardized datasets with metadata; benchmarks; testing methodologies; metrics; testbeds; and tools for accountability and auditing.[199] The AI Standards Plan notes that "While there is broad agreement that [federal policies and principles, including those that address societal and ethical issues, governance, and privacy] must factor into AI standards, it is not clear how that should be done and whether there is yet sufficient scientific and technical basis to develop those standards provisions."[200]

Standards development is not only a national but an international effort, involving the work of such entities as the International Organization for Standardization (ISO).[201] The U.S. government and other stakeholders have expressed concern about China's attempts to lead the international AI standards development efforts. China has already laid out some of these plans in white papers and is expected to release a 15-year plan to set global standards for next-generation technologies, including AI, as part of its "China Standards 2035" plan.[202] Concerns about China's focus on standards setting, particularly if the United States does not lead in these efforts, include the following.

---

requirements for accuracy, explainability, resiliency, safety, reliability, objectivity, and security."

[198] Ibid., "How Are Technical Standards Developed?" p. 9. The document also includes a list of SDOs that are developing AI standards in Appendix II. For additional information about NIST, including certain statutory authorities, see CRS Report R43908, *The National Institute of Standards and Technology: An Appropriations Overview*, by John F. Sargent Jr.

[199] Ibid., pp. 13-14.

[200] Ibid., p. 4. Social and ethical issues are discussed in the following section, "Ethics, Bias, Fairness, and Transparency."

[201] Information about the ISO Committee on AI can be found at https://www.iso.org/committee/6794475.html.

[202] The Center for Security and Emerging Technology (CSET) at Georgetown University has provided a translation of China's *Artificial Intelligence Security Standardization White*

- *Potential economic losses.* The NIST AI Standards Plan highlights this concern, stating, "AI standards developed without the appropriate level and type of involvement may exclude or disadvantage U.S.-based companies in the marketplace as well as U.S. government agencies."[203]
- *Threats to democratic norms and values.* Members of the National Security Commission on AI have expressed concern that "AI is being used in ways that are antithetical to American values. In China, AI is used as a tool for centralizing power at the expense of individual rights. The Chinese government is amassing the personal data of its people, using facial recognition software to stifle dissent and repress minorities, and exporting its surveillance technology abroad."[204] The ability of those countries leading in international standards setting to impart their societal and cultural values, such as data privacy and respect for civil liberties, into the process and outcomes, has led to concerns about China's successes in increasing its leadership positions in international standards-making bodies.[205] As NIST has stated, "standards flow from principles, and a first step toward standardization will be reaching broad consensus on a core set of AI principles."[206]

These points are discussed in greater detail in the U.S.-China Economic and Security Review Commission's 2020 annual report to Congress, which states

> In contrast to the United States, where technical standards are developed by industry in response to commercial need and adopted by consensus,

---

Paper, 2019, at https://cset.georgetown.edu/wp-content/ uploads/t0121_AI_security_standardization_white_paper_EN.pdf; regarding the forthcoming "China Standards 2035," see Arjun Kharpal, "Power Is 'Up for Grabs': Behind China's Plan to Shape the Future of Next-Generation Tech," *CNBC*, April 26, 2020, at https://www.cnbc.com/2020/04/27/china-standards-2035-explained.html.

203 NIST, *U.S. Leadership in AI: A Plan for Federal Engagement in Developing Technical Standards and Related Tools*, p. 19.

204 Eric Schmidt and Bob Work, "The US Is in Danger of Losing Its Global Leadership in AI," *The Hill*, December 5, 2019, at https://thehill.com/blogs/congress-blog/technology/473273-the-us-is-in-danger-of-losing-its-global-leadership-in-ai.

205 U.S.-China Economic and Security Review Commission, *2020 Annual Report to Congress*, December 2020, p. 107, at https://www.uscc.gov/files/001592.

206 NIST, *U.S. Leadership in AI: A Plan for Federal Engagement in Developing Technical Standards and Related Tools*, p. 15.

> Chinese state agencies formulate standards and use them to advance industrial and foreign policy objectives. Historically, Beijing has prioritized developing mandatory and unique domestic technical standards as a barrier to foreign firms' market entry and to help grow domestic industry. Now, it is also coordinating industrial policy and diplomatic strategy to expand its influence in international standards-making bodies, both to increase adoption of Chinese technology abroad and to influence norms for how technology is applied.[207]

Policy Considerations

Such concerns have generated various recommendations for robust domestic and international standards setting efforts. The AI Standards Plan included numerous recommendations to support U.S. leadership in AI standards development:

- Bolster AI standards-related knowledge, leadership, and coordination among federal agencies, including by
  - designating a Standards Coordinator within the NSTC's MLAI Subcommittee, and
  - developing clear career development and promotion paths that encourage participation and expertise in AI standards and development.
- Promote focused research to advance and accelerate broader exploration and understanding of how aspects of trustworthiness can be practically incorporated within standards and standards-related tools, including through supporting research to develop metrics, data sets, and risk management strategies for AI.
- Support and expand public-private partnerships to develop and use AI standards and related tools to advance reliable, robust, and trustworthy AI.
- Strategically engage with international parties to advance AI standards for U.S. economic and national security needs, including through accelerating information exchange with "like minded countries" through international partnerships.[208]

---

[207] U.S.-China Economic and Security Review Commission, *2020 Annual Report to Congress*, December 2020, p. 106, at https://www.uscc.gov/files/001592.

[208] NIST, *U.S. Leadership in AI: A Plan for Federal Engagement in Developing Technical Standards and Related Tools*, pp. 4-6.

In the FY2021 NDAA (Section 5301), Congress established as a mission that NIST advance collaborative frameworks, standards, guidelines; authorized NIST to work on associated methods and techniques for AI; and directed that NIST support the development of a risk-management framework for trustworthy AI systems. NIST is further directed to develop guidance and best practices for data set documentation and data sharing among industry, federally funded research and development centers, and federal agencies, including options for partnerships with universities and nonprofits. Congress may consider oversight activities to monitor the implementation of these provisions and provide subsequent direction to NIST and other federal agencies.

Ethics, Bias, Fairness, and Transparency

Along with interest in technical advances, researchers, companies, and policymakers are expressing growing concern and interest in what has been called the ethical evolution of AI, including questions about bias, fairness, and algorithm transparency. Broadly, who defines ethics and who enforces ethical design and use?[209] What constitutes an ethical decision may vary by individual, culture, economics, and geography.[210] As some analysts have asserted, "AI is only as good as the information and values of the programmers who design it, and their biases can ultimately lead to both flaws in the technology and amplified biases in the real world."[211]

Just as there are many ways of considering what is ethical in AI, "researchers studying bias in algorithms say there are many ways of defining fairness, which are sometimes contradictory," having inherent tradeoffs.[212] (For example, one computer scientist presented at the 2018 Fairness, Accountability, and Transparency (FAT*) Conference on "21 fairness

---

209 Karen Hao, "Establishing an AI Code of Ethics Will Be Harder Than People Think," *MIT Technology Review,* October 21, 2018, at https://www.technologyreview.com/2018/10/21/139647/establishing-an-ai-code-of-ethics-will-be-harder-than-people-think/.

210 Edmond Awad et al., "The Moral Machine Experiment," *Nature*, October 24, 2018.

211 Andre M. Perry and Nicol Turner Lee, "AI Is Coming to Schools, and If We're Not Careful, So Will Its Biases," *Brookings*, September 26, 2019, at https://www.brookings.edu/blog/the-avenue/2019/09/26/ai-is-coming-to-schools-and-if-were-not-careful-so-will-its-biases.

212 Rachel Courtland, "Bias Detectives: The Researchers Striving to Make Algorithms Fair," *Nature News Feature*, vol. 558 (June 20, 2018), pp. 357-360 (hereinafter, "Courtland, 2018").

definitions and their politics."[213]) The box below presents an example of the challenges of defining fairness in the criminal justice system. For some, such cases highlight the need for agencies to improve their internal processes for assessing algorithmic tools and develop training for their staff to be able not only to evaluate such tools, but also to provide developers with publicly-available metrics for fairness.[214]

Sector Example: Defining Fairness in Criminal Justice

In 2016, a team at ProPublica investigated proprietary software called COMPAS that is used during sentencing to assign defendants in the criminal justice system with risk scores, from 1 to 10, for committing another crime within two years if released (i.e., the likelihood of recidivism). The ProPublica team claimed that the algorithm was biased, because there were a disproportionate number of false positives for black defendants—people identified as high risk who were not subsequently charged with another crime (one measure of an "error rate").[215] The developers countered that the algorithm was not biased, because it was equally good at predicting whether a white or a black defendant classified as high risk would reoffend, a measure called "predictive parity." In other words, ProPublica and the developers of COMPAS were using different measures to try to conclude whether the software was fair.

Subsequent research into these analyses found that not all criteria for fairness can be satisfied when recidivism prevalence differs across groups and that disparate impact—which the researcher defined as referring "to settings where a penalty policy has unintended disproportionate adverse impact on a particular group"—may result even if a prediction instrument is fair with respect to certain criteria.[216] The researcher—citing a large body

---

213 Arvind Narayanan, "Translation Tutorial: 21 Fairness Definitions and Their Politics," Fairness, Accountability, and Transparency (FAT*) Conference, February 23, 2018; abstract and video available at https://www.youtube.com/watch? v=jIXIuYdnyyk. As noted on the conference website (https://facctconference.org/2018/program.html), "In 2018, the conference's name was FAT* and the proceedings were published in the Journal of Machine Learning Research. The conference affiliated with ACM in 2019, and changed its name to ACM FAccT immediately following the 2020 conference."

214 Courtland, 2018.

215 Julia Angwin et al., "Machine Bias," *ProPublica*, May 23, 2016, at https://www.propublica.org/article/machine-bias-risk-assessments-in-criminal-sentencing.

216 Alexandra Chouldechova, "Fair Prediction with Disparate Impact: A Study of Bias in Recidivism Prediction Instruments," *Big Data*, vol. 5, no. 2 (June 2017), pp. 153-163, at https://pubmed.ncbi.nlm.nih.gov/28632438/.

of literature showing that data-driven risk assessment instruments tend to be more accurate than professional human judgements—concluded that data-driven approaches should not be abandoned but rather proven to be free of the kinds of biases that could lead to disparate impacts in the specific contexts in which they are applied.[217]

For a more in-depth discussion of this topic, see "Concerns About Bias in Risk and Needs Assessments" in CRS Report R44087, *Risk and Needs Assessment in the Federal Prison System*, by Nathan James.

The U.S. *National AI R&D Strategic Plan* also discusses the challenges and potential approaches to designing and building ethical AI. The plan echoes concerns about the susceptibility of data-intensive AI algorithms to error and misuse without the proper collection and use of data to train the systems. It calls for researchers to design systems so that their actions and decisionmaking are more transparent and easily interpretable, and they can be examined for bias. The plan further states, "Ethics is inherently a philosophical question while AI technology depends on, and is limited by, engineering.… However, acceptable ethics reference frameworks can be developed to guide AI system reasoning and decisionmaking in order to explain and justify its conclusions and actions." To achieve these goals, the plan notes that there is a need for multidisciplinary, fundamental research in designing architectures for AI systems to incorporate ethical reasoning.[218]

While such fundamental research is being conducted, and while various groups work on developing standards and benchmarks for evaluating algorithms, some stakeholders have called for a risk-based, sector-specific approach to considering uses and potential regulations for AI algorithms. For example, some have called for more initial and ongoing testing and evaluation of algorithms and AI technologies for potential bias that directly impact U.S. citizens' lives and livelihoods (e.g., through healthcare or hiring systems)—sometimes referred to as "high risk" or "systems critical" uses.[219] Some Members of Congress have previously requested information from federal agencies about their use of AI, such as the use of facial recognition technology

[217] Ibid.

[218] NSTC Select Committee on Artificial Intelligence 2019 AI R&D Strategic Plan, pp. 21-22.

[219] See, for example, a discussion of racial bias in health care decisionmaking software used by hospitals in Heidi Leford, "Millions of Black People Affected by Racial Bias in Health-Care Algorithms," *Nature News*, vol. 574 (October 26, 2019), pp. 608-609.

in law enforcement, and how the agencies balance the potential to solve crimes and catch criminals with the potential risks to privacy and civil rights.[220]

Types of Bias

Definitions and understanding of terms such as bias and fairness can vary by discipline (e.g., technologists vs. lawyers vs. civil society), type (e.g., statistical vs. social bias), and scope (e.g., individual vs. systemic/structural). Further, there are various types of bias, and bias can show up in algorithms, including AI algorithms, in a variety of ways, including in the data, within the system, and from the people designing and using the system.

There is significant concern that biases and errors in datasets used to train AI systems will result in outcomes that reflect, and possibly amplify, those biases. For example, using a dataset that has historical inequities engrained in it—such as past employment or access to credit, both of which have a history of racial discrimination—can perpetuate bias and inequity. Limited datasets that are not representative of the population to which they will be applied may lack generalizability and subsequently not work equally well for everyone. For example, some facial analysis software has been shown to have significant gender and skin color classification bias, often accurately identifying white males while failing to accurately classify darker female faces one in three times.[221] Another study found that two prominent research-image collections display gender bias in their depiction of activities such as cooking and sports; ML algorithms trained on these collections not only mirrored, but amplified, these biases.[222]

Certain variables may reflect societal inequities and stand in as proxies for protected classes of data (e.g., race, sex), inadvertently perpetuating prohibited discriminatory practices. Practices that result in disparate impacts may violate various laws, such as equal credit or employment opportunity laws.[223] For example, the algorithm in the COMPAS tool (see the criminal

---

[220] See for example, Letter from Senator Ron Wyden et al. to Gene L. Dorado, Comptroller General of the United States, July 31, 2018, at https://www.wyden.senate.gov/download/07312018-gao-facial-recognition-request.

[221] See work conducted by the Gender Shades project by Joy Buolamwini at the Massachusetts Institute of Technology's (MIT's) Media Lab, at https://www.media.mit.edu/projects/gender-shades/overview/.

[222] Jieyu Zhao et al., "Men Also Like Shopping: Reducing Gender Bias Amplification Using Corpus-level Constraints," *Proceedings of the 2017 Conference on Empirical Methods in Natural Language Processing*, Copenhagen, Denmark, September 7, 2017, pp. 2979-2989, at https://www.aclweb.org/anthology/D17-1323.

[223] Federal Trade Commission, *Big Data: A Tool for Inclusion or Exclusion?*, January 2016, p. 19; "While specific disparate impact standards vary depending on the applicable law, in

justice box above) purports to predict the risk of future criminal activity, but it relies on inputs such as arrest history; variations in historical policing could reflect over-policing of certain communities leading to a higher number of arrests and higher correlation with crime while not accurately reflecting the likelihood of recidivism.[224]

While the above example is for a relatively simple statistical algorithm, the "black box" problem with many complex AI systems may make assessments of such bias harder to evaluate and correct. Identifying and addressing machine bias is a challenging problem, fueling a growing subfield of AI research. In trying to address pronoun gender bias in its "smart compose" feature, which automatically completes sentences for users as they type, Google opted to ban the use of gendered pronouns, stating that currently, "the only reliable technique we have is to be conservative."[225]

Beyond these arguably unintentional instances of bias perpetuation and amplification, concerns have been raised about the potential for intentional introduction of bias into algorithms through the release or use of manipulated training data.[226]

Additionally, what has been termed *automation bias* can occur when people trust the interpretations of an automated system over their own senses and instincts, expecting the algorithmic outcomes to be objective calculations since they are being performed by a computer, rather than an individual person making a decisions.[227] However, even some particularly complex AI algorithms such as deep neural networks that can work exceedingly well the majority of the time can have catastrophic failures, breaking in unpredictable ways.[228] For example, researchers have demonstrated that placing black and

---

general, disparate impact occurs when a company employs facially neutral policies or practices that have a disproportionate adverse effect or impact on a protected class."

224 Courtland, 2018.

225 Paresh Dave, "Fearful of Bias, Google Blocks Gender-Based Pronouns from New AI Tool," *Reuters*, November 27, 2018, at https://www.reuters.com/article/us-alphabet-google-ai-gender/fearful-of-bias-google-blocks-gender-based-pronouns-from-new-ai-tool-idUSKCN1NW0EF. The article further notes that gender-based pronoun biases are a widespread challenge for companies using AI for features such as natural language generation (NLG) and translation services.

226 Douglas Yeung, "When AI Misjudgment Is Not an Accident," *Scientific American*, October 19, 2018, at https://blogs.scientificamerican.com/observations/when-ai-misjudgment-is-not-an-accident.

227 John Zerilli et al., "Algorithmic Decision-Making and the Control Problem," *Minds and Machines*, vol. 29 (2019), pp. 555-578, at https://link.springer.com/article/10.1007/s11023-019-09513-7.

228 Douglas Heaven, "Why Deep-Learning AIs Are So Easy to Fool," *Nature*, vol. 574 (October 9, 2019), pp. 163-166, at https://www.nature.com/articles/d41586-019-03013-5.

white stickers on a stop sign can cause a neural network to misclassify the sign—for example, as a 45 miles-per-hour speed limit sign—over 80% of the time.[229]

Broadly, the debate around how to address bias and ethics in decisionmaking algorithms has resulted in calls for additional transparency, which raises its own sets of opportunities and challenges and questions about how best to enhance transparency. On one hand, engaging a broader set of stakeholders and providing information to those affected and journalists investigating the tools generally helps to foster trust and lead to fewer problems with bias and inequities. However, just providing all of the parameters of a model may not lead to better information about how it works. Further, providing too much information may allow people to game the system, and could provide a disincentive for private sector developers wishing to license their software. One compromise that has been proposed in this situation is to require confidential third-party auditing of proprietary software with publicly released results of such audits.[230]

Policy Considerations

Some considerations for potential policy responses to these issues include

- whether and how to increase access to public datasets to train AI systems for use in the public and private sectors;
- requirements for auditing and/or disclosing AI algorithms—particularly in high-impact areas such as social services, criminal justice, and healthcare—and direction to NIST to facilitate related standards and certifications for third-party auditors;
- mechanisms for recourse when people are subject to decisions in high-impact areas in which AI systems were used;
- facilitating the growth of multidisciplinary and diverse teams of experts for developing and training AI systems, including having people who will be using and affected by the systems as part of the design conversations;

---

[229] Kevin Eykholt et al., "Robust Physical-World Attacks on Deep Learning Visual Classification," 2018 IEEE/CVF Conference on Computer Vision and Pattern Recognition, Salt Lake City, UT, June 18-23, 2018, at https://ieeexplore.ieee.org/document/8578273.

[230] See, for example, Oren Etzioni, and Michael Li, "High-Stakes AI Decisions Need to Be Automatically Audited," *Wired*, July 18, 2019, at https://www.wired.com/story/ai-needs-to-be-audited/.

- encouraging training for AI researchers and designers in thinking about and designing systems that improve fairness, transparency, and accountability; and
- whether to continue or expand investments into AI R&D broadly and for more narrowly specified areas, such as those that facilitate transparency and auditability (e.g., explainable AI).

Disclaimer

Chapter 3

Highlights of the 2023 Executive Order on Artificial Intelligence for Congress*

Laurie Harris
and Chris Jaikaran

Abstract

On October 30, 2023, the Biden Administration released Executive Order (E.O.) 14110 on *Safe, Secure, and Trustworthy Development and Use of Artificial Intelligence*. It establishes a government-wide effort to guide responsible artificial intelligence (AI) development and deployment through federal agency leadership, regulation of industry, and engagement with international partners.

The E.O. directs over 50 federal entities to engage in more than 100 specific actions to implement the guidance set forth across eight overarching policy areas.

- *Safety and security.* The E.O. promotes the development and implementation of repeatable processes and mechanisms to understand and mitigate risks related to AI adoption, including with respect to biosecurity, cybersecurity, national security, and critical infrastructure.
- *Innovation and competition.* The E.O. compels actions to attract AI talent to the United States, understand novel intellectual property (IP) questions, protect inventors and creators, and promote AI innovation, including at startups and small businesses.

---

* This is an edited, reformatted and augmented version of Congressional Research Service, Publication No. R47843, dated April 3, 2024.

In: Artificial Intelligence
Editor: Sonja Buckley
ISBN: 979-8-89530-859-2

- *Worker support*. The E.O. states that AI adoption may be disruptive to the workforce and directs agencies to research and develop potential mitigations against such disruptions.
- *Consideration of AI bias and civil rights*. The E.O. states that AI models may perpetuate biases and their implementation may lead to civil rights violations. The E.O. includes a section on equity and civil rights considerations for use of AI in the criminal justice system and the administration of federal government programs and benefits.
- *Consumer protection.* The E.O. instructs agencies to enforce existing, technology-agnostic authorities in an effort to minimize harms to consumers, and to identify needed authorities related to AI.
- *Privacy*. The E.O. calls for the evaluation and mitigation of privacy risks—potentially exacerbated by AI— associated with the collection, use, and retention of user data.
- *Federal use of AI*. The E.O. requires the Office of Management and Budget (OMB) to establish an interagency council to coordinate AI use by federal agencies and develop guidance on AI governance and risk management activities for agencies. It acknowledges the ubiquity of generative AI (GenAI) tools, and directs agencies to move toward adoption with safeguards in place. The E.O. also calls for additional agency hiring and training activities to increase the AI workforce capacity across the federal government.
- *International leadership*. The E.O. declares that the United States should be a global leader in AI development and adoption by engaging with international allies and partners, leading efforts to develop common AI regulatory and accountability principles, and advancing responsible global technical standards for AI.

Introduction and Overview

On October 30, 2023, the Biden Administration released Executive Order (E.O.) 14110 on *Safe, Secure, and Trustworthy Development and Use of Artificial Intelligence*.[1] It establishes a government-wide effort to guide

---

[1] Executive Office of the President, "Safe, Secure, and Trustworthy Development and Use of Artificial Intelligence," 88 *Federal Register* 75191, November 1, 2023, at https://www.federalregister.gov/documents/2023/11/01/2023-24283/safe-secure-and-trustworthy-development-and-use-of-artificial-intelligence.

responsible artificial intelligence (AI) development and deployment through federal agency leadership, regulation of industry, and engagement with international partners. The E.O. states its purpose as follows.

> Artificial Intelligence (AI) holds extraordinary potential for both promise and peril. Responsible AI use has the potential to help solve urgent challenges while making our world more prosperous, productive, innovative, and secure. At the same time, irresponsible use could exacerbate societal harms such as fraud, discrimination, bias, and disinformation; displace and disempower workers; stifle competition; and pose risks to national security. Harnessing AI for good and realizing its myriad benefits requires mitigating its substantial risks. This endeavor demands a society-wide effort that includes government, the private sector, academia, and civil society.

E.O. 14110 builds on prior work to support the development of responsible AI technologies and policies, including the Office of Science and Technology Policy's (OSTP) *Blueprint for an AI Bill of Rights* and the National Institute of Standards and Technology's (NIST) *AI Risk Management Framework* (AI RMF).[2]

This CRS report provides a summary of requirements for agency action in the E.O. and timelines for their deliverables. It is organized in tables that correspond to each policy area listed in the E.O.

The E.O. describes eight overarching policy areas:

1) Safety and security;
2) Innovation and competition;
3) Worker support;
4) Consideration of AI bias and civil rights;
5) Consumer protection;
6) Privacy;
7) Federal use of AI; and
8) International leadership.

---

[2] White House, *Blueprint for an AI Bill of Rights: Making Automated Systems Work for the American People*, October 2022, at https://www.whitehouse.gov/wp-content/uploads/2022/10/Blueprint-for-an-AI-Bill-of-Rights.pdf; and National Institute of Standards and Technology, *Artificial Intelligence Risk Management Framework* (NIST AI 100-1), January 2023, at https://nvlpubs.nist.gov/nistpubs/ai/NIST.AI.100-1.pdf.

These areas and the actions listed within are further described in the section "Requirements and Deliverables," below.

To help federal departments and agencies implement the E.O., and consistent with the Artificial Intelligence in Government Act (P.L. 116-260) and the Advancing American AI Act (P.L. 117-263), OMB released a memorandum on *Advancing Governance, Innovation, and Risk Management for Agency Use of Artificial Intelligence*.[3] The stated purpose of the memorandum is to "direct[s] agencies to advance AI governance and innovation while managing risks from the use of AI, particularly those affecting the safety and rights of the public."[4]

To coordinate the timely implementation of federal AI policies, including those set forth in the E.O., it establishes the White House Artificial Intelligence Council. The Assistant to the President and Deputy Chief of Staff for Policy serves as the council's chair. The council is composed of the heads of the following departments and agencies, or their designees:

1) Department of State;
2) Department of the Treasury;
3) Department of Defense;
4) Department of Justice;
5) Department of Agriculture;
6) Department of Commerce;
7) Department of Labor;
8) Department of Health and Human Services;
9) Department of Housing and Urban Development;
10) Department of Transportation;
11) Department of Energy;
12) Department of Education;
13) Department of Veterans Affairs;
14) Department of Homeland Security;

---

[3] Office of Management and Budget, "Advancing Governance, Innovation, and Risk Management for Agency Use of Artificial Intelligence," M-24-10, March 28, 2024, https://www.whitehouse.gov/wp-content/uploads/2024/03/M-24-10-Advancing-Governance-Innovation-and-Risk-Management-for-Agency-Use-of-Artificial-Intelligence.pdf; The Artificial Intelligence in Government Act, P.L. 116-260, Division U, Title I; and The Advancing American AI Act, P.L. 117-263, Title LXXII, Subtitle B.

[4] Office of Management and Budget, "Advancing Governance, Innovation, and Risk Management for Agency Use of Artificial Intelligence," M-24-10, March 28, 2024, https://www.whitehouse.gov/wp-content/uploads/2024/03/M-24-10-Advancing-Governance-Innovation-and-Risk-Management-for-Agency-Use-of-Artificial-Intelligence.pdf.

15) Small Business Administration;
16) United States Agency for International Development;
17) Office of the Director of National Intelligence;
18) National Science Foundation;
19) Office of Management and Budget;
20) Office of Science and Technology Policy; as well as the
21) National Security Advisor;
22) Director of the Council of Economic Advisors;
23) Domestic Policy Advisor;
24) Chief of Staff to the Vice President;
25) Director of the Gender Policy Council;
26) Chairman of the Council of Economic Advisors;
27) National Cyber Director; and
28) Chairman of the Joint Chiefs of Staff.

Other agencies and executive offices may be added to the council at the discretion of the chair.

Requirements and Deliverables

E.O. 14110 directs over 50 federal entities to engage in more than 100 specific actions to implement the guidance set forth in the E.O. CRS has outlined the requirements of the E.O. (as well as any deliverables) in the tables below, organized by policy area. The tables only list requirements with explicit deliverables and due dates, as well as the responsible agency or agencies for those deliverables. The E.O. encourages independent federal regulators to engage in given tasks, but does not prescribe accompanying deadlines for those tasks. Those tasks are described below each table. Abbreviations used in the tables can be found in the Appendix.

Safety and Security

The E.O. promotes the development and implementation of repeatable processes and mechanisms to understand and mitigate risks related to AI adoption, especially with respect to biosecurity, cybersecurity, national security, and critical infrastructure risk. Actions related to this policy area are prescribed in Section 4 of the E.O. There are 27 requirements involving over 30 federal entities in this section. Table 1 lists these requirements.

Table 1. Requirements and deliverables in section 4 on safety and security; ascending by section citation

Requirements	Lead Agency (Supporting Agencies)	Due Dates	Section	Notes
Develop guidelines and best practices—with the aim of promoting consensus industry standards—and testing environments, for developing and deploying safe, secure, and trustworthy AI safety and security.	NIST (DOE, DHS, DOC, NSF)	July 26, 2024 (270 days)	4.1(a)	Includes development of companion resources to the *AI Risk Management Framework* (for GenAI) and *Secure Software Development Framework* (for GenAI and dual-use foundational models), and launching an initiative to create guidance and benchmarks for AI audits.
Develop and implement a plan to develop AI model evaluation tools and testbeds, in order to understand and mitigate AI security risks.	DOE (SRMAs)	July 26, 2024 (270 days)	4.1(b)	Efforts shall use existing solutions where possible and, at a minimum, include development of tools to evaluate security threats and hazards.
Require (1) companies developing, or intending to develop, dual-use AI models to report to the government on model training, testing, and data ownership; and (2) entities that acquire, develop, or possess potential large computing infrastructure to report	DOC	January 28, 2024 (90 days)	4.2(a)	This requirement uses Defense Production Act (DPA, 50 U.S.C. §§4501-4568) authorities to require responses.

Requirements	Lead Agency (Supporting Agencies)	Due Dates	Section	Notes
to the government on the location and amount of computing power.				
Define the set of technical conditions used to determine which models and computing infrastructure are subject to the reporting in 4.2(a).	DOC (DOS, DOD, DOE, DNI)	January 28, 2024 (90 days)	4.2(b)	The minimum computational threshold that would trigger a reporting requirement for companies currently exceeds most models in use.[a]
Propose regulations for Cloud Service Providers (CSPs) to report when foreign persons use U.S. infrastructure to train AI systems.	DOC	January 28, 2024 (90 days)	4.2(c)	This requirement follows E.O. 13984, which proposed a know-your-customer regime for CSPs.
Extend regulation from Section 4.2(c) to foreign resellers of CSP products used for AI.	DOC	April 27, 2024 (180 days)	4.2(d)	Also prescribes minimum reporting information.
Evaluate and assess potential risks related to critical infrastructure adoption and use of AI and consider ways to mitigate vulnerabilities.	SRMAs (CISA)	January 28, 2024 (90 days) and annually thereafter	4.3(a)(i)	The report shall be made to DHS.
Issue best practices for financial institutions to manage AI-specific cybersecurity risks.	Treasury	March 28, 2024 (150 days)	4.3(a)(ii)	The report shall be public.
Incorporate the *AI Risk Management Framework*, and other appropriate security guidance, into safety and security guidelines used by CI owners and operators.	DHS (DOC, SRMAs, IRAs)	April 27, 2024 (180 days)	4.3(a)(iii)	
Take steps to mandate adoption of the guidelines from Section 4.3(a)(iii).	APNSA & OMB (DHS)	December 23, 2024 (240 days from guidelines)	4.3(a)(iv)	IRAs shall consider adopting regulatory action.

Table 1. (Continued)

Requirements	Lead Agency (Supporting Agencies)	Due Dates	Section	Notes
Establish an Artificial Intelligence Safety and Security Board.	DHS	No date assigned	4.3(a)(v)	In accordance with 6 U.S.C. §451 on advisory committees.
Plan for and conduct a pilot to use AI models to discover and remediate vulnerabilities in federal IT systems.	DOD & DHS	April 27, 2024 (180 days)	4.3(b)(ii)	DOD shall carry out a pilot for national security systems; DHS shall carry out a pilot for non-national security systems.
Report (from each agency) on results of the pilot projects (Section 4.3(b)(ii)), vulnerabilities AI systems discovered, and how those vulnerabilities were mitigated.	DOD & DHS	July 26, 2024 (270 days)	4.3(b)(iii)	The reports are to the APNSA.
Evaluate potential for AI to be used to develop, produce, or counter chemical, biological, radiological, and nuclear (CBRN) threats.	DHS (DOE, OSTP)	April 27, 2024 (180 days)	4.4(a)(i)	Report shall be made to the President, including recommendations for regulating or overseeing such AI models.
Study and report on the use of AI in biology and the potential to increase biosecurity and national security risks, and make recommendations to mitigate such risks.	DOD (APNSA, OSTP)	February 27, 2024 (120 days)	4.4(a)(ii)	DOD shall contract with the National Academies of Sciences, Engineering, and Medicine for the study.
Develop a framework for providers of synthetic nucleic acids (companies that manipulate certain biologic genetic material) to encourage such providers to	OSTP (DOS, DOD, DOJ, DOC, HHS, DOE, DHS, DNI)	April 27, 2024 (180 days)	4.4(b)(i)	The stated goal is to reduce the misuse of synthetic genetic material, which might be substantially increased by AI's capabilities,

Requirements	Lead Agency (Supporting Agencies)	Due Dates	Section	Notes
implement procurement screening mechanisms, including standards and incentives.				and improve biosecurity measures for the industry.
Develop procurement screening specifications and guides, and best practices for sequence-of-concern database management and conformity-assessment, for use by nucleic acid sequence providers.	NIST & OSTP (DOS, HHS)	April 27, 2024 (180 days)	4.4(b)(ii)	
Establish requirements that life science researchers receiving federal funding must procure synthetic nucleic acids from manufacturers adhering to the framework in Section 4.4(b)(i).	All agencies that fund life sciences research	October 24, 2024 (180 days from the framework in 4.4(b)(i))	4.4(b)(iii)	The APNSA and OSTP shall review funding requirements for consistency.
Develop a framework to conduct structured evaluation and stress testing of the nucleic acid procurement screening systems.	DHS	October 24, 2024 (180 days from the framework in 4.4(b)(i))	4.4(b)(iv)	Submit an annual report, including recommendations, to the APNSA, OPPRP, and OSTP.
Identify existing and potential standards, tools, and methods for authenticating, tracking provenance of, labeling, and detecting AI-generated content.	DOC	June 26, 2024 (240 days)	4.5(a)	Report to APNSA and OMB. The report shall also consider (1) preventing GenAI from producing child sexual abuse material, (2) testing software which can be used as a tool, and (3) auditing synthetic content.

Table 1. (Continued)

Requirements	Lead Agency (Supporting Agencies)	Due Dates	Section	Notes
Develop guidance for adopting the tools and practices for digital content authentication and synthetic content detection measures identified in the report in 4.5(a).	DOC (OMB)	December 23, 2024 (180 days from report)	4.5(b)	Shall be updated periodically after development.
Issue guidance to agencies for labeling and authenticating digital and synthetic content the federal government uses.	OMB (DOS, DOD, DOJ, NIST, DHS, DNI)	June 21, 2025 (180 days from guidance in section 4.5(b))	4.5(c)	
Consider amending the Federal Acquisition Regulation to account for guidance established under section 4.5.	FARC	No date assigned	4.5(d)	
Solicit expert input and report on the risks, benefits, and policy and regulatory mechanisms on dual-use foundation AI models with widely available model weights.	NTIA (DOS)	July 26, 2024 (270 days)	4.6	Report is to be submitted to the President.
Develop guidelines for performing security reviews before releasing federal information that could be used to develop CBRN weapons or offensive cyber capabilities.	CDOC (DOD, DOC, DOE, DHS, DNI)	July 26, 2024 (270 days)	4.7(a)	
Conduct security reviews using guidelines from Section 4.7(a) and take steps to address the highest-priority potential security risks.	Agencies	January 22, 2025 (180 days from guidelines)	4.7(b)	

Requirements	Lead Agency (Supporting Agencies)	Due Dates	Section	Notes
Develop an accompanying National Security Memorandum on AI.	APNSA & DCOSP	July 26, 2024 (270 days)	4.8	Memorandum shall use an interagency development process.

Source: CRS analysis of Executive Order 14110. Executive Office of the President, "Safe, Secure, and Trustworthy Development and Use of Artificial Intelligence," 88 *Federal Register* 75191, November 1, 2023, at https://www.federalregister.gov/documents/2023/11/01/2023-24283/safe-secure-and-trustworthy-development-and-use-of-artificial-intelligence.

Notes: For a list of acronyms, please see the Appendix.

[a] For example, researchers have estimated that the computational power minimum threshold in the E.O. (10^26 floating-point operations [FLOPs]) is "more than any model trained to date" and that OpenAI's GPT-4 model was just under this threshold. See Markus Anderljung et al., "Frontier AI Regulation: Managing Emerging Risks to Public Safety," *arXiv* (non-peer reviewed), July 6, 2023, at https://arxiv.org/abs/ 2307.03718; and Rishi Bommasani et al., "Decoding the White House AI Executive Order's Achievements," Stanford University Institute for Human-Centered AI, November 2, 2023, at https://hai.stanford.edu/news/ decoding-white-house-ai-executive-orders-achievements.

Additionally, Section 4.3 encourages independent regulatory agencies to consider rulemaking to help critical infrastructure owners and operators safely adopt AI technologies and mitigate risks.

Innovation and Competition

The E.O. compels actions to attract AI talent to the United States, understand novel intellectual property (IP) questions to protect inventors and creators, and promote AI innovation, including at startups and small businesses. Actions related to this policy area are prescribed in Section 5 of the E.O. There are 21 requirements involving 10 federal entities in this section. Table 2 lists these requirements.

Section 5.2 (a)(i) encourages independent regulatory agencies to consider complementary actions to AI research resource pilots for their regulated industries. Additionally, Section 5.3(a) encourages the Federal Trade Commission (FTC) to consider rulemaking to ensure fair competition for consumers in the AI marketplace. Section 5.3(b) provides guidance to the Department of Commerce in implementing the Creating Helpful Incentives to Produce Semiconductors (CHIPS) Act of 2022 (P.L. 117-167). Sections 5.3(c) and (d) provide guidance to the Small Business Administration (SBA) on supporting small businesses' use of AI. These directions do not carry accompanying deliverables or specific due dates.

Table 2. Requirements and deliverables in section 5 on innovation and competition; ascending by section citation

Requirements	Lead Agency (Supporting Agencies)	Due Dates	Section	Notes
Streamline processes for visas for foreigners seeking to come to the United States for AI education or work.	DOS & DHS	January 28, 2024 (90 days)	5.1(a)	Also applies to other critical and emerging technologies, as identified in the White House Critical and Emerging Technologies List.[a]
Consider (1) rulemaking to establish new criteria for designating countries and critical skills for visas, and (2) implementing a visa renewal program to help highly skilled AI talent continue to work in the United States.	DOS	February 27, 2024 (120 days)	5.1(b)	
Consider rulemaking to expand nonimmigrant eligibility for the domestic visa renewal program, and establish a program to identify and attract top AI talent from overseas.	DOS	April 27, 2024 (180 days)	5.1(c)	
Review and initiate policy changes related to immigration pathways for AI experts, and consider rulemaking to enhance visa modernization processes and permanent resident pathways.	DHS	April 27, 2024 (180 days)	5.1(d)	
Solicit public input to identify AI and STEM-related occupations for which there is an inadequate number of U.S. workers, so to update the "Schedule A" list.	DOL	December 14, 2023 (45 days)	5.1(e)	Refers to Schedule A of 20 C.F.R. §656.5.

Requirements	Lead Agency (Supporting Agencies)	Due Dates	Section	Notes
Develop and publish resources to help attract and retain AI experts from other countries, and help them understand their options for working in the United States.	DHS (DOS, DOC, OSTP)	February 27, 2024 (120 days)	5.1(g)	Also includes a requirement to publish a public report with data on how AI experts have utilized the immigration system through the end of FY2023.
Launch a pilot program implementing the National AI Research Resource (NAIRR), consistent with previous recommendations.b	NSF	January 28, 2024 (90 days)	5.2(a)(i)	By December 14 (45 days) agencies are to identify resources that could be integrated into this pilot.
Fund and launch at least one NSF Regional Innovation Engine that prioritizes AI-related work.	NSF	March 28, 2024 (150 days)	5.2(a)(ii)	
Establish at least four new National AI Research Institutes.	NSF	April 22, 2025 (540 days)	5.2(a)(iii)	25 are currently funded; NSF funds 20 of those, and USDA NIFA funds 5.c
Establish a pilot program to enhance existing training programs for scientists.	DOE & NSF	February 27, 2024 (120 days)	5.2(b)	The E.O.'s goal is to reach 500 new AI researchers by 2025.
Publish guidance to USPTO patent examiners and applicants on use of AI in the inventive process.	USPTO	February 27, 2024 (120 days)	5.2(c)(i)	
Issue additional guidance to USPTO patent examiners and applicants to address other considerations at the intersection of AI and IP.	USPTO	July 26, 2024 (270 days)	5.2(c)(ii)	Could include updated guidance on patent eligibility to address innovation in AI and critical and emerging technologies.
Recommend further executive actions on copyright and AI.	USPTO	July 26, 2024 (270 days)	5.2(c)(iii)	Could also be 180 days after the U.S. Copyright Office publishes a study on AI in copyright issues pursuant to 37 C.F.R. Part 202.

Table 2. (Continued)

Requirements	Lead Agency (Supporting Agencies)	Due Dates	Section	Notes
Develop a training, analysis, and evaluation program to mitigate AI-related IP risks.	DHS (DOJ)	April 27, 2024 (180 days)	5.2(d)	This includes devoting personnel, developing guidance for the private sector, and sharing information.
Identify and prioritize funding awards—and undertake related efforts—to support responsible AI development.	HHS	No date assigned	5.2(e)	Includes collaborating with the private sector to support personalized medicine, prioritizing awards to improve health care data quality, and accelerating AIM-AHEAD program awards.
Host two three-month long AI Tech Sprint competitions.	VA	October 29, 2024 (365 days)	5.2(f)	VA is also to provide access to technical assistance, mentorship opportunities, expert feedback, and potential contract opportunities to competitors.
Issue a public report describing how AI could improve electric grid infrastructure.	DOE (FERC, OSTP, CEQ, APNCA)	April 27, 2024 (180 days)	5.2(g)(i)	The overarching goals of the requirements under Section 5.2(g) are to strengthen U.S. resilience against climate change impacts.
Develop tools to help build foundational AI models for basic and applied science, including for environmental reviews and permitting, and to mitigate climate change risks.	DOE (FERC, OSTP, CEQ, APNCA)	April 27, 2024 (180 days)	5.2(g)(ii) 5.2(g)(iii)	AI models should also improve environmental and social outcomes, and agencies should collaborate with private sector organizations and academic researchers when developing

Requirements	Lead Agency (Supporting Agencies)	Due Dates	Section	Notes
				tools to mitigate risks.
Partner with nongovernmental entities and international allies and partners to model climate risks and projects using DOE's computing capabilities and AI testbeds.	DOE (FERC, OSTP, CEQ, APNCA)	April 27, 2024 (180 days)	5.2(g)(iv)	To include partnerships that increase community preparedness, enable clean-energy deployment, and enhance grid reliability and resilience.
Establish an office in DOE to coordinate AI programs across the national laboratories.	DOE (FERC, OSTP, CEQ, APNCA)	April 27, 2024 (180 days)	5.2(g)(v)	
Report on the potential of AI for scientific research.	PCAST	April 27, 2024 (180 days)	5.2(h)	Report shall be submitted to the President and made publicly available.

Source: CRS analysis of Executive Order 14110. Executive Office of the President, "Safe, Secure, and Trustworthy Development and Use of Artificial Intelligence," 88 *Federal Register* 75191, November 1, 2023, at https://www.federalregister.gov/documents/2023/11/01/2023-24283/safe-secure-and-trustworthy-development-and-use-of-artificial-intelligence.

Notes: For a list of acronyms, please see the Appendix.

[a] Executive Office of the President, "Critical and Emerging Technologies List Update," report, February 2022, at https://www.whitehouse.gov/wp-content/uploads/2022/02/02-2022-Critical-and-Emerging-Technologies-List-Update.pdf.

[b] NSF and OSTP are jointly chairing a NAIRR Pilot Interagency Working Group, which is developing an implementation plan for the NAIRR; see NASA, "Participation in National AI Research Resource (NAIRR) Pilot Interagency Working Group," June 26, 2023, at https://science.msfc.nasa.gov/2023/06/26/participation-in-national-ai-research-resource-nairr-pilot-interagency-working-group/. Per the NSF FY2024 Budget Request to Congress, "NSF will work with agencies and the broader community on the NAIRR Pilot Option outlined in the report to provide pilot-scale access to existing computational resources, software, datasets, services, and user portals across the current national cyberinfrastructure ecosystem"; see NSF FY2024 Budget Request to Congress, March 13, 2023, p. Emerging Industries–19.

[c] James Donlon, "National Artificial Intelligence (AI) Research Institutes," Program Webinar, September 5, 2023, at https://nsf.gov/attachments/308263/public/National_AI_Research_Institutes_Webinar2023_508verified.pptx.

Worker Support

The E.O. recognizes that AI adoption may be disruptive to the workforce and directs agencies to research and develop potential mitigations against such disruptions. Actions related to this policy area are prescribed in Section 6 of the E.O. There are four requirements involving two federal entities. Table 3 lists these requirements.

Table 3. Requirements and deliverables in section 6 on worker support; ascending by section citation

Requirements	Lead Agency (Supporting Agencies)	Due Dates	Section	Notes
Report on the effects of AI on the labor market.	CEA	April 27, 2024 (180 days)	6(a)(i)	The report is to the President.
Report on the ability agencies have to assist workers displaced by AI adoption.	DOL	April 27, 2024 (180 days)	6(a)(ii)	The report is to the President.
Publish principles and best practices employers could adopt to minimize harms to employees.	DOL	April 27, 2024 (180 days)	6(b)(i) 6(b)(ii)	DOL shall also encourage adoption of these practices.
Issue guidance on complying with legal requirements for employers that deploy AI to monitor or augment employees' work.	DOL	April 27, 2024 (180 days)	6(b)(iii)	Including complying with protections ensuring worker compensation for time worked under 29 U.S.C. §201 et seq.

Source: CRS analysis of Executive Order 14110. Executive Office of the President, "Safe, Secure, and Trustworthy Development and Use of Artificial Intelligence," 88 *Federal Register* 75191, November 1, 2023, at https://www.federalregister.gov/documents/2023/11/01/2023-24283/safe-secure-and-trustworthy-development-and-use-of-artificial-intelligence.

Note: For a list of acronyms, please see the Appendix.

Section 6(c) also directs NSF to prioritize available resources to support AI-related education and AI-related workforce development through existing programs, and to consult with other federal agencies to further allocate resources for such purposes.

Consideration of AI Bias and Civil Rights

The E.O. recognizes that AI models may perpetuate biases and that their implementation may lead to civil rights violations. This section includes a focus on equity and civil rights considerations with use of AI in the criminal justice system and the administration of federal government programs and benefits. Actions related to this policy area are prescribed in Section 7 of the E.O. There are nine requirements involving eight federal entities. Table 4 lists these requirements. Numerous requirements in this section of E.O. 14110 reference requirements and deliverables from E.O. 14074, "Advancing Effective, Accountable Policing and Criminal Justice Practices to Enhance Public Trust and Public Safety."[5]

Table 4. Requirements and deliverables in section 7 on ai biases and civil rights; ascending by section citation

Requirements	Lead Agency (Supporting Agencies)	Due Dates	Section	Notes
Convene agencies and regulators to discuss how they can use their authorities to prevent algorithmic and AI-related discrimination.	DOJ	January 28, 2024 (90 days)	7.1(a)(ii)	They shall also consider improving external stakeholder engagement and developing additional training, guidance, and resources.
Report on the use of AI in the criminal justice system.	DOJ (DHS, OSTP)	October 29, 2023 (365 days)	7.1(b)	The report is to the President. The report is to address uses by police, prosecutors, and courts; and recommend best practices for safeguards and use limits for AI.
Identify and publish best practices to recruit law enforcement (LE) professionals with AI expertise and train LE professionals about responsible application of AI.	OPM	April 27, 2024 (180 days)	7.1(c)(i)	OPM is the chair of the Interagency Working Group on Policies, Best Practices for Federal Law Enforcement Agencies. This working group is responsible for this deliverable.

[5] Executive Office of the President, "Advancing Effective, Accountable Policing and Criminal Justice Practices to Enhance Public Trust and Public Safety," 87 *Federal Register* 32945-32963, May 31, 2022.

Table 4. (Continued)

Requirements	Lead Agency (Supporting Agencies)	Due Dates	Section	Notes
Review practices identified in 7.1(c)(i) and, if necessary, develop recommendations for state and local law enforcement agencies.	DOJ (DHS)	July 26, 2024 (270 days)	7.1(c)(ii)	Extends to tribal law enforcement agencies.
Assess departmental capacity to investigate cases related to AI involving the deprivation of rights by governmental agencies acting under actual or perceived authorities.	DOJ	October 29, 2024 (365 days)	7.1(c)(iii)	Pursuant to 18 U.S.C. §242.
Publish a plan addressing states' and localities' use of automated or algorithmic systems in distributing public benefits and services funded by the department.	HHS	April 27, 2024 (180 days)	7.2(b)(i)	The plan should promote equitable administration of benefits, including assessments, disclosure, and monitoring of systems and processes to appeal denials.
Issue guidance to state, local, tribal, and territorial public benefits administrators on the use of automated or algorithmic systems in distributing benefits.	USDA	April 27, 2024 (180 days)	7.2(b)(ii)	The guidance should also address the use of automated or algorithmic systems in providing customer support for benefits programs funded by USDA.
Publish guidance for federal contractors on preventing bias in AI systems used in hiring.	DOL	October 29, 2024 (365 days)	7.3(a)	
Issue guidance on AI use in housing decisions.	HUD	April 27, 2024 (180 days)	7.3(c)	

Source: CRS analysis of Executive Order 14110. Executive Office of the President, "Safe, Secure, and Trustworthy Development and Use of Artificial Intelligence," 88 *Federal Register* 75191, November 1, 2023, at https://www.federalregister.gov/documents/2023/11/01/2023-24283/safe-secure-and-trustworthy-development-and-use-of-artificial-intelligence.

Note: For a list of acronyms, please see the Appendix.

Section 7.1(a)(ii) encourages independent regulatory agencies to consider participating in DOJ's civil rights efforts. Additionally, Section 7.3(b) encourages the Federal Housing Finance Agency (FHFA) and the Consumer Financial Protection Bureau (CFPB) to consider using their authorities to govern industry use of AI in underwriting, valuation, and appraisal processes in housing markets.

Consumer Protection

The E.O. instructs agencies to enforce existing technology-agnostic authorities in an effort to minimize harms to consumers, and to identify needed authorities related to AI. Actions related to this policy area are prescribed in Section 8 of the E.O. There are nine requirements in this section involving five federal entities. Table 5 lists these requirements.

Table 5. Requirements and deliverables in section 8 on consumer protection; ascending by section citation

Requirements	Lead Agency (Supporting Agencies)	Due Dates	Section	Notes
Establish an HHS AI Task Force.	HHS (DOD, VA)	January 28, 2024 (90 days)	8(b)(i)	Within a year of its creation, the task force shall issue a plan for federal actions regarding the responsible adoption of AI in the health and human services sector.
Develop a strategy to assess AI quality, including the development of an AI assurance policy and infrastructure needs.	HHS	April 27, 2024 (180 days)	8(b)(ii)	
Consider actions to advance industry understanding of, and compliance with, federal nondiscrimination laws as they relate to AI for health and human service providers receiving federal funding.	HHS	April 27, 2024 (180 days)	8(b)(iii)	Actions may include providing technical assistance about obligations under discrimination and privacy laws as related to AI use and potential consequences of noncompliance, and issuing guidance in response to complaints.

Table 5. (Continued)

Requirements	Lead Agency (Supporting Agencies)	Due Dates	Section	Notes
Establish an AI safety program to monitor and improve AI deployment in health care through a common framework to identify AI-associated clinical errors and guidelines to avoid such harms.	HHS (DOD, VA)	October 29, 2024 (365 days)	8(b)(iv)	In partnership with Patient Safety Organizations.
Develop a strategy for the use of AI and AI-enabled tools in drug development.	HHS	October 29, 2024 (365 days)	8(b)(v)	
Task the Nontraditional and Emerging Transportation Technology (NETT) Council to assess the need for guidance regarding AI use in transportation.	DOT	November 29, 2023 (30 days)	8(c)(i)	DOT shall further direct the NETT Council to support transportation-related AI pilot programs, assess outcomes to inform regulatory actions, and establish a DOT Cross-Modal Executive Working Group.
Task DOT FACA committees to provide advice on safe and responsible AI use in transportation.	DOT	January 28, 2024 (90 days)	8(c)(ii)	
Task the Advanced Research Projects Agency–Infrastructure (ARPA-I) to explore research and development projects for AI use in transportation.	DOT	April 27, 2024 (180 days)	8(c)(iii)	
Develop resources, policies, and guidance for AI use in education.	ED	October 29, 2024(365 days)	8(d)	Shall include development of an AI toolkit for educators.

Source: CRS analysis of Executive Order 14110. Executive Office of the President, "Safe, Secure, and Trustworthy Development and Use of Artificial Intelligence," 88 *Federal Register* 75191, November 1, 2023, at https://www.federalregister.gov/documents/2023/11/01/2023-24283/safe-secure-and-trustworthy-development-and-use-of-artificial-intelligence.

Note: For a list of acronyms, please see the Appendix.

Additionally, Section 8(a) encourages independent regulatory agencies to consider using their authorities to protect American consumers from fraud, discrimination, and threats to privacy and to address other risks that may arise from the use of AI, including risks to financial stability; and to consider rulemaking, as well as emphasizing or clarifying where existing regulations and guidance apply to AI. Section 8(e) encourages the Federal Communications Commission (FCC) to consider actions related to how AI will affect communications networks and consumers, including its potential for spectrum management, and encourages efforts to combat unwanted robocalls and robotexts.

Privacy

The E.O. calls for the evaluation and mitigation of privacy risks—potentially exacerbated by AI—associated with the collection, use, and retention of Americans' data. Actions related to this policy area are prescribed in Section 9 of the E.O. There are six requirements in this section involving nine federal entities. Table 6 lists these requirements.

Table 6. Requirements and deliverables in section 9 on privacy; ascending by section citation

Requirements	Lead Agency (Supporting Agencies)	Due Dates	Section	Notes
Identify commercially available information procured by agencies.	OMB	No date assigned	9(a)(i)	Particular focus on personally identifiable information (PII). National security purposes are excluded.
Evaluate agency standards and procedures associated with agency use of commercially available information to inform ways to mitigate privacy and confidentiality risks.	OMB (FPC, ICSP)	No date assigned	9(a)(ii)	Evaluation to include looking at collection, processing, maintenance, use, sharing, and disposition of data that contains PII.

Table 6. (Continued)

Requirements	Lead Agency (Supporting Agencies)	Due Dates	Section	Notes
Solicit public comment on changes to federal guidance related to privacy and mitigating AI-related risks.	OMB (DOJ, CEA, OSTP)	April 27, 2024 (180 days)	9(a)(iii)	Take additional steps to act on feedback in implementing changes to federal guidance (Section 9(a)(iv)).
Create guidance for agencies to follow when they evaluate the use of privacy-enhancing technologies.	NIST	October 29, 2024 (365 days)	9(b)	
Fund the creation of a Research Coordination Network for advancing privacy research.	NSF (DOE)	February 27, 2024 (120 days)	9(c)(i)	Particular focus on deploying and scaling privacy-enhancing technologies.
Work with agencies to identify opportunities to incorporate privacy-enhancing technologies into their operations.	NSF	June 26, 2024 (240 days)	9(c)(ii)	Prioritize use-inspired research, including through engagements with the Research Coordination Network.

Source: CRS analysis of Executive Order 14110. Executive Office of the President, "Safe, Secure, and Trustworthy Development and Use of Artificial Intelligence," 88 *Federal Register* 75191, November 1, 2023, at https://www.federalregister.gov/documents/2023/11/01/2023-24283/safe-secure-and-trustworthy-development-and-use-of-artificial-intelligence.

Note: For a list of acronyms, please see the Appendix.

Federal Use of AI

The E.O. requires the Office of Management and Budget (OMB) to establish an interagency council to coordinate AI use by federal agencies and develop guidance on AI governance and risk management activities for agencies. The section acknowledges the ubiquity of generative AI (GenAI) tools, and directs agencies to provide access with safeguards in place. This section calls for additional agency hiring and training activities to increase the AI workforce capacity across the federal government. Actions related to this policy area are prescribed in Section 10 of the E.O. There are 29 requirements in this section involving 40 federal entities. Table 7 lists these requirements.

Table 7. Requirements and deliverables in section 10 on federal use of AI; ascending by section citation

Requirements	Lead Agency (Supporting Agencies)	Due Dates	Section	Notes
Convene and chair an interagency council on federal use of AI.	OMB	December 29, 2023 (60 days)	10.1(a)	OSTP is the vice chair of the council. CFO Act agencies (31 U.S.C. §902(b)) and DNI are members.
Issue guidance to agencies on AI use.	OMB & OSTP (Interagency council members from 10(a))	March 28, 2024 (150 days, and periodically thereafter)	10.1(b)	Guidance shall address appropriate and effective testing, use, and documentation of AI; advancing innovation; and managing AI-related risks.
Designate a Chief Artificial Intelligence Officer.	CFO Act Agencies	May 27, 2024 (60 days from guidance)	10.1 (b)(i)	This requirement shall be part of OMB's guidance from 10.1(b).
Create Artificial Intelligence Governance Boards within the agencies.	CFO Act Agencies	May 27, 2024 (60 days from guidance)	10.1 (b)(iii)	Another mechanism may be substituted for this board. This requirement shall be part of OMB's guidance from 10.1(b).
Specify minimum risk management practices for government use of AI that impact people's rights or safety.	OMB	No date specified	10.1 (b)(iv)	
Develop AI strategies and pursue high-impact AI use cases.	CFO Act Agencies	No date specified	10.1(b)(vii)	This requirement shall be part of OMB's guidance from 10.1(b).
Establish a system to track agency AI progress.	OMB	May 27, 2024 (60 days from OMB guidance and periodically thereafter)	10.1(c)	

Table 7. (Continued)

Requirements	Lead Agency (Supporting Agencies)	Due Dates	Section	Notes
Develop guidelines, tools, and practices to support implementation of the minimum risk-management practices described in the OMB guidance.	NIST (OMB, OSTP)	June 26, 2024 (90 days from OMB guidance)	10.1 (d)(i)	
Develop means to ensure that agency contracts for AI system and services procurement align with OMB guidance.	OMB	September 24, 2024 (180 days from OMB guidance)	10.1 (d)(ii)	The means should also advance aims from the Advancing American AI Act (P.L. 117-263, Div. G, Title LXXII, Subtitle B, §7224(d)(1)).
Issue instructions to agencies for the collection, reporting, and publication of agency AI use cases.	OMB	No date specified	10.1(e)	Pursuant to the Advancing American AI Act (P.L. 117-263, §7225(a)). These instructions shall include, as appropriate, an expansion of agencies' reporting on how they are managing risks from AI uses.
Develop a framework to incorporate AI in FedRAMP.	GSA & OMB (Federal Secure Cloud Advisory Committee)	January 28, 2024 (90 days)	10.1 (f)(ii)	The framework shall initially prioritize generative AI technologies.
Develop guidance for federal employee use of generative AI.	OPM & OMB	April 27, 2024 (180 days)	10.1 (f)(iii)	
Consider prioritizing funding for projects related to AI.	Technology Modernization Board	November 29, 2023 (30 days)	10.1(g)	This board administers the Technology Modernization Fund within GSA.

Requirements	Lead Agency (Supporting Agencies)	Due Dates	Section	Notes
Facilitate access to AI vendors through government-wide acquisition vehicles or tools.	GSA & OMB (DOD, DHS, DNI, NASA)	April 27, 2024 (180 days)	10.1(h)	Specified types of AI capabilities shall include generative AI and specialized computing infrastructure. Excludes AI components of national security systems.
Plan to surge AI talent in the federal government.	OSTP & OMB (APNSA, APEA, APDP, DGPC)	December 14, 2023 (45 days)	10.2(a)	Shall include identifying priority mission areas and types of AI talent to implement this E.O.
Create and convene an AI and Technology Talent Task Force.	DCOSP, OSTP, OMB (NCD)	December 14, 2023 (45 days)	10.2(b)	The task force is to accelerate and track the hiring of AI talent in the federal government.
Track, report progress on, and make recommendations on increasing AI capacity across the federal government.	AI and Technology Talent Task Force	April 27, 2024 (180 days)	10.2 (b)(i)	Recommendations are to the President. The task force shall also convene a cross-agency forum for AI professionals to share best practices and improve retention.
Develop and implement plans to support the rapid recruitment of AI talent in the federal government.	USDS, Presidential Innovation Fellowship, USDC, OPM, Agencies	December 14, 2023 (45 days)	10.2(c)	
Conduct a review of hiring authorities and workplace flexibilities needed to recruit AI talent.	OPM (OMB)	December 29, 2023 (60 days)	10.2 (d)(i)	Shall include direct-hire authorities.
Consider the use of the excepted service appointments to recruit AI talent.	OPM (OMB)	December 29, 2023 (60 days)	10.2 (d)(ii)	
Coordinate a pooled-hiring action to support AI talent recruitment.	OPM (OMB)	January 28, 2024 (90 days)	10.2 (d)(iii)	

Table 7. (Continued)

Requirements	Lead Agency (Supporting Agencies)	Due Dates	Section	Notes
Issue guidance to agencies on using existing pay flexibilities or incentive pay programs for AI, AI-enabling, and key technical positions.	OPM (OMB)	February 27, 2024 (120 days)	10.2 (d)(iv)	
Issue guidance to agencies on increasing the employment of AI, data, and technology talent from nontraditional academic backgrounds.	OPM (OMB)	April 27, 2024 (180 days)	10.2 (d)(v)	
Establish an interagency working group composed of experts in human resources and AI to inform hiring practices.	OPM (OMB)	April 27, 2024 (180 days)	10.2 (d)(vi)	
Review the qualifications for the Senior Executive Service to account for AI expertise.	OPM (OMB)	April 27, 2024 (180 days)	10.2 (d)(vii)	
Review the job description for civil engineers (and other positions) to account for, and ensure adequate, AI expertise.	OPM (OMB)	April 27, 2024 (180 days)	10.2 (d)(viii)	
Develop a position description library for data scientist jobs and a hiring guide for agencies.	CDOC	No date prescribed	10.2(f)	
Implement and/or increase the use of AI training programs among employees.	Agencies	No date prescribed	10.2(g)	Agencies should ensure employees in nontechnical roles are also eligible for AI training programs.

Requirements	Lead Agency (Supporting Agencies)	Due Dates	Section	Notes
Report on the AI talent gap in national defense, with a focus on hiring and retaining certain noncitizens.	DOD	April 27, 2024 (180 days)	10.2(h)	Report is to the APNSA and President.

Source: CRS analysis of Executive Order 14110. Executive Office of the President, "Safe, Secure, and Trustworthy Development and Use of Artificial Intelligence," 88 *Federal Register* 75191, November 1, 2023, at https://www.federalregister.gov/documents/2023/11/01/2023-24283/safe-secure-and-trustworthy-development-and-use-of-artificial-intelligence.

Note: For a list of acronyms, please see the Appendix.

International Leadership

The E.O. declares that the United States should be a global leader in AI development and adoption by engaging with international allies and partners, leading efforts to develop common AI regulatory and accountability principles, and advancing responsible global technical standards for AI. Actions related to this policy area are prescribed in Section 11 of the E.O. There are six requirements involving seven federal agencies. Table 8 lists these requirements.

Table 8. Requirements and deliverables in section 11 on international leadership; ascending by section citation

Requirements	Lead Agency (Supporting Agencies)	Due Dates	Section	Notes
Establish a global engagement plan for promoting and developing AI standards.	DOC	July 26, 2024 (270 days)	11(b)(i)	May include efforts on AI terminology, data and privacy best practices, verification and assurance of AI systems, and AI risk management.
Report to the President on priority actions taken pursuant to the plan in 11(b)(i).	DOC	January 22, 2025 (180 days after the plan in 11(b)(i))		Ensure that such efforts are guided by the NIST AI RMF and USG NSS for Critical and Emerging Technology.

Table 8. (Continued)

Requirements	Lead Agency (Supporting Agencies)	Due Dates	Section	Notes
Publish an AI in Global Development Playbook.	DOS & USAID (NIST)	October 29, 2024 (365 days)	11(c)(i)	
Develop a Global AI Research Agenda.	DOS & USAID (DOE, NSF)	No date prescribed.	11(c)(ii)	Shall include consideration of AI's potential labor market implications.
Plan for multilateral engagements on encouraging the adoption of AI safety and security guidelines among global and cross-border CI owners and operators.	DHS (DOS)	July 26, 2024 (270 days)	11(d)(i)	
Report on priority actions to mitigate cross-border risks to U.S. critical infrastructure.	DHS (DOS)	January 22, 2025 (180 days of establishing the plan in 11(d)(i))	11(d)(ii)	The report is to the President.

Source: CRS analysis of Executive Order 14110. Executive Office of the President, "Safe, Secure, and Trustworthy Development and Use of Artificial Intelligence," 88 *Federal Register* 75191, November 1, 2023, at https://www.federalregister.gov/documents/2023/11/01/2023-24283/safe-secure-and-trustworthy-development-and-use-of-artificial-intelligence.

Note: For a list of acronyms, please see the Appendix.

Appendix. Abbreviations

Abbreviations used in this report are listed below, alphabetically.

AI	Artificial Intelligence
AI RMF	NIST's AI Risk Management Framework
AIM-HEAD	National Institutes of Health Artificial Intelligence/Machine Learning Consortium to Advance Health Equity and Researcher Diversity
APDP	Assistant to the President for Domestic Policy
APEA	Assistant to the President for Economic Affairs
APNSA	Assistant to the President for National Security Affairs (a.k.a. the National Security Advisor)
CBRN	Chemical, Biological, Radiological, and Nuclear
CDOC	Chief Data Office Council

CEA	Council of Economic Advisors
CEQ	Council on Environmental Quality
CFO	Chief Financial Officer
C.F.R.	Code of Federal Regulations
CI	Critical Infrastructure
CISA	Cybersecurity and Infrastructure Security Agency
CSP	Cloud Service Provider
DCOSP	The President's Deputy Chief of Staff for Policy
DGPC	Assistant to the President and Director of the Gender Policy Council
DHS	Department of Homeland Security
DNI	Director of National Intelligence (Office of the)
DOC	Department of Commerce
DOD	Department of Defense
DOE	Department of Energy
DOJ	Department of Justice
DOL	Department of Labor
DOS	Department of State
DOT	Department of Transportation
DPA	Defense Production Act
ED	Department of Education
E.O.	Executive Order
FACA	Federal Advisory Committee Act
FARC	Federal Acquisition Regulatory Council
FedRAMP	Federal Risk and Authorization Management Program
FERC	Federal Energy Regulatory Commission
FPC	Federal Privacy Council
GSA	General Services Administration
HHS	Department of Health and Human Services
HUD	Department of Housing and Urban Development
ISCP	Interagency Council on Statistical Policy
IRA	Independent Regulatory Agencies
IP	Intellectual Property
IT	Information Technology
LE	Law Enforcement
NASA	National Aeronautics and Space Administration
NCD	National Cyber Director
NIFA	National Institute of Food and Agriculture
NIST	National Institute of Standards and Technology
NSF	National Science Foundation
NTIA	National Telecommunications and Information Administration
OMB	Office of Management and Budget
OPPRP	Office of Pandemic Preparedness and Response Policy in the White House
OPM	Office of Personnel Management
OSTP	Office of Science and Technology Policy
PCAST	President's Council of Advisors on Science and Technology
PII	Personally Identifiable Information
P.L.	Public Law
RMF	Risk Management Framework

(Continued)

SRMA	Sector Risk Management Agency
STEM	Science, Technology, Engineering, and Math
Treasury	Department of the Treasury
USAID	United States Agency for International Development
U.S.C.	United States Code
USDA	Department of Agriculture
USDC	United States Digital Corps
USDS	United States Digital Service
USG NSS	United States Government National Standards Strategy
USTPO	United States Patent and Trademark Office
VA	Department of Veterans Affairs

Disclaimer

This document was prepared by the Congressional Research Service (CRS). CRS serves as nonpartisan shared staff to congressional committees and Members of Congress. It operates solely at the behest of and under the direction of Congress. Information in a CRS Report should not be relied upon for purposes other than public understanding of information that has been provided by CRS to Members of Congress in connection with CRS's institutional role. CRS Reports, as a work of the United States Government, are not subject to copyright protection in the United States. Any CRS Report may be reproduced and distributed in its entirety without permission from CRS. However, as a CRS Report may include copyrighted images or material from a third party, you may need to obtain the permission of the copyright holder if you wish to copy or otherwise use copyrighted material.

Chapter 4

Secretary Antony J. Blinken at the Advancing Sustainable Development through Safe, Secure, and Trustworthy AI Event*

Antony J. Blinken

Secretary of State
Grand Central Station
New York City, New York

Secretary Blinken remarks at the Advancing Sustainable Development through Safe, Secure, and Trustworthy AI event.

---

* This is an edited, reformatted and augmented version of a speech by Antony J. Blinken, dated September 23, 2024.

In: Artificial Intelligence
Editor: Sonja Buckley
ISBN: 979-8-89530-859-2

SECRETARY BLINKEN: Hey, thank you. Good afternoon. Thank you, everyone.

And, first of all, to those of you who are just starting like I am on High-Level Week here at the United Nations in New York – take it from a veteran and also a native New Yorker – three simple words of advice: take the subway. (Laughter.)

Last year, we gathered on the margins on the General Assembly to discuss the future promise of artificial intelligence to advance sustainable development. And of the many events I did last year, this is one of the events that really stuck with me, because I could feel the energy, the palpable enthusiasm, the belief that AI can be a – such a force multiplier in actually moving forward on Sustainable Development Goals.

This year, that future promise is increasingly a present-day possibility. But if we're going to realize the full potential of AI to improve the lives of people around the world, that requires accelerating our efforts to ensure that this technology is genuinely inclusive. And that's what I want to spend a little bit of time talking about today.

"Inclusive" means that more people can access, understand, and develop AI to help solve the problems that they actually face in their lives. It means that AI technology benefits from – and helps preserve – cultural and linguistic diversity. It means that civil society, the private sector, governments, multilateral organizations all have a voice in shaping the governance and applications of this technology. It means that AI reduces, rather than exacerbates, the enduring inequities within and between our countries.

Around the world, we are seeing remarkable innovations in harnessing AI to actually expand opportunity.

Just to cite a few examples, in Brazil, AI chatbots are providing personalized tutoring to students with disabilities, expanding access to quality education for them.

In Indonesia, AI is helping manage and optimize renewable energy grids – bringing clean, affordable energy to more communities.

In India, farmers are using AI-driven apps to adapt to changing climate conditions, improving livelihoods, feeding more people.

The focus of this gathering – what brings us all together today – is what can we do to give more people in more places the power to unleash opportunities like these.

We know that we have our work cut out for us. Because, as we know, this revolution, this AI revolution, is leaving people behind – simply due to a lack of access or a lack of capacity. And those are really the challenges before us and the challenges that we're focused on today.

Now, this is a disparity that hurts all of us, and here's why: the more inclusive AI is, the more effective it can actually be in tackling the challenges that are affecting people everywhere, including here in the United States, including in many other countries around the world: challenges like rising temperatures, deadly viruses, things that don't stop at borders and demand that we find partners and solutions in every part of the globe; challenges like food insecurity that can lead to conflict and mass migrations. Making this technology more inclusive, it's not an act of generosity. It's in our national interest and in the interests of our firms, of our entrepreneurs, of our investors.

The foundation for making AI more inclusive is governance – the international rules, the international norms that help promote safe, secure, and trustworthy AI systems.

Now, just over the past year, the United States and our partners have made remarkable progress in building AI frameworks that promote innovation and more equitable access, while at the same time protecting human rights and safety, working with a wide range of partners in every region.

Our administration worked with leading AI companies on a set of voluntary commitments, like carrying out security tests before they release new products, developing tools to help users recognize AI-generated content.

The U.S. teamed up with our G7 partners to set out guiding principles and a code of conduct to address the impact of advanced AI systems on our societies and on our communities, and we carried this work forward at summits in the United Kingdom and then in Korea.

We put these principles at the heart of a UN General Assembly Resolution on AI that the United States developed. In March, every UN member adopted it by consensus.

And in November, the United States will host an international gathering of AI safety institutes and experts to deepen the technical foundations for implementing these governance frameworks.

In the conversations that I've had the opportunity to have around the world with government colleagues, with entrepreneurs, with advocates, with students, what I've heard is, again, this tremendous sense of optimism about the promise of AI to help tackle the problems that they're facing, to actually improve lives in tangible ways.

And at least from my own experience, I'd say that optimism, that enthusiasm, is even more widely shared in the so-called global majority countries. So today, one of the things our government is doing is putting out new resources to help our partners advance the effort to use AI in ways that actually improve lives: a playbook that identifies key actions that the United States and our development partners can take to harness AI to advance sustainable development; an agenda that sets out the principles, the priorities, the practices of advancing AI research with our international partners.

These resources add to the risk management tool that we shared in back in July, which will help organizations develop and use AI in a way that respects human rights.

Today, we're also announcing a groundbreaking new public-private partnership with leading AI companies to help expand access and capacity in the places and communities where it's needed most, especially in developing countries.

The State Department will partner with Amazon, with Anthropic, with Google, with IBM, with Meta, with Microsoft, with Nvidia, with OpenAI to expand access to AI. The Partnership for Global Inclusivity on AI will work to close the gap in three crucial areas: compute, capacity, and context, the three Cs of advancing of equity through artificial intelligence.

First on compute, we're going to expand access to cutting-edge AI models, compute credits, and more open-source tools. This means that developers, researchers, innovators in low-and-middle-income countries will be able to use models and tools that can improve their own AI applications, and better tailor them to local needs and local challenges.

Second, capacity. We will accelerate training efforts to empower people to use and adapt AI tools. Here again, just about everywhere I go, the desire to have a transfer of knowledge to enable countries to genuinely build capacity is one of the things I hear the most. I think this focus on capacity-building will really answer needs that we hear around the world.

Finally, context. We'll work with governments, with businesses, with civil society organizations, with communities to create localized, context-specific datasets, including for indigenous cultures and languages.

To catalyze this partnership, I'm also announcing today that the Department of State and USAID will spend $33 million in U.S. foreign assistance on AI development, with $10 million specifically focused on expanding access. We'll work with Congress to provide $23 million for programs to build on our efforts to develop safe, reliable, and trustworthy AI governance frameworks; use AI to advance human rights and development priorities; and promote educational and cultural exchanges on AI-related topics.

Together, we and our private sector partners are committing over $100 million to this effort.

Now, I'm eager to hand it over to those partners in just a minute. But before I do that, let me remind us of one more reason that this effort is so important. It increases our odds of creating world-changing applications.

AI's lightning evolution is, of course, being powered by rapid advances in data, in chips, in computing, in algorithms. But many of its greatest leaps are being driven not by machines, but by us – human beings, our needs, our hopes, our creativity, our ingenuity.

To get the most out of this transformative technology, we have to give more people in more places the chance to adapt it and to use it for good. None of us – no country, no community, no particular people, have a monopoly on good ideas, on innovation, on problem solving.

And one of the things that I've learned from being in this business for more than 32 years is that for virtually every problem the world faces, I'm convinced that somewhere someone has at least the beginnings of an answer. But we have to find ways to share it, and we have to find ways to empower more people to find it.

The more we unleash human creativity, human ingenuity in every part of this planet, the better off all of us are going to be. And you can just feel palpably how AI can be at the very heart of this endeavor.

So I'm so grateful to all of our partners in today's effort. For me, for the government, particularly working with the private sector, having these public-private partnerships, really is part of the secret sauce of success. And to each of you – thank you, thank you, thank you.

And so to everyone here, please join me in welcoming to the stage our teammates in the Partnership for Global Inclusivity on AI, with thanks to them and thanks to all of you. Thank you. (Applause.)

MODERATOR: We welcome to the stage from OpenAI, Sam Altman; from Microsoft, Brad Smith; from IBM, Gary Cohn; from Amazon, David Zapolsky; from Google, James Manyika; from Meta, Joelle Pineau; from Nvidia, Ned Finkle; from Anthropic, Sarah Heck. Thank you. (Applause.)

MR ALTMAN: Thank you very much, Secretary Blinken and to all of you. My name is Sam Altman, and I'm the CEO of OpenAI. It's an honor to join you and representatives from the U.S. Department of State, and other tech companies as we formally launch the new Partnership for Global Inclusivity on AI.

This program is an important part of our shared goal of expanding access to AI around the world and ensuring that its benefits reach everyone, regardless of where people live or what language they speak.

It's easy to think about AI in terms of the technological leaps themselves, which is advancing very quickly, and every day we can do new things that we would have thought impossible not that long ago. But the real power of AI doesn't come from the systems itself or the technology in the abstract – it comes from people around the world finding new ways to use the technology to solve hard problems and address the challenges facing their communities.

We want to make it easier for more people to use AI to enhance the work they're doing to support those communities. We're committed to making this partnership a success, and that's why I'm excited to announce that we're launching the OpenAI Academy, a new initiative which will give developers and organizations in low- and middle-income countries access to our latest tools and training about how to use them. It's an investment in the future of this technology and those finding new ways to use it. I can't wait to see what comes next, and thank you very much. (Applause.)

MR SMITH: Hello. Good afternoon. I'm Brad Smith, the vice chair and president of Microsoft. Thank you, Secretary Blinken, for this important initiative. I think it's worth remembering that 142 years ago – just four years after Thomas Edison first harnessed the power of electricity – the first power plant started operating here in lower Manhattan. It lit up a dark night. Tonight, more than 14 decades later, there are still 700 million people, and 43 percent of the people in Africa, who will go to bed without access to electricity. This is an initiative to ensure that we do better.

And as part of this initiative, Microsoft this year and next, in 2024 and 2025, commits we will spend more than $12 billion to build out AI data centers in Southeast Asia, in Latin America, in Africa. We will provide more than $500 million of free access to digital technology and compute to more than 30,000 nonprofits across the Global South. We will invest in local skilling. We will enable groups to work with local language AI models. We will help advance local economic development. We are one piece of the American private sector, working together with our government to advance global standards for safety, security, and trust.

We have the opportunity to do something that Thomas Edison never dreamed of doing: to bring AI to everyone In the world – not in the next 150 years but in the decade ahead. It will take all of us to do it. Thank you very much. (Applause.)

MR COHN: Hello. I'm Gary Cohn, vice chairman of IBM. First of all, I thought there'd be a bot that would cut us off after 60 seconds – (laugher) – but I guess the AI is not working as well here. Thank you, Secretary Blinken, and your entire team for your leadership in the public-private partnerships and your commitments to promote AI innovation. IBM has been involved in AI for decades and strongly believes that AI is a transformational technology of our time. The world needs innovation, training, and access to technology to create productivity and growth.

IBM has continuously committed to help vulnerable populations address environmental challenges. IBM has extended the IBM sustainability accelerator pledge of providing up to $45 million in expertise and technology, such as AI, by the end of 2028. We work with organizations such as NASA and UNDP to develop valuable datasets to make them more accessible, including the developing countries, for earth sciences, research, and energy equity. IBM provides AI training and access to technology to create a world driven by AI solutions. (Applause.)

MR ZAPOLSKY: There is a real impact on real people's lives when we deploy AI technology responsibly, and Amazon is proud to partner with the U.S. State Department to increase access to AI technology throughout the Global Majority. An example of this type of real-world impact is in Kenya that we've seen, which has one of the largest – highest maternal mortality rates. A nonprofit organization, Jacaranda Health, has AI tools to deploy an affordable and scalable solution through free text exchanges to improve health outcomes. The service includes an AI-enabled help desk, which responds to mothers' questions and sparks a rapid referral chain if a risk is identified. Jacaranda Health now reaches 1.5 million mothers who are more likely to attend prenatal care visits and twice as likely to participate in family planning services.

And later today you'll hear about Farmbyte, a digital agrofood innovator in Malaysia, who is using AWS AI technology, predictive analytics, to improve crop selection and pricing. These are just some of the critical impacts and innovations that we are seeing, and I look forward to seeing what more we can do together. Thank you. (Applause.)

MR MANYIKA: Mr. Secretary, distinguished guests, I've had the pleasure and the honor of co-chairing the UN's high-level body on AI, and we're delighted that in fact our recommendations were part of the Global Digital Compact. One of the key insights from that work was the idea that in fact we have to make sure that AI benefits everyone everywhere, and that we have to make sure that the digital divide doesn't also become the AI divide. And that's why it's really, really important that we're having this conversation. I'm a child of the Global South, so this matters to me personally and very deeply. We're – at Google, we're committed to try to make this a reality in several ways. Let me mention five key specific examples.

First, infrastructure. We're building data centers in about 140 cloud regions around the world. We've been connecting with fiber optic cables – Africa with Asia, Africa with Europe, Africa with itself – in order to bring infrastructure to these places.

Second, the Secretary mentioned the importance of rich diversity of cultural and linguistic diversity. In just over a year we've gone from Google Translate being able to handle 30-something languages to now 246 languages. In fact, we're aiming to get to a thousand languages pretty soon.

Third, most of the Global South is being ravaged by the effects of climate change, so it's going to be quite important to be able to respond to this. We've been deploying AI-enabled tools for flood forecasting. We went from about one country, Bangladesh, about a year ago to now we're doing AI-enabled flood forecasting over 80 countries, covering nearly half a billion people around the world.

Fourth, I think it's important to keep in mind that scientific development happens not just in some countries but should happen in all countries. So I work, for example, with AlphaFold program. AlphaFold program is now being used by over 2 million scientists with all – most of those actually in 190 countries, half of them in the Global South. That's very, very important.

And then finally, people. Let me talk about people. We've been investing a lot in training and giving skills to people. So far we've covered over 100 million people in the last few years, and just the other day we announced a further commitment to spend another 120 million in skills development. These are some of the capabilities that are going to be important if we're going to address these capacity gaps at scale and get to everybody.

So we're delighted about this opportunity and the further commitments we're making to continue this journey. Thank you. (Applause.)

MS PINEAU: Good afternoon. It's a pleasure to be here. It's been a little over a year since Meta signed on to the voluntary commitments from the White House. Today we are proud to sign onto this new agreement, public-private partnership, to help enable deployment of AI to accelerate progress on Sustainable Development Goals.

At Meta, we do believe that open source is crucial for democratizing access to the technology, for spurring economic growth, and for the digital inclusion of the Global South, as well as for increasing transparency and trust in AI systems. In 2004 – 2024-2025, Meta will invest over $10 million in programmatic support for open-source AI innovation. With this investment, we will directly increase access to AI to global communities in Latin America, Africa, Middle East, and Asia. We will offer grants, training, as well as deployment of open-source AI and Llama to small businesses and governments.

We're also announcing later today a collaboration between UNESCO, Hugging Face, and Meta to leverage our No Language Left Behind model to deliver translation in 200 languages, including indigenous languages. This is in addition to the billions we are investing in training the models and developing them to make sure that they are safe, open, and accessible.

We're grateful for this partnership. We know that this is just the beginning of how we can deploy AI to solve some of society's greatest challenge. Thank you. (Applause.)

MR FINKLE: Thank you, Mr. Secretary, for the opportunity to be here. Nvidia pioneered accelerated computing to tackle challenges no one else can solve. We empower communities around the world to build and grow local AI ecosystems and develop innovative solutions to some of society's greatest challenges.

Under this partnership, Nvidia is committing $10 million a year in free training programs to upskill AI developers in emerging countries. Nvidia provides compute credits and hardware grants for higher education research universities around the world.

Through Nvidia's Global Inception program, we support nearly 5,000 startups in developing countries through technical support, access to capital, hardware discounts, and free computing credits provided through our cloud partners, many of whom are here today. In 2024 alone this program mobilized more than 60 million in free compute credits for startups in developing countries.

Nvidia is committed to ensuring the benefits of safe, trustworthy AI are accessible and shared by all. Thank you. (Applause.)

MS HECK: Good afternoon. I have the distinction of being the final speaker, which you're probably very pleased about. My name is Sarah Heck, and I represent Anthropic. And we are so pleased to be a part of this partnership today.

I'm actually going to use my time as a call to action. We are an AI lab that tries to be both helpful and harmless. And the call to action today is for all of those people sitting in governments in the Global South, in the Global Majority, that are thinking about how they can use AI. This partnership is for you. Our contribution to this partnership is to ensure teams across governments can help accelerate the global development goals, to make sure – whether you're a team of two people sitting in Uganda or you're a huge team that wants API access to models that is sitting somewhere in Bosnia – we are here to help you today.

So my hope is that if you're watching online or you're sitting in the audience, you're thinking about how are you using AI in your work to build trust, to be helpful and harmless to your citizens, and how we can work together. Thanks so much. (Applause.)

Chapter 5

Artificial Intelligence and Machine Learning in Financial Services*

Paul Tierno

Abstract

The financial industry's adoption of artificial intelligence (AI) and machine learning (ML) is evolving as financial firms employ ever greater levels of technology and automation to deliver services. Expanding on earlier models of quantitative analysis, AI/ML has often been adopted in finance to solve discrete challenges, such as maximizing profit and minimizing risk. Yet the industry's adoption of the newer technology also occurs against perceptions that are steeped in tradition and historical financial regulation, and regulators want to ensure that the technology does not sidestep regulations frequently described as technology neutral. Technological advances in computer hardware, capacity, and data storage—which permit the collection and analysis of data—helped fuel the development and use of AI/ML technologies in finance. Unlike older algorithms that automated human-coded rules, new AI models can "learn" by themselves and make inferences and recommendations not identified by modelers in advance. This shift in technology has also enabled the use of new types of data including alternative data (i.e., data that the consumer credit bureaus do not traditionally use), unstructured data (images or social media posts, etc.), and unlabeled information data—which, when combined, extend the technologies' uses to new financial services or products.

* This is an edited, reformatted and augmented version of Congressional Research Service, Publication No. R47997, dated April 3, 2024.

In: Artificial Intelligence
Editor: Sonja Buckley
ISBN: 979-8-89530-859-2

Different parts of the financial services industry have adopted AI/ML technology to varying degrees and for various purposes. Some uses of AI/ML include powering chatbots in customer service functions, identifying investment opportunities and/or executing trades, augmenting lending models or (more sparingly) making lending decisions, and identifying and preventing fraud. The extent to which a sector or firm adopts various technologies reflects a variety of factors, including a firm's ability to fund internal development and regulatory requirements.

The increased use of AI/ML to deliver financial services has attracted attention and led to numerous policy issues and subsequent policy actions. Such policy actions culminated in (1) the establishment of a task force on AI in the 116th Congress and the more recent working group in the House Committee on Financial Services in the 118th and (2) 2019 and 2023 executive orders. The evolving legislative and regulatory framework regarding AI/ML use in finance is likely, at least in part, to influence the development of AI/ML financial services applications. Various financial regulators have indicated that regulated entities are subject to the full range of laws and regulations regardless of the technology used. Additionally, some regulators have identified regulations and issued guidance of particular relevance to financial firms employing AI/ML technologies.

Financial industry policymakers face competing pressures. Financial service providers and technology companies are likely to continue adopting and promoting AI/ML to save time and money and promote accessibility, accuracy, and regulatory compliance. However, challenges and risks in the form of bias, potential for systemic risk and manipulation, affordability, and consequences for employment remain. Determining whether the existing regulatory structure is sufficient—or whether one that is more closely tailored to the technological capacities of the evolving technology is necessary—has emerged as a key consideration. Should Congress consider the legislative framework governing AI/ML in finance, industry and consumers alike will expect that it weighs the benefits of innovation with existing and potential future challenges and risks.

Introduction

Artificial intelligence (AI) is the general term used to describe the process of programming computers and machines to think and operate like humans. Machine learning (ML) is a subset of AI that describes computers and programs that may be programmed to operate with minimal human intervention and can in some instances learn and/or update themselves. Various events over the past few years have helped raise the profile of AI/ML and its role in delivering financial services. OpenAI's introduction of the large language model (LLM) ChatGPT in 2022 was a rare moment when an AI/ML technology became directly accessible by the broad public. While momentum around AI/ML had been building over the past decade at least, the ubiquity of competing prominent technologies concentrated attention on all manner of applications, including those in the financial sector.

AI/ML is accelerating a long, ongoing shift in finance from face-to-face interactions conducted in a customer's community to online products and services fueled by advanced algorithms that require little or no human interaction and can occur anywhere. Such applications may have benefits for financial institutions and their clients. Relative to human operation (or models built using earlier technology), AI/ML provision of financial services may be faster and cheaper due to their speed and efficiency, and they may be able to expand service to more individuals due to their ability to analyze alternative data and find latent connections. The financial industry's use of technology is not new, and there are elements to its adoption of AI/ML that resemble past periods. While regulators are used to dealing with these cycles, there is a recognition that the growth of AI/ML is likely to be especially transformative.[1]

Adoption of the technology also brings challenges and risks. While AI may eliminate some human bias in financial services, it may also introduce or exacerbate bias. Certain AI-market specific factors—such as using the same data to train models and concentration of technology and technological capacity—may encourage monocultures, or herd-like behavior, that introduce systemic risk. The ability of certain models to learn on their own, free from human oversight, may also allow them to engage in market manipulation, conflicts of interest, or other unlawful activity.

Financial industry use of the technology has attracted policymaker interest. For example, Executive Order 14110 on the "Safe, Secure, and Trustworthy Development and Use of Artificial Intelligence" briefly discusses the Biden Administration's view of AI/ML in finance, among a host of other

[1] CNBC Television, "SEC Chair Gary Gensler: AI is the Most Transformative Technology of Our Time," YouTube video, December 14, 2023, https://www.youtube.com/watch?v=J3tT44ASl_w&t=168s.

issues. In addition, the House Committee on Financial Services created a bipartisan AI Working Group to address these issues in January 2024.[2]

This report discusses the role of AI/ML in financial services broadly. First, it provides a brief overview of some technical terms. Next, it discusses the motivations for the financial industry's use of AI/ML. It then provides an overview of some financial applications of the technology.

Finally, it addresses the regulatory framework and considers various policy issues, including any applicable regulations.

Technology Overview in Brief

What Are Artificial Intelligence and Machine Learning?[3]

AI is the broad label for technologies that give computer systems the ability to learn new concepts or tasks and to reason and draw useful conclusions about the world.[4] Earlier versions of AI were largely dependent on their human developers that programmed machines with a series of deterministic rules, such as "if … then" statements, alongside troves of subject matter content.[5] Such technology required specific syntax for questions or commands and produced responses on topics for which it had been programmed. When faced with a situation for which it had not been programmed, it would "freeze."[6] That dependency would likely disqualify it from the AI in current taxonomy and is largely disappearing. According to some, most applications of AI now are ML, so the terms as used are synonymous.[7]

---

[2] House Financial Services Committee, "McHenry, Waters Announce Creation of Bipartisan AI Working Group," press release, January 11, 2024, https://financialservices.house.gov/news/documentsingle.aspx?DocumentID=409108.

[3] This report will collectively refer to the technologies it examines as AI/ML. The individual terms (or other terms) will be used when a distinction is necessary.

[4] Shukla Shubhendu and Jaiswal Vijay, "Applicability of Artificial Intelligence in Different Fields of Life," *International Journal of Scientific Engineering and Research (IJSER)*, vol. 1, no. 1 (September 2013), https://www.ijser.in/archives/v1i1/MDExMzA5MTU=.pdf.

[5] Dorothy Leonard-Barton and John J. Sviokla, "Putting Expert Systems to Work," *Harvard Business Review*, March 1988.

[6] Marko Kolanovic and Rajesh T. Krishnamachari, *Big Data and AI Strategies: Machine Learning and Alternative Data Approach to Investing*, J. P. Morgan, May 2017, p. 16, https://cpb-us-e2.wpmucdn.com/faculty.sites.uci.edu/dist/2/51/files/2018/05/JPM-2017-MachineLearningInvestments.pdf.

[7] Sara Brown, "Machine Learning, Explained," MIT Management Sloan School, April 21, 2021, https://mitsloan.mit.edu/ideas-made-to-matter/machine-learning-explained.

ML is a subset of AI focused on constructing computer systems that can automatically improve through experiencing and determining certain characteristics inherent in *all learning systems*, which can include computers, humans, and organizations.[8] ML attempts to give computers the ability to learn and change without being reprogramed. It uses algorithms—sequenced actions designed to solve specific problems—that improve automatically with various degrees of—and often, little or no—human interaction.[9] In other words, unlike earlier AI, it is meant to be adaptable. ML systems are intended to determine relationships among variables or recognize patterns in large data sets.[10] Yet ML is not one thing, such as a discrete computer application, nor is it even one technology. Instead, it is a group of systems that is defined in part by the type of information used to train the model (labelled or unlabeled data, for example) and the amount of involvement provided by human trainers (supervised or unsupervised).

Recent Advances in Data and Technology

Technological developments in computing and telecommunications have been a boon to AI/ML, and the financial industry's use of it includes advanced performance computing, which includes hardware, cloud and edge computing, and communication technologies.[11] However, the financial industry's adoption of AI/ML depends upon the availability of data, including alternative data not traditionally used in financial decisionmaking, and the ability to process and analyze unstructured data. These technological advances move in tandem with the amassing of large quantities of data (including that which is

[8] M. I. Jordan and T. M. Mitchell, "Machine Learning: Trends, Perspectives, and Prospects," *Science*, vol. 349, no. 6245 (July 17, 2015), https://www.science.org/doi/10.1126/science.aaa8415.

[9] Financial Stability Board, *Artificial Intelligence and Machine Learning in Financial Services: Market Developments and Financial Stability Implications*, November 1, 2017, p. 10, https://www.fsb.org/wp-content/uploads/P011117.pdf.

[10] Kolanovic and Krishnamachari, *Big Data and AI Strategies*, p. 13.

[11] Gary Gensler and Lily Bailey, *Deep Learning and Financial Stability*, November 1, 2020, p. 8, https://papers.ssrn.com/sol3/papers.cfm?abstract_id=3723132; and Alessio Azzutti, Wolf-Georg Ringe, and H. Siegfried Stiehl, "Machine Learning, Market Manipulation, and Collusion on Capital Markets: Why the 'Black Box, Matters," *University of Pennsylvania Journal of International Law*, vol. 43, no. 1 (2021), p. 85, https://papers.ssrn.com/sol3/papers.cfm?abstract_id=3788872.

coming from alternative sources) that require "scalable architecture for efficient storage, manipulation, and analysis."[12]

Recently, graphics processing units—hardware previously used in gaming (and subsequently crypto mining)—has fueled development of deep learning and other advanced forms of AI.[13] Cloud computing has also increased the amount of data and programs that individuals or companies may store or access, while edge computing allows them to process data at its source in real time.

Some of today's technologies have their conceptual origins decades ago, and they are now being developed.[14] Unsupervised learning's ability to process unlabeled data may identify relationships—for example, in market interactions or among loan applications—where its programmers had not thought to look. Similarly, the ability to process unstructured and alternative data that previously could not be analyzed—such as images and social media posts— has opened it to analysis.

Big Data

Big data refers both to a type of information and how it is used. It refers to large data sets that exhibit specific characteristics such as volume, velocity, variety, and/or variability and requires "scalable architecture" to store, manage, and analyze.[15] The term also generally refers to the data use by managers, companies, and industries to facilitate business decisions.[16]

Some advances in ML have been directly attributed to the ability to process more data.[17] The specific big data used in finance depends on the

---

[12] National Institute of Standards and Technology (NIST), *NIST Big Data Interoperability Framework: Volume 1, Definitions*, October 2019, pp. 6, 9, https://nvlpubs.nist.gov/nistpubs/SpecialPublications/NIST.SP.1500-1r2.pdf.

[13] David Rotman, "We're Not Prepared for the End of Moore's Law," *MIT Technology Review*, February 24, 2020, https://www.technologyreview.com/2020/02/24/905789/were-not-prepared-for-the-end-of-moores-law/.

[14] See discussions of history at Financial Stability Board, *Artificial Intelligence and Machine Learning in Financial Services*, p. 10; and Ben Weiss, "Banks Have Used A.I. for Decades—but Now It's Going to Take Off Like Never Before," *Fortune*, July 22, 2023, https://fortune.com/2023/07/21/ai-finance-history-regressions-generative-artificial-intelligence-pagaya-kasisto/.

[15] NIST, *NIST Big Data Interoperability Framework: Volume 1, Definitions*, pp. 6, 9. For more on big data's use in finance, see CRS Report R46332, *Fintech: Overview of Innovative Financial Technology and Selected Policy Issues*, coordinated by David W. Perkins.

[16] Andrew McAfee and Erik Brynjolfsson, "Big Data: The Management Revolution," *Harvard Business Review,* October 2012, https://hbr.org/2012/10/big-data-the-management-revolution.

[17] McAfee and Brynjolfsson, "Big Data: The Management Revolution," p. 11.

sector or use case. For example, some firms may use big data—including social media—when deciding whether to make loans.[18] In a capital markets and trading environment, big data may include continuous data feeds from various stock exchanges, which can include stock prices and broader market moves and histories of transactions. Data in this environment may also include company-level data that may influence a stock performance, including financial statements and quarterly and annual regulatory filings.

Alternative data refers to information that has not traditionally been used to make financial decisions. In consumer credit underwriting, *alterative data* refers to non-credit data that has not traditionally been used in determining credit scores, such as rent and utility payments.[19] Banks and credit card and payment companies may also use alternative and *unstructured data*—such as transaction information and location or GPS data—in their fraud detection and anti-money laundering activities. Asset managers and other capital markets participants may also use GPS and satellite imagery of retailer parking lots or social media mentions that provide insight into a company's performance.[20] The availability of different forms of data and the models they use have expanded the ways financial firms may use both.

Recent interest in AI has been marked by a period of increased investment in and development and adoption of AI/ML technologies by various sectors, including the financial industry.

According to one bank's research, investment in AI is expected to climb to around $100 billion in the United States in 2025 and nearly $200 billion globally.[21] Notably, there is likely broad investment from traditional financial institutions—one market research firm suggested retail banks will spend more

---

[18] Government Accountability Office, *Data and Analytics Innovation: Emerging Opportunities and Challenges*, GAO-16-659SP, September 2016, p. 95, https://www.gao.gov/assets/gao-16-659sp.pdf.

[19] See CRS In Focus IF11630, *Alternative Data in Financial Services*, by Cheryl R. Cooper. For a description of alternative data for credit underwriting, see Consumer Financial Protection Bureau (CFPB), *Request for Information Regarding Use of Alternative Data and Modeling Techniques in the Credit Process*, February 16, 2017, https://files.consumerfinance.gov/f/documents/20170214_cfpb_Alt-Data-RFI.pdf.

[20] BlackRock, "Artificial Intelligence and Machine Learning in Asset Management," October 2019, https://www.blackrock.com/corporate/literature/whitepaper/viewpoint-artificial-intelligence-machine-learning-asset-management-october-2019.pdf.

[21] Goldman Sachs, "AI Investment Forecast to Approach $200 Billion Globally by 2025," August 1, 2023, https://www.goldmansachs.com/intelligence/pages/ai-investment-forecast-to-approach-200-billion-globally-by-2025.html.

than $4 billion on AI in 2024—with finance-focused startups attracting investment from venture capital firms.[22]

Finance and Artificial Intelligence

According to the Organisation for Economic Co-operation and Development (OECD), AI is "powering digital transformation" that has been rapidly deployed in finance.[23] Adoption of this newer technology is not surprising as finance has often been linked with cutting-edge technology. However, the industry is also known for its use of often obsolete technology and associations with traditional practices that are at odds with new technologies. While in the past, personal banking was rooted in community relationships and conducted in person, now nearly all transactions can be performed online. In capital markets transactions, electronic trading has essentially ended the need for trading to be conducted person to person at the physical location of exchanges.[24] Meanwhile, the use of AI/ML (like the related adoption of a broad set of financial technology, or "fintech") over the past few decades also has implications for regulation, which prioritizes industry transparency, explainability, and fairness.[25] Finance's adoption of AI/ML thus takes place as technology and its capacity may be evolving more rapidly than societal and regulatory expectations.

Motivation behind the financial sector's adoption of AI is not new. Finance's adoption of AI has been compared to the 13th-century development of net-present-value calculations, the more recent invention of the automated

---

[22] For banking figures, see Sherry Fairchok, "In the Global AI 'Arms Race,' Banks Are Stretching Their Tech Experimentation," *Insider Intelligence eMarketer*, June 5, 2023, https://www.insiderintelligence.com/content/global-ai-arms-race-banks-stretching-their-tech-experimentation. For a discussion on venture capital investment, see OECD, *OECD Business and Finance Outlook 2021: AI in Business and Finance*, September 24, 2021, pp. 19-21, https://doi.org/10.1787/ba682899-en.

[23] OECD, *OECD Business and Finance Outlook 2021*, p. 17.

[24] Randall Dodd, *Financial Markets: Exchange or Over the Counter*, International Monetary Fund, https://www.imf.org/en/Publications/fandd/issues/Series/Back-to-Basics/Financial-Markets. See also CRS Insight IN11447, *The Closing of the New York Stock Exchange's Trading Floor Due to COVID-19*, by Gary Shorter.

[25] For more on fintech, see CRS Report R46332, *Fintech: Overview of Innovative Financial Technology and Selected Policy Issues*, coordinated by David W. Perkins.

teller machine, use of expert systems for personal financial planning, and automated trading, all of which employed different technologies.[26]

In addition to a general gravitation to technology, various characteristics of the financial industry have made it a ripe testing ground for AI/ML. As one commentator expressed: "information processing is the central function of financial markets."[27] For example, AI/ML generally requires large quantities of data on which to train its systems. Data is a quintessential feature across the various financial sectors. The industry amasses data from economic indicators, financial markets, individual consumers and businesses, and payments and transactions, among countless other sources. Moreover, while comprised of different subsectors—with diverse functions, services, and products—finance presents quantifiable problems, the solutions for which are often reduced (perhaps overly simplistically) to maximizing returns considering a given risk tolerance while considering some number of other quantifiable variables. As such, the industry is generating large amounts of data and providing the operating environment for AI/ML technologies.

AI/ML may also increase the speed with which financial transactions may take place. For example, high-frequency trading, which is also increasingly automated and programmatic, allows trades to occur in the smallest fractions of a second, speeds at which neither human analysis nor execution are possible. Also, if a financial institution uses AI/ML to determine whether it should make a loan, the speed may be evident in multiple ways. AI/ML-induced speed may allow financial institutions to update their lending models.[28] Lenders may also use AI/ML-based lending models, integrated with digital platforms and web-interfaces, to deliver decisions to customers more quickly.

---

[26] See discussions in Gensler and Bailey, *Deep Learning and Financial Stability*, p. 8; Weiss, "Banks Have Used A.I. for Decades;" Carol E. Brown, Norma L. Nielson, and Mary Ellen Phillips, "Expert Systems for Personal Financial Planning," *Journal of Financial Planning*, vol. 3, no. 3 (July 1990), pp. 137-143, https://prism.ucalgary.ca/server/api/core/bitstreams/e044857a-17a6-4927-8ab5-c65539d61fa1/content; and K. C. Chen and Ting-Peng Liang, "PROTRADER: An Expert System for Program Trading," *Managerial Finance*, vol. 15, no. 5 (1989), pp. 1-6, http://www.ecrc.nsysu.edu.tw/liang/paper/3/PROTRADER%20An%20Expert%20System%20for%20Program%20Trading.pdf.

[27] Mihir A. Desai, "What the Finance Industry Tells Us About the Future of AI," *Harvard Business Review*, August 9, 2023, https://hbr.org/2023/08/what-the-finance-industry-tells-us-about-the-future-of-ai.

[28] Julie Lee, "AI-Driven Credit Risk Decisioning: What You Need to Know," Experian, October 27, 2022, p. 13, https://www.experian.com/blogs/insights/2022/10/ai-driven-credit-risk-decisioning/.

AI/ML Applications in Finance

Financial industry and market participants use AI for a variety of functions. These functions have multiple purposes, including improving efficiency, assisting with decisionmaking, producing analysis and forecasting, increasing profitability, managing risk, and underwriting credit.[29] Moreover, they may be used in support functions or front office functions. Back office applications may include post-trade processing, trading profit and loss reconciliations, and data analytics.[30] Other applications may include regulatory compliance functions, such as know-your-customer checks and customer identification programs, anti-money laundering and countering the financing of terrorism programs, and anti-fraud. AI may also assist in asset allocation, robo-advising, and trade execution. Many of the actions taken by financial firms are multistep and closely related, and AI may be used for and benefit from different parts of a business or phases of a business process. Moreover, there may be overlap in use cases with different definitions. For example, while asset managers may use AI to assist with asset allocation, certain asset management firms may also employ algorithmic trading. This section provides a brief overview of various financial applications and services that may use AI but is not intended to be exhaustive.

Credit Underwriting

Credit underwriting—assessing the risk of prospective borrowers defaulting on loan repayment— is one of banks' and other financial institutions' primary businesses. Loan-making financial institutions have automated the methods for making loan decisions, including through the use of electronic data.[31]

For example, for consumer loans, such methods generally entail using a mathematical formula (called a scoring model) to determine a consumer's credit score and subsequently whether the firm should make the loan and at what interest rate.[32] Various factors—including bill paying history, unpaid

---

[29] Gensler and Bailey, *Deep Learning and Financial Stability*, p. 7.

[30] OECD, *OECD Business and Finance Outlook 2021: AI in Business and Finance*, p. 39.

[31] See CRS In Focus IF12399, *Automation, Artificial Intelligence, and Machine Learning in Consumer Lending*, by Cheryl R. Cooper.

[32] CFPB, "What Is a Credit Score?," August 28, 2023, https://www.consumerfinance.gov/ask-cfpb/what-is-a-credit-score-en-315/.

debt, outstanding loans, and accounts—go into determining a credit score.[33] Recently, however, some financial companies have considered using AI/ML to augment or replace traditional credit scoring.

Lenders have been using predictive models for decades.[34] Traditionally, statistical regression methods used data from the credit reporting bureaus, assigning weights to different variables to help forecast whether an applicant would default on a loan and to determine the likelihood of on-time loan repayment.[35] More recently, firms may use ML-based measures based on their ability to analyze large amounts and different types of data—including transaction data—and their ability to discern other important relationships not visible in traditional models.[36] According to one study, some ML underwriting models are "more adaptive" and have shown improvements in predictiveness and cost savings relative to traditional models.[37]

Adoption of AI/ML for credit underwriting may differ among banks and nonbank fintech. Various regulatory requirements may make banks hesitant to use the technology for credit underwriting decisions (see "Policy Issues Regarding the Role of AI/ML in Finance"). Generally, because nonbanks may have different (and in certain ways more permissive) regulatory requirements and supervision than banks do, they may be more willing to use AI/ML technology. Some fintechs claim to have adopted the technology for underwriting, including reportedly for consumer loans, as well as for "buy now, pay later" credit products.[38] While banks may be more hesitant to use AI base models for credit underwriting decisions, some have reportedly not

---

[33] CFPB, "What Is a Credit Score?"

[34] FinRegLab, "Explainability and Fairness in Machine Learning for Credit Underwriting," December 2023, p. 7, https://finreglab.org/wp-content/uploads/2023/12/FinRegLab_2023-12-07_Research-Report_Explainability-and-Fairness-in-Machine-Learning-for-Credit-Underwriting_Policy-Analysis.pdf.

[35] FinRegLab, "Explainability and Fairness," p. 7. The predictive models were logistic regressions.

[36] FinRegLab, "Explainability and Fairness," p. 7.

[37] Amir E. Khandani, Adlar J. Kim, and Andrew W. Lo, "Consumer Credit Risk Models via Machine-Learning Algorithms," *Journal of Banking Finance*, vol. 34, no. 11 (November 2010), p. 2, https://core.ac.uk/download/pdf/ 4430264.pdf.

[38] John Adams, "Buy Now/Pay Later Fintechs Lean on AI to Survive the Banking Crisis," *American Banker*, March 27, 2023, https://www.americanbanker.com/payments/news/buy-now-pay-later-fintechs-lean-on-ai-to-survive-the-banking-crisis; and Upstart, "Our Story: Result to Date," https://www.upstart.com/our-story#results-to-date. Some researchers report success when using AI to predict corporate defaults; see reference in OECD, *OECD Business and Finance Outlook 2021: AI in Business and Finance*, p. 44. For more on "buy now, pay later," see CRS Insight IN11784, *Rapidly Growing "Buy Now, Pay Later" (BNPL) Financing: Market Developments and Policy Issues*, by Cheryl R. Cooper and Paul Tierno.

shunned the practice altogether. According to various reports, banks may use AI/ML to identify useful variables or relationships and to "explore the potential … to refine" their traditional statistical models used in the credit underwriting process.[39] Moreover, some banks—especially large ones and some solely in experimentation phases—reportedly use ML underwriting models for lending.[40]

Chatbots

Chatbots are computer programs that interact (e.g., converse and provide answers) with people online by simulating human conversation through text and voice commands. Banking chatbots provide immediate assistance 24/7, reducing wait times, addressing customer inquiries, providing information on account balances and transaction history, and guiding users through various banking processes. Chatbots used in banking provide $8 billion in cost savings annually, according to one estimate.[41]

Regtech

Regtech (regulatory technology) refers to regulated financial institutions' use of technology to meet various regulatory, compliance, and data reporting

---

[39] See FinRegLab, "The Use of Machine Learning for Credit Underwriting: Market and Data Science Context," September 2021, p. 24, https://finreglab.org/wp-content/uploads/2021/09/The-Use-of-ML-for-Credit-Underwriting-Market-and-Data-Science-Context_09-16-2021.pdf; and Federal Reserve Governor Christopher J. Waller, "Innovation and the Future of Finance," speech at the Cryptocurrency and the Future of Global Finance, Sarasota, Florida, April 20, 2023, https://www.federalreserve.gov/newsevents/speech/waller20230420a.htm.

[40] For references to large banks using ML underwriting models, see FinRegLab, *Explainability and Fairness*, pp. 12, 33; for experimentation, see Penny Crosman, "The Banks Warming to AI-Based Lending," *American Banker*, October 21, 2019, https://www.americanbanker.com/news/the-banks-warming-to-ai-based-lending.

[41] CFPB, *Chatbots in Finance*, June 6, 2023, https://www.consumerfinance.gov/data-research/research-reports/chatbots-in-consumer-finance/chatbots-in-consumer-finance/#chatbot-use-in-consumer-finance.

functions.[42] Regtech has existed for around a decade.[43] Regtech had focused on compliance with regulations related to onboarding and identifying new customers, but more recently it has been described as being instrumental in anti-money laundering, countering the financing of terrorism, fraud prevention, risk management, stress testing, and micro and macroprudential reporting.[44] For example, banks and other financial institutions use "robotics process automation" to help them comply with reporting requirements and repopulating required data on a regular basis.[45] In many cases, banks' and other financial institutions' adoption of regtech may involve partnering with third-party providers with expertise in the field.

Monitoring Fraud and Illicit Financial Activity

A key form of regtech aided by AI/ML is detecting, preventing, and reporting unauthorized and illicit financial activities for banks and other financial institutions. The shift to AI/ML solutions is due to its more adaptable approaches and its ability to leverage more types of data. Banks and other financial institutions must detect, prevent, and report on unauthorized and illicit financial activity, and there has been an increase in the number of financial institutions using AI/ML to address the issue.[46] Banks and other financial institutions can train models on huge volumes of consumer behavior data they generate, allowing the ML models to learn fraud patterns and to then detect fraudulent behavior in practice.[47] One payment processor, for example,

---

[42] For a definition and general discussion on regtech, see Financial Stability Board, *The Use of Supervisory and Regulatory Technology by Authorities and Regulated Institutions*, October 9, 2020, https://www.fsb.org/wp-content/ uploads/P091020.pdf.

[43] Matthias Memminger, Mike Baxter, and Edmund Lin, "BankThink: You've Heard of Fintech, Get Ready for 'Regtech,'" *American Banker*, September 7, 2016, https://www.americanbanker.com/opinion/youve-heard-of-fintech-get-ready-for-regtech.

[44] Memminger, Baxter, and Lin, "BankThink;" and Tobias Adrian, "AI and Regtech," International Monetary Fund, October 29, 2021, https://www.imf.org/en/ News/Articles/2021/10/29/sp102921-ai-and-regtech.

[45] American Bankers Association, "Understanding Regtech," July 25, 2018, https://www.aba.com/-/media/documents/ reference-and-guides/understanding-regtech.pdf.

[46] Unauthorized and illicit financial activity is broadly defined for the purposes of this report as including fraud, money laundering, and terrorist financing. According to one industry survey, fraud at financial institutions increased at 43% of financial institutions, with average costs increasing by 65% between 2022 and 2023. PYMNTS, "The State of Fraud and Financial Crime in the U.S. 2023," September, 2023, pp. 4, 10, https://www.pymnts.com/wp-content/uploads/2023/ 09/PYMNTS-The-State-of-Fraud-and-Financial-Crime-in-the-US-2023-September-2023.pdf.

[47] Ryan Williamson, "Benefits of AI to Fight Fraud in the Banking System," *Data Science Central*, December 22, 2022, https://www.datasciencecentral.com/benefits-of-ai-to-fight-fraud-in-the-banking-system/; Stripe, "How Machine Learning Works for Payment Fraud

has stated it uses time and location and GPS data to determine whether activity occurring in distant geographies may be fraudulent.[48] The same company also suggested that ML models can learn and subsequently evaluate certain behaviors, including swiping speed and gestures, when assessing the likelihood of fraud.[49] Similarly, there may be benefits to using the technology across the "anti-money laundering value chain," including at onboarding and client screening and with particular and immediate benefits coming from transaction monitoring.[50] In addition, researchers suggest that the technology is also useful in reducing false positives, freeing banks to dedicate resources to actual instances of fraud.[51]

Capital Markets Applications

Technology has always played a large role in the financial sector's capital markets activities. AI/ML may be seen as natural extensions of areas such as quantitative finance, which embraced advanced statistical analysis. As such, financial institutions, including the asset management industry and other investment companies, have adopted the technology to identify and exploit investment opportunities, allocate capital, execute trades, and reduce cost, with the latter ultimately allowing them to reach more customers.

Sentiment Analysis

AI/ML technologies help participants distinguish meaningful data points from noise in a practice referred to as signal processing.[52] AI has become adept at identifying events from which a viable, profitable trading strategy can be generated but where the limited information would have made devising the strategy difficult without the benefit of AI.

Detection and Prevention," June 27, 2023, https://stripe.com/resources/more/how-machine-learning-works-for-payment-fraud-detection-and-prevention; and Adrian, "AI and Regtech."

[48] Stripe, "How Machine Learning Works for Payment Fraud Detection and Prevention."

[49] Stripe, "How Machine Learning Works for Payment Fraud Detection and Prevention."

[50] P. K. Doppalapudi et al., "The Fight Against Money Laundering: Machine Learning Is a Game Changer," McKinsey and Company, October 7, 2022, https://www.mckinsey.com/capabilities/risk-and-resilience/our-insights/the-fight-against-money-laundering-machine-learning-is-a-game-changer.

[51] Adrian, "AI and Regtech."

[52] Azzutti, Ringe, and Stiehl, "Machine Learning, Market Manipulation, and Collusion on Capital Markets," footnote at p. 85.

Sentiment analysis is the analysis of financial sector news to forecast individual stock or market directions.[53] Advances in AI allow firms to analyze a wide variety of data, including unstructured data, to determine a company's popularity—for example, by surveilling social media posts and analyzing traffic through satellite imagery and GPS data. Sentiment analysis may be used across the spectrum of capital markets services where firms or individuals interpret data to allocate capital and determine strategy, including asset management and securities trading.

Structured and Unstructured Data

Some AI models are able to analyze only *structured data*, which is organized and "quantifiable," thereby limiting the data that could be used.[54]

Unstructured data, on the other hand, has no "predefined data model" and may be uniquely consumed by contemporary AI. *Unstructured data* includes data in text, audio, visual, and other formats, an example of which may be social media posts and/or connections.[55]

While sentiment analysis is not new, LLMs and computer capacity may outperform human methods and abilities to evaluate or forecast potential market moves.[56] The financial press and various researchers have suggested that LLMs may provide an edge in a number of contexts, from deciphering statements from the Federal Reserve to forecasting stock prices.[57] Some studies have shown that AI-enabled market participants (such as hedge funds) are quick to respond to new data, especially machine-readable disclosures, moving stock prices quickly.[58] Subsequently, companies have begun to adjust corporate disclosure practices to account for these market practices by learning

---

53 Gartner, "Sentiment Analysis," accessed July 19, 2023, https://www.gartner.com/en/finance/glossary/sentiment-analysis.

54 Goldman Sachs, "The Role of Big Data in Investing," July 11, 2016, https://www.gsam.com/content/dam/gsam/pdfs/common/en/public/articles/perspectives/2016/big-data/GSAMPerspectives_BigDataInvesting.pdf?sa=n&rd=n.

55 For definitions and a discussion of unstructured data, see OECD, *OECD Business and Finance Outlook 2021: AI in Business and Finance*, p. 146; and FinRegLab, "The Use of Machine Learning for Credit Underwriting," p. 69.

56 OECD, *OECD Business and Finance Outlook 2021: AI in Business and Finance*, p. 41.

57 Robin Wigglesworth, "ChatGPT vs the Markets," *Financial Times*, April 18, 2023, https://www.ft.com/content/ c76cd6c0-e965-4c76-beec-e0b2deafd1ec.

58 Sean Cao et al., *How to Talk When a Machine Is Listening? Corporate Disclosure in the Age of AI*, National Bureau of Economic Research, Working Paper no. 27950, October 2020, pp. 18-19, https://www.nber.org/papers/w27950.

"how to talk when a machine is listening," with research showing that public companies are adjusting how they speak and the language used in reporting to account for AI used by market participants.[59]

Hearing and Writing Like a Human

Natural language processing (NLP) is a branch of AI that trains computers to understand and process language as humans do.[60] NLP can be used to develop LLMs that can create content in the form of essays or computer code from prompts using techniques that predict the next word in a sequence of words based on certain probabilities.[61] This technology supports applications in finance, including powering chatbots, surveying companies' own large troves of data, and writing code.[62] LLMs are examples of *artificial neural networks* that attempt to reflect the functioning of the human brain by replicating neurons as mathematical representations, organizing layers of such so-called nodes or artificial neurons into clusters or layers.[63] Nodes receive signals from upstream nodes to which they are connected and will process signals forward if a certain threshold is met.[64] Connections between neurons can be amplified or attenuated by weights that are constantly adjusted in the model learning process.[65]

ChatGPT, which has attracted attention in recent years, is an example of an LLM. Aside from finance-specific applications, LLMs and ChatGPT in particular provided general public audiences with some of the first concrete and directly applicable examples of AI that until now had been reserved for specialists.

---

[59] Cao et al., "How to Talk When a Machine Is Listening?," p. 3.

[60] Ross Gruetzemacher, "The Power of Natural Language Processing," *Harvard Business Review*, April 19, 2022, https://hbr.org/2022/04/the-power-of-natural-language-processin.

[61] Lucas Mearian, "What Are LLMs, and How Are They Used in Generative AI?," *Computerworld*, May 30, 2023, https://www.computerworld.com/article/3697649/what-are-large-language-models-and-how-are-they-used-in-generative-ai.html.

[62] Carter Pape, "Here's How Banks Are Using and Experimenting with Generative AI," *American Banker*, July 7, 2023, https://www.americanbanker.com/news/heres-how-banks-are-using-and-experimenting-with-generative-ai.

[63] Christian Janiesch, Patrick Zschech, and Kai Heinrich, "Machine Learning and Deep Learning," *Electronic Markets*, April 8, 2021, p. 687, https://doi.org/10.1007/s12525-021-00475-2; and Larry Hardesty, "Explained: Neural Networks," *MIT News*, April 14, 2017, https://news.mit.edu/2017/explained-neural-networks-deep-learning-0414.

[64] Janiesch, Zschech, and Heinrich, "Machine Learning and Deep Learning," p. 687; and Hardesty, "Explained: Neural Networks."

[65] Janiesch, Zschech, and Heinrich, "Machine Learning and Deep Learning," p. 687; and Hardesty, "Explained: Neural Networks."

Asset Management

Asset managers are companies that manage individuals' and businesses' capital for a fee, identifying suitable investments based on stated preferences.[66] The industry has been using AI for "a number of years," according to one report, to generate ideas and for portfolio allocation.[67] Recent applications employ deep learning models, including neural networks.[68] Specifically, AI is used to perform various types of analyses to suggest asset allocations (where and how much to invest) that optimize a portfolio (to maximize profit), with evidence suggesting that they may be better at meeting targets than "traditional methods" are.[69]

Robo-advisors are a form of financial advisors under the broader asset management category that use AI to automate investment management. These digital investment advisors may employ various types of AI/ML (including NLP, LLMs, etc.) to develop a profile of an investor including budget, time horizon, and risk tolerance. They came to prominence more than a decade ago as a fintech application in part to introduce investment management to a subset of the population that may not have previously engaged with the service. Generally, these advisors may charge lower fees and require lower minimum balances than personal advisers do.[70] Additionally, robo-advisor algorithms may be programmed to rebalance a portfolio and perform "tax loss harvesting" and digital document delivery.[71]

Some asset managers have also created LLMs and generative AI models to assist with other services. Morgan Stanley, for example, announced in March 2023 that it had partnered with OpenAI (the company that created ChatGPT) to create a tool based on internal content to assist financial advisors

---

[66] "Asset management companies—also referred to as investment management companies, money managers, funds, or investment funds—are collective investment vehicles that pool money from various individual or institutional investor clients and invest on their behalf for financial returns." For this definition and more, see CRS Report R45957, *Capital Markets: Asset Management and Related Policy Issues*, by Eva Su.

[67] OECD, *OECD Business and Finance Outlook 2021: AI in Business and Finance*, pp. 39-40.

[68] Gensler and Bailey, *Deep Learning and Financial Stability*, pp. 6-7. See also Söhnke M. Bartram, Jürgen Branke, and Mehrshad Motahari, "Artificial Intelligence in Asset Management," CFA Institute Research Foundation, 2020, p. 6, https://www.cfainstitute.org/-/media/documents/book/rf-lit-review/2020/rflr-artificial-intelligence-in-asset-management.pdf for a full summary of AI/ML techniques used in asset management.

[69] Bartram, Branke, and Motahari, "Artificial Intelligence in Asset Management," p. 8.

[70] Securities and Exchange Commission, "Investor Bulletin: Robo-Advisers," press release, February 23, 2017, https://www.sec.gov/oiea/investor-alerts-bulletins/ib_robo-advisers.

[71] BlackRock, "Artificial Intelligence and Machine Learning in Asset Management," p. 4.

in serving clients.[72] The tool is said to function much like ChatGPT but uses Morgan Stanley's "own expansive range of intellectual capital" to provide answers in "an easily digestible format."[73]

Trading Applications

Algorithmic Trading and Trade Execution

Algorithmic trading is a subset of quantitative finance that dates to the 1950s that uses "mathematical models, computers, and telecommunications networks to automate the buying and selling of financial securities."[74] In earlier iterations, algorithmic trading was based on—in technological terms—"deterministic 'rules based' systems," which impose certain constraints.[75] As discussed earlier (see "Technology Overview in Brief"), these models took their cues directly from humans and lacked the ability to learn. As in other financial industry subfields, technological advances have pushed firms to use newer methods, whose algorithm-enabling trading are considered more robust, adaptable to market conditions, and capable of operating at greater levels of autonomy.[76] Traders may combine supervised (i.e., learning with the assistance of humans) and unsupervised (i.e., learning without human supervision) learning models, employing a variety of techniques based on how a firm's adoption of AI/ML capacity evolved with technology.[77] For example, one investment firm may use an LLM such as ChatGPT to develop an investment thesis that is subsequently fed into more traditional "statistical AI" models to back test a hypothesis or determine whether the theory would have been profitable based on previous data.[78]

---

[72] Morgan Stanley, "Morgan Stanley Wealth Management Announces Key Milestone in Innovation Journey with OpenAI," press release, March 14, 2023, https://www.morganstanley.com/press-releases/key-milestone-in-innovation-journey-with-openai.

[73] Morgan Stanley, "Morgan Stanley Wealth Management Announces Key Milestone."

[74] Andrei A. Kirilenko and Andrew W. Lo, "Moore's Law versus Murphy's Law: Algorithmic Trading and Its Discontents," *Journal of Economic Perspectives*, vol. 27, no. 2 (Spring 2013), pp. 52-53, https://pubs.aeaweb.org/doi/ pdfplus/10.1257/jep.27.2.51.

[75] Azzutti, Ringe, and Stiehl, "Machine Learning, Market Manipulation, and Collusion on Capital Markets," p. 85.

[76] Azzutti, Ringe, and Stiehl, "Machine Learning, Market Manipulation, and Collusion on Capital Markets," pp. 85-86.

[77] Azzutti, Ringe, and Stiehl, "Machine Learning, Market Manipulation, and Collusion on Capital Markets," p. 86.

[78] Tracy Alloway, Joe Weisenthal, and Isabel Webb Carey, "Bridgewater's Greg Jensen Explains How the World's Biggest Hedge Fund Is Investing in AI," *Bloomberg*, July 3, 2023,

Supervised and Unsupervised Learning

Supervised learning refers to a type of ML in which the system is 'fed' or trained on labeled data that allows it to make inferences about the different types of data. Supervised learning models are trained using a data set that includes inputs (the raw data that, once trained, a model may be expected to decipher) as well as labeled outputs (how that input is traditionally classified) so that the model can learn.[79] One generic example of supervised learning's use is email spam. Once trained on enough examples of "spam" versus "not spam" emails, an effective model should be able to decipher the two.[80]

Unsupervised learning uses unlabeled data—the relationship between inputs and outputs is obscured or not readily apparent—and the model is directed to find patterns among data without labels or specifications.[81]

Reinforced learning is a method in which an algorithm seeks to maximize outcomes, in successive steps, using trial and error in which successful intermediate solutions are rewarded.[82] Reinforcement learning is described as being well-equipped to deal with problems that resemble games, with rules and "incentive structures" and, by extension, capital markets applications.[83]

Various market participants may also use ML for vital process-oriented tasks such as order placement and execution, especially when *price impact* occurs—the phenomenon in which buyers or sellers of large quantities of securities experience adverse price movements brought about by market reactions to their large buy and sell orders.[84] As such, traders may employ

---

https://www.bloomberg.com/news/articles/2023-07-03/bridgewater-s-greg-jensen-explains-how-the-world-s-biggest-hedge-fund-is-investing-in-ai.

[79] Janiesch, Zschech, and Heinrich, "Machine Learning and Deep Learning," pp. 685-695.

[80] Julianna Delua, "Supervised vs. Unsupervised Learning: What's the Difference?," IBM, March 12, 2021, https://www.ibm.com/blog/supervised-vs-unsupervised-learning/.

[81] Janiesch, Zschech, and Heinrich, "Machine Learning and Deep Learning," pp. 685-695.

[82] Richard S. Sutton and Andrew G. Barto, *Reinforcement Learning: An Introduction*, 2nd ed. (Cambridge, MA: MIT Press, 2020), p. 1, http://incompleteideas.net/book/RLbook2020.pdf.

[83] Gensler and Bailey, *Deep Learning and Financial Stability*, p. 8.

[84] André F. Perold, "The Implementation Shortfall: Paper Versus Reality," *Journal of Portfolio Management*, vol. 14, no. 3 (1988), pp. 5-6, https://www.proquest.com/docview/195579087.

algorithms and, more recently, neural networks to execute orders in a dynamic way, taking into consideration market forces.[85]

AI-as-a-Service

AI-as-a-service refers to third-party service providers offering AI models to financial firms lacking their own capacity to develop them internally. In the financial services industry, BlackRock's Aladdin resembles such a service. BlackRock describes Aladdin as "end-to-end portfolio management software" that offers trading, operations, and compliance functions on a single platform.[86] The platform is used by a large number of other financial firms that, together with BlackRock, manage more than $10 trillion in assets.[87] It uses AI to develop some of its insights, including pricing data or data cleansing, extending those services to its clients. The firm reportedly offers AI/ML-fueled sustainability evaluation and assessment tools and is integrating LLM capabilities to let its clients query Aladdin to help them find information more quickly.[88] Similarly, core services providers that serve small banks and credit unions, such as Jack Henry and Fiserv, also advertise AI/ML services, including fraud detection and chatbot services.[89]

---

[85] OECD, *OECD Business and Finance Outlook 2021: AI in Business and Finance*, p. 40; and JP Morgan, "Machine Learning in FX," August 8, 2019, https://www.jpmorgan.com/insights/markets/forex/machine-learning-fx.

[86] BlackRock, "Aladdin Enterprise," https://www.blackrock.com/aladdin/offerings/aladdin-overview.

[87] Tracy Alloway, "BlackRock's Aladdin: Genie Not Included," *Financial Times*, July 11, 2014, https://www.ft.com/ content/300145d2-0841-11e4-acd8-00144feab7de; and Brooke Masters, "BlackRock to Roll Out First Generative AI Tools to Clients Next Month," *Financial Times*, December 6, 2023, https://www.ft.com/content/3f3431f1-d6dc-4310-9edc-3bc8cdc46caa. The $10 trillion figure is cited in Andrew Ross Sorkin et al., "Why BlackRock's C.E.O. Wants to Rethink Retirement," *New York Times*, March 26, 2024, https://www.nytimes.com/2024/03/26/business/dealbook/blackrock-fink-letter-retirement.html.

[88] BlackRock, "BlackRock Boosts Aladdin's Forward-Looking Sustainability Analytics and Reporting Capabilities Through Strategic Partnership with Clarity AI," press release, January 14, 2021, https://www.blackrock.com/corporate/ newsroom/press-releases/article/corporate-one/press-releases/blackrock-announced-minority-investment-in-clarity-ai; and Masters, "BlackRock to Roll Out First Generative AI Tools to Clients Next Month."

[89] See, for example, Jack Henry, "Now Is the Time to Add AI and ML to Combat Fraudsters," August 4, 2023, https://www.jackhenry.com/fintalk/now-is-the-time-to-add-ai-and-ml-to-combat-fraudsters; and Nicole Howson, "Understanding the Generative AI Industrial Revolution," Fiserv, August 30, 2023, https://www.fiserv.com/en/insights/ articles-and-blogs/understanding-the-ai-industrial-revolution.html.

Policy Issues Regarding the Role of AI/ML in Finance

Not all policy issues associated with AI/ML in finance are new, but concerns have grown as its use becomes more prevalent and as the scope of technology appears capable of exacerbating potential risks. Some policy issues, such as whether AI may introduce or magnify bias, deal with broad issues such as fairness in the provision of financial services. Others, which hinge on the scope of the technology and its potential uniformity, include whether the technology creates or increases systemic risk.

This section provides a brief treatment of the legislative and regulatory framework and selected policy issues: (1) the potential for the technology to introduce or exacerbate bias in the provision of financial services; (2) the lack of "explainability" that stems from increasing model complexity, potentially introducing risk to the financial system; (3) the ability to encourage herd-like behavior, leading to financial stability concerns; (4) data security and privacy issues; (5) the potential to promote market manipulation; (6) the evolving role of big tech's position at the intersection of data, AI/ML, and financial services; and (7) whether, and the extent to which, AI may disrupt financial sector jobs.

Legislative and Regulatory Considerations

Broadly speaking, the legal and regulatory framework applicable to financial institutions and activities are "technology neutral," meaning they do not take into consideration the specific tools or methods used by institutions. For example, lending laws apply to lending whether the lender uses a pencil and paper or a cutting-edge AI-enabled model, and securities laws apply equally to traders on an exchange floor and ultra-fast high-frequency trading rigs. Given this, many policy debates in the area relate to questions about whether existing rules, when applied to new or innovative uses of AI/ML technologies, are adequate and effective, overly restrictive and stifling to beneficial advances, or overly permissive and inadequate protections against the risks presented by the technology.

AI Executive Order

In October 2023, President Biden issued Executive Order 14110 on the *Safe, Secure, and Trustworthy Development and Use of Artificial Intelligence.*[90] The E.O. in particular acknowledges the potential for the technology as well as the risks; it broadly aims to serve as a roadmap for the technology and for use of the technology for commercial and governmental purposes.[91] The E.O. addresses financial services by, among other things, encouraging relevant agencies to use their authority to ensure regulated entities follow laws that prohibit bias and to issue guidance regarding the appropriate use of data and advertising of services that use algorithms.

Policymakers have increasingly focused their attention on AI/ML financial issues, although to date, few legislative or regulatory changes have been specifically directed at AI/ML use in finance. Meanwhile, regulators have communicated their positions and concerns about AI/ML in various areas. For example, in a March 2021 Request for Information (RFI), various federal banking regulators solicited "views on the use of AI in financial services to assist in determining whether any clarifications from the agencies would be helpful for financial institutions' use of AI." The RFI includes a list of existing laws, regulations, guidance, and other regulatory statements relevant for AI and notes that "[s]ome laws and regulations are applicable to any process or tool a financial institution employs, regardless of whether a financial institution utilizes AI or how."[92] The RFI essentially acknowledged the central issue of assessing the adequacy of existing regulation in the context of an evolving technology, acknowledging that new rules may not be immediately necessary considering that existing ones are still applicable. Yet the acknowledgement appears to be more of a reminder to financial firms of

[90] Executive Office of the President, "Safe, Secure, and Trustworthy Development and Use of Artificial Intelligence," 88 *Federal Register* 75191, November 1, 2023, https://www.federalregister.gov/documents/2023/11/01/2023-24283/safe-secure-and-trustworthy-development-and-use-of-artificial-intelligence.

[91] For an overview of E.O. 14110, see CRS Report R47843, *Highlights of the 2023 Executive Order on Artificial Intelligence for Congress*, by Laurie A. Harris and Chris Jaikaran.

[92] Comptroller of the Currency, the Federal Reserve System, the Federal Deposit Insurance Corporation, CFPB, and National Credit Union Administration, "Request for Information and Comment on Financial Institutions' Use of Artificial Intelligence, Including Machine Learning," 86 *Federal Register* 16837, March 31, 2021 https://www.federalregister.gov/documents/2021/03/31/2021-06607/request-for-information-and-comment-on-financial-institutions-use-of-artificial-intelligence.

their existing obligations and not the agencies' final stance on policy. Some commentators suggest existing laws should already motivate corporations not to engage in bad behavior and reject additional attempts to regulate as "intrusions" that will "slow American innovation."[93] Alternatively, many firms may be choosing not to use AI because of legal risks, and they may be more likely to employ the technology with clearer regulations.

AI/ML Model Bias

Bias in financial services is the overprovision, limitation, or existence of cost difference in the provision of financial services based on an individual's identity as part of a specific group. While conventional and newer AI/ML may remove one avenue for bias outcomes by eliminating the interpersonal interactions that may lead to discrimination, some believe the technology may introduce or exacerbate biases.[94] These biases generally fall into two main groups: bias introduced from data and bias introduced by models.[95] Data may introduce bias in a number of ways, including if the data on which a model is trained includes certain historical biases, which in a financial services context may include discrimination against protected classes.[96] Models trained on such data may provide credit decisions in ways that perpetuate biases and are illegal.

Model construction and training may also introduce bias. In training periods, for example, certain models may take a longer time to process observations for which there is less information and "learn" how to treat low information interactions. If institutions limit how long they train models, they may adversely affect how such models treat instances with low levels of information in practice.[97]

Regulators have addressed bias in various venues. Federal Reserve Vice Chair for Supervision Michael S. Barr cited a case in which Meta was charged

---

[93] *Wall Street Journal*, "Biden's AI Order Is Government's Bid for Dominance," November 7, 2023, https://www.wsj.com/articles/joe-biden-ai-executive-order-china-artificial-intelligence-regulation-64024988.

[94] OECD, *Artificial Intelligence, Machine Learning, and Big Data in Finance*, 2021, pp. 10, 30, https://www.oecd.org/finance/financial-markets/Artificial-intelligence-machine-learning-big-data-in-finance.pdf.

[95] FinRegLab, *The Use of Machine Learning for Credit Underwriting*, pp. 75-79.

[96] FinRegLab, *The Use of Machine Learning for Credit Underwriting*, pp. 75-79. In a services context, bias in data may include previous discrimination against protected classes.

[97] FinRegLab, *The Use of Machine Learning for Credit Underwriting*, pp. 75-79.

with violating a law that "prohibits discrimination in housing, including housing-related advertising" on the basis of protected classes.[98] On June 1, 2023, the federal banking agencies requested public comment on a proposed rule that would require companies that use automated valuation models "to adopt policies, practices, procedures, and control systems" that, among other things, ensure the models comply with nondiscrimination laws.[99] Also, in 2020, the Consumer Financial Protection Bureau issued an RFI on the Equal Credit Opportunity Act (Regulation B/ECOA)—which prohibits discrimination in credit applications because of race, color, religion, national origin, sex, marital status, or age, among others—posing the question of whether it should provide more "regulatory clarity" regarding Regulation B/ECOA to facilitate innovation that would expand credit access without unlawful discrimination.[100]

Explainability

Explainability in AI/ML generally refers to the ability of a firm or model designer to understand a model's outputs or how it came to its conclusions. A lack of explainability has significant regulatory ramifications. Regulation B/ECOA requires that when taking adverse actions (such as refusing credit), banks and other financial institutions must provide notice to applicants explaining why they were rejected.[101] Such notice should be "specific and indicate the principal reason(s) for the adverse action."[102] Therefore, a firm's use of an overly complex model whose decision and rationale cannot be

---

[98] Federal Reserve Vice Chair for Supervision Michael S. Barr, "Making the Financial System Safer and Fairer," speech at the Brookings Institution, Washington, DC, September 7, 2022, https://www.federalreserve.gov/newsevents/ speech/barr20220907a.htm; and *United States of America v. Meta Platforms, Inc. f/k/a Facebook, Inc.*, 22-cv-05187 (United States District Court Southern District of New York 2022).

[99] Comptroller of the Currency, the Federal Reserve System, the Federal Deposit Insurance Corporation, the National Credit Union Administration, the Consumer Financial Protection Bureau, and the Federal Housing Finance Agency, "Quality Control Standards for Automated Valuation Models," 88 *Federal Register* 40638, June 21, 2023, https://www.federalregister.gov/documents/2023/06/21/2023-12187/quality-control-standards-for-automated-valuation-models.

[100] Consumer Financial Protection Bureau, "Request for Information on the Equal Credit Opportunity Act and Regulation B," 85 *Federal Register* 46600, August 3, 2020.

[101] 12 C.F.R. §1002.9(b)(1). See CRS In Focus IF12399, *Automation, Artificial Intelligence, and Machine Learning in Consumer Lending*, by Cheryl R. Cooper.

[102] 12 C.F.R. §1002.9(b)(1). See CRS In Focus IF12399, *Automation, Artificial Intelligence, and Machine Learning in Consumer Lending*, by Cheryl R. Cooper.

adequately and specifically explained may directly conflict with Regulation B/ECOA. As use of AI/ML for credit underwriting expands, and as regulatory guidance evolves, determining what is a satisfactory explanation—one that is not too general nor overly technical—may emerge as a key area of negotiation between industry and regulators.

Banks also have risk management requirements, which require they understand the theory and logic of models that manage their risk.[103] Assuming that AI/ML technologies would be considered *models*, for the sake of compliance, banks' inability to explain its results may be of supervisory concern.[104]

For capital markets participants, such as traders, lack of explainability creates risks for firms insofar as traders may not be able to detect the rationale for a successful or losing strategy.[105] Lack of explainability may also cause compliance issues for market participants if a model engages in illegal practices, such as market manipulation.

There may be ways for developers to mitigate challenges from the lack of explainability and potential bias of certain AI/ML models. For example, researchers have shown that diagnostic tools and testing can address transparency-related challenges and that some such tools can identify what model features may be responsible for an adverse action.[106] In addition, policy and technology experts have recommended—including in response to a 2019 executive order— technical standards that may, among other things, eliminate the accidental or intentional promotion of bias.[107]

---

[103] Federal Reserve, *Supervisory Guidance on Model Risk Management*, April 4, 2011, p. 5, https://www.federalreserve.gov/supervisionreg/srletters/sr1107a1.pdf; and Office of the Comptroller of the Currency, "Sound Practices for Model Risk Management: Supervisory Guidance on Model Risk Management," April 4, 2011, https://www.occ.gov/news-issuances/bulletins/2011/bulletin-2011-12.html.

[104] Matthew Bisanz and Tori K. Shinohara, "Supervisory Expectations for Artificial Intelligence Outlined by US OCC," Mayer Brown, April 13, 2020, https://www.mayerbrown.com/en/perspectives-events/publications/2022/05/supervisory-expectations-for-artificial-intelligence-outlined-by-us-occ#Two.

[105] OECD, *OECD Business and Finance Outlook 2021: AI in Business and Finance*, p. 42.

[106] Laura Blattner et al., "Machine Learning Explainability and Fairness: Insights from Consumer Lending," FinRegLab, July 2023, p. 7, https://finreglab.org/wp-content/uploads/2023/07/FRL-ML-EWP_July2023.pdf.

[107] Executive Office of the President, "Maintaining American Leadership in Artificial Intelligence," 84 *Federal Register* 3967, February 14, 2019, https://www.federalregister.gov/documents/2019/02/14/2019-02544/maintaining-american-leadership-in-artificial-intelligence; NIST, "U.S. Leadership in AI: A Plan for Federal Engagement in Developing Technical Standards and Related Tools," August 10, 2019, https://nvlpubs.nist.gov/nistpubs/ SpecialPublications/NIST.SP.1500-1r2.pdf; and Darrell M. West, "Six Steps

Data-Related Policy Issues

Use of data by financial firms is subject to data protection and security requirements such as those established under the Gramm-Leach-Bliley Act (GLBA, P.L. 106-102).[108] GLBA requires that financial institutions ensure the privacy and confidentiality of customers and protect against threats and unauthorized access and use of data. GLBA also limits what financial institutions can do with information they have collected, generally requiring that they not disclose information to nonaffiliated third parties unless they notify customers and give them the opportunity to opt out.[109] To comply, banks and financial institutions subject to GLBA typically anonymize or "de-identify" their data before selling it.[110]

However, concerns about data privacy have increased as models improve and may be able to accurately identify owners of previously anonymized data.[111] In other words, anonymizing data may no longer be enough to comply with GLBA. Furthermore, because keeping data anonymous is becoming more difficult, even more information may qualify as sensitive.[112] As AI/ML models use increasingly more alternative data (see "Big Data"), more of a consumer's social behavior may become subject to commercial surveillance.[113] In other words, as financial institutions seek more alternative types of information to grant financial decisions, individuals may begin to suffer from a greater lack of privacy. While consumers may opt out of information disclosure, this may

---

to Responsible AI in the Federal Government," Brookings Institution, March 30, 2022, https://www.brookings.edu/articles/six-steps-to-responsible-ai-in-the-federal-government/.

[108] For more on financial data rights and privacy, see CRS Report R47434, *Banking, Data Privacy, and Cybersecurity Regulation*, by Andrew P. Scott and Paul Tierno; and CRS Insight IN12291, *CFPB Proposes New Regulation on Consumer Data Rights*, by Cheryl R. Cooper.

[109] P.L. 106-102, §502.

[110] Avi Gesser et al., "Alternative Data Goes Mainstream, and Gets Increased Attention from Regulators," New York University School of Law Program on Compliance and Enforcement, February 25, 2019, https://wp.nyu.edu/ compliance_enforcement/2019/02/25/ alternative-data-goes-mainstream-and-gets-increased-attention-from-regulators/.

[111] Steven T. Mnuchin and Craig S. Phillips, *A Financial System That Creates Economic Opportunities: Nonbank Financials, Fintech, and Innovation*, U.S. Department of the Treasury, July 8, 2018, p. 58, https://home.treasury.gov/ sites/default/files/2018-08/A-Financial-System-that-Creates-Economic-Opportunities—Nonbank-Financials-Fintech-and-Innovation.pdf.

[112] Mnuchin and Phillips, *A Financial System That Creates Economic Opportunities*, p. 5.

[113] U.S. Department of the Treasury, *Assessing the Impact of New Entrant Non-Bank Firms on Competition in Consumer Finance Markets*, November 2022, p. 88, https://home.treasury.gov/system/files/136/Assessing-the-Impact-of-New-Entrant-Nonbank-Firms.pdf.

limit what services they can receive, forcing them to choose between disclosure and collection or going without a service or product.[114]

Concentration Risk and Systemic Risk Concerns

The market for developing AI/ML may exhibit traditional economic forces seen in other technology sectors, such as high barriers to entry and economies of scale. The high cost to purchase equipment and hire staff may limit to large companies those that are able to develop technology and attract and retain talent.[115] Subsequently, companies that have made the investment and attracted market share may be able to offer AI/ML services broadly, profitably, and more easily than new entrants, which would have to begin making the expensive investment and then wrest market share away from the incumbents. Therefore, developing robust models may be economically feasible only for very large companies, while smaller financial institutions may not be able to develop these technologies on their own and may rely on third-party technology providers for the technology.[116]

The concentration of human capacity and model development at a handful of firms means the number of firms using the same underlying model or data may create or exacerbate systemic risk—financial market risk that poses a threat to financial stability.[117] Conditions in the market for AI/ML may create financial system risk in various ways, including through various dynamics that may create herd-like behavior.

In addition, there is a general assumption that the continued growth of data quantity and access contributes to improving AI/ML models. This may improve predictive ability and mitigate potentially harmful attributes such as myopia and human subjectivity that may precipitate asset market bubbles. An alternative theory suggests that current access to data may still not be enough to model all potential outcomes. For example, a model's predictive ability may be good for examples that are represented in the data on which it was trained, but it may be of minimal or no use for situations that do not appear in data

---

[114] U.S. Department of the Treasury, *Assessing the Impact of New Entrant Non-Bank Firms*, p. 88.

[115] OECD, *OECD Business and Finance Outlook 2021: AI in Business and Finance*, p. 40; and Gensler and Bailey, *Deep Learning and Financial Stability*, p. 23.

[116] OECD, *OECD Business and Finance Outlook 2021: AI in Business and Finance*, p. 40.

[117] See CRS In Focus IF10700, *Introduction to Financial Services: Systemic Risk*, by Marc Labonte.

(referred to as "overfit").[118] "Idiosyncratic" or once-in-a-lifetime events—such as COVID-19, for example—may introduce scenarios that were not represented in training data and for which models cannot account.[119] This could cause some AI/ML model performance to "change or deteriorate."[120]

In addition, models created using the same data sets may reach the same or similar insights, informing the collective investment decisions and encouraging similar behavior in large portions of the investment community.[121] Errors, risks, and unrepresentative conditions in the data would be propagated across the system, potentially fostering systemic risks.

Herding Behavior

Herding refers to an investment behavior wherein, for an array of reasons, investors may copy the behavior and strategy of other investors, moving markets as a result and creating risk. Literature suggests that herding has exacerbated previous financial crises and is not a new feature of finance created by AI/ML.[122] However, commentators (including regulators) suggest that herding is a key risk inherent in use of AI/ML.[123] Herding manifests itself through AI if a number of market participants use the same or sufficiently similar algorithms, models, or data sets, creating homogeneity in the market or one-way markets.[124] This may occur when firms (knowingly or not) use the same third-party provider or an "off the shelf" model employed by others or if an AI/ML vendor's technology encourages the same activity among all

---

[118] OECD, *OECD Business and Finance Outlook 2021: AI in Business and Finance*, p. 55.

[119] See OECD, *OECD Business and Finance Outlook 2021: AI in Business and Finance*, p. 56; and Alloway, Weisenthal, and Webb Carey, "Bridgewater's Greg Jensen Explains How the World's Biggest Hedge Fund Is Investing in AI" for various discussions of the issue.

[120] David Bholat, Mohammed Gharbawi, and Oliver Thew, "The Impact of Covid on Machine Learning and Data Science in UK Banking," Bank of England, December 18, 2020, https://www.bankofengland.co.uk/quarterly-bulletin/ 2020/2020-q4/the-impact-of-covid-on-machine-learning-and-data-science-in-uk-banking.

[121] See Gensler and Bailey, *Deep Learning and Financial Stability*, p. 3; and OECD, *OECD Business and Finance Outlook 2021: AI in Business and Finance* for general challenges surrounding data.

[122] Sushil Bikhchandani and Sunil Sharma, "Herd Behavior in Financial Markets," *IMF Staff Papers*, vol. 47, no. 3 (2001), https://www.imf.org/external/pubs/ft/staffp/2001/01/pdf/bikhchan.pdf.

[123] See, for example, Gary Gensler, "Isaac Newton to AI," remarks before the National Press Club, Securities and Exchange Commission, July 17, 2023; and CNBC Television, "SEC Chair Gary Gensler: AI is the Most Transformative Technology of Our Time."

[124] OECD, *OECD Business and Finance Outlook 2021: AI in Business and Finance*, p. 40. *One-way market* refers to a market in which market participants overwhelmingly favor one side of a market or trade—for example, overwhelmingly being long such that there is little appetite to sell.

clients.[125] Herding could create illiquidity or price spikes if there are not enough other market participants to take the opposite trade, which may be exacerbated in periods of stress and when financial conditions change.

Flash Crashes

Flash crashes are sudden, substantial declines in financial markets, including equity indices, individual stocks, or government securities. One potential cause is when a programmatic error induces panic selling by a large number of asset holders in a short period of time, which can destabilize financial markets, at least temporarily.[126] Panic selling is not a new phenomenon, but the signal processing and automated and recursive nature of the technology used in contemporary trading may instigate or exacerbate the associated risks.

One specific flash crash that occurred on May 6, 2010, attracted significant attention. The flash crash involved traders using technology and algorithms that resembled current or past AI/ML technology discussed in this report (programs following explicit commands, operating without the direct oversight of humans, occurring at speeds significantly faster than those at which humans operate, and based in some cases exclusively on market conditions) and identifies several distinct AI/ML-related risks. According to certain reports, the 2010 flash crash was sparked in part by a spoofing algorithm employed by a British trader in a futures contracts market that drove the price of the market lower.[127]

In addition, automated execution algorithms were programmed to execute trades based strictly on previous levels of volume traded in the

[125] Gensler, "Isaac Newton to AI;" and OECD, *OECD Business and Finance Outlook 2021: AI in Business and Finance*, p. 42.

[126] See a discussion of the 2010 flash crash in CRS Report R44443, *High Frequency Trading: Overview of Recent Developments*, by Rena S. Miller and Gary Shorter; and SEC and CFTC, *Findings Regarding the Market Events of May 6, 2010: Reports of the Staffs of the CFTC and SEC to Joint Advisory Committee on Emerging Regulatory Issues*, September 30, 2010, p. 10, https://www.sec.gov/files/marketevents-report.pdf.

[127] U.S. Department of Justice, "Futures Trader Pleads Guilty to Illegally Manipulating the Futures Market in Connection with 2010 'Flash Crash,'" press release, November 9, 2016, https://www.justice.gov/opa/pr/futures-trader-pleads-guilty-illegally-manipulating-futures-market-connection-2010-flash. See SEC and CFTC, *Findings Regarding the Market Events of May 6, 2010*, p. 10. The OECD includes this as a case study in collusion in OECD, *Algorithms and Collusion: Competition Policy in the Digital Age*, 2017, p. 25, https://www.oecd.org/daf/competition/Algorithms-and-colllusion-competition-policy-in-the-digital-age.pdf.

market. Transactions that day triggered selling by the automated traders that initiated a feedback loop among other agents using algorithmic agents, which drove prices down quickly. Thus the ever present concern of panic selling *may be* exacerbated when unrelated automated models interact with each other. Flash crashes are a microcosm of various AI/ML-related risks, including herding—represented by high frequency traders (HFTs) engaging in similar actions—and a lack of explainability, as various participants were not prepared for the outcome. (HFTs trade securities using sophisticated computers to execute trades in micro- or milliseconds.[128])

A related challenge may be that individuals capable of creating or managing systems may be concentrated in a relatively few institutions, which may drive an over-reliance on third-party vendors, comparable to other services, such as cloud computing.[129] As in other areas with a limited number of providers, concentration of third-party service providers and models may pose risk in the event of technical or other failure of the intermediary.

There are some laws and regulations governing financial institutions' use of third-party service providers, although these are not necessarily aimed at curtailing the risks of herding. For example, depository banks that rely on third-party service providers—particularly those that provide financial AI/ML services—must ensure that these vendors satisfy safety and soundness regulatory requirements under the Bank Services Company Act (P.L. 87-856). According to bank regulators' guidance, a bank's "use of third parties does not diminish its responsibility to meet these requirements to the same extent as if its activities were performed by the banking organization in-house."[130] Similarly, LabCFTC, the technology-focused division of the Commodity and Futures Trading Commission (CFTC), stipulated in a primer document that CFTC-regulated firms remain responsible for any services performed by third-party service providers of AI.[131]

---

[128] For more information on high-frequency trading, see CRS Report R44443, *High Frequency Trading: Overview of Recent Developments*, by Rena S. Miller and Gary Shorter.

[129] OECD, *OECD Business and Finance Outlook 2021: AI in Business and Finance*, p. 40. For similar challenges in cloud computing, see CRS In Focus IF11985, *Bank Use of Cloud Technology*, by Paul Tierno.

[130] Federal Reserve, Federal Deposit Insurance Corporation, Office of the Comptroller of the Currency, *Interagency Guidance on Third-Party Relationships: Risk Management*, June 7, 2023, p. 1, https://www.federalreserve.gov/ supervisionreg/srletters/SR2304a1.pdf.

[131] LabCFTC, *A Primer on Artificial Intelligence in Financial Markets*, 2019, downloads directly at https://www.cftc.gov/media/2846/LabCFTC_PrimerArtificialIntelligence102119/download.

Market Manipulation

Market manipulation occurs when an individual or firm tries to influence the supply of or demand for a security. It traditionally comes in a variety of forms, including "pump and dump" schemes in which someone engages in a series of securities transactions to make a security seem more actively traded than it is.[132] ML techniques that aim to improve profit maximization may inadvertently lead to market manipulation. Academic studies indicate that autonomous AI agents may—in an effort to optimize profitability—learn ways to manipulate markets without involving input from a developer.[133] Some manipulative tactics that AI/ML may perpetuate include "spoofing" and "pinging," both of which are intended to learn certain information about a market and use it to participants' advantage.[134] While human traders generally would and should know that these manipulative actions are illegal, AI/ML models may not know, or they may otherwise ignore the prohibition. Additionally, LLMs (and generative AI) may be used to create images or text to fabricate news stories that could move markets in a way that could prove beneficial for certain transactions.[135] Securities, commodities, and derivatives markets are governed by laws that prohibit market manipulation.[136] Therefore, manipulation would be considered illegal, regardless of the technology used to perpetrate it.

---

[132] Securities and Exchange Commission, "Market Manipulation," https://www.investor.gov/introduction-investing/investing-basics/glossary/market-manipulation.

[133] Takanobu Mizuta, "Can an AI Perform Market Manipulation at Its Own Discretion? A Genetic Algorithm Learns in an Artificial Market Simulation," 2020 IEEE Symposium Series on Computational Intelligence, 2020, https://ieeexplore.ieee.org/document/9308349.

[134] Azzutti, Ringe, and Stiehl, "Machine Learning, Market Manipulation, and Collusion on Capital Markets," p. 99. *Spoofing* refers to a trader initiating a large buy order (thus driving market price for a security higher), and placing a sell order at the higher price while cancelling the false buy order, thereby capitalizing on the sale at the elevated price. Pinging involves submitting an order into the market with the intention of determining participants' intention of selling large quantities in the future and then selling prior to such large sales moving the markets down. For a diagram, see LabCFTC, "A Primer on Artificial Intelligence in Financial Markets." See also Greg Scopino, "The Questionable Legality of High-Speed 'Pinging' and 'Front Running' in the Futures Markets," Columbia Law School, May 29, 2014, https://clsbluesky.law.columbia.edu/2014/05/29/the-questionable-legality-of-high-speed-pinging-and-frontrunning-in-the-futures-markets/.

[135] Gillian Tett, "Investors Must Beware Deepfake Market Manipulation," *Financial Times*, June 8, 2023, https://www.ft.com/content/7b352945-9295-42f5-a5d1-a01edf48ba51.

[136] See, for example, 15 U.S.C. §78i and 18 U.S.C. §1348.

Conflicts of Interest

AI/ML may create conflicts of interest between firms using the technology and their customers. As with market manipulation, AI agents that are programmed to learn on their own could conceivably maximize benefits to a firm by taking advantage of the firm's own clients. Combined with a lack of explainability and the complexity of large financial operations in general, this could create scenarios in which a conflict of interest is just another inexplicable variable in a large model.

Various securities laws and regulations are intended to protect customers from such conflicts of interest. Regulation Best Interest and the Investment Advisory fiduciary standards, established under the Investment Advisers Act of 1940, for example, oblige advisors to act in their clients' best interest and not put their own interests ahead of their clients' interests.[137] Additionally, the Securities and Exchange Commission (SEC) proposed a rule that would require firms to identify conflicts of interest that may arise from firms using "predictive data analytics" tools and related technologies and neutralize any such conflicts associated with predictive analytics technologies.[138] Some market participants have criticized the proposed rule, claiming the SEC's definition of the technology is too broad.[139]

Supervisory Technology

Financial market regulators and supervisors may also use AI/ML-driven technology to oversee companies in their jurisdiction. According to the Financial Stability Board, various drivers are precipitating the development and use of supervisory technology (i.e., "suptech"), including enhanced efficiency (the ability to demand, store, and analyze large quantities of digital

[137] Securities and Exchange Commission, "Staff Bulletin: Standards of Conduct for Broker-Dealers and Investment Advisers," August 3, 2022, https://www.sec.gov/tm/iabd-staff-bulletin-conflicts-interest.

[138] SEC, "Conflicts of Interest Associated with the Use of Predictive Data Analytics by Broker-Dealers and Investment Advisers," 88 *Federal Register* 53960, August 9, 2023, https://www.federalregister.gov/documents/2023/08/09/2023-16377/conflicts-of-interest-associated-with-the-use-of-predictive-data-analytics-by-broker-dealers-and.

[139] Sidley, "SEC Proposes Sweeping New Rules on Use of Data Analytics by Broker-Dealers and Investment Advisers," press release, August 8, 2023, https://www.sidley.com/en/insights/newsupdates/2023/08/sec-proposes-sweeping-new-rules-on-use-of-data-analytics-by-broker-dealers-and-investment-advisers.

data); real-time data analysis; and "pro-active" and "forward-looking" supervision and surveillance.[140] Supervisors may use NLP to manage and synthesize unstructured data and for sentiment and network analysis, among other uses.[141]

In testimony before the House Committee on Financial Services Task Force on Artificial Intelligence, an official from the Office of the Comptroller of the Currency addressed the agency's initiative of upgrading "core supervision systems … evaluating and exploring use of … technologies, including AI," and hiring and retaining staff with expertise.[142] The Federal Deposit Insurance Corporation also noted in its 2022-2026 strategic plan that it will expand its own use of suptech over the coming years, including ML.[143]

Market regulators such as the CFTC and SEC have begun using deep learning tools to detect market manipulation and money laundering. In its primer on AI, the CFTC has suggested it could leverage AI to identify risk, perform market and risk surveillance, and identify market manipulation and abuse.[144] It has also suggested employing AI to evaluate the troves of data to which it has access—including from registrants, clearinghouses, and public data—and to perform systemic monitoring in ways that *may* forestall crises.

Similarly, the SEC purportedly first used NLP to determine whether it should have predicted the financial crisis and has reportedly incorporated AI into several of its risk assessment programs.[145] The SEC's use of NLP has evolved, and it has since begun using a form of unsupervised learning capable of reading documents, extracting insight, and identifying themes. Likewise, the agency uses these insights to train other models using supervised learning. The SEC claims that these methods combined may help it determine the likelihood of possible fraud when it reviews documents. According to the SEC and based on back-testing analysis, algorithms are five times better than

---

[140] Financial Stability Board, *The Use of Supervisory and Regulatory Technology*, p. 5.

[141] Kenton Beerman, Jeremy Prenio, and Raihan Zamil, "Suptech Tools for Prudential Supervision and Their Use During the Pandemic," Bank for International Settlements, December 2021, pp. 2, 11, https://www.bis.org/fsi/publ/ insights37.pdf.

[142] Statement of Kevin Greenfield, Deputy Comptroller for Operational Risk Policy, OCC, before the Task Force on Artificial Intelligence, Committee on Financial Services, May 13, 2022, https://www.occ.gov/news-issuances/congressional-testimony/2022/ct-occ-2022-52-written.pdf.

[143] Federal Deposit Insurance Corporation, *2022-2026 Strategic Plan*, December 14, 2021, p. 19, https://www.fdic.gov/ news/board-matters/2021/2021-12-14-notice-sum-d-fr.pdf.

[144] LabCFTC, *A Primer on Artificial Intelligence in Financial Markets*.

[145] Scott W. Bauguess, "The Role of Big Data, Machine Learning, and AI in Assessing Risks: A Regulatory Perspective," SEC, June 21, 2017, https://www.sec.gov/news/speech/bauguess-big-data-ai.

random at identifying language that may indicate whether an investment advisor could merit enforcement referral.[146] After the flash crash in 2010, the SEC imposed requirements on national securities exchanges and the Financial Industry Regulatory Authority to "create, implement, and maintain" a consolidated audit trail (CAT) that could provide additional opportunities for AI-enabled suptech.[147] The CAT requires national securities exchanges, associations, and members to report various details of orders, providing the SEC with additional details and still more data, which it will use to improve market surveillance and likely use to develop, train, test, and then implement still newer models. Therefore, CAT was a product of a flash crash that was arguably the result of AI/ML-like technology and is expected to serve as a tool for the SEC to keep pace with various risks, including those from AI.[148] The extent to which market regulators are able to keep pace with the technologies used by regulated entities—and to develop their own techniques to manage the large quantities of data—may depend in part on how Congress evaluates their use and investments in such technologies.

Big Tech in Finance

Companies with large repositories of information may be poised to reap the benefits of that data and the models they may sustain. Big tech companies—technology-based businesses of considerable scale that have played a substantial role in transforming the internet economy, attracting billions of users—have large repositories of data and are developing their own AI models and products.[149] They have the financial capacity to make the necessary IT investments and may be best situated to capitalize on this investment by selling access to certain products or services.[150] This would represent a further consolidation of data and model creation and reinforce third-party dependency, potentially exacerbating concentration or systemic risk.

[146] Bauguess, "The Role of Big Data, Machine Learning, and AI in Assessing Risks."

[147] 17 C.F.R. §242.613.

[148] Commissioner Caroline A. Crenshaw, "Statement Regarding the Order Approving an Amendment to the National Market System Plan Governing the Consolidated Audit Trail," SEC, September 6, 2023, https://www.sec.gov/news/ statement/crenshaw-statement-cat-funding-090623.

[149] For more information, see CRS Report R47104, *Big Tech in Financial Services*, by Paul Tierno. *Big tech* typically refers to Alphabet (Google), Amazon, Apple, Meta, (formerly Facebook), and Microsoft.

[150] Gensler and Bailey, *Deep Learning and Financial Stability*, p. 23.

Another policy issue of the central role of data is that it may also create opportunities for big tech to increase its presence in financial services. Big tech companies currently have some presence in finance, mostly on the consumer products side. Their ability to accumulate and process data and AI/ML capabilities could make this transition easier, which would raise issues about regulatory arbitrage, as they are subject to uneven regulation for financial services. Separately, big-tech-related data privacy and a concentration of economic activity could be exacerbated if they successfully expand their presence in financial markets. For more information on this issue area, see CRS Report R47104, *Big Tech in Financial Services*, by Paul Tierno.

AI/ML and Financial Industry Employment

Since its origins, AI/ML has led to fears that it would disrupt the job market by replacing humans who were performing the jobs that would be automated. Some unsubstantiated recent projections suggest AI/ML may lead to a loss of 300 million jobs by 2035 across sectors.[151] Research on the impact of past technological advances on jobs has been mixed. Broadly speaking, economists generally think that automated technologies replaced routine jobs but that those job losses can be offset by gains in other industries or by new jobs actually created by new technologies.[152] The overall effect is often described as technologies having eliminated middle-income jobs and increased the portion of jobs that are either low or high paying.[153] Recent advances in AI/ML— including most recently of LLMs, such as ChatGPT—may increasingly challenge the conventional wisdom that white-collar jobs are safe from automation while only routine jobs and manual labor would be replaced. Instead, it is now widely believed that certain jobs requiring higher education may be at risk, including those in finance.[154]

---

[151] Tracy Alloway, "Job Cuts from AI Are Just Beginning, the Latest Challenger Report Suggests," *Bloomberg*, June 1, 2023, https://www.bloomberg.com/news/articles/2023-06-01/job-cuts-from-ai-are-just-beginning-the-latest-challenger-report-suggests.

[152] For a literature review of technology's impact on employment, see F. Ted Tschang and Esteve Almirall, "Artificial Intelligence as Augmenting Automation: Implications for Employment," *Academy of Management Perspectives*, vol. 35, no. 4 (2021), p. 6, https://ink.library.smu.edu.sg/lkcsb_research/6669.

[153] Tschang and Almirall, "Artificial Intelligence as Augmenting Automation," p. 6.

[154] Annie Lowrey, "How ChatGPT Will Destabilize White-Collar Work," *The Atlantic*, January 20, 2023, https://www.theatlantic.com/ideas/archive/2023/01/chatgpt-ai-economy-automation-jobs/672767/.

Use of AI/ML in finance seems poised to perpetuate the traditional dichotomy: that it will both boost and reduce demand for different types of workers. The AI/ML boom is expected to increase financial institution demand and competition for workers with AI/ML-specific skills.[155] One 2022 report suggested there may be as many as 100,000 AI/ML and related roles in banking and other financial institutions globally.[156] Whether or to what degree the technology will replace workers is up for debate, and it may be uneven across sectors. A 2023 survey of bank employees found that only 21% of those surveyed believed AI will replace many jobs in the banking industry, while 75% believe AI will change the nature of jobs but not replace human workers.[157] A slightly higher but similar number of global banking chief executives expect generative AI, in particular, to lead to a reduction of at least 5% in headcount in 2024.[158] Academic reports and empirical reviews also find that some financial services companies—such as asset management, in particular—have experienced job cuts and are likely to experience the largest number of job cuts in the near future.[159]

Conclusion

As financial industry policymakers focus their attention on AI/ML in finance, they face competing pressures. Certain financial service providers and technology companies will tout the potential for AI/ML to lower costs,

---

[155] William Shaw, "Wall Street Banks Are Poaching Rival AI Talent," *Bloomberg*, November 28, 2023, https://fortune.com/2023/11/28/goldman-sachs-ai-employees-wall-street/.

[156] Joy Macknight, "Why Talent Is Critical to the AI Revolution," *The Banker*, June 27, 2023, https://www.thebanker.com/Why-talent-is-critical-to-the-AI-revolution-1687855797. This article uses the term *banks*, *financial institutions*, and *payment providers* when discussing this topic.

[157] Claire Williams, "Will the Uncertainty Continue for Financial Institutions?," *American Banker*, December 13, 2023, https://www.americanbanker.com/research-report/will-the-uncertainty-continue-for-financial-institutions. Respondents to the survey were 65% banks or credit unions. The remaining 35% were fintechs, tech vendors, payments companies, and other companies.

[158] Sam Fleming, "Generative Artificial intelligence Will Lead to Job Cuts This Year, CEOs Say," *Financial Times*, January 15, 2024, https://www.ft.com/content/908e5465-0bc4-4de5-89cd-8d5349645dda.

[159] Bartram, Branke, and Motahari, "Artificial Intelligence in Asset Management," p. 2. In 2017, asset manager BlackRock announced a restructuring in which it eliminated roles of key stock pickers, choosing to replace them with algorithms and other models. See Amie Tsang, "Morning Agenda: The Robots Are Coming … for Your Stocks," *New York Times*, March 29, 2017, https://www.nytimes.com/2017/03/29/business/dealbook/blackrock-fink-stocks-trading.html.

increase speed and accessibility, and improve accuracy and regulatory compliance. Consumer advocates and smaller firms may oppose adoption on the grounds that it introduces bias, risk, and potential for manipulation; eliminates jobs; and is unaffordable. Policymakers may decide to balance these competing priorities while assessing whether the existing regulatory structure is sufficient or whether one that is more closely tailored to the technological capacities of the evolving technology is necessary. Any legislative proposals considered by Congress will be evaluated by industry and consumers on whether it will lead to fair outcomes, not dampen the environment for innovation, and be based on quantifiable concerns but adaptable to future technology.

Disclaimer

Chapter 6

Automation, Artificial Intelligence, and Machine Learning in Consumer Lending*

Cheryl R. Cooper

Abstract

Financial firms may use algorithms—pre-coded sets of instructions and calculations that are executed automatically—to enhance *consumer loan underwriting*, the process of evaluating the likelihood that applicants will make timely loan repayments. Lenders may rely upon forms of automated analysis to help decide whether to offer consumers loans and at what terms. Faster computing power, internet-based products, and cheaper data storage at scale have increased the prevalence of algorithms. This In Focus discusses developments in automated decisionmaking, artificial intelligence (AI), and machine learning (ML) in consumer loan underwriting. First, it focuses on market developments, then it discusses the current regulatory framework, then finally, it highlights selected policy issues.

Market Developments

Since the 1970s, consumer loan underwriting has become more automated, first with the increasing use of credit scores and more recently with new data and technologies. Credit scores are a (numeric) metric calculated with information in consumer credit reports and prepared for lenders to determine

* This is an edited, reformatted and augmented version of Congressional Research Service, Publication No. IF12399, dated May 10, 2023.

In: Artificial Intelligence
Editor: Sonja Buckley
ISBN: 979-8-89530-859-2

the likelihood of loan default. New technological innovations have been used to update automated processes, in some cases beyond traditional numeric credit scores. For example, for some lenders, the internet has been incorporated to accept applications, and new data sources are used to conduct consumer loan underwriting. *Alternative data* generally refers to information that may be used to determine a consumer's creditworthiness that the national credit reporting agencies—Equifax, Experian, and TransUnion—have not traditionally used when calculating credit scores for consumers. Further, AI and ML technologies have advanced rapidly in recent decades. AI technologies are computerized systems that work and react in ways commonly thought to require intelligence, such as solving complex problems in real-world situations. ML is often referred to as a subfield of AI with algorithms designed to automatically improve their performance through experience with little or no human input.

These technological developments potentially allow for greater speed, accuracy, and confidence in loan decisions. They are currently used more frequently in *fintech* products than in more traditional consumer lending products, particularly ML models and alternative data. *Fintech* (short for *financial technology*) refers to advances in technology incorporated into financial products and services. Many companies—both traditional financial firms and new technology-focused entrants to the market—are developing fintech products, making it a subject of increased interest for the public and policymakers.

ML Models in Consumer Loan Underwriting

Consumer loan underwriting can potentially be enhanced by ML models. ML models could improve efficiency and performance and reduce costs for financial institutions, potentially expanding credit access or making credit less expensive for some consumers. ML models could make consumer underwriting decisions more accurate by identifying new patterns, such as changing credit conditions, and by automatically updating the models to make more accurate underwriting assessments.

However, ML models can also introduce risks. One risk is a lack of *explainability*, the inability to explain why programs make particular decisions. Another risk is *dynamic updating*, which is when models evolve over time without oversight. ML models also raise concerns that they may not perform as intended, possibly resulting in higher loan losses in new market environments or discrimination against protected groups.

Current Federal Regulatory Framework

The Consumer Financial Protection Bureau (CFPB) is the primary consumer protection regulator for consumer financial products and services. One of the CFPB's statutory objectives is to ensure that "markets for consumer financial products and services operate transparently and efficiently to facilitate access and innovation." The CFPB has the authority in consumer financial markets to write regulations and enforce the law for both bank and nonbank financial institutions. However, the CFPB's supervisory authority to examine financial institutions for consumer protection compliance varies based on the charters, activities, and size of institutions. Therefore, financial regulators may monitor some nonbank fintech companies less than traditional banks.

Regulatory Uncertainty

Many financial laws and regulations that existed prior to recent ML technological developments have led to questions concerning their effectiveness achieving their designed policy goals as these potentially beneficial technologies evolve. Relevant laws and regulations may need to be reconsidered or updated in response to the future use of ML models in consumer loan underwriting. This often involves balancing efforts to encourage innovation while protecting consumers.

Federal financial regulators have been monitoring ML models in consumer lending. In March 2021, the bank and credit union regulators, along with the CFPB, requested information on financial institutions' use of AI, including ML models. In April 2023, the CFPB, along with other federal agencies, published a joint statement emphasizing that existing legal authorities still apply to automated systems and AI.

Consequently, some financial institutions, particularly many banks or other highly regulated parts of the financial system, may choose not to use ML models to approve or reject applicants for consumer credit, even if they are more accurate or efficient, due to regulatory uncertainty and compliance risks.

Policy Issues

The use of ML algorithms in credit underwriting has raised a number of policy issues of interest for financial regulators and Congress.

ML Models and Explainability Concerns

The ability of regulators or other outside parties to understand what an ML program did, and why, may be limited or nonexistent. This poses a significant challenge for companies using ML programs to ensure that they will produce outcomes that comply with applicable laws and regulations.

When a lender denies a loan application, the lender must send an adverse action notice to the applicant explaining the reason for the denial. Some question how well lenders will understand and be able to explain the reasons for adverse actions resulting from ML algorithms. To address this issue, some observers assert that regulators should set standards for how ML programs are developed, tested, and monitored, although debate exists about what these standards should include. Concerns exist about ML model fairness; the ability to provide more algorithm transparency; and developing processes to assess ML models, for example, for fairness, reliability, privacy, and security. In May 2022, the CFPB issued guidance clarifying that lenders using "complex algorithms" still need to comply with adverse action notice requirements.

Algorithmic Bias and Fair Lending

Consumer loan underwriting models using ML can introduce fair lending risks due to biases in data or model development. ML models may have training data biases, which is when a model has biases due to the limited or flawed dataset it was developed on. Historical data can reflect historical biases, potentially creating models that discriminate against protected classes. In addition, alternative data may include proxies for protected classes that might also bias ML models.

The Equal Credit Opportunity Act (ECOA; 15 U.S.C. §§1691-1691f) generally prohibits discrimination in credit transactions based upon certain protected classes, including sex, race, color, national origin, religion, marital status, age, and "because all or part of the applicant's income derives from any public assistance program." Questions exist about how lenders can comply with ECOA and other fair lending laws when using ML models for loan underwriting.

Underserved Consumers and Access to Credit

In the United States, robust consumer credit markets allow most consumers to access financial services and credit products to meet their needs in traditional financial markets. However, consumers who have difficulty entering the traditional credit reporting system face challenges accessing many consumer credit products, because lenders are unable to assess their creditworthiness. Limited credit history is correlated with age, income, race, and ethnicity, and many of these consumers are young.

Automated underwriting and ML models may expand credit access or make credit less expensive for some consumers. In particular, these technologies may increase financial inclusion for younger consumers, who may be more likely to have limited credit histories in the credit reporting system.

Data Privacy, Security, and Transparency

In credit underwriting, ML models often access sensitive consumer financial data, and the increase in digital data collection raises greater privacy and cybersecurity concerns. These data practices raise questions over what consumer information is appropriate to collect and use for loan underwriting.

Laws such as the Fair Credit Reporting Act (FCRA; 15 U.S.C. §1681) and the Gramm-Leach-Bliley Act (GLBA; P.L. 106-102) impose requirements on firms that use consumer data for credit underwriting. As data use in consumer financial services has grown, some have debated whether the scope of these laws should be expanded.

CRS Resources

CRS Report R47475, Consumer Finance and Financial Technology (Fintech), coordinated by Cheryl R. Cooper.

CRS Report R46795, Artificial Intelligence: Background, Selected Issues, and Policy Considerations, by Laurie A. Harris.

CRS In Focus IF11630, Alternative Data in Financial Services, by Cheryl R. Cooper.

CRS Report R44125, Consumer Credit Reporting, Credit Bureaus, Credit Scoring, and Related Policy Issues, by Cheryl R. Cooper and Darryl E. Getter.

CRS In Focus IF10031, Introduction to Financial Services: The Consumer Financial Protection Bureau (CFPB), by Cheryl R. Cooper and David H. Carpenter.

CRS In Focus IF11195, Financial Innovation: Reducing Fintech Regulatory Uncertainty, by David W. Perkins, Cheryl R. Cooper, and Eva Su.

Disclaimer

Chapter 7

The Macroeconomic Effects of Artificial Intelligence*

Lida R. Weinstock
and Paul Tierno

Abstract

While various forms of artificial intelligence (AI) technologies have existed and been used for decades, the recent popularization of AI products such as ChatGPT have spurred further research and debate about how these technologies could impact the economy. AI potentially has wide-ranging uses in the production of goods and services, which could affect the macroeconomy through the labor market, productivity growth, and economic growth, to name a few. However, whether AI will prove to be as economically transformational as some suggest remains to be seen and will depend on a number of complex factors.

Members of Congress are increasingly interested in AI, including its economic impacts. For example, the House announced a bipartisan task force on AI in February 2024.

* This is an edited, reformatted and augmented version of Congressional Research Service, Publication No. IF12762, dated September 12, 2024.

In: Artificial Intelligence
Editor: Sonja Buckley
ISBN: 979-8-89530-859-2

What Is Artificial Intelligence?

AI is a broad term referring to algorithms and techniques that aim to give computer systems the ability to learn new concepts or tasks and to reason and solve complex problems in a manner that mimics human intelligence.

Machine learning (ML) is generally considered a subfield of AI focused on developing systems that can learn (i.e., optimize model parameters) from data without explicit programming. AI/ML is not one thing, such as a discrete computer application, nor is it one technology. Instead, it is a group of systems that is defined in part by the type of information used to train the model and the amount of involvement provided by human trainers.

The suite of AI products in the spotlight since late 2022 are "generative AI" tools. *Generative AI* refers to AI systems that can generate content—such as written material, art, or computer code—from prompts using advanced techniques that helps models better understand how data elements influence and depend on one another. While proponents of the technology believe it can transform delivery of services in industries that rely on both general and specialized knowledge alike, it has also raised concerns of misuse by bad actors and misrepresentation in the form of "deep fakes," among others.

AI Adoption and Diffusion

The effects of AI on the economy largely depend on the extent of AI use. The overall adoption of AI by businesses to this point has been limited. According to the Census Business Trends and Outlook Survey (BTOS), the number of businesses using AI rose from 3.7% in September 2023 to 5.4% in February 2024. Further, as shown in Figure 1, adoption across sectors has varied widely. The information sector's usage of AI (18.1%) far surpasses usage in other sectors, but it nonetheless still indicates that a majority of information sector businesses are not yet using AI.

That use of AI has been somewhat limited does not necessarily indicate that it will remain so. In February 2024, businesses indicated an expected rate of AI use at 6.6% by fall 2024, an increase from earlier in the year. Other estimates indicate that certain types of AI—such as large language models, which underpin many generative AI tools—could be adopted by a large swath of businesses.

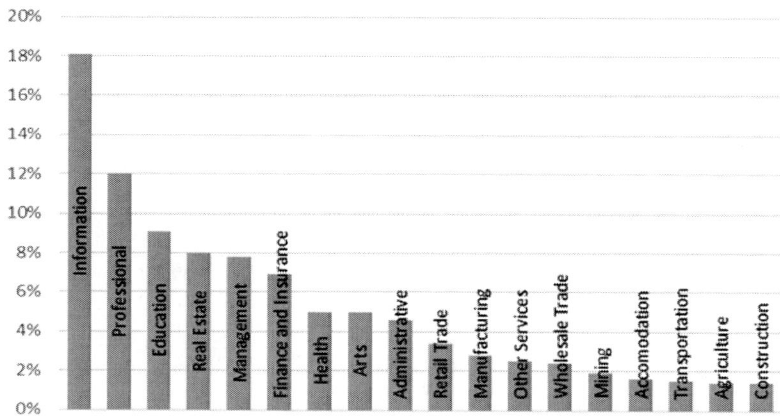

Source: Census Business Trends and Outlook Survey (BTOS).
Notes: Sector names have been shortened for brevity.

Figure 1. Sector Usage of AI; Selected Two-Week Period from February 2024 Survey.

One projection of future private U.S. investment in AI also indicates growth to $81.7 billion in 2025 from $47.4 billion in 2022. How much usage would be necessary to create structural shifts in the economy is uncertain, although the effects to this point appear somewhat limited.

Further, just because a technology has the capacity for use does not necessarily indicate that it will be used quickly and broadly across economic activity or at all. The diffusion of past technologies has varied widely. According to the Federal Reserve Bank of St. Louis, the diffusion of AI appears to be following a pattern similar to personal computers or cloud computing, which were adopted slowly over multiple decades. The extent to which AI use becomes ubiquitous in the workplace is uncertain, but current evidence suggests that workplace use of roughly 40% or more could take over a decade. As such, the effects of AI on the economy may be relatively small for the time being but may grow over time.

AI and the Labor Market

Questions around how technologies may cause structural labor market shifts are long-standing. In the past, some economists voiced concerns about the extent to which automation could replace jobs, such as in manufacturing.

Today, similar questions are being asked with regards to AI. As shown in Table 1, BTOS data indicate that while businesses that use AI report it replacing some number of tasks, employment effects in either direction are relatively small. This indicates that, as used currently, AI is not replacing workers on average. However, businesses report expectations that AI will have a growing impact on firm employment. Nonetheless, as has happened in past episodes of technological change, AI may result in a changing mix of available jobs, including the creation of new ones but not fewer total jobs in the long run.

Table 1. AI effects in the workplace; responses from February 2024 survey

	Six Months Prior to Survey	Six Months After Survey
Responses to "Number of Tasks Replaced by AI?"		
"Small Number"	84.6%	79.2%
"Moderate Number"	13.0%	17.7%
"Large Number"	2.4%	3.1%
Responses to "Effects of AI on Firm Employment?"		
"Increase"	2.8%	6.5%
"Decrease"	2.6%	6.1%
"No Change"	94.6%	87.4%

Source: BTOS.

Notes: Questions asked only to firms that responded affirmatively to using AI.

Potential Effects on Productivity

Economists generally agree that the main avenue by which AI is likely to affect the economy is labor productivity.

Many estimates suggest that AI can affect task productivity notably, although these effects may differ across skill levels. In general, studies tend to conclude that the use of AI increases task productivity and performance, although some studies have found that errors made by AI can be counterproductive. How total labor productivity may be affected by AI is harder to estimate, because it depends, in part, on how many and what types of tasks use AI. Goldman Sachs estimates that if 25% of total work tasks are automated by generative AI, labor productivity would increase 15%.

AI also has the potential to impact total factor productivity (TFP), which accounts for the impact of technological growth. If the adoption of AI results in an increased pace of research and development, this would increase the growth rate of TFP and long-run economic growth. One study suggests that in the short run (10 years), the effects of AI on TFP would be a roughly 0.53% cumulative increase.

AI and Economic Growth

Productivity growth is an important determinant of long-term economic growth and income. Gains in productivity allow for the more efficient production of goods and services, thereby increasing the productive capacity of the economy. Estimates of the effects of AI on U.S. gross domestic product (GDP) in the short and long run vary but are typically positive. The Goldman Sachs study estimates that this productivity increase could result in an up to 0.9% cumulative increase in GDP over the same time frame.

When considering the longer run, more questions arise: How many and what types of new tasks will AI create in addition to automating existing ones? Will AI-based tasks become more advanced and therefore harder to learn? Will AI adoption be even across sectors or types of tasks? How will short-run effects of AI and policy decisions in the coming years affect future economic and policy responses? One study suggests that the effects of AI on GDP in the long run could vary substantially based on a number of factors, including which industries AI adoption is concentrated in and whether or not productivity gains from AI adoption are expected. The study suggests that GDP could rise to about 35% above baseline in the long run but could be much smaller depending on the scenario.

AI and Inequality

Owing to the expected effects on productivity growth, AI has the potential to increase total income in the economy. However, this does not mean that all economic actors will benefit. For example, in recent decades, productivity gains from technological innovation have largely been concentrated among high-income, skilled workers. It is not clear whether AI use would have a similar effect.

On the one hand, evidence has suggested that within certain types of work, lower-skilled workers may benefit more from AI. For example, in a recent study the authors conducted an experiment in which customer support agents of varying experience and skill level used an AI-based conversational assistant. On average, this use of AI increased productivity significantly more for those with less experience or lower skill levels than for more experienced, higher-skilled workers. Thus, AI could potentially normalize outcomes across workers within businesses, in theory resulting in equalizing productivity and wages.

On the other hand, AI is expected to generally produce higher productivity gains for higher income and skilled workers. For example, some research suggests that productivity gains from large language models could be significantly larger for higher-income workers.

Policy Considerations

A plethora of policy questions arises from the adoption and use of AI in the production process. Many of the most frequently asked questions involve labor market outcomes, as evidenced by recent House Oversight and Accountability Committee and Joint Economic Committee hearings on AI and the labor market. Questions often consider whether AI could structurally change the nature of work and, if so, how the costs and benefits of such a change might be distributed. Congress may wish to consider policies that would either prevent or mitigate changes to the labor market or otherwise provide assistance to those workers who are fully or partially displaced once any changes do take effect.

Disclaimer

Chapter 8

Artificial Intelligence in the Biological Sciences: Uses, Safety, Security, and Oversight*

Todd Kuiken

Abstract

Artificial intelligence (AI) is a term generally thought of as computerized systems that work and react in ways commonly thought to require intelligence. AI technologies, methodologies, and applications can be used throughout the biological sciences and biology R&D, including in engineering biology (e.g., the application of engineering principles and the use of systematic design tools to reprogram cellular systems for a specific functional output). This has enabled research and development (R&D) advances across multiple application areas and industries. For example, AI can be used to analyze genomic data (e.g., DNA sequences) to determine the genetic basis of a particular trait and potentially uncover genetic markers linked with those traits. It has also been used in combination with biological design tools to aid in characterizing proteins (e.g., 3-D structure) and for designing new chemical structures that can enable specific medical applications, including for drug discovery. AI can also be used across the scientific R&D process, including the design of laboratory experiments, protocols to run certain laboratory equipment, and other "de-skilling" aspects of scientific research. The convergence of AI and other technologies associated with biology can lower technical and knowledge barriers and increase the number of actors with certain capabilities. These capabilities have potential for beneficial uses while at the same time raising certain biosafety and biosecurity concerns. For

* This is an edited, reformatted and augmented version of Congressional Research Service, Publication No. R47849, dated November 22, 2023.

In: Artificial Intelligence
Editor: Sonja Buckley
ISBN: 979-8-89530-859-2

example, some have argued that using AI for biological design can be repurposed or misused to potentially produce biological and chemical compounds of concern.

Both AI and engineering biology are multidisciplinary fields that build on advances in multiple scientific disciplines and technical developments that each have associated benefits and risks. As they converge, those benefits and risks may compound and create unique uncertainties, challenge governance systems, and, in some instances, raise new biosafety and biosecurity concerns. The U.S. Intelligence Community's 2023 Annual Threat Assessment stated that the fields of AI and biotechnology are "being developed and are proliferating faster than companies and governments can shape norms, protect privacy, and prevent dangerous outcomes." AI's use in biology sits within a broader debate on how best to manage biosafety and biosecurity, including whether that use may lower technical and knowledge barriers and increase the likelihood of malign use. The potential for the use of AI in conjunction with biological design and other types of scientific research and experimentation has prompted recommendations from various groups on how to prevent the misuse of AI applications in biology and science more broadly. These include keeping a human "in the loop," controlling access to DNA sequences and synthesis capabilities, and governance mechanisms that restrict, or monitor, who can access certain AI applications and biological design tools. Numerous bills introduced in the 118th Congress address the risks, benefits, and strategic competitiveness of AI more generally, while H.R. 4704, S. 2399, and S. 2346 focus more specifically on AI and biological threats. Other policy considerations for Congress could include the following:

- Whether AI, and its use in biology and other scientific fields, should be regulated broadly across all use cases and areas of development, regulated on a case-by-case basis focused on particular application areas or end-use products, or whether current biosafety and biosecurity oversight frameworks are sufficient.
- Whether a broad risk management approach examining the R&D system as a whole is most appropriate, including at what stage oversight is warranted (e.g., basic research stage, prototype stage, or prior to release of a final product) and what entity might conduct such oversight (e.g., a federal agency or a system of self-governance incentives).
- Whether to provide an agency (or agencies) authority to conduct oversight of various aspects of AI, create a new agency with authority over AI, or authorize agencies under current law to enforce certain oversight responsibilities. Authorizing agencies

under current law may require additional coordination amongst federal agencies in order to establish oversight responsibilities. Other types of self-governance incentives could also be examined.

Oversight and governance of the use of AI in the biological sciences involves potential benefits and risks associated with the biological design capabilities of AI models, as well as the feasibility of producing AI generated designs that pose possible biosecurity risks. Regulating AI broadly, or the use of AI in one area of R&D, could impact other areas of R&D in specific or unintended ways. For example, limiting access to AI models, restricting the types of data an AI model may be trained on, or limiting the capabilities an AI model is allowed to execute, could each impact a biological design tool's capability.

Introduction[1]

Artificial Intelligence (AI) technologies, methodologies, and applications can be used throughout the biological sciences and biology R&D. AI can generally be thought of as a multidisciplinary field that studies and develops machines that work and react in ways commonly thought to require intelligence, such as the ability to learn, solve problems, and achieve goals under uncertain and varying conditions, with varying levels of autonomy. AI is not one thing; rather, AI systems can encompass a range of technologies, methodologies, and applications, such as natural language processing, robotics, and facial recognition. Common terms used in the field of AI include machine learning (ML), deep learning (DL), and neural networks (NN). ML is an umbrella term for training computer systems to solve complex problems normally requiring human intelligence, such as predictions, classification, and association, using a large amount of data, computer algorithms, statistical models, and other computing techniques.[2] DL is a subset of ML, using techniques such as multi-layer neural networks to improve the performance and accuracy of problem-solving, for example, in image recognition. An NN represents a set of

---

[1] For a general introduction to AI and policy considerations, see CRS Report R47644, *Artificial Intelligence: Overview, Recent Advances, and Considerations for the 118th Congress*, by Laurie A. Harris.

[2] Adapted from Erik Brynjolfsson, Tom Mitchell, and Daniel Rock, "What Can Machines Learn, and What Does It Mean for Occupations and the Economy?," AEA Papers and Proceedings, vol. 108 (May 1, 2018), pp. 43-47, https://dspace.mit.edu/bitstream/handle/1721.1/120302/pandp.20181019.pdf.

algorithms and techniques that process data and extract information at multiple layers of computational nodes, based on the idea of how neurons in a nervous system signal to one another. It can be as simple as a single layer with a few nodes, or complex, containing many layers with millions of nodes. See Figure 1.

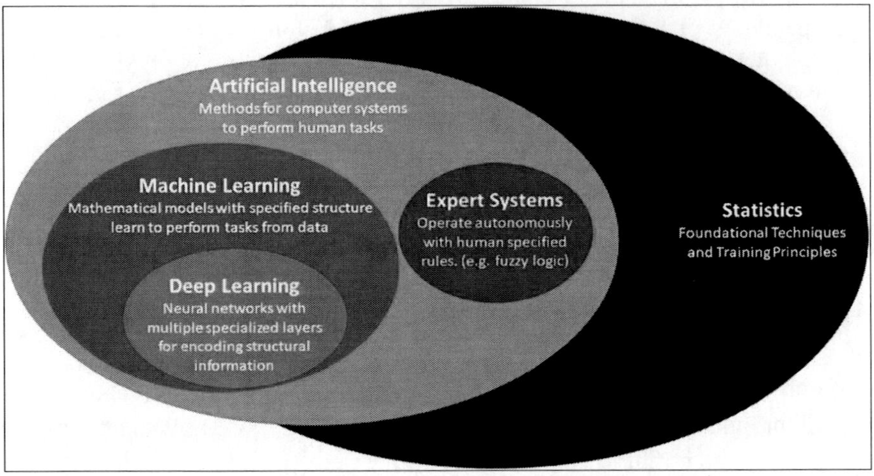

Source: Sue Ellen Haupt, David John Gagne, and William W. Hsieh, et al., "The History and Practice of AI in the Environmental Sciences," *Bulletin of the American Meteorological Society*, vol. 103, no. 5 (2022). © American Meteorological Society. Used with permission.

Figure 1. Relationship Between AI, ML, DL, Expert Systems, and Statistics.

Machine learning has been used in the biological sciences, and science in general, for some time.[3] AI's ability to process large amounts of raw, unstructured data (e.g., DNA sequence data) has reduced the time and cost to conduct certain experiments in biology, enabled others types of experiments that previously were unattainable,[4] and contributed to the broader field of engineering biology. There is no universally agreed definition of engineering biology, but it is generally thought of as the application of engineering principles and the use of systematic design tools to enable the reprogramming of cellular systems at the genetic level for a specific functional output.[5] This

[3] Joe G. Greener, Shaun M. Kandathil, and Lewis Moffat, et al., "A Guide to Machine Learning for Biologists," *Nature Reviews Molecular Cell Biology*, vol. 23 (2022).

[4] Abhaya Bhardwaj, Shristi Kishore, and Dhananjay K. Pandey, "Artificial Intelligence in Biological Sciences," *Life*, vol. 12, no. 1430 (2022).

[5] CRS Report R47265, *Synthetic/Engineering Biology: Issues for Congress*, by Todd Kuiken.

approach has increased human ability to make direct changes at the cellular level and create novel genetic material (e.g., DNA and RNA) to obtain specific functions.

Engineering biology is a multidisciplinary field that leverages a broad set of sciences and technologies.[6] Additionally, engineering biology relies on and builds upon advances in other fields such as nanotechnology, robotics, and, increasingly, artificial intelligence (see Figure 2).[7]

These technologies enable engineering biology researchers to read and write DNA. For example, sequencing technologies "read" DNA, while gene synthesis technologies can take sequence data and "write" DNA, turning the data into physical material which can then be designed or engineered for different purposes. Other terms such as synthetic biology, biotechnology, and biological sciences are used interchangeably with engineering biology in this report when discussed in relation to AI.

Policy concerns have been raised that the use of AI in the biological sciences could be repurposed or misused. For example, as part of a recent study, an AI model for drug development was retrained to design molecules for toxicity instead of designing against them. The study reported that in less than six hours the AI model generated 40,000 molecules that scored within their desired threshold of toxicity and bioactivity, which included the nerve agent VX, other known chemical warfare agents, and new molecules that were predicted to have even higher toxicities.[8]

This report focuses on the use of AI in the biological sciences, particularly engineering biology and biological design, as well as some aspects of laboratory automation and design. Biological design tools can be described as the tools and methods that enable the design and understanding of biological processes (e.g., DNA sequences/synthesis or the design of novel organisms). Such capabilities have potential positive impacts but at the same time raise certain biosafety and biosecurity concerns. AI may also have impacts on other

[6] Kent Redford, Thomas Brooks, and Nicholas Macfarlane, et al., *Genetic Frontiers for Conservation: An Assessment of Synthetic Biology and Biodiversity Conservation*, IUCN, Technical Assessment, Gland, Switzerland, 2019. National Academies of Sciences, Engineering, and Medicine, *Biodefense in the Age of Synthetic Biology*, Washington, DC, 2018, https://doi.org/10.17226/24890.

[7] Arlindo L. Oliveira, "Biotechnology, Big Data and Artificial Intelligence," *Biotechnology Journal*, vol. 14, no. 1800613 (2019).

[8] Fabio Urbina, Filippa Lentzos, and Cédric Invernizzi, et al., "Dual Use of Artificial-Intelligence-Powered Drug Discovery," *Nature Machine Intelligence*, vol. 4 (2022).

fields of science, but those are beyond the scope of this report.[9] The report aims to inform Congress as it considers potential oversight of AI, either generally, or for specific scientific application areas.

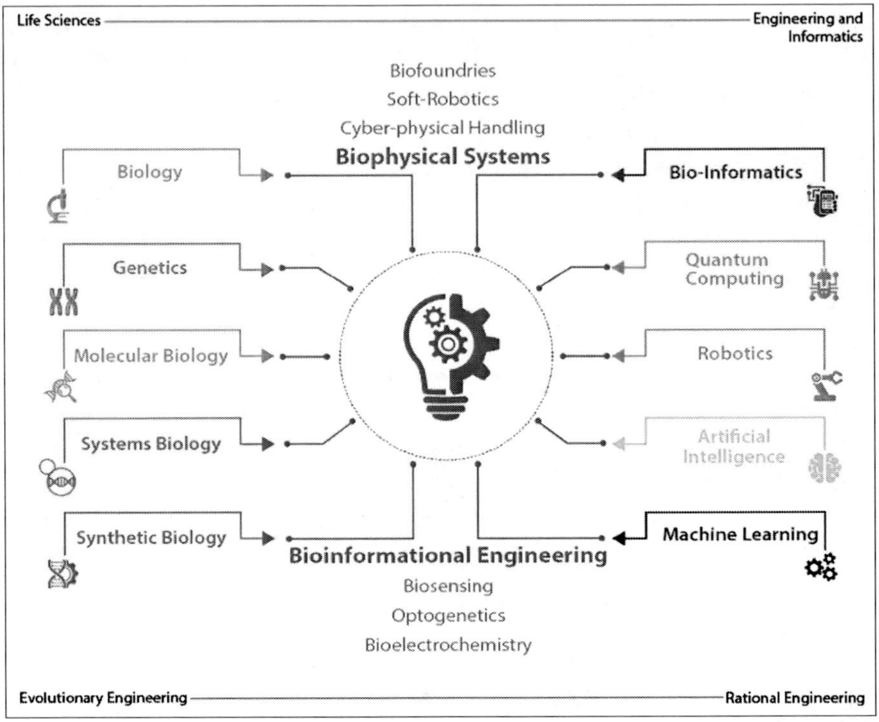

Source: Thomas A. Dixon, Paul S. Freemont, and Richard A. Johnson, et al., "A Global Forum on Synthetic Biology: The Need for International Engagement," *Nature Communications*, vol. 13, no. 3516 (2022).

Note: Machine learning is typically considered a subfield of AI, but is a specific tool used in engineering biology.

Figure 2. Associated Sciences and Technologies Enabling Engineering Biology.

[9] For examples on how AI is impacting other areas of science, see "How Scientists Are Using Artificial Intelligence," *The Economist*, 2023, https://www.economist.com/science-and-technology/2023/09/13/how-scientists-are-using-artificial-intelligence.

Convergence of AI and Biological Design

AI and the biological sciences have increasingly converged, each building upon the other's capabilities to enable new research and development across multiple areas (see Figure 3).[10] The CEO and cofounder of DeepMind, an AI subsidiary of Google, recently said of biology:

> At its most fundamental level, I think biology can be thought of as an information processing system, albeit an extraordinarily complex and dynamic one. Just as mathematics turned out to be the right description language for physics, biology may turn out to be the perfect type of regime for the application of AI.[11]

Both AI and engineering biology are multidisciplinary fields that rely on and build upon advances in other scientific disciplines and technology fields, such as nanotechnology, robotics, and increasingly big data (e.g., genetic sequence data). Each of these fields is itself a convergence of multiple sciences and technologies, so their impacts can combine to create new capabilities and concerns.[12] For example, each technology and scientific field in Figure 2 has individual benefits and risks. As they converge, those benefits and risks can layer upon one another or create unique opportunities as well as uncertainties that may challenge governance systems, and, in some instances, raise new biosafety and biosecurity concerns not present in the individual fields considered separately.

The U.S. Intelligence Community's 2023 Annual Threat Assessment stated that the fields of AI and biotechnology are "being developed and are proliferating faster than companies and governments can shape norms, protect privacy, and prevent dangerous outcomes."[13] The report went on to identify genomic sequence data as a particular area of interest, pointing toward efforts by countries, universities, and private companies that have created, or are

---

[10] Abhaya Bhardwaj, Shristi Kishore, and Dhananjay K. Pandey, "Artificial Intelligence in Biological Sciences," *Life*, vol. 12, no. 1430 (2022).

[11] Demis Hassabis, quoted in Rob Toews, "The Next Frontier for Large Language Models Is Biology," *Forbes*, July 16, 2023, https://www.forbes.com/sites/robtoews/2023/07/16/the-next-frontier-for-large-language-models-is-biology/.

[12] John T. O'Brien and Cassidy Nelson, "Assessing the Risks Posed by the Convergence of Artificial Intelligence and Biotechnology," *Health Security*, vol. 18, no. 3 (2020).

[13] Office of the Director of National Intelligence, *Annual Threat Assessment of the U.S. Intelligence Community*, 2023, https://www.dni.gov/files/ODNI/documents/assessments/ATA-2023-Unclassified-Report.pdf.

creating, centralized databases to collect, store, process, and analyze genetic data. The report further identified China's efforts to collect U.S. health and genomic data through its acquisitions of and investments in U.S. companies, as well as through cyberattacks. This analysis followed a 2021 assessment by the National Counterintelligence and Security Center suggesting that China understands that the collection and analysis of large genomic data sets from diverse populations can help foster new medical discoveries and cures with substantial commercial value, and can advance its AI and precision medicine industries.[14]

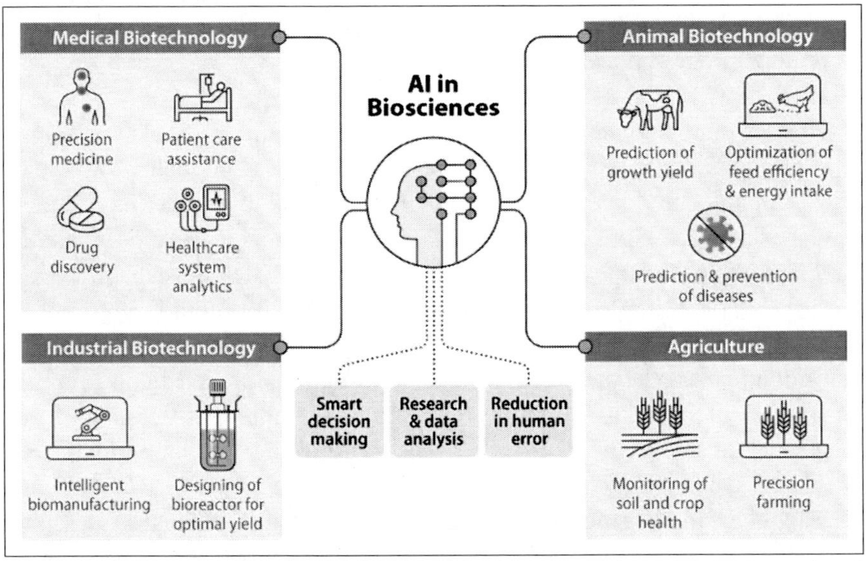

Source: CRS, adapted from Abhaya Bhardwaj, Shristi Kishore, and Dhananjay K. Pandey, "Artificial Intelligence in Biological Sciences," *Life*, vol. 12, no. 1430 (2022).

Figure 3. Example Application Areas Where AI and Biological Sciences Converge.

[14] National Counterintelligence and Security Center, *China's Collection of Genomic and Other Healthcare Data from America: Risks to Privacy and U.S. Economic and National Security*, 2021, https://www.dni.gov/files/NCSC/ documents/SafeguardingOurFuture/NCSC_China_Genomics_Fact_Sheet_2021revision20210203.pdf.

Importance of AI Related to Genetic Sequence Data and Biological Design

Some experts have suggested that AI is essential to analyzing the exponential growth of genetic sequence data.[15] According to the National Security Commission on Artificial Intelligence, "AI will be essential to fully understanding how genetic code interacts with biological processes."[16] AI has the ability to process large amounts of biological data (e.g., genetic sequence data), which can come from different biological sources. That capability is needed to understand complex biological systems[17] and has become a necessity for certain biological research, such as engineering biology.[18] For example, researchers can use AI to analyze genomic data sets to determine the genetic basis of a particular trait and potentially uncover genetic markers linked with that trait.[19] Different types of biological data can be utilized by AI and biological design tools: sequence data, molecular structure data, image data, time-series, and omics data.[20] See Figure 4. A limiting factor, however, is the quality and quantity of the biological data (e.g., DNA sequences) that the AI system is trained on.[21] For example, accurate identification of a

---

[15] Zulema Udaondo, "Big Data and Computational Advancements for Next Generation of Microbial Biotechnology," *Microbial Biotechnology*, vol. 15, no. 1 (2022); Wardah S. Alharbi and Mamoon Rashid, "A Review of Deep Learning Applications in Human Genomics Using Next-Generation Sequencing Data," *Human Genomics*, vol. 16, no. 26 (2022).

[16] National Security Commission on Artificial Intelligence, *Final Report*, 2021, https://www.nscai.gov/2021-final-report/.

[17] Abhaya Bhardwaj, Shristi Kishore, and Dhananjay K. Pandey, "Artificial Intelligence in Biological Sciences," *Life*, vol. 12, no. 1430 (2022).

[18] Arlindo L. Oliveira, "Biotechnology, Big Data and Artificial Intelligence," *Biotechnology Journal*, vol. 14 (2019).

[19] Abhaya Bhardwaj, Shristi Kishore, and Dhananjay K. Pandey, "Artificial Intelligence in Biological Sciences," *Life*, vol. 12, no. 1430 (2022). A trait is a characteristic of an organism that is expressed by genes.

[20] William A.V. Beardall, Guy-Bart Stan, and Mary J. Dunlop, "Deep Learning Concepts and Applications for Synthetic Biology," *GEN Biotechnology*, vol. 1, no. 4 (2022). Omics data refers to various disciplines in biology whose names end in the suffix -omics, such as genomics, proteomics, metabolomics, etc.

[21] Fausto Artico, Arthur L Edge III, and Kyle Langham, "The Future of Artificial Intelligence for the BioTech Big Data Landscape," *Current Opinion in Biotechnology*, vol. 76 (2022). Training a model refers to providing a model with data to learn from, often called a training dataset. After a model is trained to recognize patterns from one dataset, some models can be provided with new data and still recognize patterns or predict results. Fine-tuning a model refers to training a previously trained model on new data, or otherwise adjusting an existing model. See CRS Report R47569, *Generative Artificial Intelligence and Data Privacy: A Primer*, by Kristen E. Busch.

particular species based on DNA requires reference sequences of sufficient quality to exist and be available. Individual databases have varying standards that govern access, as well as the type and quality of information they contain. The design, management, quality standards, and data protocols for reference databases can therefore affect the utility of a particular DNA sequence and its use with AI.[22]

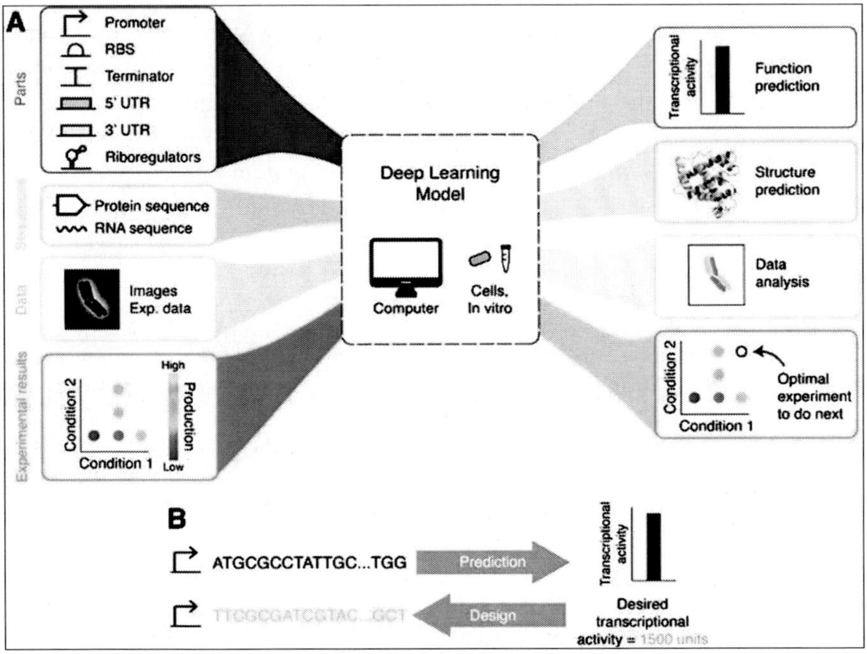

Source: William A.V. Beardall, Guy-Bart Stan, and Mary J. Dunlop, "Deep Learning Concepts and Applications for Synthetic Biology," *GEN Biotechnology*, vol. 1, no. 4 (2022).

Notes: "Parts" is a term used in engineering biology to describe a segment, or sequence, of DNA that encodes for a specific biology function.

Figure 4. Examples of AI Used in Engineering Biology.

Sequencing technologies have evolved rapidly, making it possible to sequence entire genomes more efficiently and at lower cost.[23] Gene synthesis

[22] CRS In Focus IF12285, *eDNA/eRNA: Scientific Value in What's Left Behind*, coordinated by Todd Kuiken.

[23] For additional analysis on genetic sequence data see CRS In Focus IF12356, *Digital Biology: Implications of Genetic Sequencing*, by Todd Kuiken, and CRS In Focus IF12285, *eDNA/eRNA: Scientific Value in What's Left Behind*, coordinated by Todd Kuiken.

technologies can take sequence data and "write" DNA, turning it into physical material which can then be designed or engineered for different purposes. The technologies enabling the ability to both read and write DNA is fundamental to engineering biology.[24]

DNA sequences, including human DNA sequences,[25] are stored in databases, many of which are publicly funded and freely accessible, while others are privately held. The volume of genetic sequence data has grown exponentially as sequencing technology has evolved (see Figure 5 and Figure 6). One analysis identified more than 1,700 databases incorporating data on genomics, protein sequences, protein structures, plants, and metabolic pathways, among others.[26] For example, the Protein Data Bank, a U.S.-funded data center, contains more than a terabyte of three-dimensional structure data for biological molecules, including proteins, DNA, and RNA.[27] While the Protein Data Bank is an open-source public database, other databases can be proprietary. For example, Gingko Bioworks claims to have more than 2 billion protein sequences in its proprietary database.[28] Public research groups can also produce large amounts of genetic sequence data. The Broad Institute claims to produce roughly 500 terabases (trillion bases) of genomic data per month.[29] There is great potential value in the aggregate volume of genetic datasets that can be collectively mined to discover and characterize relationships among genes.

The U.S. National Security Commission on Artificial Intelligence recommended that the U.S. fund and prioritize the development of a biobank containing a "wide range of high-quality biological and genetic data sets

---

[24] DNA is made up of two linked strands that form a double helix. These strands are connected by base pairs consisting of the following bases: Adenine (A), Thymone (T), Cytosine (C), and Guanine (G). A connects with T and C connects with G.

[25] Genetic information is considered health information and protected under the Health Insurance Portability and Accountability Act (HIPAA). For additional information on genetic research, considerations with the use and misuse of genetic information, and relevant laws see CRS Report RL34584, *The Genetic Information Nondiscrimination Act of 2008 (GINA)*, by Amanda K. Sarata.

[26] Arlindo L. Oliveira, "Biotechnology, Big Data and Artificial Intelligence," *Biotechnology Journal*, vol. 14 (2019).

[27] RCSB Protein Data Bank, *About RCSB PDB: Enabling Breakthroughs in Scientific and Biomedical Research and Education*, https://www.rcsb.org/.

[28] Ginkgo Bioworks, "Google and Ginkgo: Foundry-Scale Data Meets AI," press release, 2023, https://www.ginkgobioworks.com/2023/08/29/google-and-ginkgo-foundry-scale-data-meets-ai/.

[29] Broad Institute, *Genomics*, 2023, https://www.broadinstitute.org/genomics.

securely accessible by researchers."[30] The Commission further noted that the establishment of such a database containing a broad range of human, animal, and plant genomes would enhance and democratize biotechnology innovations and facilitate new levels of AI-enabled analysis of genetic data while also reducing U.S. researchers' reliance on foreign access to genomic databases for research.[31]

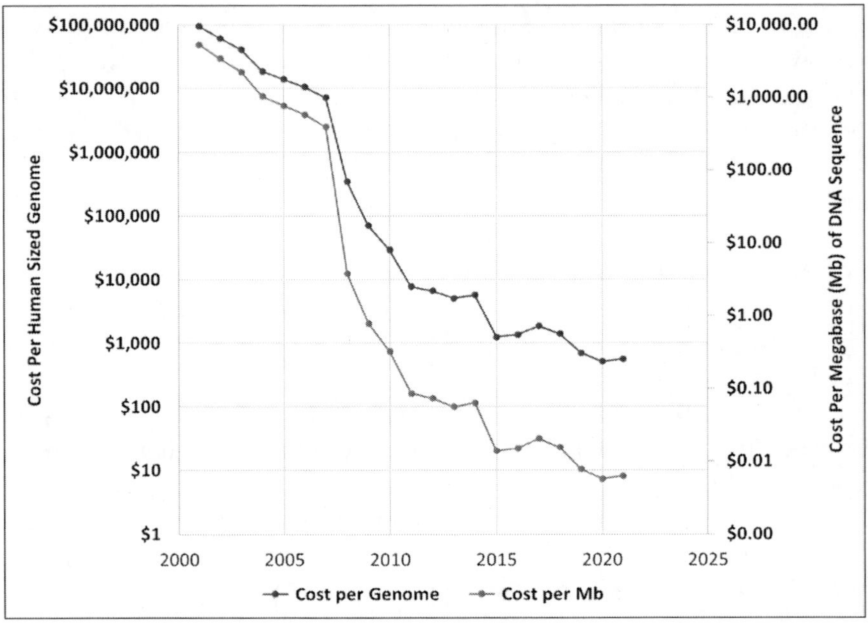

Source: CRS analysis of data from Kris A. Wetterstrand, *DNA Sequencing Costs: Data*, National Institutes of Health, National Human Genome Research Institute, 2023, https://www.genome.gov/about-genomics/fact-sheets/ DNA-Sequencing-Costs-Data.

Notes: The Y-axis is in logarithmic scale. A megabase (Mb) is a unit of measurement for DNA. One megabase = 1 million bases. The cost per genome assumes a genome size of 3,000 Mb.

Figure 5. Cost of DNA Sequencing over Time.

---

30 National Security Commission on Artificial Intelligence, *Final Report*, 2021, https://www.nscai.gov/2021-final-report/.

31 Ibid. For additional information on federal initiatives related to DNA databases see CRS In Focus IF12285, *eDNA/eRNA: Scientific Value in What's Left Behind*, coordinated by Todd Kuiken.

The availability of genetic data to train AI models, as well as decisions about the selection of genetic data for that purpose, can introduce bias. For example, training an AI model on datasets that emphasize or omit certain genetic traits can affect how that information is used and the types of applications developed, potentially privileging or disadvantaging certain populations. In addition, access to data and to AI models themselves may impact communities of differing socioeconomic status or other factors unequally.

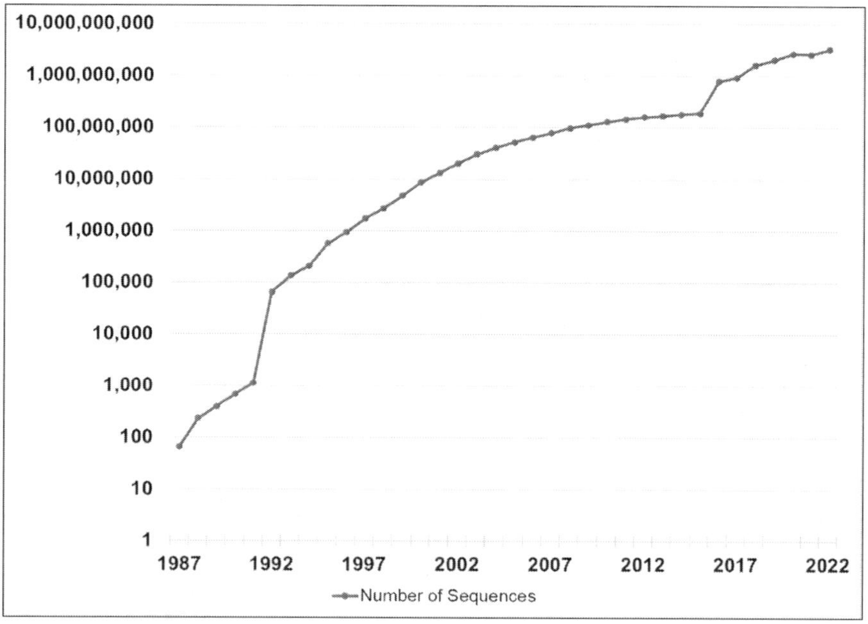

Source: CRS analysis of data from the International Nucleotide Sequence Database Collaboration (INSDC).

Notes: The Y-axis is in logarithmic scale. INSDC includes sequence data from the DNA Data Bank of Japan, the European Nucleotide Archive, and GenBank, the National Institutes of Health genetic sequence database.

Figure 6. Growth of Sequences in the International Nucleotide Sequence Database Collaboration.

AI-Enabled Biological Design Tools

Proteins are responsible for nearly every task of cellular life. Each has a unique amino acid sequence, which are the building blocks of proteins, and a complex three-dimensional physical structure.[32] Predicting the three-dimensional structure of proteins has been the focus of research for more than 50 years, with one of the first research papers on the subject published in 1973.[33] According to one paper, the structures of around 100,000 proteins have been deciphered; however, this is a fraction of the estimated billions of known protein sequences.[34] Despite the increase in genomic sequence data, scientists' ability to determine protein structures and reproduce them experimentally has remained a challenge. Understanding protein structures and how to design new proteins allows researchers to control a protein's stability and biochemical properties that can enable specific medical applications, including drug discovery.[35] The ability to predict protein structures can also impact other areas of biochemical engineering, including the identification of key protein residues and better estimates of optimal kinetic parameters, which are important for drug development.[36]

In 2021, an AI-based program called AlphaFold demonstrated the ability to predict protein structures even when no similar structures are known. The AlphaFold researchers also demonstrated that its predicted structures were accurate when compared to the experimental protein structure (i.e., physical material).[37] The AI system underpinning AlphaFold incorporated both physical and biological knowledge about protein structures and was trained on

---

[32] Clare O'Connor and Jill U. Adams, "Proteins Are Responsible for a Diverse Range of Structural and Catalytic Functions in Cells," in *Essentials of Cell Biology* (Cambridge, MA: NPG Education, 2010).

[33] Christian B. Anfinsen, "Principles That Govern the Folding of Protein Chains," *Science*, vol. 181, no. 4096 (1973).

[34] John Jumper, Richard Evans, and Alexander Pritzel, et al., "Highly Accurate Protein Structure Prediction with AlphaFold," *Nature*, vol. 596 (2021).

[35] Damiano Sgarbossa, Umberto Lupo, and Anne-Florence, "Generative Power of a Protein Language Model Trained on Multiple Sequence Alignments," *eLIfe*, vol. 12, no. e79854 (2023).

[36] Zulema Udaondo, "Big Data and Computational Advancements for Next Generation of Microbial Biotechnology," *Microbial Biotechnology*, vol. 15, no. 1 (2022). Note: Protein residues are individual amino acids that are linked by peptide bonds in the protein chain. Understanding kinetic parameters can be used for the characterization of disease processes and for monitoring treatment effects.

[37] John Jumper, Richard Evans, and Alexander Pritzel, et al., "Highly Accurate Protein Structure Prediction with AlphaFold," *Nature*, vol. 596 (2021).

the Protein Data Bank, a U.S. federally funded open-source data center.[38] Another study in 2022 suggested that AI techniques, specifically deep network hallucination,[39] can be used to design new protein structures that are different from the sequences and structures of naturally occurring proteins.[40]

Research into designing new proteins typically involves protein structures being predicted based on previous protein structures. These predictions then have to be experimentally verified for accuracy (i.e., predicted proteins have to be synthesized and tested, typically in the bacterium *E. coli*).[41] Most such predictions in the past have not been accurate, and the protein in question could not function within a living organism.[42] Recent studies suggest that AI-generated protein structures may be more accurate, which could accelerate protein engineering by reducing the number of inaccurately predicted proteins that need to be tested.

While these and other advances show promise, some argue that determining how to efficiently research and design protein structures with specific functions remains a challenge.[43] Novel AI-generated molecules will still need to be physically synthesized and evaluated to determine whether they are of any practical use or value beyond the theoretical possibility that was predicted by the AI model.[44]

AI-Enabled Laboratory Capabilities

AI-based computer models trained on biological data sets and laboratory experimental procedures could be used to design experiments to optimize specific conditions (e.g., an organism's growth rate). In many engineering and science applications, experiments are conducted and empirical models are

---

[38] RCSB Protein Data Bank, *About RCSB PDB: Enabling Breakthroughs in Scientific and Biomedical Research and Education*, https://www.rcsb.org/.

[39] Hallucination is a term sometimes used to describe the case when an AI model perceives patterns or objects that are nonexistent or imperceptible to human observers. See IBM, "What Are AI Hallucinations?," https://www.ibm.com/ topics/ai-hallucinations.

[40] B. I. M. Wicky et al., "Hallucinating Symmetric Protein Assemblies," *Science*, vol. 378 (2022).

[41] *E. coli* is a bacterium that is used in laboratory experiments to test foreign DNA and their protein products.

[42] John Jumper, Richard Evans, and Alexander Pritzel, et al., "Highly Accurate Protein Structure Prediction with AlphaFold," *Nature*, vol. 596 (2021).

[43] John Ingraham, Max Baranov, and Zak Costello, et al., *Illuminating Protein Space with a Programmable Generative Model*, Generate Biomedicines, 2022.

[44] W. Patrick Walters and Mark Murcko, "Assessing the Impact of Generative AI on Medicinal Chemistry," *Nature Biotechnology*, vol. 38 (2020).

developed with the objective of improving specific responses of interest.[45] These optimization strategies could be combined with generative AI systems,[46] including AI large language models (LLMs) to write computer code instructing laboratory robots to fulfill experimental parameters and run experiments.[47] LLMs are a subset of generative AI and are characterized as "large" due, in part, to the vast amount of data necessary for training the model to learn the rules of language.[48] This approach could eventually include the use of individual desk-top DNA synthesizers to synthesize DNA under the direction of the AI output.[49] For example, one study used LLMs, including GPT-4,[50] to generate robotic scripts from written instructions, which were able to program laboratory robots to complete experiments. The study proposed that "if LLMs can simplify the translation of experimental processes and instructions into precise robotic movements, then the cost of educating life science researchers to use robots can be substantially reduced."[51] The preliminary results suggest that LLMs can interpret and execute tasks at a level similar to a graduate student working under the guidance of a professor. However, generating scripts based on longer instructions remains a challenge. Another study attempted to develop a system, using LLMs, that could be used for autonomous design, planning, and execution of scientific experiments and concluded that the system "demonstrates exceptional reasoning and

---

[45] National Institute of Standards and Technology, *How do you optimize a process*, https://www.itl.nist.gov/div898/ handbook/pri/section5/pri53.htm.

[46] Note: Generative AI systems can generate new content—such as text, images, and videos—through learning patterns from data. See CRS Report R47569, *Generative Artificial Intelligence and Data Privacy: A Primer*, by Kristen E. Busch.

[47] Abhaya Bhardwaj, Shristi Kishore, and Dhananjay K. Pandey, "Artificial Intelligence in Biological Sciences," *Life*, vol. 12, no. 1430 (2022); Adam C. Dama, Kevin S. Kim, and Danielle M. Leyva, et al., "BacterAI Maps Microbial Metabolism Without Prior Knowledge," *Nature Microbiology*, vol. 8 (2023); Takashi Inagaki, Akari Kato, and Koichi Takahashi, et al., "LLMs Can Generate Robotic Scripts from Goal-Oriented Instructions in Biological Laboratory Automation," *arxiv (pre-print)*, 2023, https://arxiv.org/abs/2304.10267; Daniil A. Boiko, Robert MacKnight, and Gabe Gomes, "Emergent Autonomous Scientific Research Capabilities of Large Language Models," *arxiv (preprint)*, 2023, see https://arxiv.org/abs/2304.05332.

[48] CRS Report R47569, *Generative Artificial Intelligence and Data Privacy: A Primer*, by Kristen E. Busch.

[49] Sarah R. Carter, Jaime M. Yassif, and Christopher R. Isaac, *Benchtop DNA Synthesis Devices: Capabilities, Biosecurity Implications, and Governance*, Nuclear Threat Initiative, 2023, https://www.nti.org/analysis/articles/benchtop-dna-synthesis-devices-capabilities-biosecurity-implications-and-governance/.

[50] GPT-4 is an AI chatbot developed by a company called OpenAI underpinned by an LLM.

[51] Takashi Inagaki, Akari Kato, and Koichi Takahashi, et al., "LLMs Can Generate Robotic Scripts from Goal-Oriented Instructions in Biological Laboratory Automation," *arxiv (pre-print)*, 2023, https://arxiv.org/abs/2304.10267.

experimental design capabilities, effectively addressing complex problems and generating high-quality code."[52]

One commentary stated that utilizing AI to help standardize certain processes through automation may help enhance the reproducibility and predictability of biological experiments.[53] Some have argued that AI may reduce the opportunity for human creativity in science, while others suggest that AI instead will free scientists from some of the repetitive tasks of scientific research and allow more time for critical thinking.[54]

Policy Considerations

AI's use in biology and the broader scientific enterprise could raise policy concerns for Congress, particularly regarding whether additional oversight may be warranted. There have been numerous bills introduced in the 118th Congress that address the risks, benefits, and strategic competitiveness of AI more generally.[55] In addition, in July 2023, two bills were introduced that focused more specifically on AI and biological threats.

- H.R. 4704 and S. 2399, "Artificial Intelligence and Biosecurity Risk Assessment Act," would require the Department of Health and Human Services (HHS) Assistant Secretary for Preparedness and Response to "conduct risk assessments and implement strategic initiatives or activities to address whether technical advancements in artificial intelligence, such as open-source artificial intelligence models and large language models, can be used intentionally or unintentionally to develop novel pathogens, viruses, bioweapons, or chemical weapons."
- S. 2346, "Strategy for Public Health Preparedness and Response to Artificial Intelligence Threats," would require the Secretary of HHS to develop a strategy for public health preparedness and response to artificial intelligence threats, and for other purposes.

---

[52] Daniil A. Boiko, Robert MacKnight, and Gabe Gomes, "Emergent Autonomous Scientific Research Capabilities of Large Language Models," *arxiv (preprint)*, 2023, see https://arxiv.org/abs/2304.05332.

[53] Serina L. Robinson, "Artificial Intelligence for Microbial Biotechnology; Beyond the Hype," *Microbial Biotechnology*, vol. 15, no. 1 (2021).

[54] Ibid.

[55] CRS Report R47644, *Artificial Intelligence: Overview, Recent Advances, and Considerations for the 118th Congress*, by Laurie A. Harris.

Potential Biosafety and Biosecurity Concerns

Some have argued that using GenAI for biological design can be repurposed or misused, raising certain biosafety and biosecurity concerns.[56] As part of a "thought experiment" that may have implications for the Chemical and Biological Weapons Conventions,[57] Collaborations Pharmaceuticals, Inc., retrained its AI model for drug development[58] to design molecules for toxicity instead of designing against them.[59] The AI model normally penalizes predicted toxicity and rewards predicted target activity. By inverting this logic, the AI model was guided to reward both toxicity and bioactivity. The AI model was then trained with a public database of drug-like molecules and their bioactivities. The study reported that in less than six hours the AI model generated 40,000 molecules that scored within their desired threshold of toxicity and bioactivity, which included the nerve agent VX, other known chemical warfare agents, and new molecules that were predicted to have even higher toxicities. These new molecules were not included in the datasets the AI model was trained on. While the AI model was able to generate designs for these new molecules, the company did not attempt to actually synthesize and produce them.

AI's potential ability to produce molecules that have similar properties but different chemical structures or DNA sequences have raised concerns. Specifically, that current detection methods, and screening guidelines that use certain DNA sequences or other features as identifiers, may not be able to identify these new toxins of concern. For example, ricin is a plant protein toxin that is listed on the U.S. Federal Select Agent List.[60] Researchers claim that using AI, they could "take the active site of ricin, computationally remove the surrounding stabilizing protein structure, and ask a generative algorithm to

---

[56] Sean Ekins, Maximilian Brackmann, and Cedric Invernizzi, et al., "Generative Artificial Intelligence-Assisted Protein Design Must Consider Repurposing Potential," *GEN Biotechnology*, vol. 2, no. 4 (2023).

[57] Spiez Convergence Conference, 2021, https://www.spiezlab.admin.ch/en/home/meta/refconvergence.html.

[58] Fabio Urbina, Christopher Lowden, and Christopher Culberson, et al., "MegaSyn: Integrating Generative Molecule Design, Automated Analog Designer and Synthetic Viability Prediction," *ChemRxiv (Preprint)*, 2021.

[59] Fabio Urbina, Filippa Lentzos, and Cédric Invernizzi, et al., "Dual Use of Artificial-Intelligence-Powered Drug Discovery," *Nature Machine Intelligence*, vol. 4 (2022).

[60] The Department of Health and Human Services (HHS) and U.S. Department of Agriculture (USDA) Select Agent Program regulates the possession, use, and transfer of select agents and toxins deemed by HHS or USDA to pose a severe threat to public health and safety, based on a set of criteria. See http://www.selectagents.gov/.

hallucinate and imprint a new proteinaceous structure around the active site."[61] This would, in theory, remove the DNA sequence component that is screened by DNA synthesis service providers[62] and other control mechanisms (e.g., the Chemical and Biological Weapons Conventions or the U.S. Federal Select Agent Program). Note, however, that using AI to identify and design novel molecules, or DNA sequences, does not mean that the molecule could actually be produced, or a functioning living organism based on AI-generated molecules or DNA sequences. Additional scientific, technical, and other challenges would have to be overcome, such as synthesizing the DNA and getting it to function in a living organism as designed, to realize this biosecurity risk.[63]

Laboratory Automation and De-Skilling Concerns

While laboratory automation has already impacted certain research operations (e.g., liquid handling robots), the use of AI to automate certain procedures that used to require hands-on, tacit knowledge could expand the pool of individuals who can participate in the biological sciences.

While this could be a positive development in some respects, it could also potentially increase biosafety and biosecurity concerns.[64] One study examined whether such a system would provide instructions and capabilities to design certain illicit drug compounds and chemical weapons agents. While the model refused to return results for certain illicit compounds, the authors suggest this could be overcome by altering the terminology, prompting the authors to call for restrictions, particularly a mechanism that would prevent the model from moving forward without the approval of a "human" who can review and approve certain experiments.[65]

---

[61] Sean Ekins, Maximilian Brackmann, and Cedric Invernizzi, et al., "Generative Artificial Intelligence-Assisted Protein Design Must Consider Repurposing Potential," *GEN Biotechnology*, vol. 2, no. 4 (2023).

[62] International Gene Synthesis Consortium, *International Gene Synthesis Consortium Updates Screening Protocols for Synthetic DNA Products and Services*, https://genesynthesis consortium.org/.

[63] John T. O'Brien and Cassidy Nelson, "Assessing the Risks Posed by the Convergence of Artificial Intelligence and Biotechnology," *Health Security*, vol. 18, no. 3 (2020).

[64] Ibid.

[65] Daniil A. Boiko, Robert MacKnight, and Gabe Gomes, "Emergent Autonomous Scientific Research Capabilities of Large Language Models," *arxiv (preprint)*, 2023, see https://arxiv.org/abs/2304.05332.

Wider access to AI, cloud labs,[66] genetic sequence information, and gene synthesis capabilities, including desktop DNA synthesizers,[67] have raised other biosafety and biosecurity concerns— such as who should be able to access these capabilities and what limits might be placed on synthesis capabilities. The convergence of AI and other technologies associated with biology can lower technical and knowledge barriers and increase the number of actors with certain capabilities.[68] AI can enable experimentation and design of biological systems, particularly the design and synthesis of DNA sequences, without the user necessarily understanding what those biological functions represent or do.

A recent study reported that, in a course at the Massachusetts Institute of Technology (MIT), students were asked to investigate whether AI chatbots could provide information that could potentially be used to cause a pandemic. Students were able to use chatbots that suggested potential pandemic pathogens, explained how they can be generated from synthetic DNA using reverse genetics, supplied the names of DNA synthesis companies that are unlikely to screen orders, identified detailed protocols and how to troubleshoot them, and recommended that anyone lacking the skills to perform reverse genetics engage a core facility or contract research organization.[69] The authors of the study argued that increased access to AI can exacerbate the "de-skilling" of biological research and that certain restrictions and oversight may be necessary when considered alongside other advances, such as desktop synthesizers and cloud-based laboratories. Such restrictions include evaluations of, and controlled access to, LLMs, as well as screenings to evaluate what a particular person may be attempting to develop, order, or use. Others may counter that access to information does not necessarily imply the

---

[66] Cloud labs are highly automated laboratories that allow researchers to design and run experiments remotely by sending "instructions" to a contracted facility via the web. Experiments can include sample preparation, bioassays, workflows for DNA synthesis, and methods for imaging and detection, as well as AI-driven drug discovery and testing. "What Are Cloud Labs?," The Biologist, https://www.rsb.org.uk/biologist-features/the-biologist-s-guide-to-cloud-labs.

[67] Sarah R. Carter, Jaime M. Yassif, and Christopher R. Isaac, *Benchtop DNA Synthesis Devices: Capabilities, Biosecurity Implications, and Governance*, Nuclear Threat Initiative, 2023, https://www.nti.org/analysis/articles/benchtop-dna-synthesis-devices-capabilities-biosecurity-implications-and-governance/.

[68] John T. O'Brien and Cassidy Nelson, "Assessing the Risks Posed by the Convergence of Artificial Intelligence and Biotechnology," *Health Security*, vol. 18, no. 3 (2020).

[69] Emily H. Soice, Rafael Rocha, and Kimberlee Cordova, et al., "Can Large Language Models Democratize Access to Dual-Use Biotechnology?," *arxiv*, 2023, https://arxiv.org/abs/2306.03809.

scientific and technical ability to convert that information into actual harm, in this case the creation of a virus capable of causing a pandemic.

Automation and "de-skilling" could present increased biosafety and biosecurity concerns. How severe, or whether these concerns are true in actual practice, is an open debate[70] and an area that Congress may wish to examine. For example, if the output of an LLM poses certain biosafety and biosecurity risks, should there be restrictions on access to the data (e.g., certain DNA sequences of concern) on which LLMs are trained? Restricting access to certain DNA sequences may be difficult since there are a number of databases currently available globally, a large body of existing published scientific literature containing sequence data along with research results (a commonly accepted practice in the global research community), and a number of LLMs that have already been trained on data from existing databases and literature. There may also be concern that restricting data that LLMs are trained on could imperil potentially beneficial uses or create incentives for malicious actors to move certain LLMs to the dark web.

Another option could be restricting access to the LLMs themselves. Developers of the LLMs could require certain registration, authentication or screening requirements for users to access the LLM, or particular features of the LLM, that pose potential biosafety and biosecurity concerns. Additional reporting requirements could also be implemented that identified certain queries or outputs of the LLM that raised concerns, which potentially could be referred to a federal oversight or security agency.

Another concern may be the purposes of LLM outputs and what they are being used in conjunction with. For example, if an LLM is aiding in biological design then the output, or the mechanisms to produce the output, may be an area where certain restrictions could be implemented, if found necessary. As discussed below, certain aspects of this concern are addressed via DNA synthesis screening. However, if certain biological design tools become ubiquitous (e.g., desk-top DNA synthesizers), Congress may examine whether access to these tools should be restricted or whether certain aspects of these tools could be constrained. For example, could the data or biological design

---

[70] Sarah R. Carter, Nicole E. Wheeler , and Sabrina Chwalek, et al., The Convergence of Artificial Intelligence and the Life Sciences: Safeguarding Technology, Rethinking Governance, and Preventing Catastrophe, Nuclear Threat Initiative, 2023, https://www.nti.org/analysis/articles/the-convergence-of-artificial-intelligence-and-the-life-sciences/; Helena, Biosecurity in the Age of AI, 2023, https://www.helenabiosecurity.org/.

features of a desk-top synthesizer be restricted[71] to prevent certain capabilities of producing a biosafety or biosecurity hazard?

Biosafety and Biosecurity Oversight

AI's use in biology and the broader scientific enterprise sits within a debate on how best to manage laboratory biosafety and biosecurity.[72] Many of the concerns that have been raised around the convergence of AI and biology stem from information hazards. Information hazards are risks that arise from the dissemination or the potential dissemination of true information that may cause harm or enable some agent to cause harm.[73] Both AI and certain aspects of biological research can contain information hazards, either separately or collectively. Addressing these issues has led some experts to call for controlled access to certain materials, technologies, and equipment, as well as to develop international norms.[74] Some oversight mechanisms are already in place through U.S. laws and other guidance related to federally funded research,[75] as well as industry best practices that include DNA synthesis screening protocols.[76] For example, certain screening guidelines have been implemented through industry standards and other requirements for federally funded research to address biosafety and biosecurity risks associated with DNA synthesis, along with other mechanisms that may control access to certain equipment or capabilities.

Currently, the International Gene Synthesis Consortium's (IGSC's) Harmonized Screening Protocol specifies that synthetic gene sequence orders be screened against the IGSC's Regulated Pathogen Database, which contains sequences and organisms subject to regulatory control or licensing.[77] HHS developed its *Screening Framework Guidance for Providers and Users of Synthetic Nucleic Acids* to align with "Providers' and Customers' existing

---

[71] Sarah R. Carter, Jaime M. Yassif, and Christopher R. Isaac, *Benchtop DNA Synthesis Devices: Capabilities, Biosecurity Implications, and Governance*, Nuclear Threat Initiative, 2023, https://www.nti.org/analysis/articles/benchtop-dna-synthesis-devices-capabilities-biosecurity-implications-and-governance/.

[72] CRS Report R47695, *U.S. Oversight of Laboratory Biosafety and Biosecurity: Current Policies, Recommended Reforms, and Options for Congress*, by Todd Kuiken.

[73] Nick Bostrom, "Information Hazards: A Typology of Potential Harms from Knowledge," *Review of Contemporary Philosophy*, vol. 10 (2011).

[74] Helena, *Biosecurity in the Age of AI*, 2023, https://www.helenabiosecurity.org/.

[75] CRS Report R47695, *U.S. Oversight of Laboratory Biosafety and Biosecurity: Current Policies, Recommended Reforms, and Options for Congress*, by Todd Kuiken.

[76] International Gene Synthesis Consortium, "Harmonized Screening Protocol V2," 2017, https://genesynthesisconsortium.org/wp-content/uploads/IGSCHarmonizedProtocol11-21-17.pdf.

[77] Ibid.

protocols and business practices, to be implemented without unnecessary cost, and to minimize any negative impacts on the conduct of research and business operations."[78] On October 30, 2023, the White House released Executive Order 14110, *Safe, Secure, and Trustworthy Development and Use of Artificial Intelligence,* which requires federal agencies to "establish a framework, incorporating, as appropriate, existing United States Government guidance, to encourage providers of synthetic nucleic acid sequences to implement comprehensive, scalable, and verifiable synthetic nucleic acid procurement screening mechanisms, including standards and recommended incentives."[79]

Questions Congress could face in this area include whether these types of voluntary, or agency-directed, screening programs should be applied to data that AI models are trained on, whether additional oversight focused on AI's use in biology and the broader scientific enterprise is necessary, and if so, whether agencies have expertise and capacity to implement such a program, or whether current oversight systems are sufficient.

Broad-Based vs. Case-by-Case Oversight

Some have identified the importance of distinguishing the risks associated with the use of AI models to generate experimental procedures from the risks associated with the use of AI-enabled biological design tools.[80] They argue that doing so may be useful when exploring potential governance options. This could prove difficult as such biology-focused AI models and biological design tools are often developed in tandem.[81] An example of this was described in an announcement by Google Cloud and Ginkgo Bioworks, an engineering biology company, of their plans to build a "generative AI platform for

---

[78] Administration for Strategic Preparedness and Response, *Screening Framework Guidance for Providers and Users of Synthetic Nucleic Acids*, U.S. Department of Health & Human Services, 2023, https://aspr.hhs.gov/legal/synna/ Documents/SynNA-Guidance-2023.pdf.

[79] Executive Order 14110, "Safe, Secure, and Trustworthy Development and Use of Artificial Intelligence," 88 *Federal Register* 75191-75226 (2023).

[80] Jonas B. Sandbrink, "Artificial Intelligence and Biological Misuse: Differentiating Risks of Language Models and Biological Design Tools," preprint, https://arxiv.org/ abs/2306.13952.

[81] Anna Nowogrodzki, "The Automatic-Design Tools That Are Changing Synthetic Biology," *Nature*, vol. 564 (2018).

engineering biology and for biosecurity."[82] The announcement described the convergence of biological data (which includes genomic data), AI, and biodesign tools, in which biological data is designed and structured for use with the AI tools and integrated into a biofoundry. A biofoundry is a facility that provides integrated infrastructure (combination of biology, computer-aided design, robotics, and engineering principles) enabling the rapid design, construction, and testing of engineered organisms for biotechnology applications and research.[83]

The potential capabilities of AI used in conjunction with biological design and other types of scientific research and experimentation have prompted recommendations on how to prevent the misuse of AI applications in biology and science more broadly. Those recommendations include keeping a human "in the loop," controlling access to DNA sequences and synthesis capabilities, and other governance mechanisms that restrict, or monitor, who can access certain AI applications and biological design tools.[84]

Existing and proposed oversight mechanisms take different approaches, such as controlling access to a particular technology or dataset, or focusing on a particular step in the R&D process (e.g., basic research, prototypes, or release of a final product).

If further regulation or oversight in this area were deemed necessary, potential options for Congress could include

- whether AI, and its use in biology and other R&D applications, should be regulated broadly across all use cases and areas of development; or
- whether to design oversight mechanisms on a case-by-case basis (e.g., limiting access to certain tools or models), focused on particular application areas (e.g., drug development), or based on particular end-use products (e.g., certain laboratory equipment).

---

82 Ginkgo Bioworks, "Google and Ginkgo: Foundry-Scale Data Meets AI," press release, 2023, https://www.ginkgobioworks.com/2023/08/29/google-and-ginkgo-foundry-scale-data-meets-ai/.

83 CRS Report R47265, *Synthetic/Engineering Biology: Issues for Congress*, by Todd Kuiken. Nathan Hillson, Mark Caddick, and Yizhi Cai, et al., "Building a Global Alliance of Biofoundries," *Nature Communications*, vol. 10, no. 2040 (2019).

84 Fabio Urbina, Filippa Lentzos, and Cedric Invernizzi, et al., "Preventing AI From Creating Biochemical Threats," *Journal of Chemical Information and Modeling*, vol. 63 (2023). Helena, *Biosecurity in the Age of AI*, 2023, https://www.helenabiosecurity.org/.

Additional regulation and oversight could impact other areas of R&D in specific or unanticipated ways. For example, limiting access to an AI model, restricting the types of data on which an AI model is trained, or limiting the capabilities an AI model is allowed to execute could each individually impact a biological design tool's capability. Limiting AI's access to certain DNA datasets based on particular biosecurity concerns (e.g., pathogenicity) could prevent an AI model from designing certain toxins of concern. It might also, however, prevent the AI model from predicting molecular structures that could enable the development of new drug candidates.

Structured Access

Some experts have called for structured access to certain AI capabilities while others suggest a gradient approach.[85] In a structured access approach, the developer of an AI model maintains control over how the AI system can be used, modified, and reproduced.[86] Structured access could also be implemented for other research tools in the R&D process (e.g., desktop DNA synthesizers),[87] for example, by controlling the acquisition of the device itself.[88] This would not necessarily impact the AI component of the R&D process. At one university where a team of researchers was proposing to develop an AI model to predict the toxicity of chemicals and materials, its research ethics and society review panel suggested that the team think about ways to control the distribution of the software, model, and outputs in order to reduce potential misuse.[89] This type of review and oversight is similar to how the United States addresses some aspects of biosafety and biosecurity, with research institutions responsible for implementation of certain guidelines as a

---

[85] Irene Solaiman, "Generative AI Systems Aren't Just Open or Closed Source," *Wired*, 2023, https://www.wired.com/ story/generative-ai-systems-arent-just-open-or-closed-source/.

[86] Helena, *Biosecurity in the Age of AI*, 2023, https://www.helenabiosecurity.org/. Note: There are two broad categories of structured access: (1) use controls, which govern the direct use of the AI system (who, what, when, where, why, and how); and (2) modification and reproduction controls, which prevent the user from altering the AI system or building their own version in a way that circumvents use controls.

[87] Sarah R. Carter, Jaime M. Yassif, and Christopher R. Isaac, *Benchtop DNA Synthesis Devices: Capabilities, Biosecurity Implications, and Governance*, Nuclear Threat Initiative, 2023, https://www.nti.org/analysis/articles/benchtop-dna-synthesis-devices-capabilities-biosecurity-implications-and-governance/.

[88] Helena, *Biosecurity in the Age of AI*, 2023, https://www.helenabiosecurity.org/.

[89] Sadasivan Shankar and Richard N. Zare, "The Perils of Machine Learning in Designing New Chemicals and Materials," *Nature Machine Intelligence*, vol. 4 (2022).

condition for receiving federal funding.[90] Congress may examine whether federal agencies have the expertise, capacity, and authority to both develop and issue guidance requiring institutions, or other actors, who receive federal funding to conduct certain biosafety and biosecurity reviews of AI enabled R&D applications. Congress may also examine whether this type of biosafety/biosecurity review resulting in potential restricted access can be accomplished by granting authority to agencies to conduct such reviews, regardless of whether an actor receives federal funding or not.

Issues Pertaining to Genetic Sequence Data and Databases

The U.S. National Security Commission on Artificial Intelligence recommended that the U.S. fund and prioritize the development of a biobank containing a "wide range of high-quality biological and genetic data sets securely accessible by researchers." The United States currently has a number of such databases, including GenBank.[91] However, they are distributed across different agencies, contain different sources and types of sequence data, and are designed for different uses.[92] There are other sequence databases which are publicly funded and freely accessible, and others that are privately held. Some experts have raised privacy and security concerns around these databases in terms of access and potential use of the sequence data.[93]

Potential options for Congress in this area may include

- whether the United States should develop a sequence database strategy coordinating activities across the U.S. government in relation to the collection, storage, maintenance, and access to its sequence databases;
- whether certain privacy, biosafety, and biosecurity issues pertaining to access and use of sequence databases are adequately addressed, particularly related to the convergence of AI and biological design; and

---

[90] CRS Report R47695, *U.S. Oversight of Laboratory Biosafety and Biosecurity: Current Policies, Recommended Reforms, and Options for Congress*, by Todd Kuiken.

[91] NIH, GenBank, https://www.ncbi.nlm.nih.gov/genbank/.

[92] CRS In Focus IF12285, *eDNA/eRNA: Scientific Value in What's Left Behind*, coordinated by Todd Kuiken.

[93] Saadia Arshad, Junaid Arshad, and Muhammad Mubashir Khan, et al., "Analysis of Security and Privacy Challenges for DNA-Genomics Applications and Databases," *Journal of Biomedical Informatics*, vol. 119 (2021).

- whether these issues should be addressed regarding sequence databases which are publicly funded and freely accessible or privately held.

Other Policy Considerations

A general policy consideration may be whether a broader risk management approach[94] examining the R&D system as a whole is more appropriate than addressing individual components of the R&D process. This would include at what stage oversight is warranted (e.g., basic research, prototyping, or prior to release of a final product) and who might conduct such oversight (e.g., by a federal agency or through self-governance incentives). For example, would a federal agency have the authority to conduct oversight or could oversight be achieved through self-governance incentives? This could be similar to the operation of institutional review boards[95] or other industry-led programs such as the International Gene Synthesis Consortium,[96] which conducts screening for DNA synthesis orders.

Congressional options for addressing federal oversight could include whether to provide an agency (or agencies) authority to conduct oversight of various aspects of AI, create a new agency with authority over AI, or authorize agencies under current law to enforce certain oversight responsibilities. Authorizing agencies under current law may require additional coordination among federal agencies in order to establish oversight responsibilities. While it was established via an executive order, this type of coordination among agencies would be similar to how the *Coordinated Framework for Regulation of Biotechnology* established mechanisms for three federal agencies (USDA, FDA, and EPA) to share responsibility for regulating the products of biotechnology.[97]

---

[94] In January 2023 the National Institute of Standards and Technology released its *AI Risk Management Framework to better manage risks to individuals, organizations, and society associated with AI*. See https://doi.org/10.6028/ NIST.AI.100-1.

[95] U.S. Food and Drug Administration, *Institutional Review Boards Frequently Asked Questions*, 2019, https://www.fda.gov/regulatory-information/search-fda-guidance-documents/ institutional-review-boards-frequently-asked-questions.

[96] International Gene Synthesis Consortium, "Harmonized Screening Protocol V2," 2017, https://genesynthesisconsortium.org/wp-content/uploads/IGSCHarmonizedProtocol11-21-17.pdf.

[97] Executive Office of the President (EOP), Office of Science and Technology Policy, "Coordinated Framework for Regulation of Biotechnology," 51 *Federal Register* 23302, June 26, 1986. For additional information on the Coordinated Framework see CRS Report

Potential oversight and governance of the use of AI in the biological sciences both domestically and internationally, either generally or focused on particular use cases or areas of development, may have unpredicted societal and economic impacts, both positive and negative, affecting U.S. strategic competitiveness. Such concerns could include how potential U.S. oversight and governance influences, or is influenced by, policy actions taken elsewhere; whether international harmonization may be needed, and, if so, through what mechanisms (e.g., the United Nations, international standards bodies, trade policy); and how to engage in those negotiations.

Disclaimer

R46737, *Agricultural Biotechnology: Overview, Regulation, and Selected Policy Issues*, by Renée Johnson.

Chapter 9

Generative Artificial Intelligence: Overview, Issues, and Questions for Congress*

Laurie A. Harris

Abstract

Generative artificial intelligence (GenAI) refers to AI systems, in particular those using machine learning (ML) and trained on large volumes of data, that are able to generate new content. In contrast, other AI systems may have a primary goal of classifying data, such as facial recognition image data, or making decisions, such as those used in autonomous vehicles. GenAI systems, when prompted (often by a user inputting text), can create various outputs, including text responses (e.g., OpenAI's ChatGPT and Google's Bard), images (e.g., Stability AI's Stable Diffusion and Midjourney's self-titled program), videos, computer code, or music.

The recent public release of many GenAI tools, and the race by companies to develop ever-more powerful models, have generated widespread discussion of their capabilities, potential concerns with their use, and debates about their governance and regulation. This CRS InFocus describes the development and uses of GenAI, concerns raised by the use of GenAI tools, and considerations for Congress. For additional considerations related to data privacy, see CRS Report R47569, *Generative Artificial Intelligence and Data Privacy: A Primer*, by Kristen E. Busch.

---

* This is an edited, reformatted and augmented version of Congressional Research Service, Publication No. IF12426, dated June 9, 2023.

In: Artificial Intelligence
Editor: Sonja Buckley
ISBN: 979-8-89530-859-2

Background

AI can generally be thought of as computerized systems that work and react in ways commonly considered to require human intelligence, such as learning, solving problems, and achieving goals under uncertain and varying conditions, with varying levels of autonomy. AI is not one thing; AI systems can encompass a range of technologies, methodologies, and application areas, such as natural language processing, robotics, and facial recognition.

The AI technologies underpinning many GenAI tools are the result of decades of research. For example, recurrent neural networks (RNNs, a type of ML loosely modeled after the human brain that detect patterns in sequential data) underwent a period of much development and improvement in the 1980s-1990s. RNNs can generate text, but they are limited in retaining contextual information across large strings of words, are slow to train, and are not easily scaled up by increasing computational power or training data size.

More recent technical advances—notably the introduction of the Transformer architecture by Google researchers in 2017 and improvements in Generative Pre-Trained Transformer (GPT) models since around 2019—have contributed to dramatic improvement in GenAI performance. Transformer models process a sequence of whole sentences (rather than analyzing word by word), which helps them to "remember" past information. They use mathematical techniques called *attention* or *self-attention* to detect how data elements, even when far away sequentially, influence and depend on each other. These methods make GPT models faster to train, more efficient in understanding context, and highly scalable.

Other critical components to the recent GenAI advances are the availability of large amounts of data and the size of their language models. Large language models (LLMs) are AI systems that aim to model language, sometimes using millions or billions of parameters (i.e., numbers in the model that determine how inputs are converted to outputs). Repeatedly tweaking these parameters, using mathematical optimization techniques, and large amounts of data and computational power, increases model performance.

Notably, GenAI models work to match the style and appearance of the underlying training data. They also have been shown to have *capability overhang*, meaning hidden capabilities that their developers and users did not anticipate but that are emerging as the models grow larger.

Beneficial Uses and Concerns

The increase in size of recent GenAI systems (with hundreds of billions of parameters) has led to drastically improved capabilities over previous systems (with millions or a few billion parameters). For example, as released in 2020, OpenAI's GPT-3 could translate sentences from English to French with few to no training examples and outperformed previous models that were explicitly trained to solve that task. GPT-4, released in 2023, improved on various benchmarks, such as scores on simulated graduate and professional exams, and on traditional ML benchmarks.

OpenAI's ChatGPT, reportedly the fastest growing consumer application in history, uses GPT-3.5 or, for paid subscribers, GPT-4, which is the latest, most powerful version. ChatGPT is a conversational AI chatbot that can generate a variety of text outputs, such as emails, essays, and casual conversations. Microsoft has incorporated GPT-4 into its Bing search engine as a chatbot called Bing Chat, and numerous other chatbots also use the GPT-3 and GPT-4 models. In addition to GPT models, other LLM chatbots include Google's Pathways Language Model 2 (PaLM 2) in the Bard chatbot, and Hugging Face's BLOOM model in SambaNova's BLOOMChat.

Despite the impressive abilities of GenAI, its growing prominence is raising concerns. For example, the tendency of GenAI to make things up, sometimes referred to as *hallucinating*, might result in the tools generating and amplifying misinformation or being used to create and spread disinformation. OpenAI notes that even a powerful model like GPT-4 "is not fully reliable" and "great care should be taken when using language model outputs, particularly in high-stakes contexts, with the exact protocol (such as human review, grounding with additional context, or avoiding high-stakes uses altogether) matching the needs of a specific use-case." Additionally, because the models are generally trained on large amounts of data scraped from the internet, they can incorporate, reflect, and potentially amplify biases in such data.

Particular GenAI use cases, such as in education and scientific research, have also raised questions about ethical and transparent use, whether restrictions should be implemented and whether they are effective, and the accuracy of detection tools.

As GenAI use grows, analysts have begun considering how it might affect jobs and productivity. For example, will these tools complement workers' skills in existing jobs and create new jobs? Will GenAI automate some jobs, displacing workers? While these have been long-standing concerns for automation and AI technologies, the speed, capability, and widespread use of the latest GenAI models have heightened them.

LLMs have been characterized as *foundation models* (also called *general-purpose AI*), meaning models trained on broad data that can be adapted to a wide range of downstream tasks. (In contrast, many other AI systems are built, trained, and used for particular purposes.) As described by the Stanford University Institute for Human-Centered AI, foundation models may be built upon or integrated into multiple AI systems across a variety of domains, with the potential for both benefits (e.g., concentrating efforts to reduce bias and improve robustness) and drawbacks (e.g., security failures or inequities that flow out to downstream applications, amplifying their harms).

Federal AI Laws and GenAI Legislation

Numerous bills focused on AI, or including AI-focused provisions, have been enacted in prior Congresses. For example, the National Artificial Intelligence Initiative Act of 2020 (Division E of P.L. 116-283) codified the establishment of a national AI initiative and associated federal offices and committees. In the 118th Congress, at least 50 AI-related bills have been introduced.

Specifically regarding GenAI, the Identifying Outputs of Generative Adversarial Networks (IOGAN) Act (P.L. 116-258) directed federal support of research on generative adversarial networks. In the 118th Congress, at least four bills have been introduced that specifically include GenAI, including those pertaining to transparency and accountability of GenAI use in political advertisements, disclosure of GenAI outputs, and federal oversight of digital platforms.

Potential Questions for Congress

Like the private sector, federal agencies and Congress have begun testing GenAI uses, including for its potential to help with office tasks such as creating and summarizing content, writing speeches, and drafting bills. At the same time, Congress has begun considering whether and how to implement guardrails for GenAI technologies. As that work continues, along with further development and growing use of GenAI tools, Congress might consider a range of questions and potential actions.

- *Bias and ethics of use.* How are the private and public sectors using federal guidance documents and frameworks for AI evaluation and risk management to address bias and manage risk in GenAI systems? Should the deployment of GenAI models in high-risk scenarios (e.g., mental health therapy or generating forensic sketches) be restricted?
- *Testing and transparency.* The biggest models deployed today, such as GPT-4 and PaLM 2, are closed source, proprietary models. While many companies state that they conduct internal testing and are evaluating options for external validation and testing, Congress might consider whether and how to support or require independent testing and reporting of results.
- *Economic and workforce impacts.* Researchers in industry, the private sector, and academia have begun analyzing GenAI's potential widespread effects on labor. The National Academy of Sciences is currently updating a study on automation and the U.S. workforce. In addition to assessing those findings, Congress might consider the appropriate federal role in supporting U.S. workforce reskilling or upskilling in response to shifting job tasks caused by the implementation of GenAI. It might also consider whether and how to increase AI expertise in the government's own workforce.
- *Research and competition.* Estimates put training costs for GenAI models like GPT-3, with 175 billion parameters, at over $4.6 million. Some analysts have argued that cost, use of proprietary data, and access to vast computing power will create a divide between those who can train the most cutting-edge LLMs (e.g., large technology firms) and those who cannot (e.g., nonprofits, startups, universities). Congress might consider ways to support access to data, training, and computing resources, such as through codifying recommendations in the final report of the National AI Research Resource Task Force.
- *Oversight and regulation.* How might Congress regulate GenAI technologies while supporting innovation and international competitiveness? Do federal regulatory agencies have the authorities and resources to adequately oversee and regulate GenAI tools to minimize risks while supporting benefits? If not, what additional authorities are needed? How might federal oversight and regulation for GenAI be distinct from that for AI technologies more broadly?

Disclaimer

Chapter 10

Generative Artificial Intelligence and Data Privacy: A Primer*

Kristen E. Busch

Overview

Since the public release of Open AI's ChatGPT, Google's Bard, and other similar systems, some Members of Congress have expressed interest in the risks associated with "generative artificial intelligence (AI)." Although exact definitions vary, generative AI is a type of AI that can generate new content—such as text, images, and videos—through learning patterns from pre-existing data. It is a broad term that may include various technologies and techniques from AI and machine learning (ML).[1]

---

* This is an edited, reformatted and augmented version of Congressional Research Service, Publication No. R47569, dated May 23, 2023.

[1] There are various definitions of AI in statute and agency guidance. For example, the National Artificial Intelligence Initiative Act of 2020 (P.L. 116-283) defines AI as "a machine-based system that can, for a given set of human-defined objectives, make predictions, recommendations or decisions influencing real or virtual environments. Artificial intelligence systems use machine and human-based inputs to—(A) perceive real and virtual environments; (B) abstract such perceptions into models through analysis in an automated manner; and (C) use model inference to formulate options for information or action." Artificial intelligence and machine learning (ML) are often used interchangeably, but ML is a subfield of AI that focuses on systems that can "learn" and improve through experience and data. For more information on this distinction, see Columbia Engineering "Artificial Intelligence (AI) vs. Machine Learning," https://ai.engineering.columbia.edu/ai-vs-machine-learning/. For more information on artificial intelligence and machine learning, see CRS Report R46795, *Artificial Intelligence: Background, Selected Issues, and Policy Considerations*, by Laurie A. Harris.

In: Artificial Intelligence
Editor: Sonja Buckley
ISBN: 979-8-89530-859-2

Generative AI at a Glance

Major Developers and Selected Products:[2]

- OpenAI (with partnerships and funding from Microsoft)—"ChatGPT" chatbot, "DALL-E" image
- generator
- Google—"Bard" chatbot
- Meta—"LLaMA" research tool, "Make-A-Video" video generator
- Anthropic (founded by former employees of OpenAI)—"Claude" chatbot
- Stability AI—"Stable Diffusion" image generator
- Hugging Face—BLOOM language model
- NVIDIA—"NeMo" chatbot, "Picasso" visual content generator

Types of Applications:

- Chatbots—systems that simulate human conversation, often in question-and-answer format
- Image generators—systems that generate images based on an input or "prompt"
- Video generators—systems that generate videos based on an input or "prompt," sometimes called
- deepfakes
- Voice clones—systems that generate speech and voice sounds, sometimes called audio deepfakes

Generative AI models have received significant attention and scrutiny due to their potential harms, such as risks involving privacy, misinformation, copyright, and non-consensual sexual imagery. This report focuses on privacy issues and relevant policy considerations for Congress. Some policymakers and stakeholders have raised privacy concerns about how individual data may be used to develop and deploy generative models. These concerns are not new

[2] Six of the seven listed companies were identified based on participation in White House initiatives to develop "public assessments" of existing generative AI systems. Meta was not included in the White House announcement. "Fact Sheet: Biden-Harris Administration Announces New Actions to Promote Responsible AI Innovation that Protects Americans' Rights and Safety," White House, May 4, 2023, https://www.whitehouse.gov/briefing-room/statements-releases/2023/05/04/fact-sheet-biden-harris-administration-announces-new-actions-to-promote-responsible-ai-innovation-that-protects-americans-rights-and-safety/.

or unique to generative AI, but the scale, scope, and capacity of such technologies may present new privacy challenges for Congress.

What Is Generative AI?

Generative AI can generate new content—such as text, images, and videos—through learning patterns from data.[3] There are many types of generative AI models (see Figure 1), which can produce content based on different inputs or "prompts." For example, some models can produce images from text prompts (e.g., Midjourney, Stable Diffusion, DALL-E), while others create videos (e.g., Gen2 or Meta's Make-A-Video).

Image Generator

Prompt: *"The Library of Congress building in the style of Van Gogh."*

Response:

Chatbot

Prompt: *"Write a 4 sentence poem about the Library of Congress."*

Response:

"In the heart of D.C., there stands a place
A temple of knowledge, a palace of grace
The Library of Congress, a marvel to see
A monument to learning, for you and me

Rows upon rows of books, towering high
A treasury of history, never to die
Where stories and knowledge, together reside
A beacon of wisdom, that cannot be denied"

Source: Stable Diffusion and ChatGPT, via CRS. The image was generated by Stable Diffusion and the text response was generated by ChatGPT.

Figure 1. Examples of Generative AI Models.

---

[3] Generative AI models may use different technical approaches and techniques, such as generative adversarial networks (GANs) or generative pre-trained transformers (GPTs). The colloquial term "deep fakes," which refers to realistic machine-generated images, videos, and audio, may also fall under the umbrella term of "generative AI." Deepfakes are typically generated through GANs.

Some scholars and policymakers have recently coined the term "general-purpose models" (GPAI) to describe applications like ChatGPT that can complete various functions.[4] These GPAI models may have a wide range of down-stream applications compared to single-purpose models designed for a specific task. Many general-purpose AI applications are built on top of large language models (LLMs) that can recognize, predict, translate, summarize, and generate language.[5] LLMs are a subset of generative AI and are characterized as "large" due, in part, to the massive amount of data necessary for training the model to learn the rules of language.

How Do Generative AI Models Use Data?

Data is essential to train and fine-tune AI models. Generative AI models require especially large datasets for training and fine-tuning.

Definitions

Training a model refers to providing a model with data to learn from, often called a training dataset. After a model is trained to recognize patterns from one dataset, some models can be provided with new data and still recognize patterns or predict results.

Fine-tuning a model refers to training a previously trained model on new data, or otherwise adjusting an existing model.[6]

Generative AI models, particularly LLMs, require massive amounts of data. For example,

OpenAI's ChatGPT was built on a LLM that trained, in part, on over 45 terabytes of text data obtained (or "scraped") from the internet. The LLM was also trained on entries from Wikipedia and corpora of digitized books.[7] Open AI's GPT-3 models were trained on approximately 300 billion "tokens" (or

---

[4] European Parliament, "General-Purpose Artificial Intelligence," https://www.europarl.europa.eu/RegData/etudes/ATAG/2023/745708/EPRS_ATA(2023)745708_EN.pdf.

[5] Bender, Gebru, et al., "On the Dangers of Stochastic Parrots: Can Language Models Be Too Big?" March 2023, ACM Conference on Fairness, Accountability, and Transparency, https://doi.org/10.1145/3442188.3445922; Samuel Bowman, "Eight Things to Know About Large Language Models," April 2023, https://arxiv.org/pdf/2304.00612.pdf.

[6] For example, fine-tuning could include adjusting a pre-existing model's parameters.

[7] Brown, et al., "Language Models Are Few-Shot Learners," July 22, 2020, https://arxiv.org/abs/2005.14165.

pieces of words) scraped from the web and had over 175 billion parameters, which are variables that influence properties of the training and resulting model.[8]

Critics contend that such models rely on privacy-invasive methods for mass data collection, typically without the consent or compensation of the original user, creator, or owner.[9]

Additionally, some models may be trained on sensitive data and reveal personal information to users. In a company blog post, Google AI researchers noted, "Because these datasets can be large (hundreds of gigabytes) and pull from a range of sources, they can sometimes contain sensitive data, including personally identifiable information (PII)—names, phone numbers, addresses, etc., even if trained on public data."[10] Academic and industry research has found that some existing LLMs may reveal sensitive data or personal information from their training datasets.[11]

Some models are used for commercial purposes or embedded in other downstream applications. For example, companies may purchase subscription versions of ChatGPT to embed in their various services or products. Khan Academy, Duolingo, Snapchat, and other companies have partnered with OpenAI to deploy ChatGPT in their services.[12] However, individuals may not know their data was used to train models that are monetized and deployed across such applications.

Some countries have taken action against AI developers for improper use of personal information. For example, the Italian Data Protection Authority

---

[8] According to OpenAI, their models were trained on some datasets with a total of 300 billion tokens. A token is a piece of a word. One token is around ¾ of a word. Brown, et al., "Language Models Are Few-Shot Learners," July 22, 2020, https://arxiv.org/abs/2005.14165.

[9] Matt Burgess, "ChatGPT Has a Big Privacy Problem," *Wired*, April 4, 2023, https://www.wired.com/story/italy-ban-chatgpt-privacy-gdpr/.

[10] Nicholas Carlini, "Privacy Considerations in Large Language Models," December 15, 2020, Google Research Blog, https://ai.googleblog.com/2020/12/privacy-considerations-in-large.html.

[11] Nicholas Carlini et al., "Extracting Training Data from Large Language Models," Jun 15, 2021, https://arxiv.org/abs/ 2012.07805.

[12] Alex Heath, "Snapchat Is Releasing Its Own AI Chatbot Powered by ChatGPT," *The Verge*, February 27, 2023, https://www.theverge.com/2023/2/27/23614959/snapchat-my-ai-chatbot-chatgpt-openai-plus-subscription; "Introducing Duolingo Max, a Learning Experience Powered by GPT-4," March 14, 2023, Duolingo Blog, https://blog.duolingo.com/duolingo-max/; Sal Khan, "Harnessing GPT-4 So That All Students Benefit. A Nonprofit Approach for Equal Access," Khan Academy, March 14, 2023, https://blog.khanacademy.org/harnessing-ai-so-that-all-students-benefit-a-nonprofit-approach-for-equal-access/.

issued a temporary ban preventing OpenAI from using Italian users' data.[13] After agreeing to certain changes—such as allowing users to submit removal requests for personal data under the EU's General Data Protection Regulation (GDPR)—OpenAI restored access to its service for users in Italy.[14]

Where Does the Data Come from?

Many AI developers do not disclose the exact details of their training datasets. For generative AI, most training data is "scraped" from publicly available web pages before it is repackaged and sold, or in some cases, made freely available to AI developers.

Some AI developers rely on popular large datasets such as "Colossal Clean Crawled Corpus" (C4) and "Common Crawl," which are amassed through web crawling (i.e., software that systematically browses public internet sites and collects information from each available web page). Similarly, AI image generators are commonly trained on a dataset called LAION, which contains billions of images scraped from internet sites and their text descriptions.[15] Some companies might also use proprietary datasets for training.

Generative AI datasets can include information posted on publicly available internet sites, including PII and sensitive and copyrighted content. They may also include publicly available content that is erroneous, pornographic, or potentially harmful. Since data may be scraped without the creator's consent, some artists, content creators, and others have begun to use new tools such as "HaveIBeenTrained" to identify and report their own content in such databases. In a 2023 investigation, the *Washington Post* and Allen Institute for AI analyzed the websites scraped for the C4 dataset, which

[13] Italian Data Protection Data Protection Authority (Garante per la protezione dei dati personali or GPDP), March 31, 2023, https://www.gpdp.it/web/guest/home/docweb/-/docweb-display/docweb/9870847#english.

[14] Adi Robertson, "ChatGPT Returns to Italy After Ban," April 28, 2023, *The Verge*, https://www.theverge.com/2023/4/28/23702883/chatgpt-italy-ban-lifted-gpdp-data-protection-age-verification.

[15] Marissa Newman and Aggi Cantrill, "The Future of AI Relies on a High School Teacher's Free Database," Bloomberg, April 23, 2023, https://www.bloomberg.com/news/features/2023-04-24/a-high-school-teacher-s-free-image-database-powers-ai-unicorns#xj4y7vzkg.

is used by AI developers including Google, Facebook, and OpenAI.[16] The investigation found that the C4 dataset included websites with copyrighted content as well as potentially sensitive information, such as state voter registration records.

These forms of data collection may also raise questions about copyright ownership and fair use. For a discussion of copyright issues and generative AI, see CRS Legal Sidebar LSB10922, *Generative Artificial Intelligence and Copyright Law*, by Christopher T. Zirpoli.

What Happens to Data Shared with Generative AI Models?

Some critics have also raised concerns that user data shared with a generative AI application — such as a chatbot—may be misused or abused without the user's knowledge. For example, a user may reveal sensitive health information while conversing with a health care chatbot without realizing their information could be stored and used to re-train the models or for other commercial purposes. Many existing chatbots have terms of service that allow the company to re-use user data to "develop and improve their services."

These concerns may be particularly pertinent for generative models used in interactions or services that commonly result in the disclosure of sensitive information such as advising, therapy health care, legal, or financial services. In response, some critics have argued that chatbots and other generative AI models should require affirmative consent from users or provide clear disclosure of how user data is collected, used, and stored.

Policy Considerations for Congress

Existing Data Privacy and Related Laws

The United States does not currently have a comprehensive data privacy law. Congress has enacted a number of laws that create data requirements for certain industries and subcategories of data, but these statutory protections are not comprehensive. For example, the Gramm-Leach-Bliley Act (P.L. 106-

---

[16] Kevin Schaul, Szu Yu Chen, and Nitasha Tiku, "Inside the Secret List of Websites That Make AI Like ChatGPT Sound Smart," April 19, 2023, *Washington Post*, https://www.washingtonpost.com/technology/interactive/2023/ai-chatbot-learning/.

102) regulates financial institutions' use of nonpublic personal information, while the Health Insurance Portability and Accountability Act (HIPAA, P.L. 104-191) requires covered entities to protect certain health information. Under current U.S. law, generative AI may implicate certain privacy laws depending on the context, developer, type of data, and purpose of the model. For example, if a company offers a chatbot in a videogame or other online service directed at children, the company could be required to meet certain requirements under the Children's Online Privacy Protection Act (COPPA, P.L. 105-277).

Additionally, certain state laws on privacy, biometrics, and AI may have implications for generative AI applications. In many cases, the collection of personal information typically implicates certain state privacy laws that provide an individual a "right to know" what a business collects about them; how data is used and shared; the "right to access and delete" their data; or the "right to opt-out" of data transfers and sales.[17] However, some of these laws include exemptions for the collection of public data, which may raise questions about how and whether they apply to generative AI tools that use information scraped from the internet.

In the absence of a comprehensive federal data privacy law, some individuals and groups have turned to other legal frameworks (e.g., copyright, defamation, right of publicity) to address potential privacy violations from generative AI and other AI tools. For example, some companies have faced class action lawsuits for possible violations of right of publicity state laws, which protect against unauthorized use of an individual's likeness for commercial purposes.[18]

Congress may consider enacting comprehensive federal privacy legislation that specifically addresses generative AI tools and related concerns. In doing so, Congress may consider and evaluate similar state and international efforts. For example, the European Union's (EU) proposed AI Act includes various articles on data regulation, disclosures, and documentation, among other requirements. The EU AI Act recently added a

---

[17] For example, the California Consumer Privacy Act (CCPA) and California Consumer Privacy Regulation (CPRA) provide certain privacy rights to California rights. California Office of the Attorney General, "California Consumer Privacy Act (CCPA)," May 10, 2023, https://oag.ca.gov/privacy/ccpa. For more information on the CCPA or data privacy laws, see CRS Legal Sidebar LSB10213, *California Dreamin' of Privacy Regulation: The California Consumer Privacy Act and Congress*, coordinated by Eric N. Holmes; and CRS Report R45631, *Data Protection Law: An Overview*, by Stephen P. Mulligan and Chris D. Linebaugh.

[18] Isaiah Poritz, "AI Celebrity 'Deepfakes' Clash with Web of State Publicity Laws," Bloomberg Law, April 14, 2023, https://news.bloomberglaw.com/ip-law/ai-celebrity-deepfakes-clash-with-web-of-state-publicity-laws.

category for general purpose AI systems and foundation models, another term used for AI models that train on large amounts of data and can be adapted for various tasks.[19]

Proposed Privacy Legislation

Some Members of Congress have proposed various comprehensive or targeted privacy bills with requirements that could impact generative AI applications. These are three common mechanisms included in various privacy bills:

Notice and Disclosure Requirements

Currently, most generative AI applications do not provide notice or acquire consent from individuals to collect and use their data for training purposes.

Congress may consider requiring companies developing or deploying generative AI systems to (1) acquire consent from individuals before collecting or using their data, or (2) notify individuals that their data will be collected and used for certain purposes, such as training models. Some scholars dispute the efficacy of notice and consent requirements.[20]

Opt-out Requirements

Congress may consider requiring companies to provide users an option to opt-out of data collection. Of note, opt-out systems may not necessarily protect data that is publicly-scraped from the web, and may be cumbersome for individuals to exercise.

Deletion and Minimization Requirements

Congress may also consider requiring companies to provide mechanisms for users to delete their data from existing datasets or require maximum retention periods for personal data. Currently, most leading chatbots and other AI models do not provide options for users to delete their personal information.

---

[19] European Parliament, "AI Act: A Step Closer to the First Rules on Artificial Intelligence," press release, May 11, 2023, https://www.europarl.europa.eu/news/en/press-room/20230505IPR84904/ai-act-a-step-closer-to-the-first-rules-on-artificial-intelligence.

[20] Claire Park, "How "Notice and Consent" Fails to Protect Our Privacy," New America Open Technology Institute, March 23, 2020, https://www.newamerica.org/oti/blog/how-notice-and-consent-fails-to-protect-our-privacy/.

In considering such proposals, Congress may also wish to consider practical challenges users may face exercising specific privacy rights as well as potential challenges for companies in complying with certain types of legal requirements and user requests.

Existing Agency Authorities

Various federal agencies may enforce laws relevant to AI and data privacy. The Federal Trade Commission (FTC) has been active in addressing data privacy issues and has taken various actions involving AI. The FTC has applied its broad authorities over "unfair or deceptive acts or practices in commerce" to cases related to data privacy and data security. In recent months, the commission reaffirmed that its authorities also apply to new AI tools.[21] Chairman Khan stated, "there is no AI exemption to the laws on the books, and the FTC will vigorously enforce the law to combat unfair or deceptive practices or unfair methods of competition."[22]

The data collection practices of AI companies may also raise competition concerns. At the 2023 Annual Antitrust Enforcers Summit, Chair Khan stated, "As you have machine learning that depends on huge amounts of data and also depends on huge amounts of storage, we need to be very vigilant to make sure that this is not just another site for the big companies becoming bigger and really squelching rivals."[23] The development of AI models may also require

---

[21] The Federal Trade Commission (FTC) released multiple blog posts to caution companies against using AI to deceive or mislead consumers. The FTC's recent blog post states that the FTC's "unfair or deceptive acts or practices" (UDAP) authorities could apply to companies that develop, sell, or use an AI system that is "effectively designed" to deceive consumers, "even if not the system's original purpose." Michael Atleson, "Keep Your AI Claims in Check," FTC Business Blog, February 27, 2023, https://www.ftc.gov/business-guidance/blog/2023/02/keep-your-ai-claims-check; Michael Atleson, "Chatbots, Deepfakes, and Voice Clones: AI Deception for Sale," FTC Business Blog, March 20, 2023, https://www.ftc.gov/business-guidance/blog/2023/03/chatbots-deepfakes-voice-clones-ai-deception-sale.

[22] Federal Trade Commission, "FTC Chair Khan and Officials from DOJ, CFPB and EEOC Release Joint Statement on AI," press release, April 25, 2023, https://www.ftc.gov/news-events/news/press-releases/2023/04/ftc-chair-khan-officials-doj-cfpb-eeoc-release-joint-statement-ai.

[23] Adi Robertson, "The US Government Is Gearing up for an AI Antitrust Fight," *The Verge*, March 28, 2023, https://www.theverge.com/2023/3/28/23660101/ai-competition-ftc-doj-lina-khan-jonathan-kanter-antitrust-summit.

significant computational and financial resources, which may preclude new competitors and entrench incumbents.[24]

In evaluating existing agency authorities, Congress may consider updating or providing additional specific authorities to federal agencies to address AI and related privacy issues. Additionally, Congress could consider what resources federal agencies may require to conduct additional oversight of AI and privacy issues.

Regulation of Data-Scraping

There are currently no federal laws that ban the scraping of publicly available data from the internet. The Computer Fraud and Abuse Act (CFAA, 18 U.S.C. §1030) imposes liability when a person "intentionally accesses a computer without authorization or exceeds authorized access, and thereby obtains ... information from any protected computer."[25] Some court cases have held that this prohibition does not apply to public websites—meaning that scraping publicly accessible data from the internet does not violate the CFAA.[26]

Scraping publicly available information from the internet has privacy implications beyond generative AI models. The facial recognition company Clearview AI has scraped over 20 billion images from the web, including social-media profile photos, which have been used for software and databases provided to law enforcement and other entities.[27] Some technology companies have also scraped publicly available data to amass large data repositories. Web-scraping may raise competition concerns since larger companies may block competitors from scraping data.

Many researchers, journalists, and civil society groups, among others, rely on scraping to conduct research that may be in the public interest. If Congress were to consider broad legislation to limit or provide guardrails for scraping information from the internet, it might consider implications for a range of activities that it may find beneficial.

---

[24] "ChatGPT and More: Large Scale AI Models Entrench Big Tech Power," AI Now Institute, April 11, 2023, https://ainowinstitute.org/publication/large-scale-ai-models.

[25] The Computer Fraud and Abuse Act is codified at Title 18, United States Code, §1030.

[26] Zack Whittaker, "Web Scraping Is Legal, US Appeals Court Reaffirms," TechCrunch, April 18, 2022, https://techcrunch.com/2022/04/18/web-scraping-legal-court/.

[27] Alex Hern, "TechScape: Clearview AI Was Fined £7.5m for Brazenly Harvesting Your Data—Does It Care?" *The Guardian*, May 25, 2022, https://www.theguardian.com/technology/2022/may/25/techscape-clearview-ai-facial-recognition-fine.

Research and Development for Alternative Technical Approaches

Congress may wish to consider providing funds to federal agencies for intramural and extramural research to examine the development of alternative AI models or related technologies that may preserve individual privacy, such as privacy-enhancing technologies.[28] There are benefits and tradeoffs to some AI models under development that may have privacy implications. For example, smaller models that use less data or avoid transmitting and analyzing data in the cloud may minimize some privacy concerns but may amplify other issues, such as bias, by training on smaller datasets and potentially limiting the representativeness of data being used to train models.[29] Congress may consider directing agencies to conduct and fund research to support privacy-by-design[30] for AI and ML applications in order to both foster greater privacy for individuals and support the development of AI technologies and the global competitiveness of U.S. AI companies.

Disclaimer

This document was prepared by the Congressional Research Service (CRS). CRS serves as nonpartisan shared staff to congressional committees and Members of Congress. It operates solely at the behest of and under the direction of Congress. Information in a CRS Report should not be relied upon for purposes other than public understanding of information that has been provided by CRS to Members of Congress in connection with CRS's institutional role. CRS Reports, as a work of the United States Government,

---

[28] In a 2022 Request for Information, the White House Office of Science and Technology defined privacy-enhancing technologies as "a broad set of technologies that protect privacy." Examples could include "privacy-preserving data sharing and analytics technologies, which describes the set of techniques and approaches that enable data sharing and analysis among participating parties while maintaining disassociability and confidentiality. Such technologies include, but are not limited to, secure multiparty computation, homomorphic encryption, zero-knowledge proofs, federated learning, secure enclaves, differential privacy, and synthetic data generation tools." Office of Science and Technology Policy (OSTP), "Request for Information on Advancing Privacy-Enhancing Technologies," 87 *Federal Register* 35250-35252, June 9, 2022.

[29] Kyle Wiggers, "The Emerging Types of Language Models and Why They Matter," TechCrunch, April 28, 2022, https://techcrunch.com/2022/04/28/the-emerging-types-of-language-models-and-why-they-matter/.

[30] James Coker, "#DataPrivacyWeek Interview: Overcoming Privacy Challenges in AI," *Infosecurity Magazine*, January 25, 2022, https://www.infosecurity-magazine.com/interviews/data-privacy-week-privacy-ai/.

Chapter 11

Generative Artificial Intelligence and Copyright Law*

Christopher T. Zirpoli

Abstract

Innovations in artificial intelligence (AI) are raising new questions about how copyright law principles such as authorship, infringement, and fair use will apply to content created or used by AI. So-called "generative AI" computer programs—such as Open AI's DALL-E and ChatGPT programs, Stability AI's Stable Diffusion program, and Midjourney's self-titled program—are able to generate new images, texts, and other content (or "outputs") in response to a user's textual prompts (or "inputs"). These generative AI programs are trained to generate such outputs partly by exposing them to large quantities of existing works such as writings, photos, paintings, and other artworks. This Legal Sidebar explores questions that courts and the U.S. Copyright Office have begun to confront regarding whether generative AI outputs may be copyrighted and how generative AI might infringe copyrights in other works.

Copyright in Works Created with Generative AI

The widespread use of generative AI programs raises the question of who, if anyone, may hold the copyright to content created using these programs.

---

* This is an edited, reformatted and augmented version of Congressional Research Service, Publication No. LSB10922, dated September 29, 2023.

In: Artificial Intelligence
Editor: Sonja Buckley
ISBN: 979-8-89530-859-2

Do AI Outputs Enjoy Copyright Protection?

The question of whether or not copyright protection may be afforded to AI outputs—such as images created by DALL-E or texts created by ChatGPT—likely hinges at least partly on the concept of "authorship." The U.S. Constitution authorizes Congress to "secur[e] for limited Times to Authors . . . the exclusive Right to their . . . Writings." Based on this authority, the Copyright Act affords copyright protection to "original works of authorship." Although the Constitution and Copyright Act do not explicitly define who (or what) may be an "author," the U.S. Copyright Office recognizes copyright only in works "created by a human being." Courts have likewise declined to extend copyright protection to nonhuman authors, holding that a monkey who took a series of photos lacked standing to sue under the Copyright Act; that some human creativity was required to copyright a book purportedly inspired by celestial beings; and that a living garden could not be copyrighted as it lacked a human author.

A recent lawsuit challenged the human-authorship requirement in the context of works purportedly "authored" by AI. In June 2022, Stephen Thaler sued the Copyright Office for denying his application to register a visual artwork that he claims was authored "autonomously" by an AI program called the Creativity Machine. Dr. Thaler argued that human authorship is not required by the Copyright Act. On August 18, 2023, a federal district court granted summary judgment in favor of the Copyright Office. The court held that "human authorship is an essential part of a valid copyright claim," reasoning that only human authors need copyright as an incentive to create works. Dr. Thaler has stated that he plans to appeal the decision.

Assuming that a copyrightable work requires a human author, works created by humans using generative AI could still be entitled to copyright protection, depending on the nature of human involvement in the creative process. However, a recent copyright proceeding and subsequent Copyright Registration Guidance indicate that the Copyright Office is unlikely to find the requisite human authorship where an AI program generates works in response to text prompts. In September 2022, Kris Kashtanova registered a copyright for a graphic novel illustrated with images that Midjourney generated in response to text inputs. In October 2022, the Copyright Office initiated cancellation proceedings, noting that Kashtanova had not disclosed the use of AI. Kashtanova responded by arguing that the images were made via "a creative, iterative process." On February 21, 2023, the Copyright Office determined that the images were not copyrightable, deciding that Midjourney, rather than Kashtanova, authored the "visual material." In March 2023, the Copyright Office released guidance stating that, when AI "determines the expressive elements of its output, the generated material is not the product of human authorship."

Some commentators assert that some AI-generated works should receive copyright protection, arguing that AI programs are like other tools that human beings have used to create copyrighted works. For example, the Supreme Court has held since the 1884 case *Burrow-Giles Lithographic Co. v. Sarony* that photographs can be entitled to copyright protection where the photographer makes decisions regarding creative elements such as composition, arrangement, and lighting. Generative AI programs might be seen as a new tool analogous to the camera, as Kashtanova argued.

Other commentators and the Copyright Office dispute the photography analogy and question whether AI users exercise sufficient creative control for AI to be considered merely a tool. In Kashtanova's case, the Copyright Office reasoned that Midjourney was not "a tool that [] Kashtanova controlled and guided to reach [their] desired image" because it "generates images in an unpredictable way." The Copyright Office instead compared the AI user to "a client who hires an artist" and gives that artist only "general directions." The office's March 2023 guidance similarly claims that "users do not exercise ultimate creative control over how [generative AI] systems interpret prompts and generate materials." One of Kashtanova's lawyers, on the other hand, argues that the Copyright Act does not require such exacting creative control, noting that certain photographs and modern art incorporate a degree of happenstance.

Some commentators argue that the Copyright Act's distinction between copyrightable "works" and noncopyrightable "ideas" supplies another reason that copyright should not protect AI-generated works. One law professor has suggested that the human user who enters a text prompt into an AI program—for instance, asking DALL-E "to produce a painting of hedgehogs having a tea party on the beach"—has "contributed nothing more than an idea" to the finished work. According to this argument, the output image lacks a human author and cannot be copyrighted.

While the Copyright Office's actions indicate that it may be challenging to obtain copyright protection for AI-generated works, the issue remains unsettled. Applicants may file suit in U.S. district court to challenge the Copyright Office's final decisions to refuse to register a copyright (as Dr. Thaler did), and it remains to be seen whether federal courts will agree with all of the office's decisions. While the Copyright Office notes that courts sometimes give weight to the office's experience and expertise in this field, courts will not necessarily adopt the office's interpretations of the Copyright Act.

In addition, the Copyright Office's guidance accepts that works "containing" AI-generated material may be copyrighted under some circumstances, such as "sufficiently creative" human arrangements or modifications of AI-generated material or works that combine AI-generated and human-authored material. The office states that the author may only claim copyright protection "for their own contributions" to such works, and they must identify and disclaim AI-generated parts of the work if they apply to register their copyright. In September 2023, for instance, the Copyright Office Review Board affirmed the office's refusal to register a copyright for an artwork that was generated by Midjourney and then modified in various ways by the applicant, since the applicant did not disclaim the AI-generated material.

Who Owns the Copyright to Generative AI Outputs?

Assuming some AI-created works may be eligible for copyright protection, who owns that copyright? In general, the Copyright Act vests ownership "initially in the author or authors of the work." Given the lack of judicial or Copyright Office decisions recognizing copyright in AI-created works to date, however, no clear rule has emerged identifying who the "author or authors" of these works could be. Returning to the photography analogy, the AI's creator might be compared to the camera maker, while the AI user who prompts the creation of a specific work might be compared to the photographer who uses that camera to capture a specific image. On this view, the AI user would be considered the author and, therefore, the initial copyright owner. The creative choices involved in coding and training the AI, on the other hand, might give an AI's creator a stronger claim to some form of authorship than the manufacturer of a camera.

Companies that provide AI software may attempt to allocate the respective ownership rights of the company and its users via contract, such as the company's terms of service. OpenAI's Terms of Use, for example, appear to assign any copyright to the user: "OpenAI hereby assigns to you all its right, title and interest in and to Output." A previous version, by contrast, purported to give OpenAI such rights. As one scholar commented, OpenAI appears to "bypass most copyright questions through contract."

Copyright Infringement by Generative AI

Generative AI also raises questions about copyright infringement. Commentators and courts have begun to address whether generative AI programs may infringe copyright in existing works, either by making copies of existing works to train the AI or by generating outputs that resemble those existing works.

Does the AI Training Process Infringe Copyright in Other Works?

AI systems are "trained" to create literary, visual, and other artistic works by exposing the program to large amounts of data, which may include text, images, and other works downloaded from the internet. This training process involves making digital copies of existing works. As the U.S. Patent and Trademark Office has described, this process "will almost by definition involve the reproduction of entire works or substantial portions thereof." OpenAI, for example, acknowledges that its programs are trained on "large, publicly available datasets that include copyrighted works" and that this process "involves first making copies of the data to be analyzed" (although it now offers an option to remove images from training future image generation models). Creating such copies without permission may infringe the copyright holders' exclusive right to make reproductions of their work.

AI companies may argue that their training processes constitute fair use and are therefore noninfringing. Whether or not copying constitutes fair use depends on four statutory factors under 17 U.S.C. § 107:

1) the purpose and character of the use, including whether such use is of a commercial nature or is for nonprofit educational purposes;
2) the nature of the copyrighted work;
3) the amount and substantiality of the portion used in relation to the copyrighted work as a whole; and
4) the effect of the use upon the potential market for or value of the copyrighted work.

Some stakeholders argue that the use of copyrighted works to train AI programs should be considered a fair use under these factors. Regarding the first factor, OpenAI argues its purpose is "transformative" as opposed to "expressive" because the training process creates "a useful generative AI system." OpenAI also contends that the third factor supports fair use because the copies are not made available to the public but are used only to train the program. For support, OpenAI cites *The Authors Guild, Inc. v. Google, Inc.*, in which the U.S. Court of Appeals for the Second Circuit held that Google's copying of entire books to create a searchable database that displayed excerpts of those books constituted fair use.

Regarding the fourth fair use factor, some generative AI applications have raised concern that training AI programs on copyrighted works allows them to generate similar works that compete with the originals. For example, an AI-generated song called "Heart on My Sleeve," made to sound like the artists Drake and The Weeknd, was heard millions of times on streaming services. Universal Music Group, which has deals with both artists, argues that AI companies violate copyright by using these artists' songs in training data. OpenAI states that its visual art program DALL-E 3 "is designed to decline requests that ask for an image in the style of a living artist."

Plaintiffs have filed multiple lawsuits claiming the training process for AI programs infringed their copyrights in written and visual works. These include lawsuits by the Authors Guild and authors Paul Tremblay, Michael Chabon, Sarah Silverman, and others against OpenAI; separate lawsuits by Michael Chabon, Sarah Silverman, and others against Meta Platforms; proposed class action lawsuits against Alphabet Inc. and Stability AI and Midjourney; and a lawsuit by Getty Images against Stability AI. The Getty Images lawsuit, for instance, alleges that "Stability AI has copied at least 12 million copyrighted images from Getty Images' websites . . . in order to train its Stable Diffusion model." This lawsuit appears to dispute any characterization of fair use, arguing that Stable Diffusion is a commercial product, weighing against fair use under the first statutory factor, and that the program undermines the market for the original works, weighing against fair use under the fourth factor.

In September 2023, a U.S. district court ruled that a jury trial would be needed to determine whether it was fair use for an AI company to copy case summaries from Westlaw, a legal research platform, to train an AI program to quote pertinent passages from legal opinions in response to questions from a user. The court found that, while the defendant's use was "undoubtedly commercial," a jury would need to resolve factual disputes concerning whether the use was "transformative" (factor 1), to what extent the nature of the plaintiff's work favored fair use (factor 2), whether the defendant copied more than needed to train the AI program (factor 3), and whether the AI program would constitute a "market substitute" for Westlaw (factor 4). While the AI program at issue might not be considered "generative" AI, the same kinds of facts might be relevant to a court's fair-use analysis of making copies to train generative AI models.

Do AI Outputs Infringe Copyrights in Other Works?

AI programs might also infringe copyright by generating outputs that resemble existing works. Under U.S. case law, copyright owners may be able to show that such outputs infringe their copyrights if the AI program both (1) had access to their works and (2) created "substantially similar" outputs.

First, to establish copyright infringement, a plaintiff must prove the infringer "actually copied" the underlying work. This is sometimes proven circumstantially by evidence that the infringer "had access to the work." For AI outputs, access might be shown by evidence that the AI program was trained using the underlying work. For instance, the underlying work might be part of a publicly accessible internet site that was downloaded or "scraped" to train the AI program.

Second, a plaintiff must prove the new work is "substantially similar" to the underlying work to establish infringement. The substantial similarity test is difficult to define and varies across U.S. courts. Courts have variously described the test as requiring, for example, that the works have "a substantially similar total concept and feel" or "overall look and feel" or that "the ordinary reasonable person would fail to differentiate between the two works." Leading cases have also stated that this determination considers both "the qualitative and quantitative significance of the copied portion in relation to the plaintiff's work as a whole." For AI-generated outputs, no less than traditional works, the "substantial similarity" analysis may require courts to make these kinds of comparisons between the AI output and the underlying work.

There is significant disagreement as to how likely it is that generative AI programs will copy existing works in their outputs. OpenAI argues that "[w]ell-constructed AI systems generally do not regenerate, in any nontrivial portion, unaltered data from any particular work in their training corpus." Thus, OpenAI states, infringement "is an unlikely accidental outcome." By contrast, the Getty Images lawsuit alleges that "Stable Diffusion at times produces images that are highly similar to and derivative of the Getty Images." One study has found "a significant amount of copying" in less than 2% of the images created by Stable Diffusion, but the authors claimed that their methodology "likely underestimates the true rate" of copying.

Two kinds of AI outputs may raise special concerns. First, some AI programs may be used to create works involving existing fictional characters. These works may run a heightened risk of copyright infringement insofar as characters sometimes enjoy copyright protection in and of themselves. Second, some AI programs may be prompted to create artistic or literary works "in the style of" a particular artist or author, although—as noted above—some AI programs may now be designed to "decline" such prompts. These outputs are not necessarily infringing, as copyright law generally prohibits the copying of specific works rather than an artist's overall style. Regarding the AI-generated song "Heart on My Sleeve," for instance, one commentator notes that the imitation of Drake's voice appears not to violate copyright law, although it may raise concerns under state right-of-publicity laws. Nevertheless, some artists are concerned that AI programs are uniquely capable of mass-producing works that copy their style, potentially undercutting the value of their work. Plaintiffs in one lawsuit against Stable Diffusion, for example, claim that few human artists can successfully mimic another artist's style, whereas "AI Image Products do so with ease."

A final question is who is (or should be) liable if generative AI outputs do infringe copyrights in existing works. Under current doctrines, both the AI user and the AI company could potentially be liable. For instance, even if a user were directly liable for infringement, the AI company could potentially face liability under the doctrine of "vicarious infringement," which applies to defendants who have "the right and ability to supervise the infringing activity" and "a direct financial interest in such activities." The lawsuit against Stable Diffusion, for instance, claims that the defendant AI companies are vicariously liable for copyright infringement. One complication of AI programs is that the user might not be aware of—or have access to—a work that was copied in response to the user's prompt. Under current law, this may make it challenging to analyze whether the user is liable for copyright infringement.

Considerations for Congress

Congress may consider whether any of the copyright law questions raised by generative AI programs require amendments to the Copyright Act or other legislation. Congress may, for example, consider legislation clarifying whether AI-generated works are copyrightable, who should be considered the author of such works, or when the process of training generative AI programs constitutes fair use. Given how little opportunity the courts and Copyright

Office have had to address these issues, Congress may adopt a wait-and-see approach. As the courts gain experience handling cases involving generative AI, they may be able to provide greater guidance and predictability in this area through judicial opinions. Based on the outcomes of these cases, Congress may reassess whether legislative action is needed.

Disclaimer

Chapter 12

Section 230 Immunity and Generative Artificial Intelligence*

Peter J. Benson
and Valerie C. Brannon

Abstract

Over the past year, technology companies have expanded access to services capable of creating content using artificial intelligence (AI). In February 2023, Microsoft announced an "all new, AI-powered Bing search engine" that "can help you write an email, create a 5-day itinerary for a dream vacation to Hawaii, with links to book your travel and accommodations, prep for a job interview or create a quiz for trivia night." Google introduced Bard, an "experimental conversational AI service," the same month.

Applications such as these that are capable of generating new content like text, images, and videos form a subset of AI applications often referred to as "generative AI."

As access to AI tools has expanded and the underlying models have become more powerful, Congress has shown interest in regulating AI models. Committees have held hearings, and Members have introduced bills to regulate AI (or announced a framework for doing so). Some Members have called for a task force or commission to recommend rules. The executive branch has also weighed in. The White House issued an Executive Order, in October 2023, tasking agencies with actions to address the advent of AI models.

---

* This is an edited, reformatted and augmented version of Congressional Research Service, Publication No. LSB11097, dated December 28, 2023.

In: Artificial Intelligence
Editor: Sonja Buckley
ISBN: 979-8-89530-859-2

Generative AI poses unique policy and legal issues. One question raised by the introduction of generative AI products is the extent to which companies that provide the products could be held liable for illegal content generated by the AI. The answer likely depends in part on an existing legal framework: Section 230 of the Communications Act of 1934, a federal statute that, subject to some exceptions, immunizes interactive computer service providers from being sued as the publisher or speaker of information provided by another party. If this immunity extends to claims based on an output from a generative AI product, plaintiffs defamed by an AI output (for example) may be barred from suing a company that provided the AI product. The potential application of Section 230 to generative AI has already garnered comments at a Supreme Court oral argument and from Section 230's primary authors. This Sidebar discusses how Section 230 might apply to legal claims involving generative AI products.

Section 230

Section 230 creates a federal immunity for publishing another person's content online, as explained in a longer CRS report. Specifically, Section 230, enacted in the Communications Decency Act of 1996, prevents providers and users of "interactive computer services" from being held liable—that is, legally responsible—as the "publisher or speaker" of information provided by another person. "Interactive computer service" is defined as any service that "provides or enables computer access by multiple users to a computer server." This broad term encompasses services such as Facebook, Google, and Amazon. There are exceptions to Section 230 immunity, such as for intellectual property law.

Section 230 only provides immunity for content provided by *another* person and does not apply if a provider or user of an interactive computer service helped create or develop the content. Although the Supreme Court has never interpreted Section 230, many federal and state courts have considered when a lawsuit would attempt to hold a defendant liable for another's content or for the defendant's own content. A number of courts have settled on a "material contribution" test, under which Section 230 immunity does not apply if the provider or user materially contributed to the alleged unlawfulness of the content.

This inquiry is highly fact-specific. The U.S. Court of Appeals for the Ninth Circuit, for example, decided in one case that Section 230 barred housing discrimination claims against the operator of the website Roommates.com based on one portion of the website but did not bar claims based on a different portion of the site. The court said an open text field where roommate seekers could describe "what [they] are looking for in a roommate" did not materially contribute to discrimination, even if users' descriptions ended up facilitating discriminatory searches. In contrast, the court held that "search and email systems [designed] to limit the listings available to subscribers based on sex, sexual orientation and presence of children" did materially contribute to alleged discrimination. The court suggested sites could provide "*neutral* tools" to post user content so long as the tools do not materially contribute to illegal activity.

Citing this "neutral tools" analysis, some federal courts of appeals have held that Section 230 barred lawsuits against service providers for promoting harmful content through algorithms, where the algorithms used objective factors that treated the harmful content similarly to other content. Beyond content recommendation algorithms, courts have held that other choices about how to present material— and even actions that rearrange or slightly edit material—can also be immunized by Section 230. In *O'Kroley v. Fastcase, Inc.*, a federal appeals court concluded that Section 230 barred a defamation lawsuit challenging the way Google presented its search results. The plaintiff alleged that when he searched his name, one entry on the search results page inaccurately suggested that he had been involved in a case regarding indecency with a child. The court held that even though Google "performed some automated editorial acts on" content provided by other parties, "such as removing spaces and altering font," these alterations did not materially contribute to the alleged defamatory nature of the content.

In contrast, in *FTC v. Accusearch Inc.*, a federal appeals court held Section 230 immunity did not apply because the website operator that was sued had helped to develop third-party information. The website sold information contained in telephone records. Although the website acquired the records from other parties, it solicited and paid for them. The legal harm came from the publication of the records: the FTC alleged the website operator violated a federal provision limiting disclosure of certain personal information. The court said the website operator was responsible for developing the information and thus not protected by Section 230, as it "contributed mightily to the unlawful conduct" by paying researchers to acquire confidential records with the intent of making them public contrary to federal law.

Even if Section 230 does not apply, a service provider will only be liable in a lawsuit if a plaintiff can prove their underlying legal claims. For example, if a copyright lawsuit falls within the Section 230 exception for intellectual property law, the plaintiff will still have to prove the provider in fact violated copyright law. Other CRS products may be relevant to that inquiry. For example, other products provide an introduction to tort law and discuss generative AI and copyright law or campaign advertising.

Generative AI

"Artificial intelligence" is a broad term referring to computerized systems that act in ways commonly thought to imitate human intelligence. Generative AI is a type of AI that uses machine learning to generate new content, as discussed in this In Focus. For instance, a user can provide a text prompt that the generative AI uses to create an image or other content. Machine learning algorithms allow computers to learn at least partially without explicit instructions. Programmers gather and prepare training data, then they feed that data into a machine learning model. There are different types of generative AI, but applications based on large language models, such as OpenAI's ChatGPT, were trained by providing the model with massive amounts of existing data scraped from the internet. (This CRS report discusses some of the data privacy concerns with generative AI.)

Accordingly, when generative AI creates new content, it draws from this existing information created by other parties and attempts to match the style and content of the underlying data. However, the new content may not be identical to the training data. Generative AI may sometimes produce so-called "hallucinated" outputs that, for instance, go beyond the scope of the training data or have incorrectly decoded that data.

The generative outputs are also influenced by the specific text of the prompt itself—because the algorithms generate content based on statistical probabilities that the underlying training data are associated with the words in the prompt, changes to the words in the prompt can change the output. Even the same prompt provided to a generative AI system multiple times can result in different outputs.

Potential Application of Section 230 to Generative AI

Courts have not yet decided whether or how Section 230 may be used as a defense against claims based on outputs from recently released generative AI products, but they may soon be asked to address the issue. Outputs from generative AI products have already led to lawsuits. In June 2023, for example, a radio host sued OpenAI, alleging that ChatGPT defamed him. In a second defamation case, a plaintiff alleged that searching for his name on Microsoft's Bing search engine returned an AI-generated summary that commingled facts about him with facts about a different individual who had a similar name and who once pleaded guilty to seditious conspiracy. Although no defendant in these cases has yet raised Section 230 as a defense, the claims are similar to those that have given rise to Section 230 defenses in the past. In each case, the plaintiff alleges that a defendant published information using a tool that relies at least in part on user inputs and data created by other parties. At least one commentator has asserted that generative AI companies might attempt to invoke Section 230 in similar circumstances. Even if raised, the courts deciding these cases may not address the issue. The cases could settle or be resolved on the merits or another defense. Still, these or future lawsuits alleging that generative AI outputs are defamatory, negligent, or cause other legal harms may test whether the providers of the tools or users who requested those outputs materially contributed to the harmfulness of the challenged content such that Section 230 immunity would not apply.

If Section 230 were to be invoked in such circumstances, past cases suggest Section 230 would be applied in a fact-specific manner. Thus, a Section 230 inquiry in a lawsuit challenging any given AI-generated output would likely depend on the particular legal claim and underlying facts. Not all generative AI products function the same way, and not all legal claims would necessarily turn on the same aspects of a given product. As one group of scholars asserts, generative AI products "operate on something like a spectrum between a retrieval search engine (more likely to be covered by Section 230) and a creative engine (less likely to be covered)." Section 230's application could therefore vary across different generative AI products, different applications of a single product, and different legal claims about an application or product.

As such, commentators have made different predictions about how courts would resolve Section 230 defenses based in part on which aspects of generative AI the arguments focus on. Some commentators contend that "AI programs' output is composed by the programs themselves," so the AI providers should be viewed as information creators or developers that receive no Section 230 immunity. Large language models, for example, can "draft[] text on a topic in response to a user request or develop[] text to summarize the results of a search inquiry." A commentator has argued that this aspect of the technology would likely lead courts to conclude that large language models develop text themselves. A large language model's output can "hallucinate," creating brand new "text on a topic" that no other party has ever written. If generated content contains claims or assertions that do not appear in its training data, the claims or assertions could be seen as entirely new information created by the providers rather than by another person. Even if an AI program assembles facts or claims from training data into new material that does not appear elsewhere on the internet, this may be viewed as similar to *Accusearch*, where the website operator was deemed "responsible for the development of the specific content that was the source of the alleged liability" and thus was unprotected by Section 230.

On the other hand, another commentator argues that the current iteration of ChatGPT (as of March 2023) "is entirely driven by third-party input" and "does not invent, create, or develop outputs absent any prompting from an information content provider." When it receives a prompt, ChatGPT "uses predictive algorithms and an array of data made up entirely of publicly available information online to respond to [the] user-created inputs." Outside the context of Section 230, OpenAI has claimed that the "content" associated with any particular ChatGPT interaction includes both the machine-generated outputs and the user-generated inputs that prompted them. Courts focusing on these aspects of the product could consider ChatGPT analogous to search engines that use algorithms to generate lists and illustrative snippets of websites in response to user inputs. As discussed, federal appeals courts have held that Section 230 shields internet search engines from liability for claims based on the results returned by users' searches.

Autocomplete features are another potential analogy, given that some generative AI operates by predicting and assembling plausible text outputs that it associates with user prompts and patterns learned from training datasets. Although there is relatively little case law on point, two federal trial courts have held that Section 230 immunizes search engines from claims that auto-generated, suggested search terms were defamatory. The courts reasoned that the "auto-generated terms 'indicate[] only that other websites and users have connected plaintiff's name' with certain terms," meaning that the allegedly harmful content was created by another party. This reasoning could apply to an AI product that completes a sentence by "predict[ing] probabilities for the next plausible word or phrase given previous words or phrases."

Similarly, some courts have held, under the neutral tools test, that other algorithmic processes do not develop content for the purposes of Section 230. For example, the U.S. Court of Appeals for the Second Circuit held that Facebook does not develop or create content that its algorithms arrange and display on a user's page when the algorithms "take the information provided by . . . users and 'match' it to other users . . . based on objective factors applicable to any content." As mentioned, a large language model can be "trained simply to predict probabilities for the next plausible word or phrase given previous words or phrases." Some scholars have argued that this sort of probabilistic compilation could likewise be considered a tool that operates neutrally, regardless of the particular content to which it is being applied. The same algorithmic process that generates an output containing defamation or other illegal content in response to some user interactions could generate lawful outputs in response to other interactions. The neutral tools test, however, has been criticized by some, including with respect to how it might apply to AI products. A court could deny Section 230 immunity without resorting to the neutral tools test if it concluded in a given case that an AI output was created by the AI provider rather than information created by *another* person.

In all of these potential analyses, details will matter. Regardless of how the contours of the analysis are ultimately defined, current case law suggests that courts applying Section 230 to claims involving generative AI products would need to look closely at how the particular AI product at issue generates an output and what aspect of the output the plaintiff alleges to be illegal. Because generative AI products are not all the same, are likely to continue to evolve, and can rely on data and inputs from disparate sources, Section 230 analysis may lead to different outcomes in different cases.

Considerations for Congress

As Congress contemplates regulating generative AI, it may consider whether any proposals that would impose liability on generative AI companies would potentially conflict with Section 230 immunity. If so, Congress might consider creating Section 230 carveouts in any new legislation. Without such a carveout, courts may construe a law that imposes civil liability on generative AI companies to be limited by Section 230. For instance, Congress could create a new private right of action for harms stemming from generative AI outputs. The new right of action could define the elements a plaintiff would have to prove to establish liability and could specify whether Section 230 provides a defense. Congress might also consider creating new immunities to legal claims that relate to generative AI outputs. A new immunity could preclude liability regardless of whether Section 230 may also apply.

In addition, Congress could amend Section 230 to address generative AI directly. This sort of amendment could extend immunity to claims arising from generative AI products, withhold immunity from such claims, or extend immunity to certain types of claims and withhold it from others. A bill introduced in the 118th Congress (S. 1993), for example, would withhold Section 230 immunity "if the conduct underlying the claim or charge involves the use or provision of generative artificial intelligence by the interactive computer service." This bill would remove immunity not only for generative AI providers but also in any claim *involving* a provider's *use* of generative AI. Alternatively, Congress could wait to see how courts address defenses under the current version of Section 230 in cases based on outputs from generative AI.

Other proposals to more broadly amend Section 230 could also have implications for generative AI. For instance, the DISCOURSE Act (S. 921) would effectively create an exception for certain service providers that modify or alter others' information. This approach could sweep in generative AI that edits third-party content in creating new outputs.

Congress's ability to regulate in this area could be limited by the First Amendment's Free Speech Clause. Some scholars have argued that generative AI output is protected by the First Amendment, either because the creators use the program as a means of expression or because the program's users have a right to use generative AI as a method of creating or receiving expression. The Supreme Court has ruled that "the creation and dissemination of information are speech within the meaning of the First Amendment," such that even factual information (and sometimes false information) can be constitutionally protected. These cases suggest a law creating or allowing liability for using generative AI could implicate free speech interests. If Section 230 did not bar a lawsuit, whether under existing interpretations of the law or because Congress created a new exception, the protections of the First Amendment might still apply.

A law that affects speech is not necessarily unconstitutional, however. First Amendment protections are not absolute. Instead, courts apply different types of constitutional scrutiny depending on the type of speech being regulated and how the regulation affects that speech. A law amending when Section 230 immunity applies might be scrutinized differently than a law more directly regulating generative AI activity. Further, for example, laws that regulate speech based on its content are generally subject to stricter constitutional scrutiny than content-neutral regulations. Thus, the constitutionality of a law regulating generative AI, including through an amendment to Section 230, may depend in part on whether the law targets the function of a generative AI program or its expressive output and on whether it targets specific types of AI outputs based on their content.

Disclaimer

Chapter 13

Artificial Intelligence Prompts Renewed Consideration of a Federal Right of Publicity*

Christopher T. Zirpoli

Abstract

Recent uses of artificial intelligence (AI) to create realistic images, videos, replicas, or voice simulations of real people have prompted some Members of Congress to call for federal legislation to protect the "right of publicity" (or ROP, for short). The ROP is often defined as the right to prevent unauthorized commercial uses of one's name, image, or likeness (NIL) or other aspects of one's identity (such as one's voice). The ROP is not comprehensively protected by current federal laws.

This Legal Sidebar surveys existing state-level legal protections for the ROP, explains how they intersect with federal laws regarding intellectual property (IP), describes potential ROP concerns raised by AI, and presents constitutional and other legal considerations for Congress. Another Legal Sidebar discusses questions AI raises for copyright law, while a separate Legal Sidebar and a CRS report discuss the ability of college student-athletes to receive compensation for uses of their NIL.

State Right of Publicity Laws

The ROP is protected in some form by the laws of most U.S. states, and the number of states that recognize this right has expanded over the past several

---

* This is an edited, reformatted and augmented version of Congressional Research Service, Publication No. LSB11052, dated January 29, 2024.

In: Artificial Intelligence
Editor: Sonja Buckley
ISBN: 979-8-89530-859-2

decades. One study found that 35 states recognized the ROP as of 2020. ROP laws generally create a private right of action for the unauthorized commercial use of another person's NIL. For example, if a manufacturer uses a famous athlete's name or face in a TV commercial without her permission, the athlete could sue the manufacturer for violating her ROP, and a court could order the manufacturer to pay damages and stop showing the commercial.

What constitutes an unauthorized commercial use of NIL can vary from state to state. Some states' ROP laws may apply only to advertising, while others more broadly apply to any use that commercially benefits the user, such as video game or comic book characters based on real people.

Other notable differences between the ROP laws of various states concern questions such as:

- *Is the ROP protected by statute, common law, or both?* Twenty-five states have enacted statutes protecting the ROP. In some of these states, including California, the ROP is protected by both statutes and common law (law derived from court opinions). In other states, including Delaware, the ROP is protected by common law only, sometimes as an application of a common law "right of privacy."
- *What parts of a person's identity does the ROP protect?* The ROP often only protects a person's NIL, voice, and signature. In some states, the ROP also includes someone's "distinctive appearance, gestures, or mannerisms." Courts have construed certain states' ROP laws to protect more abstract aspects of personal identity, finding defendants liable for using an image of a famous driver's race car, a blonde robot performing Vanna White's role on a game show, or the catch phrase "here's Johnny."
- *Do all individuals enjoy the ROP?* State laws vary as to whether all persons or only those with "commercially valuable" NIL (such as celebrities) may assert ROP claims.
- *Does the ROP survive a person's death?* In some states, the ROP is *descendible*, meaning it can be asserted by one's heirs after a person dies. States that recognize a descendible (or postmortem) ROP differ as to their duration, with postmortem rights lasting 20 years in Virginia, 70 years in California, and 100 years in Oklahoma, for instance. Under Tennessee law, postmortem ROP may last indefinitely. In other states, the ROP is not descendible, or else courts have not resolved the issue.

Often, the law of the state in which a person is domiciled—or, where they were domiciled when they died—governs their ROP. Indiana's ROP statute, however, allows suit "regardless of a personality's domicile" for infringing materials "disseminated within Indiana." This law may allow non-Indiana plaintiffs to sue for infringing materials that are made available in Indiana via television or the internet.

Intersection of Right of Publicity and Federal IP Laws

Although the ROP is distinct from the forms of IP already protected by federal law, it is related in some ways to trademarks and copyrights. If Congress chooses to regulate the ROP via federal law, it may consider how best to harmonize the ROP with existing trademark and copyright laws.

Trademarks

While the ROP generally protects commercial uses of a person's identity, trademarks protect commercial uses of words, names, and other symbols that distinguish one person's goods from others. The ROP may overlap with trademarks in cases where aspects of a person's NIL can be trademarked. A person's name, for instance, may be trademarked if it acquires a distinctive meaning and is used commercially to identify goods or services (e.g., McDonald's). The ROP may be seen as serving a similar function to trademarks, although some scholars have criticized the theoretical foundations and expansion of the ROP.

Trademark infringement occurs when someone without authorization uses a trademark in a way that creates a likelihood of confusion for consumers. The Lanham Act—the federal trademark law—also establishes a cause of action for "false endorsement," which provides additional protection that overlaps with the ROP. False endorsement occurs when a person's identity is used in a way that is likely to confuse consumers into believing that the person recommends a product. In 2023, for instance, actor Tom Hanks alerted fans that an AI-generated replica of him was being used to advertise a dental plan without his permission; such scenarios might give rise to both state ROP and Lanham Act false endorsement claims.

State ROP laws can provide broader protection than the Lanham Act, however, as they often prohibit unauthorized commercial uses of NIL regardless of whether they imply any sponsorship or confuse consumers. In addition, some courts have held only individuals with “recognizability” (such as Hanks) may sue for false endorsement, whereas many state laws allow all individuals to sue for ROP violations.

Copyrights

Copyrights protect original works of authorship that are “fixed” (i.e., recorded) in a “tangible medium,” including books, paintings, music recordings, and films. The Copyright Act gives copyright owners the “exclusive right” to reproduce (copy), perform, display, and distribute copyrighted works and to make derivative works (adaptations) from them. Generally, a work’s author automatically owns the copyright but may sell or license it to others. In short, whereas ROP laws prohibit unauthorized uses of another person’s identity, copyright law prohibits unauthorized uses of another’s creative works. As one illustration, in January 2024, the estate of comedian George Carlin filed a lawsuit based on an unauthorized comedy program delivered in an AI-generated imitation of Carlin’s voice. The complaint claims defendants infringed their copyrights by making copies of Carlin’s works to train the AI model— similar to other AI-related copyright lawsuits noted in a separate Legal Sidebar—and that defendants violated Carlin’s ROP under California law by using his NIL to promote the comedy program and other media.

The ROP intersects with copyright law inasmuch as both fictional and nonfictional copyrighted works often include the NIL of real people, including descriptions, portrayals, recordings, or performances of those people. For example, people depicted in photographs often do not hold the copyright, since the photographer is usually considered the author, but they may have ROP interests implicated by how those photos are used. These rights may come into conflict, such as when a copyright owner displays photographs in a way that commercially exploits the NIL of people shown in the photographs.

Section 301 of the Copyright Act provides that the Copyright Act preempts (supersedes) any state law rights that are “equivalent to” a copyright holder’s exclusive rights. Some commentators argue courts have inconsistently applied Section 301 in cases where copyrights conflict with the ROP. Some courts have dismissed lawsuits that allege copyright holders violated the ROP by exercising their exclusive rights under the Copyright Act. For instance, in 2017, one court held that Section 301 preempted a suit claiming the sale of photographs of NCAA athletes violated the athletes' ROP. Other courts have held that Section 301 does not preempt ROP claims based on advertising. For example, one court held that a sports announcer's ROP claim was not preempted where an excerpt of his voice from a copyrighted broadcast was used in a commercial for a video game. Congress could clarify the scope of copyright preemption of ROP claims by amending Section 301. In addition, if Congress enacts any new protections for ROP at the federal level, it may specify under what circumstances copyright would preempt such protections.

ROP laws can protect commercial interests in live performances, which cannot be copyrighted unless they are "fixed" (e.g., filmed). In the Supreme Court's only ROP case to date, for instance, a performer sued a television company for broadcasting his "human cannonball" act, undermining ticket sales for the act. The Supreme Court held that the First Amendment did not prevent the performer from asserting a ROP claim against the company. As an exception to the rule that live performances have no copyright protection, in 1994 Congress provided criminal and civil liability for recording and distributing live music performances without permission, although some courts have questioned these laws' constitutionality.

Right of Publicity Concerns Regarding AI

Recent advances in generative AI systems, which are trained on large volumes of data to generate new content that may mimic likenesses, voices, or other aspects of real people's identities, have stimulated congressional interest. Like the above-noted uses of AI to imitate Tom Hanks and George Carlin, the examples below illustrate that some AI uses raise concerns under both ROP laws and myriad other laws.

One example of AI's capability to imitate voices was an AI-generated song called "Heart on My Sleeve," which sounded like it was sung by the artist Drake and was heard by millions of listeners in 2023.

Simulating an artist's voice in this manner could make one liable under ROP laws, although these laws differ as to whether they cover voice imitations or vocal styles as opposed to the artist's actual voice. Voice imitations are not, however, prohibited by copyright laws. For example, the alleged copyright violation that caused YouTube to remove "Heart on My Sleeve"—namely, that it sampled another recording without permission—was unrelated to the

Drake voice imitation. In August 2023, Google and Universal Music were in discussions to license artists' melodies and voices for AI-generated songs.

The potential for AI to replicate both voices and likenesses was also a point of contention in last year's negotiations for a collective bargaining agreement between the Screen Actors Guild-American Federation of Television and Radio Artists (SAG-AFTRA)—a union that represents movie, television, and radio actors—and television and movie studios, including streaming services. SAG-AFTRA expressed concern that AI could be used to alter or replace actors' performances without their permission, such as by using real film recordings to train AI to create "digital replicas" of actors and voice actors. The Memorandum of Agreement between SAG-AFTRA and studios approved in December 2023 requires studios to obtain "clear and conspicuous" consent from an actor or background actor to create or use a digital replica of the actor or to digitally alter the actor's performance, with certain exceptions. It also requires that the actor's consent for use of a digital replica or digital alterations be based on a "reasonably specific description" of the intended use or alteration. The agreement provides that consent continues after the actor's death unless "explicitly limited," while consent for additional postmortem uses must be obtained from the actor's authorized representative or—if a representative cannot be identified or located—from the union.

In January 2024, SAG-AFTRA announced it had also reached an agreement with a voice technology company regarding voice replicas for video games, while a negotiation to update SAG-AFTRA's agreement with video game publishers is reportedly ongoing.

Commentators have also raised concern with deceptive AI-generated or AI-altered content known as "deepfakes," including some videos with sexually explicit content and others meant to denigrate public officials. To the extent this content includes real people's NIL and is used commercially, ROP laws might provide a remedy. Where deepfakes are used to promote products or services—such as the AI replica of Tom Hanks used in a dental plan ad—they may also constitute false endorsement under the Lanham Act. In addition to these laws, some states have enacted laws prohibiting sexually explicit deepfakes, with California and New York giving victims a civil claim and Georgia and Virginia imposing criminal liability. In addition, Section 1309 of the federal Violence Against Women Act Reauthorization Act of 2022 (VAWA 2022) provides a civil claim for nonconsensual disclosure of "intimate visual depictions," which might be interpreted to prohibit intimate deepfakes—as might some states' "revenge porn" laws. A bill introduced in the House of Representatives in May 2023, the Preventing Deepfakes of

Intimate Images Act, H.R. 3106, would amend VAWA 2022 by creating a separate civil claim for disclosing certain "intimate digital depictions" without the written consent of the depicted individual, as well as providing criminal liability for certain actual or threatened disclosures. Deepfakes may also give rise to liability under state defamation laws where a party uses them to communicate reputation-damaging falsehoods about a person with a requisite degree of fault.

Regarding the use of AI in political advertisements, some proposed legislation would prohibit deepfakes or require disclaimers for them in federal campaigns, although such proposals may raise First Amendment concerns. The Protect Elections from Deceptive AI Act, S. 2770 (118th Cong.), for instance, would ban the use of AI to generate materially deceptive content falsely depicting federal candidates in political ads to influence federal elections, while excluding news, commentary, satires, and parodies from liability.

Google announced that, as of mid-November 2023, verified election advertisers on its platform "must prominently disclose when their ads contain synthetic content that inauthentically depicts real or realistic-looking people or events."

Another concern some commentators raise is that AI-generated material might be falsely attributed to real persons without their permission. One writer who focuses on the publishing industry, for instance, found that books apparently generated by AI were being sold under her name on Amazon. Although the company ultimately removed these titles, the writer claimed that her "initial infringement claim with Amazon went nowhere," since her name was not trademarked and the books did not infringe existing copyrights. As she noted, however, this scenario might give rise to claims under state ROP laws as well as the Lanham Act. In addition, the Federal Trade Commission (FTC) states that "books sold as if authored by humans but in fact reflecting the output of [AI]" violate the FTC Act and may result in civil fines.

It is unclear how Section 230 of the Communications Act of 1934 might apply when ROP-infringing content from a third party, including content made with AI, is disseminated through social media and other interactive computer services. Although the law generally bars any lawsuits that would hold online service providers and users liable for third party content, there is an exception allowing lawsuits under "any law pertaining to intellectual property." Courts differ as to whether state ROP laws and the Lanham Act's prohibition on false endorsement are laws "pertaining to" IP within the meaning of Section 230.

Another Legal Sidebar discusses the application of Section 230 to generative AI more broadly.

Considerations for Congress

Some commentators have called for federal ROP legislation to provide more uniform and predictable protection for the ROP in the United States. Others have argued that Congress should leave ROP protection to the states on federalism grounds. If Congress decides to craft federal ROP legislation, it might consider the scope of the ROP protections it seeks to enact, the effect of those enactments on state ROP laws, and constitutional authorities and limitations on Congress's power to enact ROP protections. As noted below, some Members have proposed legislation that would prohibit certain unauthorized uses of digital replicas or depictions of individuals while leaving state ROP laws in place.

Scope and Preemptive Effect of Federal ROP Legislation

Congress has many options to determine how broadly to protect the ROP via possible federal legislation. Federal ROP legislation might specify, for instance, which aspects of a person's identity are protected, whether individuals without a commercially valuable identity may assert the ROP, and how long—if at all—the ROP survives a person's death. Legislation might also specify whether a federal ROP applies broadly to all uses of NIL or only to specific uses. For example, a discussion draft circulated in October 2023 by four Senators, the NO FAKES Act of 2023, would create a civil action for producing, publishing, distributing, or transmitting a "digital replica" of a real person's image, voice, or likeness without consent, with some exceptions. A bill introduced in the House of Representatives in January 2024, the No AI FRAUD Act, H.R. 6943, would create a civil action for certain conduct involving "digital depictions," "personalized cloning services," and "digital voice replicas" of real people without their consent. These proposals differ as to how long postmortem rights may last, among other differences.

Additionally, Congress may consider whether federal ROP legislation should preempt or leave in place existing state ROP laws. Existing federal IP laws provide examples of both approaches, as the Patent Act and Copyright

Act largely preempt state laws while the Lanham Act and Defend Trade Secrets Act do not. Some commentators argue Congress should preempt state ROP laws to promote greater uniformity and predictability. Alternatively, Congress could create a minimum level of ROP protection under federal law, letting individual states provide greater ROP protections if they wish. The NO FAKES Act of 2023 and No AI FRAUD Act, for instance, state that they do not preempt other ROP protections.

Constitutional Authority and Limitations for Federal ROP Legislation

While Congress has express constitutional authority to enact patent and copyright laws, its power to protect other IP, such as trademarks and trade secrets, derives from its authority to regulate interstate commerce. Some have argued the Commerce Clause of the Constitution gives Congress the power to establish a federal ROP and preempt state ROP laws. ROP laws would likely fall within Congress's commerce authority so long as they regulate uses of NIL in or substantially affecting interstate commerce.

ROP laws create civil liability for certain NIL-containing speech—potentially including media such as books, films, and video games—and therefore raise questions about defendants' First Amendment rights. Some scholars argue that courts apply inconsistent tests to resolve clashes between the ROP and First Amendment protections. The Ninth Circuit, for example, held that the First Amendment did not shield the use of football players' avatars in a video game from a ROP lawsuit, since the avatars were not a "transformative use" of the players' identity under a test first articulated by the Supreme Court of California. The Ninth Circuit reached a different result in a Lanham Act false endorsement case involving another football player's avatar, holding that the use of the plaintiff's NIL was "artistically relevant" to the video game and therefore protected under a test developed by the Second Circuit. In a third case, the Ninth Circuit held that the film portrayal of an army veteran was not subject to the transformative use test because, unlike the football players, the veteran had not built up "a marketable performance or identity." The court therefore applied strict scrutiny, a standard requiring that a law be narrowly tailored to serve a compelling governmental interest. The court held that application of California's ROP statute would violate the First

Amendment because the plaintiff could not demonstrate a "compelling state interest," given his lack of a marketable identity.

Congress might have more latitude to enact ROP laws aimed at commercial speech, such as advertising, which merely proposes a commercial transaction or relates solely to the speaker's and the audience's economic interests. Courts typically subject commercial speech regulations to intermediate scrutiny, a less stringent standard than strict scrutiny that requires the government to show that its regulation directly advances a substantial government interest and is not broader than necessary to serve that interest.

If Congress enacts federal protections for the ROP, it may seek to mitigate the need for judicial resolution of conflicts between the ROP and the First Amendment, or it may try to give wider latitude to free speech than courts might hold is constitutionally required. To limit the reach of ROP claims, Congress could consider enacting statutory exceptions to ROP liability, possibly similar to the "fair use" defenses in the Copyright Act and the Lanham Act. Congress could also consider limiting federal ROP protections to commercial speech.

Disclaimer

Chapter 14

Law Enforcement Use of Artificial Intelligence and Directives in the 2023 Executive Order*

Kristin Finklea

The use of artificial intelligence (AI) has expanded in a variety of arenas, including by law enforcement. AI has been broadly conceptualized as computerized systems operating in ways often thought to require human intelligence. It is defined in the *U.S. Code* (15 U.S.C. §9401(3)) as

> a machine-based system that can, for a given set of human-defined objectives, make predictions, recommendations or decisions influencing real or virtual environments. Artificial intelligence systems use machine and human-based inputs to-
>
> - perceive real and virtual environments;
> - abstract such perceptions into models through analysis in an automated manner; and
> - use model inference to formulate options for information or action.

AI involves a host of technologies and applications. In the law enforcement realm, researchers note that while the use of AI is not yet widespread, existing tools may be enhanced with AI to expand law enforcement *capabilities* and increase their *efficiency*. Examples include the following:

* This is an edited, reformatted and augmented version of Congressional Research Service, Publication No. IN12289, dated December 15, 2023.

In: Artificial Intelligence
Editor: Sonja Buckley
ISBN: 979-8-89530-859-2

- Automated license plate readers can be leveraged to employ machine, or computer, vision for capabilities such as automating the issuance of red-light violation tickets.
- Security cameras outfitted with certain AI-embedded hardware can be used for real-time facial recognition of potential suspects.
- Facial recognition technology and text analysis tools can be enhanced with AI to scan online advertisements to help identify potential crimes such as human trafficking.
- In addition to gunshot detection technology that can detect shots fired, security cameras can be outfitted with AI-enhanced software to detect weapons and alert police before shots are fired.
- AI redaction capabilities can be used to reduce possible bias in officers' narratives by removing certain identifying characteristics of suspects and victims—such as race—that could influence charges brought by prosecutors.
- Body-worn cameras can use AI software to redact or blur faces or sensitive footage before it is released to the public.
- Automated speech recognition software can use AI to help properly identify speakers' voices in audiovisual materials such as witness testimonies or interrogations.
- First responders use computer aided dispatch (CAD) systems to capture data that inform decisions on resource deployment; AI-enhanced CAD systems can improve resource allocation by using historical data, making predictions, and automating workflow.
- AI can be used along with predictive policing models to help identify individuals or places most at risk of being involved in crime.
- Law enforcement agencies can employ AI to enhance its communications with the public; they can use chatbots to respond to questions and push out emergency information.

A number of concerns have been raised about law enforcement use of AI, including whether its use perpetuates biases; one criticism is that the data on which the software are trained contain bias, thus training bias into the AI systems. Another concern is whether reliance on AI technology may lead police to ignore contradictory evidence. Policymakers may consider increased oversight over police use of AI systems to help evaluate and alleviate some of the shortcomings.

On October 30, 2023, President Biden issued Executive Order (E.O.) 14110 on the *Safe, Secure, and Trustworthy Development and Use of Artificial Intelligence*. This E.O. advances a government-wide approach to "governing the development and use of AI safely and responsibly" and directs efforts in AI policy areas involving safety and security, innovation and competition, worker support, equity and civil rights, individual protections, privacy protections, federal AI use, and international leadership.

E.O. 14110 acknowledges the risk of AI exacerbating discrimination and directs federal law enforcement in various ways. (In doing so, it references accountability focused directives for federal law enforcement previously outlined in the May 25, 2022, E.O. 14074 on *Advancing Effective, Accountable Policing and Criminal Justice Practices to Enhance Public Trust and Public Safety*.) Directives in E.O. 14110 include the following:

- The Attorney General (AG) shall coordinate and support enforcement of federal laws addressing discrimination and violations of civil rights and civil liberties related to AI. The Department of Justice's Civil Rights Division shall also coordinate with other federal civil rights offices to assess how their offices can prevent and address discrimination in automated systems—including algorithmic discrimination.
- The AG, with the Homeland Security Secretary and Office of Science and Technology Policy Director, shall submit a report to the President on the use of AI in the criminal justice system, including how AI can enhance law enforcement efficiency and accuracy, consistent with privacy, civil rights, and civil liberties protections. The report should also recommend best practices for law enforcement, including guidance on AI use, to address concerns outlined in E.O. 14074 with respect to law enforcement use of "facial recognition technology, other technologies using biometric information, and predictive algorithms, as well as data storage and access regarding such technologies."
- The interagency working group established by E.O. 14074 shall share best practices for recruiting law enforcement professionals with AI expertise and training them on responsible AI use. The AG, along with the Homeland Security Secretary, may review these and recommend best practices for state, local, tribal, and territorial law enforcement.

- The AG shall review the Justice Department's capacity to "investigate law enforcement deprivation of rights under color of law resulting from the use of AI," including through increasing or improving training for federal law enforcement officers and prosecutors.

Policymakers conducting oversight of executive branch activities to ensure that AI is used in a fair and equitable manner may examine not only these elements of E.O. 14110 that specifically relate to federal law enforcement but also other elements—such as the development of industry standards on AI—that may in turn affect law enforcement use of AI. They may also explore whether there should be specific standards for AI use in the criminal justice sector or AI-specific requirements for criminal justice entities receiving federal grants. Additionally, policymakers may continue to debate law enforcement use of *specific* AI technologies in its toolbox such as facial recognition technology.

Disclaimer

This document was prepared by the Congressional Research Service (CRS). CRS serves as nonpartisan shared staff to congressional committees and Members of Congress. It operates solely at the behest of and under the direction of Congress. Information in a CRS Report should not be relied upon for purposes other than public understanding of information that has been provided by CRS to Members of Congress in connection with CRS's institutional role.

Chapter 15

Artificial Intelligence (AI) in Federal Election Campaigns: Legal Background and Constitutional Considerations for Legislation*

L. Paige Whitaker

Introduction

Federal campaign finance law does not specifically regulate the use of artificial intelligence (AI) in political campaign advertising. As technology continues to evolve, concerns have grown regarding the use of AI-generated campaign ads and their potential to spread misinformation. At the same time, there are questions about whether regulation of such ads would run afoul of the First Amendment. This CRS In Focus discusses provisions of federal campaign finance law that may be relevant should Congress consider regulating AI-generated campaign ads. It then discusses pivotal Supreme Court rulings on campaign finance law and constitutional considerations for possible legislation. For a related policy discussion, see CRS product, *Artificial Intelligence (AI) and Campaign Finance Policy: Recent Developments*, by R. Sam Garrett.

---

* This is an edited, reformatted and augmented version of Congressional Research Service, Publication No. IF12468, dated August 17, 2023.

In: Artificial Intelligence
Editor: Sonja Buckley
ISBN: 979-8-89530-859-2

Federal Campaign Finance Law

The Federal Election Campaign Act (FECA or Act), codified at 52 U.S.C. §§ 30101–30146, does not specifically regulate the use of AI in political campaign ads. Two FECA provisions, however, may be relevant to this issue: the prohibition on fraudulent misrepresentation of campaign authority and the requirement of *disclaimers*, which are statements of attribution that appear directly on certain campaign communications.

FECA Prohibition on Fraudulent Misrepresentation of Campaign Authority

FECA prohibits a federal office candidate, including employees and agents of such a candidate, from fraudulently misrepresenting another candidate or political party "on a matter which is damaging to such other candidate or political party." The Act further prohibits anyone from fraudulently soliciting campaign contributions whereby the solicitor misrepresents that he or she is fundraising on behalf of a candidate or party. 52 U.S.C. § 30124.

On August 16, 2023 the Federal Election Commission (FEC) published a petition for rulemaking to amend its regulation on fraudulent misrepresentation of campaign authority, 11 C.F.R. §110.16, to clarify that the related statute, 52 U.S.C. § 30124, applies if "candidates or their agents fraudulently misrepresent other candidates or political parties through deliberately false AI-generated content in campaign ads or other communications." It approved the petition on August 10, 2023. (On June 22, the FEC had discussed, but not approve, a similar petition).

FECA Disclaimer Requirements

FECA requires that any public political advertising financed by a political committee—including candidate committees—include disclaimers. FECA and Supreme Court precedent define *political committee* to include "any committee ... or other group of persons that receives contributions or makes expenditures aggregating in excess of $1,000 during a calendar year" whose major purpose is to elect federal candidates to office. 52 U.S.C. § 30101(4); see *Buckley v. Valeo*, 424 U.S. 1, 79 (1976). FECA further defines *contribution* and *expenditure* as monies or anything of value "for the purpose of influencing any election for Federal office." 52 U.S.C. § 30101(8), (9).

For radio and television advertisements by candidate committees, FECA generally requires that the communication state who financed the ad, along with an audio statement by the candidate identifying the candidate and stating that the candidate "has approved" the message. In the case of television ads, the candidate statement is also required to be conveyed by an unobscured, full-screen view of the candidate making the statement or, if the candidate message is conveyed by voice-over, accompanied by a clearly identifiable image of the candidate, along with a written message of attribution at the end of the communication. 52 U.S.C. § 30120(a).

In addition, regardless of the financing source, FECA requires a disclaimer on (1) communications that expressly advocate for the election or defeat of a clearly identified candidate, (2) electioneering communications (defined to include broadcast ads that refer to a clearly identified federal candidate that are run 60 days before a general election or 30 days before a primary), and (3) public communications that solicit contributions. These communications can include ads financed by outside groups, corporations, or labor unions. For such ads, FECA generally requires that a disclaimer clearly state certain contact information of the entity that paid for the communication and that the communication was not authorized by any candidate or candidate committee. In radio and television advertisements, such disclaimers are required to include, in a clearly spoken manner, an audio statement saying who is responsible for the content of the advertising. In television ads, the statement is required to be conveyed by an unobscured, full-screen view of a representative of the entity paying for the ad, in a voice-over, along with a written message of attribution at the end of the communication. 52 U.S.C. § 30120(a), (c), (d).

Effective March 1, 2023, the FEC promulgated new regulations that broaden the disclaimer requirements for public internet communications. Previously, the regulations generally required disclaimers on public communications— defined to include ads that are "placed for a fee on another person's website"—that were made by political committees, contained express advocacy, or solicited campaign contributions. The new regulations specify that this requirement also applies to "communications placed for a fee on another person's ... digital device, application, or advertising platform." 87 Fed. Reg. 77467–77480 (Dec. 19, 2022).

Regardless of whether a campaign communication is created with AI, FECA's disclaimer requirements would apply as discussed. However, the Act does not require such disclaimers to indicate that the ad was created with AI.

FECA Penalties

In addition to a series of civil penalties, FECA sets forth criminal penalties for knowing and willful violations of the Act. Generally, FECA provides that any person who knowingly and willfully violates any provision of the Act that involves the making, receiving, or reporting of any contribution, donation, or expenditure of $25,000 or more per calendar year shall be fined under Title 18 of the *U.S. Code*, imprisoned for not more than five years, or both. If the amount involved is $2,000 or more per calendar year, but less than $25,000, the Act provides for a fine or imprisonment for not more than one year, or both. Should Congress amend FECA to regulate AI-generated campaign ads, unless otherwise provided in the legislation, FECA's civil and criminal penalties would apply.

Constitutional Considerations for Legislation

In the 118th Congress, legislation has been introduced that would regulate AI in federal election campaigns. For example, H.R. 3044 and S. 1596, which are companion bills, would amend FECA's disclaimer requirements to require additional disclaimers. Specifically, for an ad that contains an image or video generated, entirely or in part, by AI, the legislation would require the ad to include a statement indicating that fact.

Should Congress consider legislation to amend FECA establishing an AI disclaimer requirement, the Supreme Court's campaign finance jurisprudence may be relevant in evaluating the constitutional bounds of such legislation. For example, the Court upheld the facial validity of FECA's disclaimer requirements against a First Amendment challenge, determining that the disclaimer requirements "bear[] a sufficient relationship to the important governmental interest of 'shedding the light of publicity on campaign financing.'" *McConnell v. FEC*, 540 U.S. 93, 231 (2003). Similarly, the Court upheld FECA's disclaimer requirements as applied to a film regarding a presidential candidate and related promotional broadcast ads. Quoting *Buckley* and *McConnell*, the Court in *Citizens United* determined that while disclaimer requirements may burden the ability to speak under the First Amendment, they "impose no ceiling on campaign-related activities" and "do not prevent anyone from speaking." According to the Court, FECA's disclaimer requirements "provid[e] the electorate with information" and "insure that the voters are fully informed" about who is speaking. Moreover, they facilitate the ability of a listener or viewer to judge more effectively the arguments they are hearing, the Court observed. *Citizens United v. FEC*, 558 U.S. 310, 368 (2010).

In *McConnell* and *Citizens United*, the Court applied a standard of "exacting scrutiny" that requires a substantial relation between the disclaimer requirement and a sufficiently important governmental interest. These precedents suggest that courts could uphold the constitutionality of a FECA AI-disclaimer requirement to the extent the government could show that the requirement furthers the informational interests of the electorate. However, it is uncertain whether courts will determine that notifying the electorate that an ad was created with AI is as sufficiently an important governmental interest as informing the electorate as to who financed or approved of an ad, as mandated by the current FECA disclaimer requirements.

Exacting scrutiny also requires a court to evaluate the burden on speech. As the Court appeared to rely on the fact that FECA's current disclaimer requirements did not prevent anyone from speaking, if such a requirement is so burdensome that it impedes the ability of a candidate or group to speak—for example, if a required disclaimer comprises a relatively long period of time in an ad—it could violate the First Amendment. *Citizens United v. FEC,* 558 U.S. at 366–71.

Possibly casting further doubt on the constitutionality of an AI disclaimer requirement, the Court recently invalidated a state disclosure law under a potentially more rigorous standard of exacting scrutiny that requires a "narrow tailoring" to a sufficiently important governmental interest. *Americans for Prosperity Foundation v. Bonta*, 141 S. Ct. 2373, 2389 (2021). While *Bonta* is not a campaign finance case, some lower courts have since applied this version of exacting scrutiny in cases challenging campaign disclaimer laws. In evaluating an AI disclaimer requirement under this potentially more rigorous standard, a court might be less likely to uphold the law. Nonetheless, some appellate courts have approved of campaign finance disclaimer laws under this narrow tailoring standard. See *No on E v. Chiu*, 62 F.4th 529, 533 (9th Cir. 2023) and *Gaspee Project v. Mederos*, 13 F.4th 79, 95–96 (1st Cir. 2021), *cert. Denied* 142 S. Ct. 2647 (2022).

In contrast to a disclaimer requirement, it appears that courts would likely determine that a *prohibition* on AI-generated campaign ads is unconstitutional under the First Amendment. In evaluating a prohibition on certain campaign communications, the Supreme Court applied a "strict scrutiny" standard of review. Strict scrutiny requires the government to show that the law is the least restrictive means to achieve a compelling interest, which is a difficult standard to meet. Hence, applying strict scrutiny, the Court invalidated a FECA provision that prohibited corporations and unions from directly funding independent expenditures and electioneering communications. *Citizens United v. FEC*, 558 U.S. at 372. Accordingly, it appears that a prohibition on AI-generated campaign ads would likely be invalidated under a strict scrutiny standard of review unless the government could show that the law achieves a compelling government interest.

Disclaimer

Chapter 16

Artificial Intelligence (AI) and Campaign Finance Policy: Recent Developments[*]

R. Sam Garrett

Abstract

No federal statute or regulation specifically addresses artificial intelligence (AI) in political campaigns. The Federal Election Campaign Act (FECA) and Federal Election Commission (FEC) regulations govern conduct that calls for election or defeat of federal candidates or solicits funds. They also regulate some advertisements (*electioneering communications*) that refer to clearly identified federal candidates during preelection periods that do not call for election or defeat. Disclaimer requirements that mandate attribution for communications regulated by campaign finance law appear to apply to ads created with AI. Those requirements do not mandate that such advertising alert the audience, or regulators, to the presence of AI-generated content. Campaign management decisions, such as which technology to use, are generally not subject to regulation.

This updated CRS Insight discusses recent developments that could be relevant as Congress monitors or considers legislation related to AI and campaign finance policy. It does not address legal issues. Other CRS products provide information on generative AI and other AI policy areas.

---

[*] This is an edited, reformatted and augmented version of Congressional Research Service, Publication No. IN12222, dated September 25, 2024.

In: Artificial Intelligence
Editor: Sonja Buckley
ISBN: 979-8-89530-859-2

AI in Political Campaigns, and Recent Legislative Developments

Recent policy attention to AI in campaigns focuses on "deepfakes," referring to artificially manipulated audio or video content in political advertising. Such advertising appears to present new challenges for campaigns and voters about how to determine whether communications are authentic.

Recent legislation proposes disclaimers, reporting requirements, or prohibitions on deepfakes in federal campaigns or elections. Bills introduced in the 118th Congress include H.R. 3044; H.R. 3106; H.R. 3831; H.R. 4611; H.R. 5586; H.R. 8384; H.R. 8668; H.R. 9639; S. 686; S. 1596; S. 2770; and S. 3875. The Senate Committee on Rules and Administration reported an amended version of S. 3875 on May 15, 2024. The bill would amend FECA to require disclaimers on certain political advertisements that are generated using AI. Legislation (H.R. 1; H.R. 5314) addressing various elections topics, including some provisions concerning deepfakes, passed the House in the 117th Congress but was not enacted.

In May 2023, the American Association of Political Consultants (AAPC) issued a statement explaining that its board of directors unanimously "condemn[ed] use of deceptive generative AI content in political campaigns" as inconsistent with the organization's code of ethics. The AAPC position represents a voluntary professional standard, not a regulatory requirement. The AAPC also stated its support for a February 2024 Federal Communications Commission (FCC) declaratory ruling that calls made with AI-generated voices are "artificial" under the Automated Telephone Consumer Protection Act of 1991 (47 U.S.C. §227), and that using AI-generated voice for robocalls absent prior consumer consent is "illegal." FCC activity on robocalls is otherwise beyond the scope of this Insight.

Despite the focus on AI's role in political advertising, AI also can serve campaign-management functions. For example, political professionals or volunteers could use AI to automate, or supplement human labor to complete, various internal campaign tasks. According to media reports, campaigns have used AI to perform data analysis, compile opposition research, or draft fundraising appeals.

Federal Election Commission Rulemaking Activity

On June 22, 2023, members of the FEC deadlocked on whether to issue a notice of availability (NOA) to receive comments on an AI rulemaking petition from the interest group Public Citizen. The request asked the FEC to issue rules specifying that the FEC fraudulent misrepresentation of campaign authority prohibition (52 U.S.C. §30124) applied to AI-generated ads. At the June 22 meeting, some commissioners expressed skepticism about the agency's statutory authority to regulate AI ads; others expressed support for a rulemaking. On July 13, 2023, several Members of Congress wrote to the commission expressing "disappoint[ment]" with the FEC's action and requested additional information.

The commission considered a second Public Citizen rulemaking petition on August 10, 2023. In this case, it approved an NOA. Discussion at the August 10 meeting suggested that at least some commissioners continued to have reservations about the commission's authority concerning regulating AI ads in particular; about the appropriateness of the FECA fraudulent misrepresentation provision as an avenue to do so; or both. Fifty-two Members of Congress submitted joint comments encouraging the FEC to adopt rules specifying that the fraudulent-misrepresentation provisions apply to ads created using generative AI, and to require disclaimers on ads created with the technology. The matter remained under consideration for the next year.

On September 19, 2024, the commission took two actions.

- It approved a notice of disposition (NOD) to resolve the July 2023 Public Citizen petition without issuing new rules. The NOD notes that the fraudulent-misrepresentation provision is "technology neutral and applies on its face to all means" of fraudulent misrepresentation, "including AI-assisted media."
- It approved an interpretive rule, based on existing regulation and statute, confirming that the FECA fraudulent misrepresentation provision also covers communications generated using AI.

To summarize, the commission did not issue new rules concerning AI. It clarified that the existing fraudulent misrepresentation provisions in FECA and FEC regulations (11 C.F.R. §110.16(a)) apply to communications generated using AI. Those actions do not affect AI or campaign finance beyond the fraudulent misrepresentation provision, nor do they require additional disclaimers on political advertising. Discussion at the open meeting suggests that a majority of the commission believes that it currently lacks legislative authority to issue broader rules concerning AI.

FEC Responses to Federal Communications Commission Activity

Some House and Senate activity has examined a proposed FCC rulemaking that does not directly implicate campaign finance policy and which is largely beyond the scope of this Insight. On July 25, 2024, the FCC approved a notice of proposed rulemaking (NPRM), published in the *Federal Register* on August 5. If approved, the rules would require certain licensees (e.g., broadcasters) to (1) announce on air that a political ad contains "AI-generated content"; and (2) include the information in their "political files" of advertising contracts. Another CRS product discusses identification requirements on political advertising in telecommunications law and regulation.

On June 3, 2024, FEC Chair Sean Cooksey wrote to FCC Chair Jessica Rosenworcel, stating that the reportedly forthcoming FCC proposed rules would infringe on FEC jurisdiction and could cause confusion before the general election. Three days later, FEC Vice Chair Ellen Weintraub wrote to Rosenworcel stating that the FCC could add telecommunications expertise to AI regulation. It is unclear how or whether the FEC might respond if the FCC adopted the proposed rules.

Potential Policy Considerations for Congress

If pursuing legislation, Congress might need to determine whether to do so narrowly, such as by addressing specific AI issues, or to also address other campaign finance or elections topics. Congress has pursued both approaches to campaign finance regulation recently. If Congress chose to task the FEC with pursuing rulemaking without also providing additional statutory guidance, it is possible that the commission would be unable to agree, with the four of six minimum required votes, about how to proceed.

Maintaining the status quo likely would reinforce the emerging debate about whether additional regulation is needed, including about what role industry should play. Congress could also require agency (or committee or task force) study of AI issues before, or in addition to, other policymaking.

Amending FECA would be a typical approach to further regulate ads that are made by political committees; or that solicit funds, engage in express advocacy, or refer to federal candidates through electioneering communications. Although Congress could also amend FECA or another statute to require disclaimers on ads that do not meet those requirements (e.g., issue advocacy), federal campaign finance law currently generally does not regulate issue advocacy. As noted above, amending telecommunications law or regulation could affect broadcasters or other entities that transmit ads, and could affect issue advocacy in ways that campaign finance law and regulation do not. Prohibiting AI-generated ads or requiring additional disclaimers might raise First Amendment concerns, such as those discussed in another CRS campaign finance product.

Disclaimer

Chapter 17

Semiconductors and Artificial Intelligence*

Laurie A. Harris

Abstract

The increasing popularity of artificial intelligence (AI) has drawn congressional attention, and many Members are considering proposals to regulate the quickly evolving landscape. Technical progress in AI has been enabled in large part by advances in the underlying computational hardware—also known as semiconductors, integrated circuits, microelectronics, or simply *chips*—that offer increased processing power to improve the development of AI systems. This In Focus describes the types of semiconductors used in AI, concerns related to their supply chains, and challenges for the regulation of semiconductors to promote U.S. competitiveness in AI.

Artificial Intelligence Models

AI refers broadly to computational systems that can learn from data and make decisions such as predictions, recommendations, or classifications. AI systems can be implemented for diverse applications, including speech/visual recognition, autonomous driving, robotic process automation, and as virtual assistants.

A popular class of AI systems is deep neural networks, which use algorithms, or models, to mimic neurons in the brain to identify complex

* This is an edited, reformatted and augmented version of Congressional Research Service, Publication No. IF12497, dated September 18, 2023.

In: Artificial Intelligence
Editor: Sonja Buckley
ISBN: 979-8-89530-859-2

patterns. This AI model typically involves two stages: training and inference. In the training phase, the model is fed data that can be labeled (e.g., thousands of pictures of dogs to learn all the variations of dogs) or unlabeled to identify patterns. In the inference phase, the trained model is used to enable predictions and guide decisions, such as autonomous driving systems recognizing dogs as obstacles to avoid. The training phase typically requires the most computational power.

Generally, the accuracy of AI models increases with training on larger amounts of data, which in turn requires more computational power. Popular large language models, such as GPT-3, are trained on billions or trillions of text data to process and generate text. Given the large data sets associated with AI models, some of the largest AI models can take weeks or months to train, using thousands of chips and costing millions of dollars. These high costs are due in large part to the electricity required to operate the hardware.

Semiconductor Use in AI Models

Semiconductors are tiny electronic devices designed to enable functions such as processing, storing, sensing, and moving data or signals. AI models employ different types of chips, including memory chips to store large amounts of data and logic chips to process the data. According to forecasts from Gartner, revenues from semiconductors used in AI may increase rapidly from around $44 billion in 2022 to $120 billion in 2027.

Early AI models used commercial, off-the-shelf logic chips called *central processing units* (CPUs) for training and inference. Although CPUs are still sufficient for inference, leading AI models now primarily train using *graphics processor units* (GPUs) originally designed for video rendering. GPUs enable parallel processing of information; by contrast, CPUs process information serially. Parallel processing allows the AI model to train faster using large amounts of data by dividing tasks and executing them simultaneously. Additionally, many chip design firms are increasingly offering custom logic chips designed for particular applications, including AI training, called *application-specific integrated circuits* (ASIC) or *accelerators*. Logic chips used for AI applications are also referred to generally as *AI chips*.

To train the largest AI models, many logic chips are connected together in large clusters with other semiconductor hardware (e.g., memory and networking chips) in data centers or supercomputing facilities. For example, Meta is building a supercomputer for AI research that is anticipated to contain

16,000 GPUs, and a startup called Inflection AI is building a cluster of 22,000 GPUs for its AI model. Some supercomputers built by private firms such as Meta, Tesla, and NVIDIA are larger than many nationally owned supercomputers around the world.

Companies that train AI models may purchase and maintain their own chip hardware infrastructure or may train their models remotely using the cloud by paying fees to access the hardware they need. According to the Federal Trade Commission, "cloud services can be expensive and are currently provided by only a handful of firms, raising the risk of anticompetitive practices." Top cloud service providers in the United States for AI applications include Amazon Web AI Services, Microsoft Azure AI, and Google Cloud AI.

AI training typically benefits from improving two technical parameters for AI chips: higher processing power and faster chip-to-chip transfer speeds. A common metric used to market the processing power of different AI chips is a measurement of the number of mathematical operations a chip can do in one second, calculated in trillions of operations per second (TOPS). Chip-to-chip transfer speeds are generally reported by measuring how fast a chip can send information, or bytes, into and out of the chip in gigabytes per second (1 gigabyte is 1 billion bytes).

Many large AI models, such as GPT models from OpenAI, and leading AI research papers do not explicitly report the amount of computational power used to train the AI model. Additionally, there are no standard methods or tools to measure the amount of computational power used to train AI models, as TOPS may be calculated differently by different companies and may not be the most optimal metric to evaluate and compare AI models. Transparency in computing usage for AI training and standard methods for measuring computing power globally may support regulatory efforts for AI.

AI Chip Design and Manufacturing

U.S.-headquartered companies, both established firms and start-ups, lead globally in the design of specialized logic chips for AI applications. However, the large majority of these chip-design firms rely wholly on contract manufacturing services to produce and package their designs. As the highest performance AI chips require the most advanced manufacturing processes in the world, the majority of AI chip designers rely on the two logic chip manufacturing firms currently capable of producing their designs: Taiwan Semiconductor Manufacturing Company (TSMC) and Samsung.

The top AI chip designer by revenue and usage in AI research is U.S.-headquartered NVIDIA, one of the first companies to mass market GPUs in the early 2000s. Leading GPU products from NVIDIA used in AI applications, in order of increasing computational power, are marketed by the names V100 (2017), A100 (2020), and H100 (2022). Each successor chip can transfer information into and out of the chip faster than its predecessor, enabling higher-speed communications between large clusters of chips and faster AI training. These higher performance metrics may enable an AI model to train faster than it would using other commercially available GPUs and, in turn, may lead to relatively lower costs.

Top U.S.-headquartered AI chip design start-ups include, by company valuation, SambaNova, Cerebras, and Graphcore. Smaller entities such as start-ups often face challenges to prototyping and producing their designs due to the high cost of and limited access to contract manufacturing services from companies such as TSMC. As competitiveness in AI benefits from advancements in chip hardware, promoting access to prototyping and manufacturing services for U.S.-based firms may boost long-term innovation.

Export Controls on AI Chips

In October 2022, the Department of Commerce implemented controls that require licenses for exports to China and Macau of certain advanced logic and other chips that can be used for applications such as AI training and for building supercomputers. Controls apply to those logic chips with chip-to-chip transfer speeds of 600 gigabytes per second or more and computational power over 600 TOPS.

Under this definition, exports of leading AI chips, including NVIDIA's A100 and H100, to China and Macau are restricted. In recent years, China accounted for about a quarter of total annual revenues for NVIDIA. In November 2022, NVIDIA began marketing an A800 chip, which had a lower chip-to-chip transfer speed of 400 gigabytes per second (compared with 600 gigabytes per second in the A100), to "provide alternative products not subject to the new license requirements" to customers in China, according to its annual report. Similarly, in March 2023, NVIDIA marketed an H800 chip that does not require a license as an alternative to the newest H100 products, which fall under the controls.

Additionally, the October 2022 export controls restrict chip manufacturing facilities globally from manufacturing certain advanced chips for Chinese-headquartered chip design firms without a license if the manufacturer uses U.S.-origin technology or software (i.e., Advanced Computing Foreign Direct Product Rule). As the United States is a global leader in the production of semiconductor manufacturing equipment, this rule would apply to most foreign chip manufacturing firms, including TSMC, which previously produced advanced chips for Chinese AI chip design companies such as Biren. The rules require licenses to export certain advanced manufacturing equipment to chip manufacturers in China and Macau to impede the manufacturers' ability to produce advanced chips.

The export controls are designed to limit the ability of China and Macau to buy or produce certain advanced chips that can be used for AI applications. However, there are no controls on Chinese AI firms to use cloud service providers inside or outside of the country to train AI models.

Selected Federal Actions and Considerations for Congress

In January 2021, Congress enacted the National Artificial Intelligence Initiative Act of 2020 (Division E of P.L. 116-283), which seeks to advance U.S. leadership in AI research and development. Part of the act seeks to establish a roadmap for a National AI Research Resource, a shared research infrastructure for AI researchers and students.

Directed by Executive Order 13859, the National Institute of Standards and Technology conducted a study that recommended the federal government "commit to deeper, consistent, long-term engagement in AI standards development activities," including the development of "metrics to quantifiably measure and characterize AI technologies, including but not limited to aspects of hardware and its performance."

In August 2022, President Biden signed P.L. 117-167, known as the CHIPS and Science Act. The act appropriated $39 billion to expand domestic semiconductor manufacturing capacity and $11 billion for research and development of next-generation semiconductor technologies. Congress may exercise its oversight authority with respect to the effectiveness of expanding domestic manufacturing capacity for advanced logic chips and improving manufacturing accessibility for smaller entities.

Additionally, as many AI models are trained using cloud services, Congress may consider export control reforms that enable the Department of

Commerce to exercise regulatory authority over providers of cloud services that sell access to large amounts of computational power.

A previous version of this In Focus was authored by Manpreet Singh.

Disclaimer

This document was prepared by the Congressional Research Service (CRS). CRS serves as nonpartisan shared staff to congressional committees and Members of Congress. It operates solely at the behest of and under the direction of Congress. Information in a CRS Report should not be relied upon for purposes other than public understanding of information that has been provided by CRS to Members of Congress in connection with CRS's institutional role. CRS Reports, as a work of the United States Government, are not subject to copyright protection in the United States. Any CRS Report may be reproduced and distributed in its entirety without permission from CRS. However, as a CRS Report may include copyrighted images or material from a third party, you may need to obtain the permission of the copyright holder if you wish to copy or otherwise use copyrighted material.

Chapter 18

United States and Eight Companies Launch the Partnership for Global Inclusivity on AI*

U.S. Department of State

Today in New York City, on the margins of the 79th Session of the United Nations General Assembly, Secretary of State Antony Blinken launched the Partnership for Global Inclusivity on AI and announced other initiatives to harness the rapid advancement of artificial intelligence (AI) to advance sustainable development globally.

The Partnership for Global Inclusivity on AI (PGIAI) brings together the Department of State, Amazon, Anthropic, Google, IBM, Meta, Microsoft, Nvidia, and OpenAI. Together they commit more than $100 million leveraging their combined expertise, resources, and networks to unlock AI's potential as a powerful tool for sustainable development and improved quality of life in developing countries, while maintaining an unwavering commitment to safety, security, and trustworthiness in AI systems. This effort recognizes that effective and equitable AI solutions must be rooted in an understanding and respect for the diverse cultures, languages, and traditions of the communities they serve. To this end, the PGIAI will focus on three areas: 1) Compute: increasing access to AI models, compute credit, and other AI tools; 2) Capacity: building human technical capacity; and 3) Context: expanding local datasets.

---

* This is an edited, reformatted and augmented version of U.S. Department of State, dated September 23, 2024.

In: Artificial Intelligence
Editor: Sonja Buckley
ISBN: 979-8-89530-859-2

In conjunction with the Partnership, Secretary Blinken announced:

- *The Department of State intends to provide $10 million in Foreign Assistance,* subject to the availability of funds, to close the AI access gap and promote the objectives of the Partnership, including access to compute credits.
- *The Department of State plans to provide an additional $23 million in funding,* working with Congress, to promote the responsible use and governance of AI globally, among other objectives, to include programs that leverage AI tools to help countries achieve the UN Sustainable Development Goals. Examples of these programs include:
    - *Over $12 million* for programs using AI as a tool to advance democracy, promote human and labor rights, and foster justice and accountability.
    - *Approximately $5 million in Education and Cultural Exchanges* funding for programs that contribute to AI capacity building. These include academic programs, professional and cultural exchanges, private sector exchanges, as well as policy and monitoring evaluation learning and innovation activities.
    - *Over $3 million* for programs that employ AI to identify mis- and disinformation and prevent online hate from spreading to offline violence for members of religious minority communities.
    - *A $1.2 million project* to develop a Safe, Secure, and Trustworthy AI Policy Framework and Ecosystem in member states of the Organization of American States.
    - *$1.3 million* to launch USAID's Responsible AI funding to conduct AI-related programs through the Digital Forward mechanism.

Participating companies announced the following commitments:

- *Amazon Web Services:* Amazon Web Services (AWS) announced a donation of $10 million in credits in support of this partnership to help close the AI access gap around the world. Amazon is committed to offering skills training to empower the next generation of innovators and has already trained over 31 million learners across 200 countries and territories in cloud computing skills. Additionally, AWS has committed to provide free AI-specific skills training to two million more people globally by 2025—underscoring Amazon's commitment to cultivating an inclusive, diverse pipeline of cloud talent to drive innovation.

- *Anthropic:* AI models can play a crucial role in supporting and accelerating developing countries' work to address SDGs and better support their citizens. As part of the Partnership for Global Inclusivity on AI, Anthropic will provide up to $1 million in API access to Claude and Claude for Teams to government projects focused on improving citizen services, advancing democracy, and supporting the UN sustainable development goals.
- *Google:* Google is providing $120 million to support a Global AI Opportunity Fund to make AI education and training available throughout the world. Google is partnering with nonprofit and civil society organizations to provide training in local languages based on foundational AI courses designed by Google and others. This is in addition to $275 million in Google.org funding to support development of AI solutions to address the SDGs as well as Research efforts, which include Flood Forecasting in over 80 countries, wildfire detection, and AlphaFold which is being used by over 2 million scientists in over 190 countries toward novel research. Of this, $10 million will specifically support the aims of the MOU signed today with the US State Department. In addition, Google has announced a number of submarine cable investments over the last year that will expand the reach, reliability, and resilience of the global internet. This includes Umoja, the first submarine cable connecting Africa directly to Australia. These cables provide vital connectivity, driving economic growth and job creation.
- *IBM:* IBM believes AI is the transformative technology of our time, and that the world needs innovation, access to technology and partnerships like this, to create a more sustainable and equitable future. To help vulnerable populations address environmental challenges, this year, we have extended our pledge through the IBM Sustainability Accelerator to provide up to $45 million in expertise and technologies, such as AI, by the end of 2028. In addition, we work with organizations such as NASA and UNDP to develop valuable data sets and make them more accessible – including in developing countries – for earth science research and energy equity. We also

continue our commitment to train two million learners in AI globally by 2026, helping to democratize AI opportunity and close the growing skills gap. We are making progress towards this goal through our IBM SkillsBuild program providing the following: AI training to education organizations and adult learners, access to technology, and opportunities for university students to apply IBM's watsonx technology to create real-world AI solutions.

- *Meta:* In 2024 and 2025, Meta will invest more than $10 million in programmatic support globally to expand open-source AI innovation. With this investment, they will increase access to open-source AI globally, including in Latin America, Africa, Middle East and Asia by: offering grants, training and ad credits to developers and organizations leveraging Meta's Llama 3 and Llama 3.1 models for social impact projects; and by funding global trainings on open-source AI and Llama to small businesses and governments. Meta has invested billions to make AI open and accessible, including through their Fundamental AI Research Lab. Meta, UNESCO and Hugging Face also announced a collaboration to leverage Meta's "No Language Left Behind" model to deliver translations in 200 languages, including indigenous languages. Meta has made over 200 datasets publicly available, including AI-powered population and poverty maps helping accelerate access to water, electrification and financial assistance throughout the global south.
- *Microsoft:* In 2024 and 2025, Microsoft is contributing to the Partnership for Global Inclusivity on AI by investing more than $12 billion in AI data center infrastructure, connectivity, and skilling in the Global South. In Southeast Asia, Africa, and Latin America, the company is expanding and building new datacenters, boosting cybersecurity capacity, providing broad digital skilling at scale, nonprofit technical and financial support, and local R&D. Partnering with local providers, the company's Airband Initiative aims to provide broadband connectivity for 250 million unserved and underserved people in the Global South, including 100 million in Africa. During this same time frame, it will provide AI and digital skilling for five million people in the Global South.
- *Nvidia:* NVIDIA is committed to democratizing AI and empowering businesses and governments around the world to harness the transformational power of AI. NVIDIA works with startups,

universities, and developers in every region to help them build and grow local AI ecosystems and develop innovative solutions to some of society's biggest challenges. Under this partnership, NVIDIA will provide $10m/year in training programs to upskill developers and IT professionals in emerging economies. NVIDIA also provides compute credits and hardware grants for higher education research to universities around the world. Through NVIDIA's global Inception program, NVIDIA supports nearly 5,000 start-ups in emerging economies with technical expertise, go-to-market support, hardware and software discounts, and access to free cloud computing credits provided through NVIDIA partners. In 2024 alone, this program has mobilized more than $60 million in free cloud compute credits for start-ups in emerging economies.

- *OpenAI:* OpenAI is launching the OpenAI Academy, which will invest in developers and organizations in low- and middle-income countries who are leveraging AI to help solve hard problems and spur economic growth in their communities. To support this initiative, OpenAI will distribute an initial $1 million in API credits and provide training and technical guidance. Our goal is to support the creation of thriving AI ecosystems around the world by ensuring broad access to the technology and empowering those developing innovative new ways of using it.

Secretary Blinken also announced the official release of the *Global AI Research Agenda* and *AI in Global Development Playbook* – two complementary documents developed by the U.S. government to foster future research collaborations on AI and guide the development community in leveraging AI to advance progress in addressing global development challenges. He also highlighted the Risk Management Profile for AI and Human Rights, released in July 2024, which provides concrete recommendations on assessing and managing the human rights impacts of AI technologies.

These new announcements add to the U.S government's ongoing efforts to promote inclusivity, respect for human rights, digital solidarity, and equitable access to the benefits of AI globally. In 2023, the U.S. government announced $15 million in foreign assistance funding at the 78th Session of the UN General Assembly to build global capacity to develop and govern AI in ways that advance the Sustainable Development Goals. In March 2024, the UN General Assembly adopted its first-ever resolution on AI, introduced by the United States. In September 2024, the United States signed the Council of Europe's Framework Convention in Artificial Intelligence and Human Rights, Democracy, and the Rule of Law, underscoring the importance we place on respect for human rights, democracy, and the rule of law in the context of AI. The Department of State and the Department of Commerce will launch the International Network of AI Safety Institutes in San Francisco in November 2024 to advance the science of AI safety.

Chapter 19

AI in Global Development Playbook*

U.S. Agency for International Development

Disclaimer

This document contains links to external resources. The links reflect the URL information available at the time of drafting. The United States makes no representations concerning the accuracy of the linked content, and linking does not constitute U.S. endorsement of the linked material. Except where a U.S. government resource is linked below, the document should be read as acknowledging the views of the authors of the resource and not the adoption of those views or perspectives by the United States.

Glossary of Terms

ADD: Advancing Digital Democracy
AI RMF: National Institute of Standards and Technology Artificial Intelligence Risk Management Framework
AI: Artificial Intelligence
ANCIR: African Network of Centers for Investigative Reporting
APIs: Application Programming Interfaces
CCTV: Closed-circuit Television
CEDI: Clean Energy Demand Initiative
CfA: Code for Africa

---

* This is an edited, reformatted and augmented version of a U.S. Agency for International Development publication, *AI in Global Development Playbook* dated 2023.

In: Artificial Intelligence
Editor: Sonja Buckley
ISBN: 979-8-89530-859-2

COVID-19: Coronavirus Disease 2019

DOE: U.S. Department of Energy

DPGA: Digital Public Goods Alliance

DPGs: Digital Public Goods

FAAST: Frontiers in Artificial Intelligence for Science, Security and Technology

FCDO: United Kingdom Foreign, Commonwealth and Development Office

FLAIR: First Languages AI Reality

GAIRA: Global Artificial Intelligence Research Agenda

GIZ: Deutsche Gesellschaft für Internationale Zusammenarbeit (German International Cooperation)

GPAI: Global Partnership on AI

GPT-4: Generative Pre-trained Transformer 4

GPU: Graphics Processing Unit

HP: Hewlett-Packard

HPC: High-performance Computing

IBM: International Business Machines

IDRC: Canada International Development Research Centre

ILO: International Labour Organization

IMDA: Singapore Infocomm Media Development Authority

LGBTQI+: Lesbian, Gay, Bisexual, Transgender, Queer, Intersex, and Others

LLMs: Large Language Models

LMICs: Low- and Middle-Income Countries

MCV: Mozilla Common Voice

Mila: Quebec Artificial Intelligence Institute

NASA: National Aeronautics and Space Administration

NCII: Non-consensual Intimate Imagery

NIST: National Institute of Standards and Technology

NTIA: National Telecommunications and Information Administration

Open RAN: Open Radio Access Network

OPG: Open Government Partnership

Playbook: AI in Global Development Playbook

R&D: Research and Development

RCC: Responsible Computing Challenge

RFI: Request For Information

SDGs: United Nations Sustainable Development Goals

SMEs: Small- and Medium-sized Enterprises

STEM: Science, Technology, Engineering, and Math
TB: Tuberculosis
U.S.: United States
UN: United Nations
UNESCO: United Nations Educational, Scientific and Cultural Organization
UNFCCC: United Nations Framework Convention on Climate Change, secretariat "UN Climate Change"
UNGA: United Nations General Assembly
URL: Uniform Resource Locator, web address
USAID: United States Agency for International Development
WIPO: World Intellectual Property Organization

Executive Summary

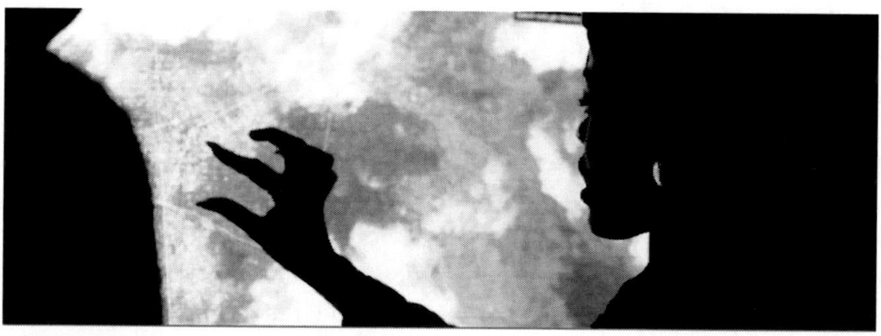

Photo Credit: USAID.

The world stands at a precarious moment as we work towards shared prosperity. The global community is on track to meet just 17% of the United Nations Sustainable Development Goals (SDGs) by 2030, and progress has plateaued or regressed in many areas. When used effectively and responsibly, artificial intelligence (AI) holds the potential to accelerate progress on sustainable development and close digital divides, but it also poses risks that could further impede progress toward these goals. With the right enabling environment and ecosystem of actors, AI can enhance efficiency and accelerate development outcomes in sectors such as health, education, agriculture, energy, manufacturing, and delivering public services. The United

States aims to ensure that the benefits of AI are shared equitably across the globe.

As President Joseph R. Biden said in remarks before the United Nations General Assembly in September 2023, the United States is committed "to ensur[ing] we harness the power of artificial intelligence for good." In March 2024, the United States led the adoption by consensus of the first-ever standalone resolution on AI at the United Nations General Assembly, "Seizing the opportunities of safe, secure and trustworthy artificial intelligence systems for sustainable development," which established a global concurrence on twin imperatives: harness the promise of AI and mitigate its risks. The U.S. government has continued to expand work on AI solutions with global impact and local relevance and to partner with the private sector, civil society, and international partners to strengthen AI enabling environments, while at the same time helping ensure adequate safeguards are in place to protect human rights and public safety.

Building on these efforts and the U.S. government's long history of digital development and efforts to foster safe, secure, and trustworthy AI, the AI in Global Development Playbook[1] (Playbook) maps a set of key actions for the United States and its development partners, such as other governments, the private sector, and philanthropies, to foster responsible AI ecosystems worldwide, advance sustainable development, create opportunities for partnership and collaboration, and address some of the world's greatest challenges.

This Playbook is a roadmap to develop the capacity, ecosystems, frameworks, partnerships, applications, and institutions to leverage safe, secure, and trustworthy AI for sustainable development. All of these characteristics comprise a good governance regime for AI, which is a cross-cutting theme throughout the Playbook. Good governance measures can foster trust among citizens, trust can foster adoption, and adoption can drive innovation.

[1] The AI in Global Development Playbook (Playbook) is published pursuant to Section 11(c)(i) of the United States Executive Order on the Safe, Secure, and Trustworthy Development and Use of Artificial Intelligence. The Executive Order tasks the U.S. Secretary of State and the Administrator of the United States Agency for International Development (USAID), in coordination with the National Institute of Standards and Technology (NIST), to publish an AI in Global Development Playbook that incorporates the principles, guidelines, and recommended practices of NIST's AI Risk Management Framework (AI RMF) into the social, technical, economic, governance, human rights, and security conditions of contexts beyond United States borders, and to draw on lessons learned from programmatic uses of AI in global development.

The Playbook is intended to synthesize existing work and offer recommendations for the design, deployment, and use of safe, secure, and trustworthy AI for sustainable development—including some of the steps the United States intends to take to support AI ecosystems worldwide. To provide practical guidance, the Playbook also includes a series of case studies. These case studies highlight existing initiatives and organizations doing exemplary work in the identified areas. By showcasing these real-world examples, the Playbook aims to inspire and guide others.

Photo Credit: Jack Gordon for USAID.

The Playbook is especially relevant for development practitioners, policymakers, development and philanthropic organizations, and private sector actors looking to contribute to sustainable development especially in low-and middle-income countries (LMICs). As technological advances in AI continue, each of these stakeholder groups should be aware of the benefits and risks and each of their important roles in building safeguards and approaches for supporting responsible AI ecosystems in global development.

The diffuse, fast-changing nature of AI technology means no one group of stakeholders alone will be successful in delivering the benefits of AI or mitigating its risks. Collaboration between governments, the private sector, civil society, and academia (both within and between countries) is a central element of our approach in this document.

Photo Credit: Angela Rucker.

The Playbook maps opportunities and challenges across key themes relevant to global development and humanitarian assistance. Addressing AI's risks is the first step toward realizing its benefits. This Playbook, in alignment with and building off the AI Risk Management Framework from NIST, identifies how risks (such as harm to individuals, communities, organizations, ecosystems, or societies) can be mitigated in the design, deployment, and use of AI.

The Playbook's recommendations—distilled from consultation with hundreds of government officials, non-governmental organizations, technology firms and startups, and individuals from around the world—are constructed around several focal areas:

- *Enhancing Capacity, Promoting AI-Related Skills Across All Sectors and Levels, and Protecting the Workforce.* Addressing gaps in the AI workforce by equipping a broader range of individuals with AI skills can allow countries to tap into economic opportunities, drive local innovation, and create jobs that contribute to sustainable development. At the same time, AI brings about changes in the labor landscape that necessitate robust social safety nets for workers, action to prevent and address any new risks to workers' rights, and social dialogue processes that include workers and unions.

- *Building Trusted and Sustainable Digital Infrastructure.* In addition to playing a pivotal role in development more broadly, widespread Internet connectivity and reliable energy resources can enable AI for sustainable development. Partnering to enhance digital infrastructure will not only improve access to AI technologies but also stimulate economic growth and enable communities to leverage AI for addressing local challenges and enhancing quality of life. Priority should be given to energy efficiency in AI systems, with careful consideration of climate and environmental impacts to not perpetuate existing issues.
- *Broadening Access to Data Storage and Compute Resources.* AI innovators need access to large-scale computing and data storage resources to support model inference, training, and deployment. Making compute more affordable and accessible by expanding access to application programming interfaces (APIs), trusted cloud computing services, and other resources can accelerate the development of AI applications that meet local needs.
- *Creating Representative, Locally Relevant Datasets and Preserving Cultural Heritage.* Locally, linguistically, and culturally relevant datasets that reflect the racial and ethnic diversity of LMICs and their local context and realities, can enable the development and use of AI models that address community needs, are better-suited for use in local contexts, and drive sustainable development. By building representative datasets, stakeholders can work together to enable AI solutions that are more accurate, equitable, and impactful, ultimately fostering inclusive growth and innovation.
- *Developing Strategies to Deliver the Promise of AI in Practice.* Rigorous testing and benchmarking of AI in development contexts and the broad, public sharing of research findings, are essential to ensuring that AI and AI-enabled interventions are grounded in evidence of what works. This evidence is critical to guiding the scale-up of AI solutions, helping to ensure that they provide broad, public

value while addressing established development challenges. Systematic assessment of AI initiatives can highlight success stories, inform best practices, and guide investments, making it possible to replicate and scale effective solutions across different sectors and regions.

- *Advancing Good Governance Frameworks for the Development and Use of Safe and Rights-Respecting AI Systems.* AI has the potential to be misused by malicious actors in ways that harm individuals and societies, such as through unlawful or arbitrary surveillance and by facilitating cyber threats, disinformation campaigns, political manipulation, or deepfakes—including synthetic non-consensual intimate images and child sexual abuse material. Proactive measures to advance good governance frameworks must be taken to safeguard democratic processes; enhance transparency; protect cybersecurity, intellectual property, and privacy; ensure alignment with applicable legal frameworks; ensure equitable access to goods and services; and promote human rights, which can help foster trust and resilience in societies.
- *Fostering Trust in AI through Openness, Transparency, and Explainability.* Improving transparency in AI models, development processes, organizational practices, and AI policymaking can enhance reliability, fairness, protection of and respect for intellectual property rights, and accountability. Embracing openness and explainability in how AI systems are designed, deployed, and used can encourage adoption, facilitate transparency, and promote trust in AI systems.
- *Deploying AI Sustainably and for Climate Action.* Seizing opportunities where AI can contribute to energy savings across sectors can play an urgent and important role in addressing the changing climate. Emphasizing sustainability will reduce the net environmental footprint of AI technologies while leveraging AI to enhance energy efficiency in various industries, thereby contributing to global efforts to combat climate change.

The United States is steadfast in its support for sustainable development, responsible AI use globally, and collaborative efforts to enhance AI safeguards. By helping address the challenges outlined in the Playbook—through policy, funding, engagement, partnership, and other mechanisms—

the United States hopes to encourage and engage more stakeholders to commit to safe, secure, and trustworthy design, deployment, and use of AI technologies.

Introduction

Photo Credit: André Josué Anchecta Oseguera.

To maximize the benefits of AI while mitigating its risks, it is crucial to support the ecosystems and the people designing, deploying, and using AI systems. With the right safeguards and enabling conditions, AI can drive greater efficiency and accelerate development outcomes across various sectors, including health, education, agriculture and food security, energy, governance, and public service delivery.

Promoting the benefits of AI requires multi-stakeholder and multi-disciplinary collaboration, leveraging the expertise of local communities, the private sector, workers and their organizations, academia, civil society, and others to identify opportunities, navigate barriers, and manage risks to cultivate a responsible AI ecosystem.

The Playbooks is a key deliverable in the U.S. Executive Order on the Safe, Secure, and Trustworthy Development and Use of Artificial Intelligence, published on October 30, 2023. The intent of the Playbook is to characterize the opportunities and challenges of AI in contexts beyond United States borders, especially in LMICs, providing recommendations to help ensure that actors involved in AI ecosystems can collaborate, partner, and align priorities with sustainable development, including protecting the free exercise of human rights.[2]

---

[2] Artificial intelligence refers to a machine-based system that can, for a given set of human-defined objectives, make predictions, recommendations, or decisions influencing real or virtual environments. Artificial intelligence systems use machine- and human-based inputs

There are significant gaps around the world on safe, secure, and trustworthy AI, with nearly 6 billion people across the world living in countries without robust measures on responsible AI governance. In areas such as privacy, data protection, accountability, transparency, bias, discrimination, cybersecurity, and linguistic diversity, the world has a long way to go toward ensuring that AI systems are designed and deployed in a responsible way.

Responsible AI

An approach to AI that aligns the design, deployment, and use of AI with the core values of democracy, reliability, safety, security, trustworthiness, inclusion, transparency, privacy, cybersecurity, fairness, human rights, and accountability.[3]

What does a local AI ecosystem look like?

In any country, the AI ecosystem is an integral part of the broader digital ecosystem. This includes processes and policies for digital data collection, storage, management, and sharing; a local workforce involved in research, development, and private sector activities; an engaged civil society; and governance and policy frameworks. The ecosystem involves a diverse range of stakeholders, including government agencies, businesses and startups, universities and training institutes, as well as civil society organizations.

Understanding the impact of AI on development requires acknowledging the differences in circumstances across countries, regions, communities, and contexts. Even among countries in the same region or with similar income levels, there can be significant disparities in access to AI technologies and in how AI is deployed, ultimately affecting individuals and communities in diverse ways.

A meaningful approach to global development must prioritize locally led and relevant solutions, not just at the national level but also within individual communities. This involves understanding and adapting to the unique political, social, cultural, economic, and environmental conditions

---

to perceive real and virtual environments; abstract such perceptions into models through analysis in an automated manner; and use model inference to formulate options for information or action.

[3] A succinct summary of Responsible AI in the context of global development and humanitarian assistance from the USAID AI Action Plan.

of each context, recognizing that there is no "one-size-fits-all" approach. This is particularly crucial in promoting responsible AI deployment, as it ensures that AI technologies are tailored to meet the specific needs and challenges of different populations. Additionally, this approach allows for the implementation of safeguards that address the particular risks associated with AI in each context.

There are a range of existing tools that stakeholders can use to better understand how AI fits into their local contexts, including indices such as the Global Index on Responsible AI, the AI Index from Stanford University, the UNESCO Readiness Assessment Methodology, the Government AI Readiness Index, and the Microsoft AI Engagement Index. Each of these tracks AI at different levels and can help in understanding which aspects of the AI ecosystem could be prioritized or strengthened.

Approach

Before drafting the AI in Global Development Playbook, subject matter experts at USAID, the U.S. Department of State, and the U.S. Department of Commerce (among other interagency partners) released a Request for Information (RFI) aimed at gathering a wide range of perspectives from the public and relevant partners in the AI development ecosystem. More than 60 organizations and individuals provided responses. The themes identified in this RFI were informed by desk research comprising existing literature, reports, initiatives, case studies, and data on AI in global development and humanitarian assistance. The research team then held 13 virtual consultation sessions with representatives from governments of countries from around the world at all levels of development, civil society, development organizations, philanthropies, and the private sector. The Playbook is a distillation and analysis of the information gathered through the research, the request for information, and consultations.[4]

[4] While the AI in Global Development Playbook aims to address many of the foundational issues gathered from consultations, we recognize it cannot cover all the possible areas of concern around AI and choose the areas of the greatest relevance while providing as comprehensive of an approach as possible. We encourage readers to reach out to aiplaybook@usaid.gov with general feedback, suggestions, or areas of focus that should be included in the United States government's approach to AI in the future.

The Playbook addresses the ecosystem-level opportunities and challenges for the safe, secure, and trustworthy design, deployment, and use of AI in the context of global development. Building on the risks identified in the AI Risk Management Framework, there are unique questions that should be considered: What are the necessary skills required to build safe, secure, and trustworthy AI systems to address global development challenges? Which partnerships and initiatives can bridge the infrastructure gaps impeding safe, secure, and trustworthy AI development in LMICs? What does diverse and equitable representation in data mean for communities with limited Internet connectivity? How should AI systems be designed with participation and partnership from local users and affected communities, and deployed in a way that represents the rich diversity of human experiences? What are the gaps in evaluations of AI models that could make them most useful for local communities? How can we prevent and mitigate harmful applications of AI? What incentives can be put in place to ensure AI is appropriately open, transparent, and explainable? Finally, how can we align the design, deployment, and use of AI with the goals of environmental sustainability and taking action against climate change?

These considerations inform not just the organizations building AI systems, but the ecosystem of actors shaping the design, deployment, use, and ultimate impact of these systems on people and communities. As a result, the Playbook takes a wide view of AI ecosystems that could apply across a variety of sectors and issue areas,[5] aiming to shift the broader landscape to leverage the opportunities and mitigate the risks that AI actors will encounter in the future.

United States Efforts to Promote Responsible AI in Global Development

Given the inherently intersectional nature of AI and its many cross-cutting effects, the U.S. government has created the AI.gov website to provide a

---

[5] Through the research and consultation process, issues areas of most relevance were AI solutions in health; education; agriculture and food security; energy including energy consumption and production; climate including climate change mitigation and adaptations; transportation including roads, ports, airports, railways; and delivering public services. To a lesser degree we also heard the need for solutions related to the financial sector and industrial manufacturing.

comprehensive review of actions taken to support safe, secure, and trustworthy AI.

In the context of global development specifically, USAID launched the AI Action Plan in 2022, setting a strategic vision for the U.S. Government's role and commitment to advancing responsible AI to address critical global challenges. The Action Plan describes how USAID integrates AI into development programming across different sectors, how it is supporting digital ecosystems to encourage responsible AI, and how it is partnering to shape a global agenda on AI in development. The Action Plan focuses on building local capacity in partner countries, ensuring respect for human rights, and fostering collaboration with diverse stakeholders. Among these partnerships, USAID has joined forces with other international development donors to support responsible AI ecosystems worldwide, including the United Kingdom's Foreign, Commonwealth and Development Office (FCDO), Canada's International Development Research Centre (IDRC), Germany's Corporation for International Cooperation (GIZ), and the Gates Foundation. Also in partnership, USAID and IDRC have launched the Donor Principles for Human Rights in the Digital Age at the United Nations' Internet Governance Forum, which aims to center human rights and democratic values in governmental actions related to digital engagement and investments. The Principles specifically highlight the need for security and safety both in development and humanitarian assistance programs as well as the responsibility of donors to conduct human rights due diligence assessments.

In September 2023, Secretary Blinken announced at a global event on "Artificial Intelligence for Accelerating Progress on the Sustainable Development Goals: Addressing Society's Greatest Challenges" on the margins of the UNGA high-level week working with Congress, a commitment to provide $15 million in foreign assistance over five years to promote the responsible use and governance of AI globally, among other objectives, to include programs that leverage AI tools to help countries achieve SDGs. Additionally, the U.S. private sector committed $21 million to leverage AI to bolster the SDGs and provide training to four million people in developing countries, including at least 2 million people in Africa. Alongside the United States, some of the co-convening countries announced significant future funding and resources, together totaling more than $9 billion in investments in AI startups and scaleups as well as risk analysis globally. The event highlighted private sector initiatives in developing countries in areas such as health, education, agriculture and food security, energy, and more.

The Executive Order on the Safe, Secure, and Trustworthy Development and Use of Artificial Intelligence issued in October 2023 outlines a whole-of-government strategy on AI. This includes promoting global practices for AI through multilateral fora, strengthening partnerships with allies and international organizations to address shared AI challenges, and supporting capacity building initiatives worldwide. The AI in Global Development Playbook is a deliverable under the Executive Order aimed at promoting the responsible use of AI for global good while mitigating potential risks and challenges. The Global AI Research Agenda, another deliverable identified in the AI Executive Order, is a companion document to the Playbook. The Research Agenda guides the objectives and implementation of AI-related research in contexts beyond the U.S.'s borders, and includes principles, guidelines, priorities, and best practices aimed at ensuring the safe, responsible, beneficial, and sustainable development and adoption of AI.

Photo Credit: U.S. Department of State.

On March 21, 2024, the United Nations General Assembly adopted by consensus the U.S.-led resolution "Seizing the opportunities of safe, secure and trustworthy artificial intelligence systems for sustainable development." This resolution underscores a global commitment to harness AI's potential to achieve the SDGs. Generally speaking, the resolution calls for international cooperation to ensure AI systems are developed responsibly, addressing risks related to privacy, security, and inequity.

Finally, as part of efforts to support Section 11 of the Executive Order, the U.S. Department of State, in coordination with NIST and USAID, developed a "Risk Management Profile for Artificial Intelligence and Human Rights." This Profile of the NIST AI Risk Management Framework (AI RMF) draws on multi stakeholder consultations to identify examples of potential unintentional and intentional human rights impacts that can arise from the design, deployment, and use of AI. The Profile then provides voluntary recommendations for governments, private sector, and civil society globally on how to incorporate human rights considerations into select actions from the AI RMF to manage such risks.

Opportunities, Challenges, and Recommendations on AI in Global Development

Enhancing Capacity, Promoting AI-Related Skills Across All Sectors and Levels, and Protecting the Workforce

In many LMICs there is a critical shortage of AI expertise, hindering the potential benefits of AI for sustainable development. Investing in responsible AI skills in LMICs (including in the public sector) is essential for building the AI workforce and ensuring that the benefits of safe, secure, and trustworthy AI are equitably distributed.

Opportunity and Challenge
Many countries face challenges in developing a robust AI workforce and in building a resilient labor market in the face of technological change. Yet by investing in upskilling and promoting respect for workers' rights, countries have the opportunity to foster diverse talent pools and create resilient labor

markets, enabling them to develop and adapt AI tools tailored to their unique contexts and drive sustainable development.

Diverse Skills for Diverse Populations

Developing locally relevant expertise in AI across a wide variety of sectors can lead to the creation of innovative solutions tailored to local and regional challenges in healthcare, agriculture, education, and other fields.

The development and use of safe, secure, and trustworthy AI technologies benefits from diverse pools of talent, representing all segments of the population. As highlighted by UNESCO, voices and perspectives from LMICs are critical in identifying and addressing biases and helping ensure that AI solutions are tailored to local contexts. Yet there is, in general, a lack of diversity in technology ecosystems across different stages of AI design, deployment, and use. For example example, of professionals in AI & data science fields those researching and developing the technology, less than 22% of professionals in AI & data science fields are women. And this lack of diversity is not just an issue on the basis of gender—barriers also exist for racial or ethnic minorities, people with disabilities, individuals in rural contexts, older people, and other populations.

Relevant school curricula are also important in this context. While responsible AI skills should include proficiency in data science, machine learning, software development, cybersecurity, and sector and industry-specific relevant technical skills, responsible AI education also benefits from an understanding of AI's societal implications, including how issues such as bias, fairness, and transparency impact digital divides in communities, regions, and sectors around the world. In this regard, perspectives from experts in areas such as gender studies, history, cybersecurity and privacy, behavioral economics, psychology, political science, anthropology, sociology, and linguistics are key to informing the designs of systems that work for their intended users, managing risks, and unpacking and addressing AI's societal implications. These are the educational foundations for a responsible approach to AI.

As AI continues to evolve, it is crucial to invest in retraining, reskilling, upskilling, and professional development programs to help workers transition to new roles. Governments, businesses, and educational institutions can collaborate to develop comprehensive retraining programs that equip workers with the skills demanded by the AI-driven economy. These programs should have a dual focus on advancing technical and generalized skills; specifically efforts should be made to educate individuals in areas such as digital literacy;

the implication of AI's usage; methods of applying and developing AI tools, especially in legacy industries; methods of anticipating, identifying, contextualizing, and responding to an AI system's impacts; stakeholder and community engagement; problem-solving; and adaptability. Online courses, vocational training, and partnerships with the private sector and academia can provide accessible and flexible learning opportunities. One such example is Equitech Futures' Civic Tech Institute: a 10-week program for emerging leaders in government, non-profits, or social enterprise to "practice the data and technology skills critical to achieving impact at scale." By connecting the needs of employers with individuals willing to learn and advance their skills, efforts like these have the potential to support good jobs and resilient labor markets.

Rights- and Labor-Respecting Approaches to AI

AI also poses new questions for the changing nature of work and labor markets. The Partnership on AI, a non-profit coalition of stakeholders in the AI ecosystem, for example, has conducted extensive research on the "data enrichment" economy—composed of people that collect and annotate data used in AI systems—and has developed guidelines for responsible sourcing of data enrichment services. These guidelines aim to ensure fair compensation, fair labor practices, and better working conditions for data enrichment workers. The International Labor Organization and the UN Office of the Secretary General's Envoy on Technology have also released a report highlighting the need to both build AI skills and encourage social dialogue with workers to ensure that technological advancements respect workers' rights and improve job quality.

Protecting workers also means protecting their labor fundamental rights, including freedom of association and the right to collective bargaining, which can give workers and their representatives the ability to negotiate and provide meaningful input into the development, use, and monitoring of AI in the workplace, especially given the changing nature of work.

The potential impact of AI on labor markets also reinforces the importance of robust systems to support those affected by automation. Ensuring workers benefit from new opportunities created by AI and are protected from its potential harms will require a consistent focus on worker empowerment, as recommended by the Principles for AI and Workers by the U.S. Department of Labor. This may mean prioritizing strengthening unemployment benefits, healthcare access, training opportunities, and social services to support and provide a safety net for workers during periods of transition and unemployment. Community-based support systems, mental health services, and career counseling could also help workers navigate the challenges of career transitions and maintain well-being. The Global AI Research Agenda further addresses these issues and provides research and policy directions on the impact of AI on labor markets, the AI value chain, and workers impacted by the changes presented by AI.

Responsible Computing Challenge — Training the Next Generation of Technologists

The Mozilla Foundation's Responsible Computing Challenge (RCC) underscores the importance of investing in responsible AI skills in LMICs. By targeting universities and educational institutions, RCC seeks to integrate responsible AI practices into technology curricula, ensuring that future technologists are equipped with the skills to build ethical AI systems and understand the broader social, political, and environmental implications of their work.

RCC emphasizes interdisciplinary education, fosters industry connections and partnerships and tailors curricula to address local community needs. This approach aims to drive an industry-wide shift toward responsible AI.

For example, at Kisii University in Kenya, undergraduate AI courses were redesigned to integrate ethical principles, with industry practitioners co-teaching to facilitate a pipeline from education to employment. RCC also reaches students beyond traditional computer science programs through workshops and events, impacting thousands of students. From 2018 to 2023, RCC has funded 50 higher education institutions in the United States, India, and Kenya, with additional countries to follow. RCC has also compiled learnings into a Responsible Computing Challenge Playbook and Curriculum Library, aiming to spur change beyond the funded institutions.

By providing resources and support, RCC enables emerging technologists to develop AI solutions tailored to their communities, ensuring these technologies are socially and culturally relevant and ultimately contributing to sustainable development.

Karya — "Creating high quality datasets while enabling economic opportunities for rural Indians"

Karya is an Indian social enterprise focused on creating fair and sustainable work opportunities in the AI economy. The organization aims to empower communities by providing dignified and fairly compensated work in data labeling and other digital tasks essential for AI development, including categorizing images, transcribing audio, and tagging data.

Karya offers training programs designed to equip workers with digital literacy and technical skills, covering basic computer skills, data management, and specific tools used in data labeling. The goal of these programs is to enhance workers' technical capabilities and prepare them for future job opportunities in the global digital economy.

Karya provides fair compensation for workers by reinvesting profits into wages, thereby promoting financial stability and economic empowerment for people otherwise left out of the digital economy.

Central to Karya's approach is engagement directly with local communities to train workers. By collaborating with community leaders and organizations, Karya aims to ensure its initiatives and employment opportunities support economic development from the bottom up. This community-centric approach is intended to foster trust and collaboration, thus creating a supportive environment for workers and further ensures that its initiatives are culturally relevant and meet the specific needs of the communities they serve.

Karya's initiatives are particularly aimed at benefiting women, who often face barriers to gainful employment due to prevailing gender norms. By providing flexible, home-based work opportunities in data labeling and digital tasks that require little infrastructure development (in this case using readily available smartphones), Karya supports women to earn fair wages in communities where women's work is traditionally undervalued. Additionally, Karya emphasizes digital literacy and skills training to empower women with the technical expertise needed to succeed in the global AI economy.

According to Karya, thus far, they have been able to reach 40,000 people across 27 states in rural India, and have distributed over $1,000,000 wages to workers for 40 million tasks.

Photo Credit: Riaz Jahanpour for USAID.

African Content Moderators Union — a grassroots effort to protect workers' rights in the AI ecosystem

Data labelers, moderators, and other workers who complete tasks essential for AI design, deployment, and use are often contracted by technology companies.

The African Content Moderators Union and other grassroots organizations have long worked to champion safe employment practices and environments. They have been at the forefront of collective bargaining for improved labor conditions, supported by Foxglove, which itself is supported by the Ford Foundation, Luminate, and the Open Society Foundation, among others. In addition, the African Content Moderators Union has attempted to bolster governmental responses to harmful labor practices and supported legal disputes against employers that they allege have created unsafe working environments.

The Union advocates that contractors be paid fairly for their work, highlighting that greater support for these workers has the potential for positive change to the AI value chain overall and promote socioeconomic development among the communities that these technology companies engage with.

Empowering and supporting grassroots and locally led efforts have the power to lead to change across the AI value chain. Through efforts such as greater government protections, funding support, and technical assistance (such as access to legal support), grassroots efforts can help mitigate many labor challenges associated with data labeling economy and contribute to community-wide economic development.

Recommendations for Enhancing Capacity, Promoting AI-Related Skills, and Protecting the Workforce

Government

- Integrate responsible and contextually relevant AI education into state, national, and regional curricula at all levels, from primary and university-level education to public-facing or professionally oriented upskilling and education efforts. Encourage educational institutions to provide necessary resources such as instructor training and engagement with relevant government agencies for teaching safe, secure, and trustworthy AI, with a special focus on bridging digital divides.
- These could create incentives for the private sector to collaborate with educational and workforce development institutions on AI education and upskilling initiatives and workforce development. This can include tax benefits, grants, and public recognition for companies that actively contribute to safe, secure, and trustworthy AI capacity building.
- Prioritize training, unemployment benefits, healthcare access, and social services to support workers in industries affected or prone to labor disruption from AI.
- Enforce and monitor compliance with domestic labor laws and international labor standards to prevent worker exploitation and help ensure decent work in and across the AI value chain.
- Take special efforts to ensure that underrepresented groups—especially women, girls, and gender-diverse people—are encouraged to participate in AI programs and education, with the goal of bridging disparities in STEM education.

United States' Support

The United States supports a range of AI capacity building efforts, including AI Connect, the Responsible Computing Challenge, a partnership with Google under the Future Growth Initiative, and the Equitable AI Challenge.

The United States is committed to expanding these existing programs, developing new programs focused on AI policy capacity building, and working with private sector firms and through multilateral bodies to increase global capacity building efforts on AI, tailored to local contexts.

Private Sector

- Develop AI training and curricula, certifications, and credentialing programs in meaningful partnership with development experts, civil society organizations including educational and workforce development organizations, and local communities, focusing squarely on the needs of LMICs and the skills that can support AI ecosystem strengthening in those countries.
- Prioritize the safe, secure, and trustworthy development and implementation of AI systems within the organizational culture so that AI is deployed around the world in a manner that meets local needs and incorporates local perspectives.
- Provide decent work for data enrichment workers throughout the AI value chain, and support and respect workers' right to collective bargaining.
- Support and respect workers' right to collective bargaining so they may negotiate the design, deployment, and use of AI systems in the workplace as well as the collection and use of data in the workplace.
- Support inclusive hiring, promotion, professional development, and skilling efforts to support all people, especially women, girls, and gender-diverse people as well as other under-represented groups often left out of STEM-related fields.

Photo Credit: Jack Gordon for USAID.

Development Donors and Philanthropic Organizations

- Allocate funds to universities and educational institutions in LMICs to develop and implement responsible AI curricula focused on the impacts of technology on society, bias and fairness, transparency, cybersecurity, and domain-specific knowledge relevant to key sectors in AI (e.g., health, education, agriculture and food security, energy, climate change, transportation, and public service delivery). These curricula should be designed to be fit-for-purpose by those who understand the local context.
- Invest in research initiatives that focus on responsible AI and encourage collaboration between institutions in LMICs and established AI research centers in other parts of the world. This can be facilitated through grants, joint research programs, scholarships, and international conferences.
- Support unions and other civil society organizations advocating for workers' rights in the context of AI. Raise awareness about exploitative labor practices and promote the fundamental principles and rights at work.

Building Trusted and Sustainable Digital Infrastructure

Safe, secure, and trustworthy AI technology depends on broader trusted digital infrastructure. Bridging digital divides and addressing these digital infrastructure challenges, including AI's impacts on the environment, is crucial for fostering local innovation and economic development and can allow AI technologies to be developed and deployed inclusively and sustainably.

Opportunity and Challenge

Many LMICs face limited Internet connectivity and unreliable power. Addressing these infrastructure gaps, especially due to AI's significant energy costs, not only supports technological advancement and economic growth, but also enables the development and use of targeted AI solutions for sustainable development.

Electricity and Connectivity Challenges

Internet penetration rates are still limited in many LMICs. For instance, while global Internet usage reached 63% in 2022, in Africa and South Asia the rates were just 36% and 43% respectively.

Meanwhile, several connectivity digital divides need to be addressed: gender digital divides, between urban and rural areas, and disability-related divides, among many others. Expanding connectivity can enable individuals, organizations, and businesses to access and build AI technologies and allow for more locally relevant data generation to improve the quality of these AI models.

Frequent power outages and unstable electricity supply in many LMICs are also a barrier for people trying to build and use AI systems (in addition to their broader repercussions). Outages disrupt the consistent operation of AI systems, hinder data processing and model training, and complicate efforts to maintain reliable and sustainable AI infrastructure.

AI's Energy Costs

AI interacts in many ways with climate sustainability. Training and deploying AI technologies, particularly the foundation models commonly used in generative AI, requires substantial computational resources, which in turn, cost natural resources. This compute comes with substantial electricity demands from the power grid, which, if not met with clean energy resources, will result in growing greenhouse gas emissions. Increasing clean energy deployment is critical to ensuring that AI systems are sustainable in the long run, and—at least until sufficiently powerful models can be trained with less energy—to enable organizations of all sizes to build and deploy custom AI systems.

Throughout the life cycle of an AI system, energy is required to power data centers and water is needed for cooling systems. As AI development has accelerated, this energy and water consumption has increased in tandem. The embodied emissions of data centers in some cases will have more of a negative impact than the electricity used to run them. The International Energy Agency estimates that, "electricity consumption from data centers, artificial intelligence (AI) and the cryptocurrency sector could double by 2026." Meeting this increased energy consumption sustainably is imperative due to the urgent global need to transition away from fossil fuels, in order to limit global warming to 1.5 degrees Celsius and avoid the worst effects of climate change.

Photo Credit: Gretchen Robleto Lupiac.

As a consequence, there is active research into methods to reduce the energy requirements of AI systems to reach the same model performance with less computation. For example, techniques such as model pruning, quantization, and knowledge distillation may be able to significantly reduce the computational resources required for many AI applications without significantly compromising performance.

While efficiency measures should be pursued continuously, companies deploying AI systems should also pursue options to expand the availability and use of clean energy to power these systems. Powering AI systems through clean energy sources avoids the greenhouse gas emissions created by the burning of unabated fossil fuels. Supporting the expansion of clean energy, and the infrastructure needed to incorporate clean energy sources into the grid where relevant, avoids displacing emissions from fossil energy elsewhere within the energy system. Furthermore, leveraging the large energy demand from AI systems can spur innovation and drive commercialization and cost reductions of clean power generation and storage technologies. Likewise, flexing operations to match electricity demand with variable renewable energy output can aid grid operators in incorporating larger amounts of wind and solar.

While there are efforts to measure the energy consumption of various AI systems, the methods and metrics are not standardized, and data on energy use is not always available from the companies designing and deploying AI. Making this data available, and transitioning to clean energy sources for powering computational infrastructure, could substantially reduce the carbon emissions associated with AI. Similar efforts are also required to measure and address water consumption by data servers used for server cooling.

Another key mechanism for reducing AI's energy usage is selecting the most appropriate AI models for a given task. While multi-purpose generative models are highly adaptable and receive much of the public attention, they are often orders of magnitude more compute-intensive than similarly performant task-specific models. This phenomenon is observed not only during model development and training, but also during the inference stage – when a model makes decisions as part of production operations. By selecting and designing models carefully, and continuously replacing inefficient models with more efficient alternatives, practitioners can both reduce carbon emissions and make their systems easier to deploy in environments with limited compute access.

Microsoft's Phi-3 model – Innovating in AI while reducing energy demands

The Phi-3 language model developed by Microsoft represents an advancement for more energy-efficient AI technologies. Designed to maintain high performance while significantly reducing energy consumption, Phi-3 systematically eliminates unnecessary parameters within the model, thereby reducing the amount of computational power needed. This approach not only helps cut down the carbon footprint associated with the system, but also potentially makes the model more accessible for deployment in compute-constrained environments or situations where fast response times are essential.

By focusing on reducing the carbon emissions of AI models, the Phi-3 project aims not only to address immediate environmental concerns but also set a precedent for future AI research and development. By integrating energy efficiency into the design of AI technologies, developers can contribute to global sustainability efforts while also enhancing the practicality of AI applications in diverse settings. This approach highlights the importance of continued innovation in the field to balance technological advancement with environmental responsibility.

Recommendations for Building Trusted and Sustainable Digital Infrastructure

Government

- Create policy and institutional frameworks that encourage collaboration between government, private sector, and civil society to improve trusted digital infrastructure and create a conducive investment environment for connectivity and energy.
- Provide incentives that de-risk investment, such as tax benefits, grants, advanced market commitments, guaranteed contracts, and public recognition for companies to invest in trusted, sustainable infrastructure.
- Collaborate with the private sector to contribute to projects that provide affordable access to the Internet to underserved areas, and support local capacity building to use those connectivity resources.

United States' Support

The United States supports a range of infrastructure projects focused on investing directly or de-risking investment from the private sector, including Power Africa, Digital Invest, the Asia Open Radio Access Network (Open RAN) Academy, a partnership with Amazon Web Services in Indonesia, and the Digital Connectivity and Cybersecurity Partnership.

The National Institute of Standards and Technology (NIST) is convening a community of experts and stakeholders, including via a new task force within the AI Safety Institute Consortium, to study measurement of AI's environmental impacts, including energy and water usage. The project will survey the landscape of measurement methods for impact measurement, identify gaps, and possibly establish an expert group to develop rigorous shared measurement metrics.

Private Sector

- Regularly release data about the energy use and environmental costs of AI systems, from training through to deployment, and invest in R&D to decrease energy needs for these systems. Work to improve and standardize measurement and disclosure methodologies.
- Partner with governments, philanthropic organizations, and local organizations to invest in expanding trusted broadband networks and energy infrastructure.

Photo Credit: Riaz Jahanpour for USAID Tanzania.

Development Donors and Philanthropic Organizations

- Support advocacy initiatives that promote transparency in AI energy consumption by encouraging companies to disclose their energy use data, facilitating better understanding and accountability in the industry.
- Continue to build on existing investments and allocate funds to expand sustainable broadband networks and improve Internet access in underserved regions, particularly in the last mile and for LMICs.
- Establish mechanisms for monitoring and reporting on digital infrastructure needs and barriers AI ecosystems, particularly those that contribute to persistent digital divides. Use this information to support civil society advocacy efforts, and share it with governments and industry to inform their efforts.

Broadening Access to Data Storage and Compute Resources

Opportunity and Challenge

In order to develop AI systems that meet local needs, innovators in LMICs need access to compute resources for training and inference. Making compute more accessible and affordable can lower barriers to entry for AI innovation, leading to more useful and relevant AI applications.

Both cloud access and on-premises computing in many parts of the world are difficult to access or afford. Relevant computing resources, including access to trusted cloud providers and on-premises computing where appropriate, can enable LMICs to develop and use AI systems tailored to their local challenges. The cost of access to relevant computing resources can hinder the ability of local AI developers to experiment, innovate, and participate in the global AI ecosystem. A lack of access to data centers and infrastructure can potentially lead to increased latency and higher operational costs.

Initiatives that promote public-private partnerships, regional collaborations, and innovative financing models— such as shared infrastructure projects or subsidized access to cloud services—can help overcome these barriers. Additionally, fostering local expertise through targeted training programs and capacity-building initiatives can empower communities to manage and optimize the use of these resources, helping to ensure that AI technologies are not only accessible but also effectively leveraged to address local needs.

Fair Transition Initiative — Expanding Access to Compute

The Fair Transition Initiative (a partnership between Uwazi Foundation, NVIDIA, and HP) enables access to high-performance computing (HPC) to support the development of AI models.

The Fair Transition Initiative's action plan includes several strategic initiatives aimed at bridging this gap. One prominent example is the National Compute Infrastructure project in partnership with the Government of Barbados, which aims to transform the island nation into a global technology hub. By establishing state-of-the-art data centers, Barbados can provide local entrepreneurs, students, and researchers with the necessary compute resources to develop and deploy AI technologies. These data centers will enable the processing and storage of large datasets and serve as innovation sandboxes.

Additionally, the initiative is working to empower Kenyan youth with access to compute. Through this collaboration, local data scientists were equipped with GPU-powered workstations, enabling them to fine-tune and deploy AI models up to 23 times faster. This partnership enhances local capacity and ensures that AI solutions are tailored to the specific needs and contexts of LMICs.

Efforts like this, focused on public-private partnerships rooted in local needs, have the power to change the landscape of access to technology and AI, enabling the benefits of AI to be directly applied by local communities for their needs and interests. In Kenya, youth were able to fine-tune, adapt, and deploy an earth science and climate-related AI model in an attempt to address local challenges. Future efforts on compute should adopt a similar approach: conduct thorough needs assessments with local stakeholders and community organizations, and then develop public-private partnerships to meaningfully address compute gaps in those contexts.

Recommendations for Broadening Access to Data Storage and Compute Resources

United States' Support

The U.S. National Science Foundation is working to broaden participation in cutting edge AI research through the National AI Research Resource pilot, in which government agencies are collaborating with government-supported and non-governmental partners to connect researchers and educators to computational, data, and training resources. In addition, USAID will be working with international partners to broaden access to compute resources for innovators and entrepreneurs across the globe.

Government

Create policy and institutional frameworks that encourage collaboration between government, private sector, and civil society to expand access to compute resources, including trusted cloud providers.

Private Sector
Consider product packages and tiered pricing models for cloud compute that account for local needs, conditions, and usage patterns.

Development Donors and Philanthropic Organizations
Provide grants and resources for cloud compute access and de-risk investment in high-performance computing facilities to serve LMICs. Develop capacity building programs so these facilities can best enable local researchers, developers, and businesses to innovate and build safe, secure, and trustworthy AI systems to address local challenges.

Creating Representative, Locally Useful Datasets and Preserving Cultural Heritage

Opportunity and Challenge: Locally relevant, diverse, multilingual, and multicultural datasets for LMICs are relatively scarce. But when these datasets are created in meaningful partnership with local communities they can enable the development and use of AI models that are better fit for use in local contexts and drive equitable development.

The Consequences of Unrepresentative Data…
Data quality and availability are important to AI development and use, yet locally relevant datasets are scarce for many LMICs, or data has not been digitized.

To take one example, off-the-shelf healthcare AI tools may not accurately diagnose conditions prevalent in LMICs without sufficient local, diverse, and relevant data —a phenomenon that is relevant for many sectors and contexts.

Opportunity and Challenge
Locally relevant, diverse, multilingual, and multicultural datasets for LMICs are relatively scarce. But when these datasets are created in meaningful partnership with local communities they can enable the development and use of AI models that are better fit for use in local contexts and drive equitable development.

These potential gaps in data underscore the importance of probing AI models for representativeness and bias to improve the effectiveness of AI solutions. In 2023, USAID funded a project between a consortium of civil society organizations and a state government in Mexico to review an AI-based early alert system. This system aimed to improve school retention and graduation rates by identifying at-risk students and providing them support. However, a critical gender bias in the system would have prevented it from identifying more than 4000 girls who needed help to stay in school. This evaluation enabled the system to be updated to recognize and mitigate gender biases in source datasets, making it more effective for its intended purposes. Importantly, this project identified this gender bias early, before the AI tool was further institutionalized. Early stage and regular bias detection through local datasets can be critical to addressing these rapidly scalable information gaps, and this project produced a tool to support these efforts. Similar biases have shown up in other contexts; for example, language models that evaluate resumes can be biased against people who reference that they have a disability. It is critical to not only examine datasets for underrepresentation of particular groups, but also to consider the ways that data may reflect inequalities in society (e.g., related to gender, race, ethnicity, caste, or ability) such that AI tools then learn from and reinforce these inequalities.

...And the Benefits of Investing in Representative Data

Investing in more representative datasets is crucial for several reasons. First, it can help ensure that AI technologies are better able to address the specific challenges faced by LMICs, leading to more effective and culturally relevant solutions. By capturing the diversity of languages, dialects, and cultural contexts within these regions, AI models can be trained to perform more accurately and fairly across a broader range of scenarios. Furthermore, representative datasets contribute to the global AI ecosystem by providing a more complete and nuanced understanding of underrepresented populations, helping to avoid the perpetuation of biases and inaccuracies in widely used AI tools. This not only improves the inclusivity and fairness of AI applications globally but also enables countries to participate more fully in the design, deployment, and use of AI technologies, fostering innovation and economic growth within their own borders.

The representativeness of data (or lack thereof) also plays a role in how today's foundation models are evaluated. Benchmark tests are routinely used to evaluate how well generative AI models can make truthful statements, avoid problematic outputs, and resist jailbreaking and similar attacks. Comparing the results of such tests across different languages can provide insight into the capabilities and limitations of these models, but creating locally relevant benchmarks demands locally relevant datasets. Many organizations are also now beginning to develop evaluation benchmarks for different languages to assess models across a range of local contexts.

Photo Credit: Beso Gulashvili for USAID.

There are a range of organizations stepping up to strengthen and create these datasets. For example, Masakhane—a collaborative community of African researchers aiming to focus data collection and research efforts on under-resourced African languages—has a range of projects to generate and use high-quality text and speech datasets. One other example is SustainBench, a collection of eleven datasets to drive and measure progress across seven SDGs that facilitates greater academic and research input into the fight for the SDGs, including by providing "standard benchmarks for evaluating machine learning models on tasks across a variety of SDGs." Beyond these civil society-led initiatives, there is also a critical role for governments and public-private partnerships in creating open data systems that innovators and universities can use to build locally relevant AI models.

Supporting Indigenous Communities to Preserve and Promote Their Cultures

Also of critical importance in this context is the role that AI can play in supporting and advancing local communities, especially for Indigenous communities around the world.

For example, AI can support Indigenous language preservation and revitalization, enable translation services amongst marginalized languages, and empower Indigenous communities through supporting them in controlling their own data and leveraging AI for different purposes as decided by Indigenous community members.

Photo Credit: KC Nwakalor for USAID.

Public-private partnerships and creative funding initiatives such as the use of prizes are also unlocking ways for AI technology to be harnessed for cultural preservation. For example, OpenAI, the government of Iceland, and local Icelandic technology firms partnered to improve the performance of OpenAI's GPT-4 model in the Icelandic language, incorporating culturally sensitive feedback from local communities and individuals. Similarly, Anthropic, in partnership with Singapore's Infocomm Media Development Authority (IMDA) and AI Verify Foundation, engaged in capacity building efforts by engaging with local populations to test (or "red-team") AI systems for language competency and on topics relevant to their communities. This red-teaming took place in English, Tamil, Mandarin, and Malay (the national languages of Singapore) and focused on topics relevant to those populations.

Lacuna Fund — "Putting the benefits of machine learning within reach of data scientists, researchers, and social entrepreneurs worldwide"

Established in 2020, Lacuna Fund addresses data gaps that impede the development of AI solutions tailored to the needs of LMICs. By providing financial support and technical assistance for the creation and maintenance of datasets, this coalition of funders and data scientists provides a foundation for locally relevant AI design and use. Currently, the Fund is administered by Meridian Institute and includes resources contributed by The Rockefeller Foundation, Canada's International Development Research Centre (IDRC), Google.org, German Federal Ministry for Economic Cooperation and Development (GIZ), Wellcome, Gordon & Betty Moore Foundation, Patrick J. McGovern Foundation, and Robert Wood Johnson Foundation.

Lacuna Fund has supported dataset creation in health, agriculture, under-resourced languages, and climate. For example, in agriculture, Lacuna Fund supported labeled datasets on smallholder farmers' fields that includes "georeferenced crop images along with labels on input use, crop management, phenology, crop damage, and yields, collected across 8 counties in Kenya." By focusing on locally relevant data, AI tools will be better suited to address the specific challenges faced by farmers in the region, leading to more effective agricultural practices.

True to the mission of Lacuna Fund, every dataset is locally developed and owned but openly available to the international community. Lacuna Fund also emphasizes the importance of responsible data management practices and community involvement. Projects funded by Lacuna Fund are required to adhere to strict guidelines, ensuring that data is collected and used in a manner that respects the rights, autonomy, and privacy of individuals. Additionally, the fund promotes the involvement of local researchers and communities in data collection efforts, which helps to ensure that the datasets are culturally and contextually appropriate.

Lacuna Fund's principles of "accessibility, equity, ethics, participatory approach, quality, and transformational impact" guide their selection of projects, which includes over 30 datasets. To date, these datasets have been downloaded more than 1,600,000 times.

Photo Credit: Emily Mahoney.

Common Voice — Collecting inclusive voice data

Speech recognition is a rapidly growing market and the rise of large language models (LLMs) and generative AI has accelerated this growth. Despite over 7,000 languages in the world, only a few are recognized by voice assistants. Proprietary datasets are costly to create, buy, maintain, and adapt, typically focusing on well-resourced languages like English. Additionally, existing speech training datasets often embed biases related to culture, race, gender, and socio-economic status, favoring educated, urban users.

Mozilla Common Voice (MCV) seeks to address these disparities by providing an open-source, high-quality speech corpus for languages worldwide. MCV is the largest and most diverse public participation multilingual speech corpus, centered around inclusion, community-driven efforts, and rights-conscious development. Presently, MCV has over 30,000 recorded hours, 120+ languages, and approximately 2.5 million downloads. MCV has also taken a gender responsive approach to ensure gender representative data set curating resources such as the gender action plan and expanding gender options on the platform.

In 2024, MCV expanded its core Scripted platform to include domain-specific corpora and increased linguistic diversity by offering end-to-end support for language variants and accents. This expansion enables community members to contribute to variants and accents that are often excluded, ensuring greater representation of marginalized voices.

MCV has also launched the beta version of a new platform for Spontaneous Speech, moving beyond read speech to capture more organic, natural speech patterns, including code-switching and languages rooted in oral-first cultures. MCV aims to reach 100,000 hours of crowdsourced, diverse speech within the next two years and continues to explore ways to support marginalized language communities in the era of LLMs and AI.

MCV has worked collaboratively with GIZ, the Gates Foundation, and FCDO to invest in building data sets and use cases for three East African Languages—Kinyarwanda spoken in Rwanda, Luganda in Uganda, and Kiswahili with a focus on Democratic Republic of Congo, Kenya and Tanzania. The work built on Mozilla's approach of fellowships and grant making as a means of growing leadership and community. The work has been led by fellows and partners such Digital Umuganda and Makerere AI Lab. These dataset were built during the COVID-19 pandemic and relied on building trust for community engagement for their success. Out of this investment - solutions have been built to provide information on COVID-19 in a local language as well as information for land rights, financial and agriculture services.

Te Hiku Media — Māori Data Preservation

Te Hiku Media is a Māori-owned and operated non-profit media organization based in New Zealand. The organization focuses on preserving and promoting the Māori language (te reo Māori) and culture. In 2018, they launched a competition in which Māori speakers across New Zealand recorded over 300 hours of annotated audio. With this, they built AI tools for automatic speech recognition and pronunciation of te reo Māori. As stated by the Chief Technology Officer of Te Hiku Media, Keoni Mahelona: "You have to be mindful that the access to data is huge… Globally there is an interest in te reo Māori, and Māori need to be leading that on their terms and conditions."

Te Hiku Media created various AI technologies and tools for Māori (e.g., automatic speech recognition, auto tagging, real time language feedback), and many of its tools are available as APIs through its digital language platform, Papa Reo. They also established new data protection protocols and worked with Māori-led organizations to develop AI tools that support the community. At the same time, they worked with other Indigenous communities to leverage the Te Hiku language database to train language models for other Indigenous groups – such as on Cooks Island, where language models reached around 70% accuracy with only ten hours of data.

With this strong basis of community-led solutions, public private partnerships also played a role: Te Hiku Media worked with NVIDIA to gain access to more affordable compute, enabling them to build and train these AI systems. This demonstrates how a responsible approach to AI and meaningful partnerships between local communities and technology firms can help bridge digital divides.

First Languages AI Reality — Revitalizing Indigenous languages

First Languages AI Reality (FLAIR), an initiative from the Quebec Artificial Intelligence Institute (Mila), addresses the imminent threat of language extinction, particularly among swiftly disappearing Indigenous languages.

FLAIR's mission is to empower Indigenous communities by providing them with tools and the autonomy to sustain their languages and the cultures that have evolved in tandem with these languages. This involves developing speech recognition systems tailored to Indigenous languages, which can be used for language learning, audio transcription, and voice-controlled technology. FLAIR aims to rapidly create custom models even for languages with limited available data and few remaining speakers—which characterizes many languages across the world. Central to FLAIR's work is accounting for the unique nuances in North American Indigenous languages, compared to European languages, within the design of AI systems and creating inclusive methods of collecting data led by communities and based on community consent.

FLAIR emphasizes the importance of open-source solutions and community involvement. All tools and models developed through FLAIR are shared publicly, ensuring that other communities can benefit from the advancements. This open approach is designed to empower Indigenous communities worldwide, facilitating the preservation and revitalization of thousands of under-resourced languages. By focusing on flexible model development approaches, as opposed to custom built models only for one language, FLAIR allows for rapid scaling, helping ensure that this technology can be deployed in a variety of contexts and thus mitigate language extinction.

Recommendations for Creating Representative, Locally Useful Datasets and Preserving Cultural Heritage

United States' Support

The United States open government data portal facilitates access to hundreds of thousands of datasets, is supporting a program to preserve Tibetan culture using AI, and is creating an AI-enabled system for documenting damage to cultural heritage and national infrastructure across Ukraine.

Yet there is more the United States intends to do to strengthen data quality and availability for our partners, including by investing in the creation of more inclusive benchmarks for AI systems and to ensure that off-the-shelf AI tools are as useful as possible for communities across the globe.

Government

- Encourage and support local data collection efforts by providing funding, resources, and policy support. Partner with educational institutions, local leaders, and civil society organizations to gather and curate comprehensive datasets with meaningful, informed consent.
- Formulate and apply policies that ensure the secure and safe handling of data. These policies should promote data privacy, protect individuals and communities, and facilitate data governance approaches that allow for seamless data sharing between trusted parties.
- Advocate for efforts to preserve Indigenous and historically marginalized populations' languages and cultures, and for Indigenous and historically marginalized populations to manage the collection, ownership, and application of their own data.

Private Sector

- Continuously evaluate AI systems pre- and post-deployment to identify and mitigate cultural, regional, and linguistic biases as well as discriminatory, and harmful outputs.
- Collaborate with governments, non-profits, and local technology firms to develop AI tools that support cultural preservation. Work with local stakeholders to improve AI models in ways that are culturally sensitive and beneficial to preserving local languages.
- Fund and provide technical support for community-led projects to ensure that the development and use of AI tools are aligned with communities' needs. This can include providing access to resources, training, and platforms for developing AI technologies.

Development Donors and Philanthropic Organizations

- Allocate funds to projects that focus on collecting and curating high-quality, locally relevant, sector-specific datasets, under-resourced language datasets, and foundation model benchmarks (all with meaningful informed consent and appropriate privacy protections) in LMICs. Ensure that funding efforts include funding to keep data relevant, updated, and usable. At the same time, support local communities in data gathering to ensure cultural relevance and meaningful consent in data collection.
- Invest in the development and implementation of data governance frameworks that facilitate the free flow of data with trust, safety, and security across borders while also seeking to ensure that data producers can benefit from these data flows. Provide resources for training and capacity building in data privacy and security practices, and advocate for responsible data practices and the inclusion of local voices and civil society in data governance discussions.
- Support Indigenous groups, marginalized populations, and cultural heritage institutions to convene and discuss their goals and desires as it relates to AI technologies, and then fund their resulting ideas. This may include developing and curating datasets and AI technologies, and supporting choices about how those datasets are used and distributed.
- Enable opportunities for Indigenous communities and marginalized populations to partner with policy makers or AI developers to actively participate in AI policymaking and/or AI development in ways that

center their empowerment and agency.

Developing Strategies to Deliver the Promise of AI in Practice

Continuous Improvement and Evaluation

AI has the potential to transform multiple sectors, driving progress towards the SDGs. Scaling AI use cases, however, requires solid evidence to measure effectiveness. Systematically assessing how AI systems contribute to addressing development challenges can instill confidence in the interventions that should be invested in or discontinued. While the need for rigorous evaluation of global development programs is not specific to AI, there is much to be learned from the history of development evaluation and implementation science. Evaluating for program impact often means pushing the "finish line" of evaluation further downstream. An AI model with a low error rate may not be sufficient; measuring real-life outcomes and consequences, or the closest possible proxy to those measurements, can be more meaningful.

Opportunity and Challenge

Many AI projects do not reach scale and produce meaningful impact, either because of a failure to robustly evaluate whether the AI system works in the local context, or because of a lack of sustained investment. Grounding AI interventions in solid evidence and scaling up successful approaches is essential for addressing global development challenges and maximizing the societal impact of AI.

For example, AI-driven diagnostic tools may enhance diagnostic accuracy in lab settings, but their real-world performance should be monitored to ensure they are properly used and integrated with healthcare workflows to genuinely improve patient outcomes, save time for medical professionals, or lower costs. When these kinds of AI technologies are deployed, metrics such as reduced diagnostic errors, improved health biomarkers, or increased access to healthcare information and services should all be tracked to validate whether a given AI system is providing marginal value.

In education, AI has the potential to personalize learning experiences and improve student engagement. But real-world impact on student performance and access to high-quality education should be measured to contextualize the efficacy of AI-enabled interventions such that they can scale across the sector. Student retention rates, graduation rates, and improvements in educational outcomes in underserved areas are all metrics that together could help evaluate the impact of introducing and using AI systems.

The same premise applies to other AI applications such as optimizing agricultural yields or predicting natural disasters and optimizing relief efforts. In each of these areas, it is essential for developers and deployers to ask: how is this AI system providing marginal value compared to relevant alternatives, and are there complementary policies or tools that can enhance their efficacy or mitigate harmful outcomes? By focusing on transparent and evidence-based results, we can help ensure that AI interventions are beneficial at the individual or project level, and worthy of investing in further.

Photo Credit: Des Syafrizal for USAID.

Sustainable Scaling of AI Applications

Rigorous evaluation alone is insufficient for AI's promise to deliver in practice. To scale the AI interventions that prove effective, sustainable investment in and collaboration across companies and organizations developing and deploying these technologies is crucial. By promoting and supporting such investments, we can help ensure that proven AI solutions not only sustain their impact but also expand their reach. Investing more in locally owned startups across diverse countries and locations will encourage sustainable solutions to local problems—and there is no shortage of promising research labs and startups in LMICs.

Addressing barriers to capital is critical. Venture capital and impact investment funds could be structured to better meet the needs of local entrepreneurs, including offering smaller ticket sizes, longer-term horizons, and greater flexibility to accommodate the unique challenges faced in these markets. Collaborative models, such as innovation hubs and accelerators that provide mentorship, networking opportunities, and exposure to global markets, can also play a pivotal role in scaling successful AI solutions.

Finally, fostering partnerships between local innovators and global technology firms can accelerate the design, deployment, and use of AI solutions. These partnerships can provide access to global expertise, advanced tools, and platforms that might otherwise be out of reach. Additionally, such collaborations can help bridge the gap between local needs and global technology trends, helping ensure that AI solutions are not only scalable but also relevant and impactful in the local context.

The TRACE-TB project – Scaling AI solutions in the fight against tuberculosis

The TRACE-TB project, funded by USAID and implemented by Wadhwani AI, is a prime example of how careful evaluation of AI systems can lead to change at scale. Tuberculosis (TB) remains a significant health challenge globally, particularly in countries like India. The project's goal is to integrate AI solutions into the TB care lifecycle to enhance prevention, detection, and treatment, ultimately aiming to eliminate TB in India.

The TRACE-TB project includes a screening tool that analyzes cough sounds to predict TB likelihood, a computer vision program for interpreting drug-resistant TB lab results, and a predictive tool for assessing the risk of patients not completing their TB treatment. These tools are tailored to address specific challenges in TB care, such as early detection and adherence to treatment regimens. The cough sound screening tool, for example, leverages deep learning neural networks trained on a substantial dataset of audio recordings, enabling rapid and non-invasive TB screening in both healthcare facilities and at home.

The project's evaluation process highlights the importance of measuring the effectiveness of AI solutions before scaling up. TRACE-TB has screened over 100,000 individuals through its cough detection tool, identifying more than 15,000 presumptive TB cases which then increased patient diagnosis by 12%. And, it has helped identify more than 26,000 patients who need more intensive care, resulting in a 16% decrease in negative outcomes like discontinued treatment plans, permanent lung damage, and mortality. Now, USAID and Wadhwani AI are scaling the program country-wide in partnership with the Government of India.

Overall, the TRACE-TB project serves as a model for how AI systems can be evaluated and scaled responsibly. By focusing on effectiveness and integration with existing healthcare infrastructure, the project demonstrates a pathway for leveraging AI to tackle complex health challenges globally.

Recommendations for Developing Strategies to Deliver AI's Promise in Practice

United States' Support

The United States has supported a range of projects to assess AI's real-world impact and support sustained investment in interventions that show promise: evaluating gender bias in AI-based wealth estimates, inclusive finance, testing and scaling of an AI-based literacy program, improving maternal and neonatal outcomes, and using AI to reduce HIV treatment interruptions, among others.

This year USAID is standing up a Responsible AI Fund, which will support and rigorously evaluate interventions for strengthening AI ecosystems worldwide. This is in addition to existing efforts to evaluate AI in healthcare settings, in education programs, and other sectors.

Government

- Fund and facilitate the creation of platforms for sharing best practices and lessons learned about the development and evaluation of AI interventions.
- Partner with independent evaluators, academic institutions, or auditors to assess the impact of AI interventions using metrics tied to real-world outcomes. Share data and insights with external experts to enhance the credibility, transparency, and efficacy of impact evaluations. Scale up interventions that show promise, and allocate resources away from projects that do not.

- Invest in government upskilling and continuous learning to ensure that staff have the knowledge and skills to make informed decisions about AI technologies.

Private Sector

- Create or contribute to dedicated AI impact funds aimed at supporting startups and organizations developing AI technologies with proven socioeconomic benefits, particularly from LMICs.
- Prioritize investments and partnerships in AI solutions that have demonstrated positive outcomes for advancing sustainable development.

Development Donors and Philanthropic Organizations

- Pair durable, sustained project funding with evaluation funding and technical support for measuring the impact of AI projects. Evaluate projects based in part on the quality of their plans for deployment, scaling, and evaluation. Support initiatives that establish standardized metrics and methodologies for evaluating the contributions of AI to development interventions. Ensure that the metrics used reflect the needs and priorities of local communities.

Developing Good Governance Frameworks for the Development and Use of Safe and Rights-Respecting AI

AI has the potential to be misused in ways that harm people and societies, undermining human rights and weakening democratic norms. Advances in AI systems are accelerating these risks, including through use by state and nonstate actors to further disinformation campaigns, malicious cyber activity, deepfakes, inequitable outcomes, infringement of intellectual property rights, and unlawful or arbitrary surveillance. Preventing and mitigating these misuses— while promoting rights-respecting AI—should be a top priority in efforts to promote global development and provide humanitarian assistance. Ensuring that AI is rights-respecting includes the central need for the protection of privacy rights. Adopting such an approach requires the embedding of human rights, privacy, and security principles at all levels of AI design, deployment, and use such as lawfulness, fairness, data minimization and purpose limitation, integrity, and confidentiality."

Governance is a central component of efforts to build safe and rights respecting AI, with great responsibility placed on governments and policymakers to effectively develop and implement balanced and effective frameworks to harness the benefits and manage the risks that AI presents. Such measures can foster trust among citizens; that trust can foster adoption, and adoption can drive innovation. Also critical in this context of governance is the need for sector specificity and integration with existing regulatory mechanisms. As AI is a general-purpose technology, its benefits and risks depend on the specific context of the technology's development and use. Many governments are therefore well-placed to leverage their existing regulatory agencies to address AI by sector, adding on to existing sector-specific expertise and capacity already developed. In this context of AI systems, and especially in the context of the new, cross-cutting challenges posed by synthetic content, including false and misleading information, and privacy concerns, policymakers are still gathering information and consulting stakeholders to better define and approach the issue. These are also areas where voluntary guidance can provide safeguards for the private sector and other actors, without prematurely imposing regulation as technologists and policymakers both develop a better technical understanding of AI technology.

Photo Credit: USAID.

Mitigating the Risk of the Spread of False and Misleading Information

Opportunity and Challenge
AI has the potential to be misused in ways that harm societies, including through disinformation campaigns, political manipulation, deepfakes, unlawful or arbitrary surveillance, and human rights abuses. However, by supporting the stakeholders confronting these abuses, promoting responsible AI practices, and fostering international cooperation, we can leverage AI for positive societal impact and protect democratic values and international human rights.

AI can be used to create false or misleading information, and algorithmic content recommendations often scale the spread of disinformation, often using content protected by intellectual property rights, an especially significant issue in the global sphere, which increases the likelihood of the undermining of democracy and human rights violations and abuses. AI-powered disinformation is particularly concerning in contexts with pre-existing political and social tensions, fragile institutions, or limited media and digital literacy. Generative models may lower the threshold for scaling persuasive disinformation campaigns further still, allowing actors with limited funding and resources to wield considerable influence online. Ultimately, this could facilitate the usage of AI to overwhelm and skew democratic engagement, such as through hyper-targeting or vote suppression campaigns, which has profound consequences for the preservation of democratic values. Just as large language models can produce convincing text, image generators can produce plausible but fabricated audio, images, or videos of people and events—sometimes called "deepfakes." In Moldova, a deepfake video of Moldovan President Maia Sandu promoting a pro-Russian candidate went viral on Facebook, seen by over one million users. In another instance, in the days before the Presidential election in Slovakia, AI-generated audio was released that purportedly showed one of the candidates describing how he would rig the election. These tools are especially concerning in lower-resourced contexts, such as local elections or countries with smaller numbers of tech platform users, due to less content moderation and rapid, independent fact checking.

One of the most pervasive and harmful applications of generative AI tools is the creation of fake and sexually explicit depictions of women and girls—a form of technology-facilitated gender-based violence—with women making up 99% of the individuals targeted in deepfake pornography. Deepfakes are also used to target women and girls in political and public life, often playing on sexist or misogynist tropes to create gendered disinformation, with the goal of discouraging the exercise of freedom of expression. As the creation of deepfakes becomes easier, the potential for malicious actors to manipulate public opinion, exploit and harm individuals, and undermine democratic processes grows in parallel. And in an era of increasing global interconnectedness, the ramifications of AI-enabled content extend far beyond the borders of any single nation, threatening to hinder progress on critical issues such as democratic resilience, public health, economic development, gender equity, privacy protection, intellectual property protection, and social cohesion.

> In this context of potential harms created by synthetic content, it is important to note the issue of intellectual property concerns. Intellectual property issues related to artificial intelligence are complex, rapidly evolving, and involve numerous legal, policy, ethical, and technical considerations. As such, the United Nations' World Intellectual Property Organization has drafted principles to help address some of these issues and to reinforce the need for the respect of intellectual property considerations when it comes to their use in the design, deployment, and use of AI technologies.

Mitigating the risks of AI-powered disinformation and deepfakes means investing further in technical safeguards such as provenance, data tracking, and watermarking, as well as a range of non-technical measures. Technical methods that facilitate labels for users must be paired with efforts to help users make sense of and react appropriately to those labels. More broadly, bolstering local capacity in institutions like AI forensics, data privacy protection instruments, investigative journalism, independent media, and fact-checking organizations, particularly those with a regional focus, is paramount. In conjunction with advances in the development and deployment of technical safeguards and labeling, media and digital literacy training should teach citizens how to identify the hallmarks of AI manipulated media and understand the limitations of what technical safeguards can and cannot do and how existing societal biases and division can be exploited.

Addressing Privacy and Surveillance Concerns

In tandem with the increase in AI-enabled disinformation, AI-powered surveillance systems are being deployed globally, often unlawfully and arbitrarily, with significant investments and misuse from both government and private sectors. These systems leverage AI to analyze data from various sources, including CCTV cameras and social media. What makes the current landscape particularly troubling is the increasingly blurred line between surveillance with broad social benefits (e.g., disease tracking in public health) and unlawful or arbitrary AI-powered surveillance to target political activists, workers and unionists, journalists, minority groups, or others. Additionally, there is the significant issue of unintended harms, such as the disproportionate effects of such AI systems on already vulnerable or marginalized communities, often due to biases in training data.

Photo Credit: Amir Mohebali.

According to some observers, in many countries, the adoption of AI technologies by both governments and the private sector for unethical, unlawful, and arbitrary surveillance is growing, and the use of these technologies often outpaces the development and application of domestic legal frameworks to protect the rights of unions, civil society, and individuals. This imbalance can make it easier to engage in unlawful or arbitrary surveillance, and the use of AI in surveillance can disproportionately impact marginalized communities due to explicit targeting or inadvertently due to implicit biases in datasets, exacerbating existing social inequalities and generating fear and mistrust. As a consequence, AI surveillance technologies should be deployed only in circumstances where they can be used responsibly, with the utmost safeguards in place.

With privacy violations and surveillance concerns comes the significant issue of aggressive and targeted censorship, with serious potential violations of the freedom of expression. Such AI-driven tools enhance the capacity of authoritarian state and non-state actors to monitor, control, and suppress information, which, reduces the opportunity for truly free and open conversation, dissent, and disagreement, which may restricts access to information and informed decision-making.

AI and National Security

The challenges that AI presents are not limited to those detailed above– conscious efforts must be taken to ensure that AI design, deployment, and use as well as its unintended consequences are taken into account to both be addressed and mitigated. In a national security context, AI system implementation, in key areas such as autonomous weapons and casualty assessment, and usage bring up potential ethical or legal concerns. Unifying efforts such as the U.S. Department of State's Political Declaration on Responsible Military Use of Artificial Intelligence and Autonomy, already endorsed by over 50 states, are increasingly necessary to protect international humanitarian law and international human rights, due to the imperative of protecting civilians and civilian objects in armed conflict, unintended bias mitigation, adoption and insurance of critical safety features, and the need for transparency and oversight by relevant defense personnel. Human rights assessments can also help identify and address risks. It is important to note that the challenges detailed here are not comprehensive and in an ever changing landscape of AI design, deployment, and use, comprehensive and continuous efforts must be taken to facilitate good governance and rights-respecting use.

Photo Credit: Angela Rucker.

Code for Africa – Safeguarding the information ecosystem in the age of AI

Code for Africa (CfA) is a civic technology initiative that leverages data and technology to promote transparency, fight disinformation, and strengthen digital democracy in Africa.

CfA has launched various initiatives to combat disinformation and promote accurate information. For example, its PesaCheck project is Africa's largest Indigenous fact-checking initiative. PesaCheck verifies the accuracy of news and social media content in multiple languages, helping to curb the spread of false information. Using a systematic process of identifying claims, finding data, verifying that data, and publishing findings, PesaCheck can efficiently identify and debunk misinformation based on reviews from multiple editors.

As another example, CfA's WanaData network is a pan-African initiative that supports women data scientists and journalists in producing data-driven stories. This network enhances transparency and accountability by leveraging data to uncover and report on issues such as corruption, governance, and social justice. By empowering local journalists with the tools and skills to analyze and report data, CfA fosters a more informed and engaged citizenry. This peer-to-peer collaborative approach of upskilling and meaningfully supporting local experts, each connected to their individual communities, proves to be a useful approach in addressing community needs such as combating disinformation.

Finally, CfA also focuses on improving digital literacy and civic engagement through programs like the African Network of Centers for Investigative Reporting (ANCIR). ANCIR provides training, resources, and collaboration platforms for investigative journalists, equipping them with the skills to use digital tools effectively. This initiative helps journalists produce high-quality investigative work that can hold power to account and inform the public.

Especially clear through many of CfA's projects is its meaningful approach to collaboration—bringing together community leaders, subject matter experts, emerging leaders, civil society organizations, and the private sector to champion shared goals and vision for Africa and promote digital democracy.

Recommendations for Developing Good Governance Frameworks for the Development and Use of Safe and Rights-Respecting AI

United States' Support

The United States is supporting a range of policy efforts, funded projects, and tools to support rights-respecting AI. This includes the Blueprint for an AI Bill of Rights, the Risk Management Profile for AI and Human Rights, an AI Accountability Report from the National Telecommunications and Information Administration, a report focused on Reducing Risks Posed by Synthetic Content, and a project on building capacity for responsible, inclusive, and rights-respecting approaches to AI.

In the coming years, USAID's Advancing Digital Democracy (ADD) initiative will support dozens of countries' AI ecosystems against misuse and harms from AI. ADD will support local actors' efforts to strengthen legal frameworks for rights-respecting AI governance, while promoting increased investment for startups, tech hubs and other innovations that advance responsible, trustworthy and rights-respecting AI systems.

Government

- Develop, implement, and enforce whole-of-government governance and oversight frameworks that specifically address the misuse of AI technologies, including disinformation, deepfakes and non-consensual intimate imagery, cyber attacks, censorship, public safety, individual harms, and unlawful and arbitrary surveillance abuses by both state and non-state actors. These laws and frameworks should protect privacy, protect intellectual property rights, safeguard democratic institutions, and protect human rights. These laws and frameworks should also incorporate a gender lens to account for the unique and disproportionate targeting of women and girls, and LGBTQI+ political and public figures with deepfake image-based sexual abuse.
- Develop, implement, and advance international standards and compatibility frameworks to facilitate international collaboration, rights-respecting procurement, partnership, and coordination as it relates to AI design, deployment, and use.
- Adopt efforts to support foreign investors and developers in resource constrained environments to receive technical support in navigating

local regulations around AI, such as through designated AI officers to provide on-the-ground connections and support for rights-respecting AI innovation.

- Ensure that government procurement, contracting, and AI technology usage facilitates efforts to enhance privacy, well-being, and human rights, with built-in technical and non-technical safeguards.

Private Sector

- Support exchanges of information between government officials, policymakers, workers and their organizations and other stakeholders to voice concerns around how AI is designed and deployed in LMICs, and factor this guidance into product development.
- Invest in privacy and transparency enhancing technologies and other technological solutions that minimize the risks of potential misuse.
- Design AI tools to make rights-respecting uses easier and non-rights-respecting uses harder. Perform human rights due diligence before releasing AI tools and build in safeguards such as those referenced in the NIST AI RMF Generative Artificial Intelligence Profile for known harms and misuse, such as AI-generated non-consensual intimate imagery and child sexual abuse material.
- Vet customers adequately to prevent malicious uses of such technology, including by by non-democratic governments and by malign non-state actors, especially if such technology has the capacity to be used to violate civil liberties, human rights, and personal privacy. Source data ethically, including the use of informed consent.

Development Donors and Philanthropic Organizations

- Support research initiatives to develop tools to detect and mitigate AI misuse, and safeguards to prevent that misuse. Invest in initiatives that promote transparency, accountability, and the responsible use of AI technologies.
- Invest in local journalism, fact checking organizations, and oversight mechanisms, especially in vulnerable contexts such as during elections, to identify and respond to deepfakes and other forms of disinformation.
- Support the development and use of content provenance and authentication tools, along with public awareness campaigns to promote media literacy and false information detection skills as well

as clear communication of the limits of these technologies.

- Support civil society organizations working to counter the gendered impacts of disinformation on women and LGBTQI+ political and public figures, especially in the contexts of elections.
- Advocate for policies that protect privacy and promote respect for human rights in the use of AI technologies. Develop and support existing mechanisms for monitoring the implementation of AI governance frameworks, and support civil society advocacy efforts to improve adherence to these frameworks.

Fostering Trust in AI through Openness, Transparency, and Explainability

Transparency (or lack thereof) is relevant at many levels: in the data used to train an AI model, within an AI model, in how AI is implemented, at the organizational level, and ultimately at the policymaking level. Addressing transparency is essential to ensure safe, secure, and trustworthy AI.

Opportunity and Challenge

Lack of transparency in AI can pose barriers for trust and accountability. By promoting openness in AI ecosystems and in the technology itself, we can foster greater trust, inclusive innovation, and public participation in AI policy and governance.

Explainable AI Systems

AI models, especially deep learning neural networks, are often described as "black boxes." This lack of transparency—at the model level, what's often referred to as "explainability"—can exacerbate concerns about potential bias; concerns related to reliability, fairness, protection of and respect for intellectual property rights; accountability; or unintended behaviors of AI systems. Black-box behavior may be difficult to avoid for some kinds of algorithms or levels of performance and other mechanisms can often provide the benefits desired from explanations. But in some sectors and applications, explainability in AI models can help recipients understand the AI's outputs and how and when to trust them. To this end, finding techniques to explain AI model behaviors is an active area of research and should be invested in further.

Transparency in Model Design and Deployment

Even for black box models, measures can be taken to improve transparency in how AI systems are developed and deployed. Transparency can help people understand how well a model will work in a particular context and can include things like the AI system's data sources, model training process, validation process, and the situations in which a model is best suited or avoided (model cards and datasheets for datasets are two useful tools for this).

Photo Credit: Power Africa.

Another kind of openness can also be helpful: AI models can be released "open" or "closed" in various ways and to varying extents, with different modalities bringing different contextual strengths and weaknesses. Open models (frequently referred to as "open-source AI" models, though these terms can mean different things) can provide significant benefits, in particular for small- and medium-sized enterprises. One benefit is that open models generally allow greater ability for researchers to conduct audits. Another is that developers can better adapt and tailor the models to their use case and do so at a fraction of the cost.

For these reasons, open AI models may also help empower a more diverse range of AI developers. By enabling greater customization and adaptation, open models could help communities tailor models to their particular needs and contexts. This is one of the justifications for exploring the concept of AI systems as digital public goods (DPGs).

At the same time, dual-use foundation models with widely available weights present a variety of ethical and policy challenges, due to their potential for misuse and the near impossibility of "recalling" an open-source model after its release. A recent report by the National Telecommunications and Information Administration reviews these policy concerns and recommends actively monitoring risks while taking steps to ensure that the government is prepared to act if heightened risks emerge.

Transparency within Organizations and in AI Governance

Transparency at the organizational level involves clear communication about the design, deployment, and use of AI systems. Organizations should establish policies and practices that can ensure accountability and responsible use of AI. This includes providing information about the objectives, limitations, and potential impacts of AI systems, as well as the steps taken to meet compliance with relevant standards or policies. Tools like the NIST AI Risk Management Framework and the Blueprint for an AI Bill of Rights are especially helpful for this.

One level up, policymaking in AI should also be open and transparent to help ensure that regulations and standards are developed in an inclusive manner. Transparent policymaking involves open consultations with diverse stakeholders, including industry representatives, academia, civil society, workers and unions, and the general public. This participatory approach helps in identifying the societal impacts of AI and in developing balanced policies that protect public interests while promoting innovation. For example, when NIST was developing the AI RMF, and as the White House developed the Blueprint for an AI Bill of Rights, they held a series of listening sessions and open public workshops, released requests for information, and offered public drafts for comment. In sum, this approach produced a document that incorporated a wide range of perspectives.

Photo Credit: USAID.

Data Nutrition Project – Improving data transparency for better AI systems

The Data Nutrition Project is an initiative aimed at improving the quality and transparency of datasets used in AI. Inspired by the nutrition labels on food products, the project creates "Dataset Nutrition Labels" that provide detailed information about the composition, provenance, and potential biases in AI systems. These labels help practitioners make informed decisions about which datasets to use for specific AI applications, thus fostering more responsible AI development.

The Data Nutrition Labels include various metrics and indicators that assess dataset quality along several dimensions, such as ethical considerations, data composition, and potential for harm. This standardized framework for dataset evaluation can promote transparency allowing users to better understand the strengths and limitations of certain AI systems trained on those underlying datasets, and potentially even the contexts in which they should and shouldn't be used based on known weaknesses in the data. Initiatives like the Data Nutrition Project offer a model for how to increase transparency in AI, highlighting the importance of scrutinizing and improving the data that fuels AI systems.

Project AEDES – Creating open, adaptable AI systems for public health

Project AEDES is focused on improving public health responses against dengue in the Philippines by leveraging digital and climate data. Recognized as a Digital Public Good by the Digital Public Goods Alliance (DPGA), Project AEDES is committed to creating open-source solutions that address critical health challenges.

Project AEDES operates as an advanced early detection and exploration service aimed at predicting dengue cases from climate and digital data while identifying potential hotspots using satellite data. This initiative is particularly significant given the epidemic's impact, and particularly high rates of dengue in the Philippines.

One of the distinguishing features of Project AEDES is its commitment to open data and open models, making it accessible and adaptable for public use. The project harnesses real-time data from various sources, including climate readings and Google search trends, to model and predict dengue outbreaks. Additionally, it utilizes satellite imagery to pinpoint areas with stagnant water, which are potential breeding grounds for dengue-carrying mosquitoes.

Algorithmic Accountability for the Public Sector

In 2021, Ada Lovelace Institute, the AI Now Institute, and the Open Government Partnership (OGP) initiated a collaborative project focused on increasing algorithmic accountability in the public sector. Recognizing the growing use of algorithms to aid and automate decision-making in areas such as welfare entitlements, unemployment fraud detection, and urban planning, this initiative addresses the need for transparency and accountability in these systems.

The project emphasizes the importance of transparency in AI policymaking and the implementation of AI tools. It highlights that many algorithmic systems currently lack transparency and accountability, which can (for example) inadvertently reinforce discrimination.

To tackle these issues, the project reviews and analyzes various policy mechanisms designed to enhance transparency and accountability. These include impact assessments, audits and regulatory inspections, external oversight bodies, rights to hearings and appeals, and procurement conditions. These mechanisms aim to provide transparency into how algorithmic systems function, identify and mitigate potential biases or flaws, and strengthen accountability for their use. At the same time, the project underscores the need for public transparency by providing information about algorithmic systems to the general public. This transparency allows individuals and groups to learn about these systems and demand justifications for why an AI system is used in a particular context. This report also stresses the importance of public participation in policymaking to ensure that the needs of affected communities are met and that policies are both effective and equitable.

By compiling lessons from the first wave of algorithmic accountability policies implemented across various jurisdictions, the project offers practical guidance for policymakers and public-sector workers. It aims to support the consistent and effective implementation of accountability mechanisms, promote public participation, and encourage coordination across sectors and levels of governance.

Recommendations for Fostering Trust in AI through Openness, Transparency, and Explainability

United States' Support

Through engagement with the world's largest technology firms, including by securing voluntary commitments to manage the risks posed by AI, the United States is working toward openness, transparency, and explainability in AI ecosystems. In addition, USAID has supported grantees to increase transparency in AI applications and is working with the government of Colombia to build an AI system to increase transparency and improve community based organizations access to infrastructure programs.

Government

- Implement governance frameworks that promote transparency in AI design, deployment, and use, including regular audits and appropriate disclosures about data sources, algorithms, deployment processes, and post-deployment oversight processes. Ensure these policies and frameworks related to transparency, accuracy, and fairness in AI are developed through open consultations with a wide range of stakeholders.

Private Sector

- Implement transparency practices in AI design, deployment, use, and oversight processes, including clear documentation of data sources and algorithms. Invest in research on explainable AI techniques and other ways of helping users interpret, trust, and act on AI system outputs. Be transparent and clear to end users in ways that are understandable to them, including through participatory research and development and user experience design with end users.

Development Donors and Philanthropic Organizations

- Support research initiatives that focus on developing practical transparency tools and explainable AI systems, including tools geared to different audiences (e.g., technical and non-technical), and evaluating the downstream impact of their explainability or transparency features.
- Invest in projects that promote appropriate, rights-respecting open model development and the sharing of best practices and opportunities for transparency and collaboration; support civil society organizations advocating for transparent AI governance.

Deploying AI for Climate Action

While the energy costs and greenhouse gas emissions associated with AI are a major concern, it is also true that AI technologies, especially more traditional predictive machine learning systems (i.e., non-generative AI), hold significant potential to accelerate efforts to adapt to climate change and mitigate carbon emissions, including in LMICs. For example, there is an active area of research on using AI to improve energy grid efficiency and efficiency in data centers themselves. For energy grids, AI can help in demand forecasting and grid monitoring, reducing outages and potentially enhancing energy distribution efficiency. AI is being used to predict deforestation, allowing countries to address potential land clearing before it occurs.

Additionally, AI is actively being used in the management of climate change's effects, supporting climate adaptation and resilience. Examples include the ongoing use of AI in targeting natural disaster and emergency response, including predicting floods and wildfires and informing response plans. AI is also being used to accelerate the deployment of clean energy infrastructure.

Opportunity and Challenge

A wide range of AI-enabled applications are currently supporting progress on climate action and have the potential to further accelerate progress. Promising areas for AI in climate include energy efficiency, clean energy deployment, and other climate mitigation objectives as well as climate adaptation and resilience.

Weather-climate foundation models such as NASA and IBM's Prithvi can be applied to better track weather-related disasters and improve the accuracy of forecasts. AI also is being used to protect natural resources. For example, GIZ's FAIR Forward initiative is working with local communities to build and deploy AI applications to protect forested land in Indonesia. In a parallel effort, IDRC is supporting an AI and climate change innovation research network, which aims to develop and scale AI solutions for climate action and provide funding for students at the intersection of AI and climate change.

In 2021, the Global Partnership on AI (GPAI), along with Climate Change AI and the Center for AI & Climate, released a report titled "Climate Change and AI: Recommendations for Government Action." This work highlights key areas where AI can contribute to climate action and provides recommendations where governments can better collaborate to reduce AI's negative impacts on the climate. It also notes where AI can be especially useful, such as predicting solar power production, optimizing heating and cooling systems, and detecting deforestation from satellite imagery. At the same time, AI could prove useful in scientific research by modeling climate systems, discovering new materials for energy storage, simulating increasingly complex climate scenarios, and mapping climate-vulnerable populations.

AI + Climate Futures in Asia – A roadmap for action at the intersection of AI and climate

The AI + Climate Futures in Asia project, implemented by Digital Futures Lab and supported by Rockefeller Foundation, conducted research to create a comprehensive understanding of the intersection between AI and climate action. This research project provides insights and recommendations for how we might use AI to support climate mitigation, adaptation, and resilience.

This is especially relevant in many parts of Asia that are highly vulnerable to the effects of climate change: flooding, increased storms, heat waves, droughts, air pollution, and other effects—all of which pose risks to human livelihoods.

AI + Climate Futures in Asia focuses on several key areas across 9 Asian countries: agriculture and food systems, power and energy transitions, and disaster response and preparedness. Overall, the work recommends a range of actions, highly aligned with the recommendations throughout this Playbook: open data sharing, rigorous evaluation of pilot projects, interdisciplinary collaboration, localized and participatory data collection, and investment in greener computing, among others.

Recommendations for Deploying AI for Climate Action

United States' Support

The United States has been at the forefront of multilateral cooperation to apply AI technologies in support of climate action and clean energy deployment, particularly in developing countries through the UN Climate Change #AI4ClimateAction initiative and the United States launched Net-Zero World Initiative. Additionally, through a program called SERVIR, NASA and USAID are using geospatial technology and AI to bolster sustainability and climate resilience. With the COOLERCHIPS program, the United States is investing in R&D to reduce total cooling energy expenditures at data centers.

Through the Clean Energy Demand Initiative (CEDI), the U.S. Department of State is connecting tech companies with governments in key markets to support the adoption of clean energy policies that ensure companies can access and buy the clean energy for their operations.

In July 2024, the U.S. Department of Energy (DOE) announced the AI for Science, Security, and Technology (FASST) initiative, which leverages DOE and its 17 national laboratories to support energy efficient AI hardware through AI testbeds, develop safe and trustworthy models with an eye towards energy efficiency, and supercharge AI to help scientists discover new energy materials. The DOE is also using its national laboratories to support clean energy generation across the globe, including through the National Solar Radiation Database.

Government

- Implement policies and regulatory frameworks that promote investment in clean energy generation and storage, grid infrastructure, and energy efficiency measures and enable private sector procurement of clean energy to reduce carbon emissions associated with AI systems.
- Foster collaboration between local firms, research institutions, and international partners to develop AI solutions that address climate change.
- Direct scientific research funding toward mitigating climate impacts of AI and applying AI for climate-relevant applications.
- Encourage investment in renewable energy sources for data centers and computational infrastructure to reduce carbon emissions associated with AI technologies.

Private Sector

- Work to ensure that AI development is sustainable and minimally greenhouse gas-emitting by investing in and sourcing from clean energy solutions.
- Select projects and partners for AI deployment who are working on applications with climate benefits. Avoid projects that stand to further exacerbate climate change.

Development Donors and Philanthropic Organizations

- Fund R&D of energy-efficient AI technologies to reduce the computational resources required for training and operating AI

models and ensure their sustainability.
- Support initiatives that apply AI solutions to climate mitigation and adaptation efforts, particularly in partnership with LMIC stakeholders.

Conclusion

AI presents significant opportunities for advancing sustainable development. This Playbook, developed as a key deliverable of President Biden's Executive Order on the Safe, Secure, and Trustworthy Development and Use of Artificial Intelligence, seeks to underscore AI as a uniquely global opportunity with far-reaching impacts and potential risks. It highlights that safe, secure, and trustworthy design, deployment, and use of AI is not only possible but essential. A consistent theme throughout the case studies and examples in this Playbook as a way of achieving this responsible design, deployment, and use is the critical importance of active and diverse stakeholder engagement, ensuring meaningful representation of the populations who may use or be affected by AI systems.

This Playbook also marks another step in the United States' commitment to the responsible deployment and use of AI on a global scale, rooted in human rights.

The United States' current efforts are grounded in the belief that AI, when developed and deployed responsibly, can be a powerful force for achieving the Sustainable Development Goals and addressing some of the world's most urgent challenges. Looking ahead, the United States will continue to support LMICs through funding, advocacy, and convening efforts–collectively navigating the complexities of the digital age and working toward a future in which the benefits of technological development are widely shared.

We acknowledge that much work remains to be done in this area, and this Playbook is only one of many actions required to advance sustainable development. Recognizing that international cooperation and multi-stakeholder partnerships are key in achieving progress, we invite others to contribute their expertise, resources, and perspectives to enrich and expand this framework. The true measure of progress in responsible AI is not in the sophistication of our machines but in the quality of life the technology enhances. Together we can work toward ensuring the promise of AI is realized in service of this goal.

Annex

Resources

- USAID Digital Ecosystem Framework
- USAID AI Action Plan
- Risk Management Profile for AI and Human Rights
- Artificial Intelligence Risk Management Framework: Generative Artificial Intelligence Profile
- Blueprint for an AI Bill of Rights
- Reflecting the Past, Shaping the Future: Making AI Work for International Development
- Artificial Intelligence at the Department of State
- AI.gov
- Global AI Research Agenda

Chapter 20

The Global AI Research Agenda*

U.S. Department of State and U.S. Agency for International Development

Glossary of Terms

AI: Artificial Intelligence
R&D: Research and Development
GAIRA: Global Artificial Intelligence Research Agenda
G7: Group of Seven
OECD: Organisation for Economic Co-operation and Development
UNGA: United Nations General Assembly
RFI: Request For Information
E.O.: Executive Order
U.S.: United States
G20: Group of Twenty
NIST: National Institute of Standards and Technology
NSF: National Science Foundation
UNESCO: United Nations Educational, Scientific and Cultural Organization
GBV: Gender-based Violence
TFGBV: Technology-facilitated Gender-based Violence
LMICs: Low- and Middle-Income Countries
SDGs: United Nations Sustainable Development Goals
AgTech: Agricultural Technology
LLMs: Large Language Models

---

* This is an edited, reformatted and augmented version of a U.S. Agency for International Development publication, *The Global AI Research Agenda* dated 2024.

In: Artificial Intelligence
Editor: Sonja Buckley
ISBN: 979-8-89530-859-2

LGBTQ+: Lesbian, Gay, Bisexual, Transgender, Queer, and Intersex
ISO: International Organization for Standardization
IEC: International Electrotechnical Commission
SDOs: Standards Developing Organizations
HICs: High-Income Countries
SMEs: Small- and Medium-sized Enterprises
PTSD: Post-traumatic Stress Disorder
B Corp: Benefit Corporation
ILO: International Labour Organization
STEM: Science, Technology, Engineering, and Math
EU: European Union
PPPs: Public-Private Partnerships
USAID: United States Agency for International Development

Section 1: Executive Summary

Photo Credit: USAID.

The rapid development of AI technologies is taking place in an interconnected landscape, where funding, data, talent, information, and computing resources flow across borders. Despite this global relevance, AI research and development (R&D) policies are most commonly driven by domestic priorities; funding silos and other barriers to collaboration can contribute to isolated networks that undermine the potential benefits of international scientific cooperation. The global research ecosystem should be founded on the scientific values of reciprocity, openness, and transparency, including for the study of AI systems.

The Global AI Research Agenda (GAIRA) recommends principles, priorities, and practices for AI research and development (R&D) to advance safe, secure, and trustworthy development of AI systems in international contexts. It aims to strengthen collaboration in researching the interactions between individuals, communities, and society with AI systems, foster innovation, and support equitable access to the benefits of AI. The conclusions presented serve as a starting point to align a global research vision, in which research communities continuously assess the state of AI research, review current publications addressing the presented priorities, and identify gaps to guide future research, focusing on global needs.

There is no international consensus on guiding principles for AI research, reflecting the still evolving state of AI research communities. In consideration of this lack of consensus, this agenda will be guided by three recommended principles for AI research: 1) Inclusion and Equity, 2) Responsible Research Conduct, and 3) Partnership and Collaboration. These principles emphasize the importance of building AI systems that benefit individuals, communities, and society, upholding the highest standards for preserving autonomy, dignity, and privacy, involving impacted people as collaborators, and striving for sustainability of systems and research. They resonate broadly with prior work outlined by researchers, funders, and multilateral forums and reflect a collective commitment to create an AI ecosystem that prioritizes human well-being and societal values, including respect for human rights. When designed, developed, deployed and used in a rights-respecting manner, AI can propel technological advances that benefit societies and individuals. These principles were developed through thematic analysis of both U.S. domestic and international guiding documents – namely Executive Order 14110, the G7 Common Values and Principles on Research Integrity and Research Security, the Organization for Economic Cooperation and Development (OECD) AI Principles, and the United Nations General Assembly Resolution on "Seizing the Opportunities of Safe, Secure, and Trustworthy AI Systems for Sustainable Development."

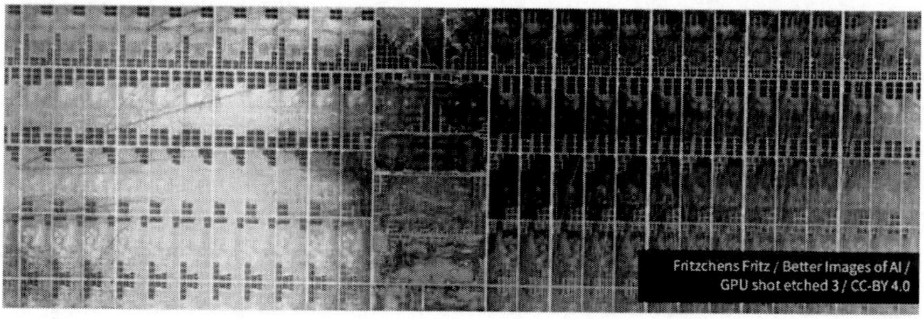

The *research priorities to advance safe, secure, inclusive, and trustworthy AI* presented in this document broadly align with the following themes:

- *Sociotechnical Research* - There is an urgent need for research that can deepen understanding of interactions between technology and society and guide the design and deployment of AI systems that enhance human well-being. The need to understand AI systems as sociotechnical systems—one in which technology interacts with and influences human behavior, culture, and institutions—is even more acute in a global context in which technologists and researchers may develop or deploy AI tools in unfamiliar environments. Research to monitor and evaluate the impacts of AI development and deployment in real-world settings is important to identify tangible benefits and risks of AI applications and promote and protect human rights and fundamental freedoms for all.
- *Inclusive Research Infrastructure* - A critical element for AI research progress is enabling researcher access to data, compute power, and research platforms, with appropriate safeguards to protect privacy and international human rights, that can support innovation in AI technologies and systems. Research infrastructure should be available for researcher access to foster innovation, high-quality research, and the dissemination of findings. Diverse perspectives will drive important discoveries, applications, and sensitivities critical to advancing AI technology around the world.
- *Research to Support AI for Global Challenges* - Prioritizing AI applications to address global challenges can promote environmental stewardship, economic resilience, and social well-being. Additionally, collaborative efforts can make AI systems, equipment, and infrastructure more sustainable, and performing applied research can advance a safer, healthier, and more prosperous world.
- *Fundamental Research on AI, including AI Safety, Security, and Trustworthiness* - AI is still in an early stage of development and more technical advancements are needed to advance the state-of-the-art and drive towards safe, secure, and trustworthy systems. To support these developments and contribute to international discussions on AI governance, researchers must also address issues related to information integrity, cybersecurity, and measurement and evaluation, among others.

- *Research on AI's Global Labor Market Implications* - AI's potential to automate processes and increase labor efficiency calls for research into the labor market impacts of AI. This section outlines opportunities to address research gaps, understand disruptions, and propose risk mitigation measures that fit within different global and economic contexts. Researchers should consider labor market shifts, the emergence of new types of work, and impacts on wealth distribution and income inequality.

The last section in this document lists *recommended practices for AI research* based in part on input received from the Request For Information (RFI),[1] informed by respondents from various regions, industries, and Backgrounds. It provides a global perspective on what implementation practices could look like for research funders, research ecosystem hubs, and research teams. This section can serve as a guide for stakeholders to align actions with the agenda's goals.

- For Research Funders:
    - Elevate Transparency
    - Open Funding Calls to Support International AI Research Collaboration
    - Promote Research Infrastructure Accessibility for Diverse Demographics
    - Offer Connection Opportunities
    - Pursue Public-Private Partnerships
- For Research Ecosystem Hubs:
    - Incentivize Reproducibility of Research
    - Foster Broadly Accepted Practices Around Research Publications
    - Coordinate and Collaborate Around AI Research Guidelines
    - Support Research Beyond Topics Prioritized by the Private Sector
    - Provide Guidance to Navigate the Evolving Regulatory Landscape
- For Research Teams:

[1] "Global AI Research Agenda." 2024. Federal Register. March 14, 2024. https://www.federalregister.gov/documents/2024/03/14/2024-05357/ global-ai-research-agenda.

- Prioritize Multidisciplinary Teams
- Collaborate with Local Researchers
- Make Use of Sociotechnical Methodologies and Research Design
- Incorporate Risk Assessments

This research agenda, as part of a broad body of national and international literature,[2] underscores the importance of AI research collaboration, enabling stakeholders to leverage resources and competitive advantages to facilitate cutting edge AI research that upholds fundamental values, such as international human rights and the protection of privacy. By focusing efforts on both the technical advancements of AI systems and the interactions between AI and communities, the global research community can foster safe, secure, and trustworthy AI development. Progress in creating this balanced ecosystem should be based upon promotion of these priority areas within international research networks and enduring conversations with global research stakeholders as the field transforms.

Section 2: Introduction

Image by Alan Warburton / © BBC /.

Better Images of AI / Nature / CC-BY 4.0.

[2] Kerry, Cameron F., Joshua P. Meltzer, and Andrea Renda. "AI Cooperation on the Ground: AI Research and Development on a Global Scale." Brookings, November 4, 2022. https://www.brookings.edu/articles/ai-cooperation-on-the-ground-ai-research-and-development-on-a-global- scale/.

2.1. Executive Order on Safe, Secure, and Trustworthy Development and Use of AI

The Global AI Research Agenda (GAIRA) is published pursuant to Section 11(c)(ii) of Executive Order 14110,[3] Safe, Secure, and Trustworthy Development and Use of Artificial Intelligence. The Executive Order outlines a whole-of-government strategy, promoting global practices through multilateral fora, strengthening partnerships to address shared AI challenges, and supporting global capacity building.The Executive Order states: "[t]he Secretary of State and the Administrator of the United States Agency for International Development, in collaboration with the Secretary of Energy and the Director of NSF, shall develop a Global AI Research Agenda to guide the objectives and implementation of AI-related research in contexts beyond United States borders. The Agenda shall:

a) include principles, guidelines, priorities, and best practices aimed at ensuring the safe, responsible, beneficial, and sustainable global development and adoption of AI; and
b) address AI's labor-market implications across international contexts, including by recommending risk mitigations."

Complementary to the concepts outlined in this Global AI Research Agenda is another E.O. deliverable, the AI in Global Development Playbook,[4] which aims at promoting the responsible use of AI for global good while mitigating potential risks and challenges.

2.2. National AI R&D Strategic Plan

The GAIRA is meant to supplement the U.S. National AI R&D Strategic Plan,[5] updated in May 2023, by exploring tangible opportunities to advance

---

[3] "Safe, Secure, and Trustworthy Development and Use of Artificial Intelligence." 2023. Federal Register. November 1, 2023. https://www. federalregister.gov/documents/ 2023/11/01/2023-24283/safe-secure-and-trustworthy-development-and-use-of-artificial-intelligence.

[4] "U.S. Agency for International Development. AI in Global Development Playbook. Washington, D.C.: USAID, 2024. http://www.usaid.gov/digital-development/ai-global-development-playbook.

[5] Select Committee On Artificial Intelligence, National Science and Technology Council, Arati Prabhakar, Kei Koizumi, Laurie Locascio, Sethuraman Panchanathan, Geraldine

international research collaboration for safe, secure, and trustworthy AI systems in global contexts. Namely, this agenda explores more in-depth the opportunities to galvanize the research community towards the following priorities:

- *Strategy #1:* Make Long-Term Investments in Fundamental and Responsible AI Research
- *Strategy #2:* Develop Effective Methods for Human-AI Collaboration
- *Strategy #5:* Develop Shared Public Datasets and Environments for AI Training and Testing
- *Strategy #9:* Establish a Principled and Coordinated Approach to International Collaboration in AI Research

U.S. Government science funding agencies, such as the National Science Foundation and Department of Energy, actively contribute to global AI research, in line with the National AI R&D Strategic Plan. The publication of the GAIRA is not accompanied by any additional U.S. Government funding, but it does serve as an outline and expansion of key areas for AI research already funded by science agencies. The GAIRA emphasizes the need for international collaboration and coordination to address these areas and to derive the positive benefits of developing safe, secure, and trustworthy AI systems through existing U.S. research funding commitments.

2.3. International AI Research Efforts

Principle 2.1[6] of the OECD Principles for Trustworthy AI[7] calls for governments to facilitate public and private investment in AI research and development, emphasizing the importance of basic research and acknowledging the extended timeframes involved in research policy. The principle highlights long-term public investment, investment in open science, and interdisciplinary efforts as essential to spur innovation in trustworthy AI,

---

Richmond, et al. 2023. "National Artificial Intelligence Research and Development Strategic Plan 2023 Update." https://www.whitehouse.gov/wp-content/uploads/2023/05/National-Artificial-Intelligence-Research-and-Development-Strategic-Plan-2023-Update.pdf.

6 "Investing in AI Research and Development (OECD AI Principle) - OECD.AI." n.d. https://oecd.ai/en/dashboards/ai-principles/P10.

7 "AI Principles Overview - OECD.AI." n.d. https://oecd.ai/en/ai-principles.

as scientific breakthroughs enabled by AI could help solve societal challenges and create entirely new industries. This type of investment, paired with evidence-based understanding of the risks, capabilities, and limitations of AI systems, and when tailored to the appropriate level of AI-preparedness,[8] is essential to drive and shape trustworthy AI innovation and ensure beneficial outcomes for all.

Many organizations, fora, and countries are actively pursuing research priorities, and the GAIRA is complementary to a mosaic of existing research globally. This includes research outputs as directed and published by the United Nations, OECD, Global Partnership on AI, G20, G7, and the International Scientific Report on the Safety of Advanced AI, among others.

2.4. Defining the Global Artificial Intelligence Research Agenda

The Global Artificial Intelligence Research Agenda (GAIRA) aims to inform the objectives and implementation of AI-related research, globally. To achieve this ambition, it has four interrelated subgoals:

1) *Advance multifaceted research collaborations and leverage them to promote the safe, secure, and trustworthy development of AI technologies around the world in a manner that is both inclusive and sustainable.* Building stronger international partnerships to address global priorities and promoting responsible research practices can positively influence AI development and help achieve this subgoal.
2) *Outline important areas of inquiry, including the impacts of the development and use of AI systems on economies and societies around the world.* Researchers are still in the early stage of understanding many technical aspects of recent AI advances and how they may interact with and influence economies, societies, and cultures. Since the development and use of these technologies can impact across national borders, these inquiries need to take into consideration language, culture, geography, environment, socioeconomic development, economic competitive dynamics, international human rights and fundamental freedoms, and conflict dynamics. AI's global spread will also be shaped by digital divides,

[8] International Monetary Fund. "Artificial Intelligence Potential Index (AIPI)." IMF DataMapper. Accessed September 12, 2024.

in which the costs and benefits of AI will accrue differently to people with different levels of connectivity, access, and digital literacy.

3) *Elevate opportunities for academics and researchers globally to contribute to a body of evidence to guide policy and decisionmakers towards promoting equitable access to the benefits of AI and support implementation of the AI in Global Development Playbook.* The AI in Global Development Playbook offers a roadmap to develop the capacity, ecosystems, frameworks, partnerships, and institutions to leverage safe, secure, and trustworthy AI for sustainable development and foster good governance regimes for AI. While the Playbook recommendations are geared towards governmental, private sector, and development donor and philanthropic stakeholders, the diffuse, fast-changing nature of AI technology means no small group of stakeholders alone will be successful in delivering the benefits of AI or mitigating its risks. Collaboration between researchers and academia globally can bolster a robust body of research necessary to inform evidence-based decision-making amongst these stakeholders long-term.

Shutterstock Standard License / Photo contributor Boijonell Prod

4) *Outline needed areas of research on the labor market implications of AI systems across international contexts.* AI's impacts on employment and labor may lead to unpredictable changes in the

quantity, profitability, safety, quality, and nature of work, driving new concerns about the well-being of workers, particularly in diverse global settings. These changes are impacting different economies around the world in disparate ways, as AI can also create job opportunities and drive economic growth, particularly in developing regions, by enabling access to new markets and fostering innovation. Research into the varied aspects of how AI is impacting the labor market and workers can offer a more nuanced analysis of the benefits and risks of applications.

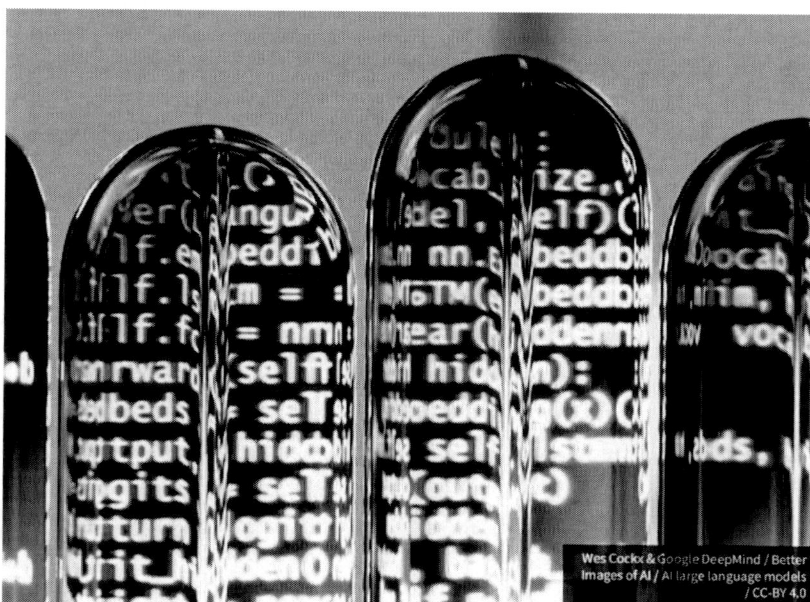

2.5. Focus and Audience

The rapid advancement of AI technologies holds significant implications for economies and societies, globally. Uneven international uptake of AI can be detrimental if societal impacts and implications are overlooked. This research agenda proposes a holistic plan to advance AI's interaction with human societies and technical systems addressing gaps in understanding AI's impacts, promoting evidence-based assessments, and encouraging international collaboration around the technical underpinnings of AI systems.

The audience of the GAIRA includes research funders, policymakers, and practitioners globally, aiming to promote responsible AI design and adoption through research partnerships and to deploy AI for positive economic benefit.

The GAIRA drafting team invited the scientific community and global stakeholders to help shape the principles, guidelines, priorities, and recommended practices outlined in this research agenda and sought stakeholder feedback via an RFI. Doing so ensured the GAIRA content was informed by both local and global perspectives, fostering international collaboration and promoting cooperative practices across regions.

Section 3: Recommended Principles for AI Research

Principles can help to inform research priorities as well as behaviors and actions of the research community. Since 2016, numerous documents[9] articulating principles for responsible and ethical AI have been released by companies, governments, professional organizations, multilateral forums, and nonprofits.

Researchers have identified some thematic convergence[10] around high-level principles, and many governments have begun to adopt internationally-negotiated principles such as the OECD's Principles for Trustworthy AI. Research integrity and security principles are also an active focus of scientific stakeholders, and of countries domestically and internationally. At the same time, there is still a lack of consensus on exactly what unique principles should apply to AI research – , as opposed to AI systems themselves or the research process writ large.

The GAIRA will be guided by a set of three recommended principles that resonate broadly with existing frameworks in this space.

- *Inclusion and Equity* – Research should focus on developing AI systems that are representative, flexible, and fit for their context. Technology systems impact the social contexts into which they are deployed; to support holistic research evaluation and analysis, and

[9] "AI Ethics Guidelines Global Inventory - AlgorithmWatch." n.d. AlgorithmWatch. https://algorithmwatch.org/en/ai-ethics-guidelines-global- inventory/.

[10] Jobin, Anna, Marcello Ienca, and Effy Vayena. 2019. "The Global Landscape of AI Ethics Guidelines." Nature Machine Intelligence 1 (9): 389–99. https://doi.org/10.1038/s42256-019-0088-2.

equitable access to the benefits of AI systems, researchers should strive for inclusive research processes.

- *Responsible Research Conduct* – AI research should uphold the highest standards for preserving the autonomy, dignity, well-being, and privacy of people who are directly and indirectly impacted by the research and the development of any resulting systems, including data subjects, platform testers, end users, and workers engaged through data enrichment or crowdsourcing platforms. Researchers should implement frameworks to systematically evaluate and optimize practices, to help ensure the process and outputs are both sustainable and responsible.
- *Partnership and Collaboration* – AI researchers should seek ways to involve impacted individuals, communities, and organizations as collaborators early in the research process, especially in international contexts where local stakeholders have necessary and valuable perspectives about potential use cases, benefits, and risks of the research. Tools, guidelines, and training for participatory AI design[11] and research are urgently needed to make these practices more accessible for AI practitioners.

These recommended principles draw from converging areas discussed in relevant national and international documents, such as the following:

- *Executive Order 14110:* At the national level, the President of the United States signed E.O. 14110 "Safe, Secure, and Trustworthy Development and Use of Artificial Intelligence" in October 2023, which in addition to driving federal actions, also outlines a set of guiding principles to guide the federal government in addressing AI. These include promoting responsible innovation, competition, and collaboration; advancing equity and civil rights; protecting privacy and civil liberties; among others.
- *G7 Common Values and Principles on Research Security and Research Integrity:* In the 2021 G7 Research Compact[12]

---

[11] Madaio, Michael A., Shivani Kapania, Rida Qadri, Ding Wang, et al. "Learning about Responsible AI On-The-Job: Learning Pathways, Orientations, and Aspirations." In Proceedings of the 2024 ACM Conference on Fairness, Accountability, and Transparency (FAccT), 2024. https://doi.org/10.1145/3630106.3658988.

[12] "G7 Common Values and Principles on Research Security and Research IntegrityFootnote 1." 2023. September 13, 2023. https://science.gc.ca/ site/science/en/safeguarding-your-

governments committed to the promotion of international research cooperation and the conditions of freedom, independence, openness, reciprocity, and transparency under which it flourishes. The G7 Principles of Research Security[13] subsequently outlined by the G7 provide a common framework to guide responses to research security risks in domestic and international research and recognizes the foundational importance of research integrity to academic discovery. Importantly, the framework notes that openness and security are not contradictory, but complementary and mutually reinforcing.

- *OECD AI Principles:* At the multilateral level, in 2024, the OECD revised its AI Principles[14] which were initially released in 2019. These reflect important considerations for risk management, as outlined in the NIST AI Risk Management Framework,[15] and define a values-based approach to the creation and management of AI systems which should also drive the global policy and research agenda. These include inclusive growth, sustainable development and well-being; human rights and democratic values, including fairness, civil liberties, and privacy; transparency and explainability; robustness, security, and safety; and accountability.
- *UNGA AI Resolution:* At the global level, in 2024, The United Nations General Assembly 2024 resolution A/78/L.49[16] on "Seizing the Opportunities of Safe, Secure, and Trustworthy AI Systems for Sustainable Development" fostered a global vision to inform the design, development, and use of AI. The resolution outlines a shared vision for AI systems that are: (1) human-centric, (2) reliable, (3) explainable, (4) ethical, (5) inclusive, (6) privacy preserving, and (7) responsible. By combining a "sustainable development oriented" view of AI "in full respect, promotion, and protection of human rights

---

research/general-information-research-security/international-research-security-resources/g7-common- values-and-principles-research-security-and-research-integrity.

[13] G7 Working Group on the Security and Integrity of the Global Research Ecosystem (SIGRE). 2022. "G7 Common Values and Principles on Research Security and Research Integrity." https://www.bmbf.de/SharedDocs/Downloads/de/2022/220812-g7-sigre-paper.pdf?blob=publicationFile&v=2.

[14] "OECD Legal Instruments." n.d. https://legalinstruments.oecd.org/en/instruments/OECD-LEGAL-0449.

[15] U.S. Department of Commerce, National Institute of Standards and Technology. 2023. "Artificial Intelligence Risk Management Framework (AI RMF 1.0)." NIST AI 100-1. https://nvlpubs.nist.gov/nistpubs/ai/nist.ai.100-1.pdf.

[16] "General Assembly Adopts Landmark Resolution on Artificial Intelligence." 2024. UN News. March 21, 2024. https://news.un.org/en/ story/2024/03/1147831.

and international law," this document affirmed the compatibility of human rights-respecting AI and sustainable development, and that nations support pursuit of both together.

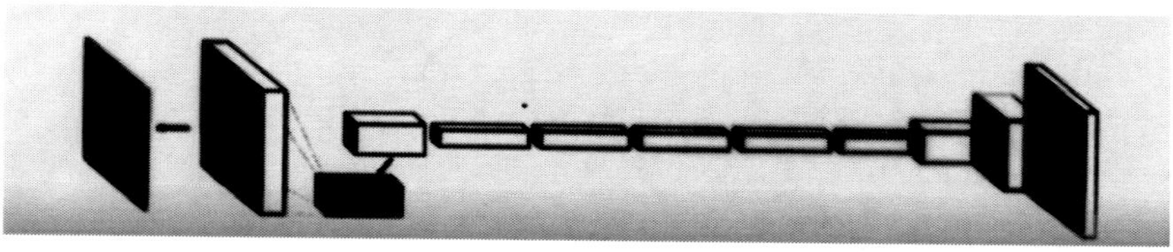

Philipp Schmitt / Better Images of AI/.
Neural network diagram / CC-BY 4.0.

Section 4: Research Priorities to Advance Safe, Secure, Inclusive, and Trustworthy AI

The following section covers four broad priorities to advance AI research fields towards safe, secure, and trustworthy AI. These priorities encompass methodologies, research infrastructure needs, applied research, and fundamental research. International cooperation is crucial to facilitate the sharing of resources and best practices across borders, fostering a collaborative environment that accelerates innovation and supports equitable access to AI benefits.

4.1. Sociotechnical Research

As AI tools become more widespread, they will become more integrated within economies and societies. Sociotechnical research methods can enhance understanding of the interactions between people and technology, improving researchers' ability both to design and use AI to advance human well-being and to support effective AI governance and policymaking. The following sociotechnical research priorities help to advance these goals.

4.1.1. Interactions between AI, People, and Societal Systems

AI technologies do not operate in a vacuum; rather they emerge from and constantly interact with people and societal structures. These systems reflect the values, perspectives, biases, and decisions of their developers. In turn, people are directly and indirectly impacted and influenced by AI systems: they are present (or not) in the underlying datasets; they act on and react to system outputs; and their lives can be positively or negatively shaped even by systems they did not interact with. Understanding AI's benefits and risks thus requires understanding the broader interactions between individuals, technology, and the contexts in which they operate. It also requires understanding what inequalities or biases AI tools may reflect—not simply quantifying bias but assessing how technologies impact marginalized people in different contexts, and the broader and longer-term implications of AI and automation more generally on equity, democracy, and human rights and fundamental freedoms. Effective research into these interactions will benefit from collaboration between technologists and experts in social sciences and the humanities fields, such as psychology, design science, law, sociology, anthropology, political science, and economics, among others.

Global Research Opportunities:

- Understand the needs of global stakeholders for AI systems and document the experiences of AI users and other individuals and communities across a variety of contexts, with particular emphasis on improving well-being for marginalized groups.
- Develop human-AI interaction paradigms that are useful for diverse users and help people build any necessary mental models about the systems. This includes paradigms to help people understand how AI systems arrive at their outputs, when they can be relied upon, and situations in which they should not be used, and to build resiliency to automation bias.
- Develop methodologies and testbeds for evaluating AI systems that go beyond computer modeling performance evaluation to investigate real world interactions with individuals and groups.
- Study the impacts of AI tools on social systems across cultures, such as measuring family formation, religious belief, and community cohesion, as well as individual and community-based health outcomes such as for mental health.
- Characterize how people around the world make sense of and react to AI system outputs, such as predictions, recommendations, or content, including how their reactions vary depending on system design and context and how those reactions relate to trust.

- Identify how AI may create systemic risks to economies, societies, cultures, and governments, including systemic harms that may arise from effects that are beneficial on the individual level.

4.1.2. Global Perspectives on AI Misuse

People around the world are grappling with the risks of AI misuse— ranging from individual-level fraud and impersonation scams to unlawful and arbitrary surveillance, information manipulation, and censorship. State and nonstate actors are increasingly using AI tools to undermine democracies through false and misleading information, influence in international institutions, and surveillance of opponents. Globally, AI misuse can exacerbate repression and contribute to active conflicts. Research into AI misuse and its impacts can provide policymakers, lawmakers, and technology leaders with insight into how to build effective legal, normative, and technical safeguards to mitigate misuse.

Global Research Opportunities:

- Document the ways and the extent to which AI tools are being used for repressive or illegal aims, and how patterns of misuse are affected by technological and political change.
- Understand which legal, normative, and technical safeguards and interventions are most effective at preventing the misuse of AI by governments and state-affiliated actors, during periods of both active conflict and relative political stability.
- Explore which aspects of AI system design can make those systems more difficult to misuse. This could include protections related to data (such as privacy-enhancing technologies) or emerging techniques designed to constrain the behavior of generative AI systems.

4.1.3. Gender Implications and & Gender-Based Violence

Women and girls are common targets of AI-facilitated abuse – the vast majority[17] of synthetic content videos created by AI involve sexual depictions of women and girls. In addition, a 2024 UNESCO report[18] highlights a variety of ways in which generative AI tools could be used to facilitate gender-based violence[19] (GBV).

Technology-facilitated gender-based violence (TFGBV)[20] is a subset of gender-based violence that describes any act that is committed, assisted, aggravated, or amplified by the use of information communication technologies or other digital tools, that results in or is likely to result in harm, or other infringements of rights and freedoms. These problems are likely to become even more acute as the use of AI increases globally, intersecting with the gender digital divide.[21]

Global Research Opportunities:

- Determine which legal, normative, and technical safeguards and interventions are most effective at preventing AI systems from being used to facilitate gender-based violence and how robust these safeguards are across languages and models.
- Explore the extent to which common risk management strategies, such as algorithmic auditing and gender- inclusive design teams, result in AI systems that more effectively promote gender equity and safe access to and use of AI systems.
- Document the extent of technology-facilitated gender-based violence globally and the prevalence and impacts of that violence, with

[17] "2023 State of Deepfakes: Realities, Threats, and Impact." n.d. https://www.securityhero.io/state-of-deepfakes/.

[18] UNESCO, Rumman Chowdhury, and Dhanya Lakshmi. 2023. "Your opinion doesn't matter, anyway": exposing technology-facilitated gender- based violence in an era of generative AI. Vol. World trends in freedom of expression and media development. https://unesdoc.unesco.org/ ark:/48223/pf0000387483.

[19] "United States Strategy to Prevent and Respond to Gender-Based Violence Globally 2022 - United States Department of State." 2023. United States Department of State. February 27, 2023. https://www.state.gov/reports/united-states-strategy-to-prevent-and-respond-to-gender- based-violence-globally-2022/.

[20] "Frequently Asked Questions: Tech-facilitated Gender-based Violence." n.d. UN Women – Headquarters. https://www.unwomen.org/en/what-we-do/ending-violence-against-women/faqs/tech-facilitated-gender-based-violence.

[21] Ramundo Media for DAI and Miles Sedgwick, Rana Labs. 2020. The Gender Digital Divide Primer. https://www.usaid.gov/sites/default/files/2022-05/DAI-1089_GDD_Primer-web_rev1_9.6.21.pdf.

particular attention to intersectional aspects such as ethnicity, religion, disability, sexual orientation, gender identity, and socioeconomic status.

- Evaluate opportunities of AI systems to address gender inequality and the perpetuation of gender biases, with particular attention to intersectional aspects such as ethnicity, nationality, religion, disability, sexual orientation, gender identity, and socioeconomic status.

4.2. Inclusive Research Infrastructure

Trusted international AI research infrastructure refers to a trusted global network of facilities, resources, and standards that support AI research and development technologies. Trusted international research infrastructure is crucial for enabling researchers everywhere to participate in cutting-edge AI research, and can access resources, best practices, and knowledge across borders on voluntary and mutually agreed terms. Building robust and interconnected research infrastructures on a global scale will also help promote interoperable and globally accepted practices from the bottom-up, promoting consistency and trust in AI systems worldwide. Accessible and widely available research infrastructure can also facilitate the participation of researchers from marginalized groups into the AI research and development ecosystem, ensuring that diverse perspectives are represented and potentially reduce bias in the development and training of AI systems.

4.2.1. Open-Source AI Software, Widely Available Model Weights, Open Datasets, and Open Source Enabling Tools

Multiple forms of openness in AI models, training data, and enabling software have long been an essential part of the AI research and development ecosystem. Open-source software used to train, evaluate, and deploy models in industry and academia makes robust and well-documented design patterns in machine learning accessible to range of researchers. The wide availability of training data is also useful in advancing the state of the art, including by allowing researchers to compare approaches, algorithms, and models across common benchmarks, though in some cases this utility needs to be carefully balanced against data privacy and confidentiality concerns. Fully open and reproducible AI models – where associated code, training data, and model weights are all made public – allow a wide set of researchers to approach otherwise impossible or prohibitively expensive research questions, such as questions related to the training procedures of large models. These forms of openness clearly foster innovation and collaboration in the AI community, allowing researchers to share their work globally and accelerate scientific progress. Researchers can leverage existing tools and software libraries reducing redundancy, development time, cost, and lowering barriers to entry. Openness also furthers transparency and reproducibility, enables more fulsome peer review and validation, and enhances the credibility and reproducibility of research results. Many open-source projects encourage continuous improvement and updates from the research community, keeping open-source products and tools up-to-date and at the state-of-the-art. Supporting the continued development of open and reproducible AI research means developing a better understanding of how openness and confidentiality across training data, model weights, and tooling interact.

Global Research Opportunities:

- Develop new tools, training, and communities of practice to make open models, datasets, and libraries more collaborative, accessible, and transparent to researchers across and within a variety of application areas.

- Characterize the relationship between training data and model behavior, including risks related to training on low quality data, data specific to the local context where the AI tool is being used, or on the wide release of model weights trained on confidential data.
- In AI application areas that facilitate scientific discovery, enhance open science practices and access to relevant datasets amongst researchers.
- Advance efforts to meaningfully evaluate and review open models across dimensions, including safety, security, trustworthiness, capabilities, limitations, and risk.

4.2.2. Linguistic, Cultural, and Geographic Contexts

While leading generative AI tools respond to prompts in various languages, today's models are often trained on data from majority-spoken languages and images from dominant cultures. As a result, they tend to produce more accurate, less biased, and higher-quality responses to prompts in relation to these representations. For AI to be globally inclusive, it must perform well across the world's linguistic, cultural, and geographic diversity, including those languages and cultures that are not well-represented on the Internet, or where there have been fewer resources devoted to training and refining AI systems in the past. Governments, academia, and the private sector should collaborate to ensure AI tools perform well across a wide variety of languages and cultural contexts, including those from smaller communities. Voluntary partnerships across sectors and across borders may improve the availability of data from more cultural contexts. This may include enhancing multilingual and multicultural capacity of mainstream AI models, or embarking on collaborative smaller, targeted applications. Incorporating more assorted languages and culturally accurate images into AI systems—and evaluating system performance within those contexts—is crucial for technological enhancement, social equity, and economic inclusivity.

Global Research Opportunities:

- Identify good practices for language and image data collection and attribution in collaboration with affected communities, recognizing that cultural and social norms around data sharing may vary widely.

Consider enhancing capacity-building of these communities so they can be stewards of their linguistic and cultural resources and help to ensure that benefits and results from AI research reach their communities.

- Establish and support consortia dedicated to advancing AI technologies that enhance linguistic and image-based cultural diversity, involving state actors, stakeholder communities, language speakers, prominent AI research bodies, academic institutions, and private-sector firms, including through building more representative datasets in partnership with affected communities.
- Investigate gaps in AI models' performance for culturally diverse inputs, and the extent to which these gaps can be mitigated through data curation, data development, translation efforts, fine-tuning, algorithmic advances, or other means.
- Improve AI modeling techniques for low-resource languages, focusing on making the most of limited data and capturing the nuances of dialects and local variations.

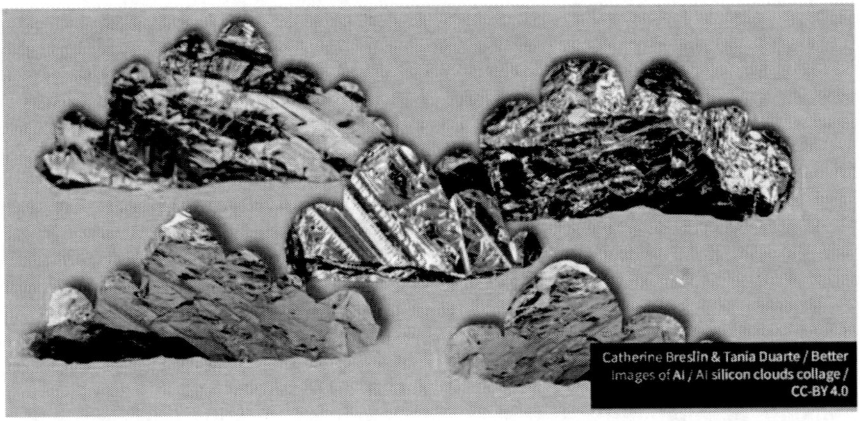

4.2.3. Increasing Access and Inclusion in AI Research Infrastructure

With appropriate safeguards, increasing access to data, compute, and other research infrastructure is essential for AI system and tool development, and can strengthen the capabilities of the global AI workforce while enabling inclusivity in the AI research ecosystem. AI research faces challenges due to varying data sharing requirements and data localization laws. Data is important for developing AI systems and applications, and researchers ultimately benefit from trusted cross-border data sharing. Under-resourced institutions, especially in low- and middle-income countries (LMICs), may face challenges related to access for data, compute, testing resources, and software. To support these areas, the AI research community should advance the availability of compute, datasets, testbeds, testing frameworks, and open-source libraries and toolkits.

Global Research Opportunities:

- Develop international guidance on how to conduct ethical and privacy-preserving research, particularly for the development of appropriate safeguards around the use of shared research infrastructure.
- Digitize scientific and historical data still stored in analog formats to expand and improve the quality and diversity of training data to ensure it is sufficiently representative across different dimensions.
- Explore linking trusted research infrastructure in national, regional, and international contexts to advance researcher access to diverse datasets, knowledge bases, testbeds, testing frameworks, and open-source libraries and toolkits.
- Evaluate the efficiency and scalability of computational resources in handling large-scale data processing tasks and develop optimization techniques that enhance performance and reduce resource consumption.
- Define globally accepted, machine-readable formats for scientific data to increase the interoperability of datasets internationally and their use for training and fine-tuning AI systems and tools to facilitate AI data readiness.

4.3. Research to Support AI for Global Challenges

AI can revolutionize the production and utilization of knowledge to tackle global challenges, particularly those related to the United Nations Sustainable Development Goals (SDGs), by designing new tools and conducting applied research to create a safer, healthier, more prosperous world. Research to support AI tools, that address global challenges, should be a focus of the international research community, as it fosters collaboration and entails pooling resources and expertise across borders to tackle pressing issues, such as climate change, global health, and food insecurity.This section explores ways in which international cooperation in applied AI research can leverage innovative solutions in pursuit of global sustainability.

4.3.1. Climate, Energy, and the Environment

Joint research initiatives can contribute to reduction of the negative impacts of AI on climate, energy, and the environment, particularly by leading to breakthroughs which could reduce electricity consumption associated with AI. International research can also accelerate the development and deployment of AI-driven solutions and AI-informed climate models and can facilitate data sharing that will help empower countries, communities, and individuals to address climate, environmental, and energy challenges. New AI methods can contribute[22] tools towards responding to the climate crisis by enhancing climate modeling, prediction,[23] adaptation, resilience, and mitigation efforts. Additionally, the clean energy transition requires modernizing and decarbonizing global energy systems. AI can advance this by managing energy use, incentivizing customer behavior, integrating renewable sources, discovering new energy materials, developing clean energy technologies, assisting in obtaining permits for these technologies, and accelerating the resilience of power systems for severe weather. AI research and collaboration can also drive novel insights from disparate data sources to improve the decision-making process and promote a wider range of mitigation, adaptation, and resilience strategies to support more coordinated efforts in tackling the impacts of climate change to build a more resilient future. Increased capabilities in AI can help integrate local and Indigenous knowledges and can incorporate context-specific data to ground-truth assumptions and validate model predictions. International cooperation is essential to share best practices, technologies, and innovations, minimizing AI risks and maximizing its benefits for the international community, particularly in developing countries.

Global Research Opportunities:

- Explore pathways for international collaboration to enable the development of novel AI systems to predict and combat climate

---

[22] "Climate Change AI - Interactive Summaries." n.d. Climate Change AI. https://www.climatechange.ai/summaries.

[23] "AI4ESP | Artificial Intelligence for Earth System Predictability." n.d. https://ai4esp.org/.

change. This includes establishing comprehensive and detailed digital twins of the planet, modeling climate scenarios and response options for warming, sea-level rise, flooding, wildfires, and other slow-onset and extreme weather events, as well as assessing climate impacts on human migration and biodiversity.

- Share best practices and develop technologies to reduce AI's resource demands, including energy, water, and critical minerals, through hardware, software, and efficiency measures. This holistic approach to sustainable AI considers performance, reliability, usability, and sustainability. Additionally, accelerate efforts to quantify and reduce the global environmental effects of AI, particularly energy and water consumption.

- Focus a subset of research on the next generation of energy efficient AI-enabled supercomputing platforms and unlocking new clean energy sources, optimizing energy production, improving grid resilience, and building tomorrow's advanced energy economy.
- Develop AI tools to evaluate scenarios to reduce greenhouse gas emissions while balancing their deployment with the protection of the world's natural and cultural resources, such as promoting climate-smart agriculture, sustainable land use, and biodiversity protection (see also section on Agriculture and Food Security below).
- Develop and define tools that leverage global geospatial data, satellite imagery, climate data, and text to enhance situational awareness and

design responses for natural disasters enhancing multi-hazard early warning systems, while also improving machine learning methodologies to handle thc complex structured and unstructured data types central to climate work to aid in mitigation and recovery efforts.

- Develop tools that leverage climate and other relevant data to provide early warning for climate-sensitive disease outbreaks and other impacts to more effectively mitigate risks to the well-being of individuals and populations.

4.3.2. Health

AI has the potential to accelerate the impact of digital health systems and initiatives. It can positively impact global health by supporting health systems, healthcare delivery, and health science. AI could drive down healthcare costs by optimizing market efficiencies, such as streamlining administrative processes and reducing waste. Additionally, AI could support prevention and public health strategies by enabling early detection of diseases and personalized health interventions, ultimately reducing the need for expensive treatments. A recent United States Agency for International Development analysis[24] of AI applications in the global health context highlighted opportunities across four domains—population health, individual health, health systems, and pharmaceutical and medical technologies— and identifies AI use cases for addressing aspects in each of those areas. The use of AI techniques, such as computer vision and natural language processing, can streamline data entry and improve data quality and analytics for better and faster decision-making. AI-enabled tools can assist with clinical decision support, ensure treatment regimen compliance, improve diagnosis accuracy, and provide personalized health coaching and other innovative wellness services. AI-based technologies and services can help patients better understand their medical information to enable deeper engagement in their health care.

As researchers look to use AI systems and develop AI tools to advance health outcomes, it is important that local perspectives are prioritized to identify relevant and impactful use cases, and that locally relevant data is

[24] USAID's Center for Innovation and Impact (CII), Bill & Melinda Gates Foundation, The Rockefeller Foundation, and Boston Consulting Group. 2021. "Artificial Intelligence in Global Health: Defining a Collective Path Forward." CII's Innovating for Impact Series. USAID's Center for Innovation and Impact (CII). https://www.usaid.gov/sites/default/files/2022-05/AI-in-Global-Health_webFinal_508.pdf.

available and incorporated to train these models for optimal performance, relevance, and sustainability. Safety, security, and privacy approaches to health-relevant data and outputs is of utmost importance and approaches may vary significantly by country. Developing health-related benchmark datasets in multiple languages and applicable to various geographies will be key to supporting AI research in health. AI tools should be designed to integrate into existing health systems, digital health architectures, and healthcare workflows, improving efficiencies and enhancing capacities rather than replacing them. Finally, it is essential to identify ways to measure the impact of AI systems on health systems and outcomes to identify and prioritize tools for scaling and integration.

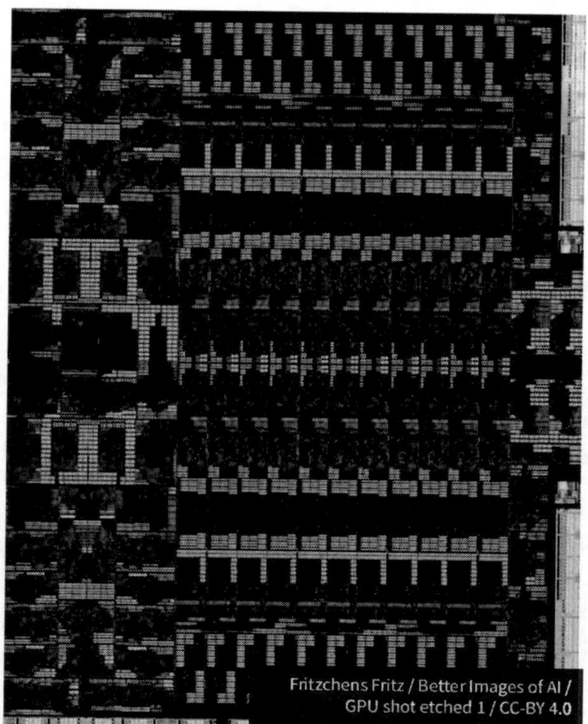
Fritzchens Fritz / Better Images of AI / GPU shot etched 1 / CC-BY 4.0

Global Research Opportunities:

- Design AI-based health applications specifically for and with LMICs, to help ensure such applications address unique challenges and needs, rather than simply applying existing applications across all countries.

- Develop common AI standards, reporting, and terminology to align with broader digital health and health data standardization and interoperability efforts, improving data management and curation for AI systems and tools development.
- Advance efforts to prepare for, detect and monitor, and respond to, emerging global health threats, including pandemics, combining disparate and localized data to protect population and individual health and global health security.
- Explore methods of protecting patient data privacy and meaningful consent and address ethical and integration challenges of AI deployment in global health settings.
- Examine approaches for vetting the quality and safety of AI applications used by providers and patients including misinformation, disinformation, and malicious uses.
- Build an implementation science evidence base to support understanding for the factors that promote effective health worker and patient uptake of AI-based tools to improve health outcomes. Build off the extensive lessons learned, research outcomes, implementation science and principles developed for the broader digital health ecosystems.

4.3.3. Agriculture and Food Security

In high-income countries, AI applications for industrial-scale agriculture[25] are used to maximize yields, minimize inputs, and manage environmental impact. Increasingly in the developed world, agricultural technology (AgTech) innovators and some government agencies are adapting precision agriculture for smallholder farmers, who produce around a third of the world's food consumption and are concentrated in LMICs. These include yield forecasting systems which can help offer tailored advice to individual farmers, low-cost distributed sensor networks, supply chain resiliency systems, robotic systems to augment farm labor support, animal health monitoring systems, and smartphone-based systems for image-based diagnosis of plant diseases and pests. Beyond precision agriculture, AI is being used to supplement inadequate extension systems with agriculture advisory chatbots and to improve credit and insurance modeling, customizing financial services to make them more attractive for smallholder farmers.

Global Research Opportunities:

- Increase efforts to protect and support smallholder farmers, who produce around a third of the world's food, by understanding AI tools applicable in low-resource environments to boost yields, engagement in formal economies, and optimized distribution.
- Integrate data sources such as climate modeling, satellite imagery, and affordable in situ sensors to build more effective models to predict and improve farming practices and yields.
- Work with agricultural scientists, behavioral scientists, and others to develop AI-enabled agricultural decision support tools that can help farmers effectively use model outputs.
- Develop participatory design practices that can be used to include rural actors, including smallholder farmers, in the design and governance of AI tools and datasets.
- Promote AI applications that can be used to improve food and agricultural resilience, especially in the context of mitigating the effects of and adapting to increased prevalence of natural disasters and other consequences of climate change.

---

[25] "Can AI Inclusively Advance Agri-food Systems?" n.d. https://www.genesis-analytics.com/reports-and-other-documents/can-ai-inclusively-advance-agri-food-systems.

4.3.4. AI in Science and Engineering

AI is already enhancing and improving scientific and engineering workflows,[26] from autonomous laboratories creating new materials to deep learning algorithms analyzing how pathogen evolution affects disease spread. New AI techniques could support the continued growth and expansion of science infrastructure, especially when handling large and complex data. Increasingly, scientific applications are shifting from human-in-the-loop to AI-driven design, discovery, and evaluation. Scientists are more frequently leveraging AI to structure processes, optimize large-scale simulations, and operate next-generation instruments. International collaboration is essential to share AI advances and integrate diverse expertise, accelerating global scientific progress. Joint efforts, when paired with appropriate risk mitigation strategies, can help standardize AI methodologies and ensure that innovations benefit a wide range of scientific domains and researchers across different countries.

[26] President's Council of Advisors on Science and Technology. 2024. "Supercharging Research: Harnessing Artificial Intelligence to Meet Global Challenges." Report to the President. https://www.whitehouse.gov/wp-content/uploads/2024/04/AI-Report_Upload_29APRIL2024_SEND-2.pdf.

Global Research Opportunities:

- Expand secure and responsible access of anonymized government datasets for critical research needs with appropriate protections and safeguards.
- Support basic, translational, and applied research in AI that involves collaborations across academia, industry, government laboratories, and agencies.
- Adopt accountability and other methods designed to promote responsible, transparent, and trustworthy AI use throughout all stages of the scientific research process to manage the risks of inaccurate or non-replicable findings from scientific uses of AI.
- Encourage innovative approaches to integrating AI assistance into scientific workflows to support researchers conducting high quality science that utilizes AI assistance responsibly.

4.4. Fundamental Research on AI, including AI Safety, Security, and Trust

AI is still in its early stages of development, and fundamental advances in AI technology and governance are necessary before some AI systems can be considered safe or trustworthy. Recent generative models, such as large language models (LLMs), introduce or exacerbate various risks[27] including issues of robustness, information integrity, and privacy preservation that impact many other types of AI systems (likely including future generations of AI technology). This section focuses on four priority areas where international research cooperation is particularly crucial.

4.4.1. Synthetic content and Information Integrity

While generative AI may bring many benefits, the potential misuse of generative AI to create misleading or harmful content remains a concern - images, audio, video, and text that have been generated or manipulated by AI – can be challenging to identify and understand its lineage. When AI is

[27] National Institute of Standards and Technology. 2024. "Artificial Intelligence Risk Management Framework: Generative Artificial Intelligence Profile." NIST AI 600-1. NIST Trustworthy and Responsible AI. U.S. Department of Commerce. https://doi.org/10.6028/NIST.AI.600-1.

misused to spread dis- or misinformation, it can undermine public health, individual well-being, and trust in institutions, governance structures, news industries, and media, ultimately threatening information integrity in the global digital ecosystem. AI-manipulated content can be particularly dangerous because it can be quickly customized, created, and deployed to reach and influence audiences on a large scale. This could have widespread implications. As the use of AI to create or manipulate digital content becomes more prevalent, it is important for people all over the world to be aware of digital content's origins and ability to detect whether it was manipulated or altered. Research is vital to manage these risks.

Research can help policymakers understand public perceptions and the societal impacts of an increased presence of and exposure to synthetic and authentic content, and identify techniques to enhance digital content transparency, media literacy, and information integrity globally. Addressing this challenge will require a suite of localized approaches, deployed at scale and informed by research, to safeguard the efficacy and authenticity of information online, and empower global audiences to better understand where digital content came from and whether and how it was manipulated. This suite includes algorithms for labeling, watermarking, metadata recording, and synthetic content detection.

Global Research Opportunities:

- Identify mechanisms for enhancing societal awareness, digital media literacy, and transparency about the origins of digital content, including synthetic content. Ensure that these mechanisms work in low-literacy contexts and for people not explicitly or regularly exposed to AI.
- Identify reliable techniques for disclosing and tracking the provenance of digital content (e.g., AI-manipulated images, audio, videos and text), to include watermarking and metadata, that can be applied at scale across platforms, across languages, and across institutions. Assess the robustness, security, and other tradeoffs of these techniques across content modalities.
- Identify data-driven best practices for labeling digital content regarding its provenance in a way that builds trust, promotes transparency, and considers different languages and cultures. Also

explore designing effective user experiences beyond labels that enhance digital content transparency.

- Explore and assess the effectiveness of techniques for the reliable detection of synthetic content, including voice clones, along with safeguards to mitigate the consequences of false positives or negatives. Explore how user interface design can help users respond appropriately to uncertainty in detection results.
- Conduct research to monitor and understand the sociotechnical effects of increased exposure to synthetic content, labeling synthetic and authentic content, and the resulting impacts on the information environment, as well as implications for democratic processes, including by the tactical use of synthetic content against women and LGBTQ+ political and public figures by foreign state and non-state actors and further investigate future harmful uses of synthetic media as technology evolves.

4.4.2. AI and Cybersecurity

International cooperation on AI is essential for improving cybersecurity, including cybersecurity of AI systems and the use of AI for cyber defense. Malicious cyber activity against one country can quickly extend to networks across borders, posing threats to security and stability. Recognizing cyber incidents frequently have global impacts, preventing and responding to these incidents also requires international cooperation. AI is particularly powerful in international social engineering attempts because it provides the ability to tailor cyberattacks in the recipient's native language. Through efforts like the U.S.-led International Countering Ransomware Initiative,[28] global cooperation to address cyber threats is growing. However, more coordination is needed on cybersecurity research and development to identify emerging threats that are unique to or exacerbated by AI systems and to leverage AI to develop effective ways to mitigate security threats.

---

[28] The White House 2023. "International Counter Ransomware Initiative 2023 Joint Statement." The White House. November 2, 2023. https://www.whitehouse.gov/briefing-room/statements-releases/2023/11/01/international-counter-ransomware-initiative-2023-joint-statement/.

Global Research Opportunities:

- Develop AI-driven systems for real-time threat detection, automated response to cyber incidents, and proactive defense measures, leveraging global data sharing, collaboration, and advanced analytics to improve accuracy, effectiveness, compliance with global cybersecurity regulations, and resilience against evolving cyber threats.
- Research methods to enhance the security and robustness of AI systems, including protection from cyberattacks,[29] to ensure confidentiality, integrity, and availability.
- Explore AI techniques that enhance cybersecurity while preserving user privacy to ensure data protection across international borders.
- Advance applications of AI to secure critical infrastructure sectors, such as energy, transportation, and healthcare, against sophisticated cyber threats. This includes developing AI solutions tailored to the specific needs and vulnerabilities of these sectors.

4.4.3. Evaluate AI Systems Using Benchmarks, and Develop Technical Standards based on Pre-standardization Research and Collaboration

Benchmarks, frameworks, and standards for AI as part of efforts to enable greater safety, security, and trustworthiness are still nascent. Benchmarks are standardized tests that can measure AI system performance. To date, most AI benchmarks have used data drawn from a select set of sources, creating a risk that future AI systems may underperform for users and applications in different contexts. In recent years there has been progress in using more representative benchmark datasets (i.e., curated data collections used to evaluate AI capabilities); however, significant work remains. Such work is essential, as researchers are incentivized to demonstrate the performance of new systems and approaches using robust methods. If benchmarks can be made more robust and representative, then diversity (and accuracy) of output may be a valued feature of new AI models, not an afterthought. Similarly, AI standards for testing, evaluation, verification, and validation methods will be most useful if they respond to the needs of diverse demographics around the

---

[29] Vassilev, Apostol, Alina Oprea, Alie Fordyce, Hyrum Anderson, National Institute of Standards and Technology, Northeastern University, and Robust Intelligence, Inc. 2024. "Adversarial Machine Learning: A Taxonomy and Terminology of Attacks and Mitigations." NIST Trustworthy and Responsible AI. https://nvlpubs.nist.gov/nistpubs/ai/NIST.AI.100-2e2023.pdf.

world.[30] AI has been an important focus of activity within standards development organizations, such as the work being done by Subcommittee 42 of the International Organization for Standardization (ISO) and the International Electrotechnical Commission (IEC) Joint Technical Committee 1 (ISO/ IEC JTC 1/SC 42). In support of efforts conducted within Standards Developing Organizations (SDOs), researchers have an important role to play in pre-standardization activities. Pre-standardization research and stakeholder collaboration lay the foundation for future standards development efforts. Robust standards development processes often reflect the widely-accepted principles of transparency, openness, impartiality and consensus, effectiveness and relevance, and coherence. Researchers may also wish to contribute their technical expertise directly to standards projects.

Global Research Opportunities:

- Foster AI standards development through evidence-based practices that are scientifically sound, open, transparent, and reflect the needs and inputs of diverse global stakeholders.
- Build researcher contributions to standardization work into research funding programs.
- Prioritize pre-standardization research into topics where standardization is urgently needed, including terminology and taxonomy, risk mitigation, bias and discrimination, provenance, generated content, and transparency standards about system and data characteristics.
- Build more globally representative benchmark datasets, including datasets that support the implementation of standards.

[30] U.S. Department of Commerce, Gina M. Raimondo, and Laurie E. Locascio. 2024. "A Plan for Global Engagement on AI Standards." NIST Trustworthy and Responsible AI. National Institute of Standards and Technology. https://doi.org/10.6028/NIST.AI.100-5.

Shutterstock Standard License / Photo contributor Gorodenkoff

4.4.4. Fundamental Developments in AI System Design and Implementation

There is significant opportunity for improvements in AI systems' functionality, reliability, and performance to enable use-cases beyond today's state-of-the-art designs. Maximizing the potential benefits of AI technologies will require continuous research into fundamental scientific and engineering dimensions of AI system design and implementation. The improvements this research can drive are crucial for addressing the diverse needs of various applications and industries and have the potential to address constraints faced by researchers in low- and middle-income countries (LMICs). Interoperability, accessibility, and reproducibility of data and research products should also be considered in fundamental developments of AI system design.

Global Research Opportunities:

- Identify avenues for improving the multi-modal performance of AI systems, enabling systems to perform reliably in mixed-media contexts, such as those combining audio, video, and textual inference tasks.

- Explore topics relating to the performance and computational efficiency of AI systems, such as designs for improved data-caching, speculative decoding, or parallelism during training and inference.
- Advance the development of AI systems that better preserve the privacy of users and individuals represented in training datasets, such as through differential privacy and federated learning techniques.
- Improve methods to detect and mitigate potential bias in AI systems and datasets.
- Advance transfer learning methods that enable greater performance in low-data languages, geographic or cultural settings, or other underrepresented application contexts.

4.5. Research on AI's Global Labor Market Implications

Adopting human-centered, socially responsible, safe, secure, and trustworthy AI can deliver substantial economic benefits and accelerate progress on many of the SDGs, including improved labor productivity,[31] management processes,[32] safety, health,[33] fair and equitable hiring, and job quality.[34] AI can positively augment work by replacing and automating repetitive tasks or assisting with routine activities and decisions, which may reduce the burden on some workers and allow them to better perform other tasks. At the same time, labor-related AI implementation carries risks[35] including increased work intensity, mental distress, and reduced agency in managerial decisions related to hiring, evaluation and dismissal, and fair remuneration. Gender disparities, including the gender digital divide, and other asymmetries could be

[31] Kane, Aidan T., and Martin Neil Baily. 2024. "How Will AI Affect Productivity?" Brookings, May 2, 2024. https://www.brookings.edu/articles/ how-will-ai-affect-productivity/.

[32] Nieto-Rodriguez, Antonio. 2023. "How AI Will Transform Project Management." Harvard Business Review. October 3, 2023. https://hbr. org/2023/02/how-ai-will-transform-project-management.

[33] Reinhold, Karin, Marina Järvis, Tallin University of Technology, Aleksandr Christenko, Vaida Jankauskaitė, Agnė Paliokaitė, Visionary Analytics, et al. 2022. "Artificial Intelligence for Worker Management: Implications for Occupational Safety and Health." European Agency for Safety and Health at Work. https://doi.org/10.2802/76354.

[34] Khattar, Rose. 2024. "Will AI Benefit or Harm Workers?" CAP 20. 2024. https://www.americanprogress.org/article/will-ai-benefit-or-harm- workers/.

[35] Lane, Marguerita, Morgan Williams, and Stijn Broecke. 2023. "The Impact of AI on the Workplace: Main Findings From the OECD AI Surveys of Employers and Workers." OECD Social Employment and Migration Working Papers. https://doi.org/10.1787/ea0a0fe1-en.

exacerbated, with a range of disproportionate consequences across diverse sectors and regions. Unequal access to and use of AI in labor markets could also lead to increased imbalances among firms and workers, within and across countries. Additionally, certain uses of AI in the workplace – including for increased worker monitoring – have the potential to undermine collective bargaining and other fundamental principles and rights at work, including freedom of association, non-discrimination, and a safe and healthy working environment.

This section explores research directions touching on several aspects of AI's impacts on labor. In addition to highlighting important research needs, this section closes with strategies to mitigate potential negative labor market implications of AI that are grounded in current evidence and can be refined by further research.

4.5.1. Job Augmentation and Automation

AI, like many past technological advances, has potential to increase productivity, add complexity to jobs, change the nature of some tasks, and fully automate others. Generative AI, in particular, could broaden the scope of the types of tasks that can be augmented or automated, though there is still much uncertainty about how these changes will develop. Effects of AI will vary between countries, but also within countries by occupation, gender, income level, and other factors. Recent research suggests certain types of AI may lead to greater augmentation and automation of tasks in HICs, compared to LMICs, due in part to the prominence of digitized workplaces in these countries.[36] However, more research is needed to examine potential impacts of different types and uses of AI on job tasks, globally, and how this may change with future advancements.[37]

---

[36] Cazzaniga, Mauro, Florence Jaumotte, Longji Li, Giovanni Melina, Augustus J. Panton, Carlo Pizzinelli, Emma Rockall, and Marina M. Tavares. 2024. "Gen-AI: Artificial Intelligence and the Future of Work." Staff Discussion Notes No. 2024/001. International Monetary Fund. https://www.imf.org/en/Publications/Staff-Discussion-Notes/Issues/2024/01/14/Gen-AI-Artificial-Intelligence-and-the-Future-of-Work-542379?cid=bl-com-SDNEA2024001.

[37] Gmyrek, Paweł, Janine Berg, David Bescond, and International Labour Organization. 2023. "Generative AI and Jobs: A Global Analysis of Potential Effects on Job Quantity and Quality." ILO Working Paper 96. International Labour Office. https://doi.org/10.54394/FHEM8239.

Global Research Opportunities:

- Forecast employment trends by studying AI's impacts on tasks in specific sectors and occupations, and how these trends may change based on projections of how AI capabilities and limitations might evolve in the future.
- Conduct analyses of AI adoption and forecast its labor market impacts – including, for example, whether AI may decrease the availability of middle-skilled occupations – on various countries, regions, sectors, and occupations, considering various aspects of identity and social factors including gender, age, geography, language, sexual orientation, race, disability, immigration status, documentation status, ethnicity, and nationality.
- Map AI-related risks and benefits for job design and distribution, task complexity and receptiveness, productivity and wage distribution across contexts. Assess how these risks and benefits may impact job recruitment, satisfaction, and retention, as well as how changes in these factors will impact the larger global economy.
- With particular focus on women and marginalized groups, examine patterns of worker transitions between occupations and industries in response to AI, including whether they are transitioning to higher- or lower-wage jobs, if they are transitioning to jobs in sectors with higher or lower degrees of formality, and if internal or cross-border labor migration is involved in their transitions.
- Perform gap analyses of national labor market data collection systems, especially in LMICs, to determine whether countries can collect robust and accurate data related to AI and work, and to inform the design of indicators of labor market impacts from AI development, deployment, and use.
- Use gender-responsive research methods from different fields of study, including ethnography, anthropology, sociology, and social work, to ensure meaningful inclusion of diverse perspectives in AI labor market research.

4.5.2. New Jobs Resulting from AI Development, Deployment, and Use

As AI continues to develop, so does its value chain and the type and amount of human labor required to support it. Globally, millions of data enrichment workers—who label and validate data to train AI models—work in pay-per-task environments. These workers are primarily from LMICs,[38] recruited for this work due to lower costs to technology companies in HICs. While some data enrichment workers are employed full-time in settings similar to call centers, most work through task-based online platforms.[39] Basic facts about these workers, such as their numbers, locations, working time on the platform, and tasks are unknown. In some cases, these workers may be tasked with reviewing toxic and inappropriate content. As demand for data enrichment grows, more research is needed to understand this sector and develop strategies and frameworks to ensure workers' protections, benefits, and grievance mechanisms.

---

[38] United Nations. n.d. "Valuing Data Enrichment Workers: The Case for a Human-Centric Approach to AI Development | United Nations." https://www.un.org/en/un-chronicle/valuing-data-enrichment-workers-case-human-centric-approach-ai-development.

[39] Tan, Rebecca, and Regine Cabato. 2023. "Behind the AI boom, an army of overseas workers in 'digital sweatshops.'" The Washington Post, August 28, 2023. https://www.washingtonpost.com/world/2023/08/28/scale-ai-remotasks-philippines-artificial-intelligence/.

Beyond data enrichment, it is likely other new jobs and industries will emerge in response to AI, as seen with previous technological advancements.[40] More research is needed to anticipate where these jobs and industries will emerge.

Global Research Opportunities:

- Map the AI value chain to identify jobs that support the development and deployment of AI systems, those created as a result of AI systems, and those negatively impacted by AI systems. Document within these jobs their locations, industries, quality, tasks, impact on worker well-being, relationship to AI, and to whom they are accessible, prioritizing direct engagement with workers.
- Analyze how AI systems are shaped and influenced by the contributions of data enrichment workers of various educational, cultural, linguistic backgrounds, employment classifications, and under different labor conditions and workplace exposure to AI. Assess the effectiveness of unionization efforts and labor regulations to protect and empower these workers.
- Forecast potential global, national, and regional economic impacts of jobs created by, or related to the AI value chain.
- Project how new jobs resulting from AI design, development, and use, including data enrichment work, will change over time, including by studying whether these jobs may require increasingly skilled or specialized labor.

4.5.3. Effects on Inequality

AI development may impact income distribution differently across different groups, countries, regions, and sectors. One study suggests AI deployment may reduce intra-occupational inequalities[41] by benefitting less experienced workers. Overall, more research is needed to understand AI's contribution to global inequality and its distribution along the value chain.

High Income Countries – As different tasks in HICs are automated and augmented, there may be a polarizing effect on labor markets, increasing

---

[40] Agrawal, Ajay, J., Joshua Gans, and Avi Goldfarb. n.d. "An Economic Framework for Understanding Artificial Intelligence." In Chapter 7, 243–45. https://www.whitehouse.gov/wp-content/uploads/2024/03/ERP-2024-CHAPTER-7.pdf.

[41] Brynjolfsson, Erik, Danielle Li, and Lindsey Raymond. 2023. "Generative AI at Work." https://danielle-li.github.io/assets/docs/ GenerativeAIatWork.pdf.

income inequalities. However, mature industries, strong digital infrastructures, and non-routine occupations may help HICs benefit from AI early on, potentially softening harmful labor market impacts. The development of AI-complementary industries in HICs could mitigate the negative effects of automation in these countries.

Low-to Middle-Income Countries – AI will affect each LMIC in different ways, depending on its current ability to develop and deploy AI. Recent research[42] estimates LMICs that rely on manual labor and more traditional industries may benefit less from AI deployment than HICs or other LMICs. The offshoring of work by companies in HICs to lower-cost operations in LMICs – ranging from call centers to manufacturing – has contributed to economic development in many LMICs. While it's possible that offshored jobs may be augmented or new types of jobs created because of AI, the technology could potentially disrupt development offshoring by automating certain tasks, rendering some of these jobs obsolete. Additionally, since many LMICs may lack the digital infrastructure to utilize AI technologies to complement certain tasks, it is possible that companies may reshore labor to technologically advanced countries, potentially widening inequalities between LMICs and HICs. More research is needed to determine how AI may impact jobs that have been offshored by companies in HICs.

Global Research Opportunities:

- Evaluate how AI may impact income inequality and wealth distribution within and between countries, among various worker demographics, sectors, occupations, and regions.
- Assess the impact of AI on small- and medium-sized enterprises (SMEs) and examine factors that may enhance their effective and ethical AI use.
- Research the prevalence and patterns of AI-related outsourcing and nearshoring across and within countries, regions, and sectors. Examine how changes in these practices caused by AI will impact economies on national, regional, and global levels.

---

[42] Cazzaniga, Mauro, Florence Jaumotte, Longji Li, Giovanni Melina, Augustus J. Panton, Carlo Pizzinelli, Emma Rockall, and Marina M. Tavares. 2024. "Gen-AI: Artificial Intelligence and the Future of Work." Staff Discussion Notes No. 2024/001. International Monetary Fund. https://www.imf.org/en/Publications/Staff-Discussion-Notes/Issues/2024/01/14/Gen-AI-Artificial-Intelligence-and-the-Future-of-Work-542379?cid=bl-com-SDNEA2024001.

4.5.4. Risks for Workers

AI's impact on workers' rights may be significant, with risks spanning the global labor market and potentially affecting certain groups of workers, countries, sectors, and occupations more prominently. More research is needed to identify which of the following risks may impact workers around the world – especially for vulnerable populations.

Algorithmic Management and Decision-Making - Algorithmic management uses AI to support, inform, or automate management decisions or tasks, often resulting in increased collection of data and expanded monitoring of workers. Algorithmic management is regularly used[43] in digital platforms and is being increasingly used in warehouses, retail and hospitality, and in manufacturing. This practice can lead to increased work intensity, loss of worker autonomy, reduced job satisfaction, discrimination, and privacy infringement.

Deskilling - As AI augments tasks, some workers' jobs can become simpler and more repetitive, leading to a downward pressure on wages[44] and stalled career growth, especially if workers lack access to reskilling programs.

Wellbeing - AI system deployment may lead to negative health effects[45] for workers in particular sectors and in certain countries and regions due to increased pressure for productivity, diminished human interaction, anxiety related to job security, the assignment of fewer meaningful tasks, and downward pressure on wages. Jobs in the AI value chain, such as content moderation, also present mental health challenges to workers. For example, PTSD caused by constant exposure to violent and graphic subject matter has been documented[46].

Discrimination in Hiring Practices - The use of AI in employment decisions raises concerns[47] about how potential biases in the technology may

---

[43] Aloisi, Antonio, and De Stefano Valerio. 2022. "Introduction — Your Boss Is an Algorithm. Artificial Intelligence, Platform Work and Labour." July 14, 2022. https://papers.ssrn.com/sol3/papers.cfm?abstract_id=4139319.

[44] "OECD Employment Outlook 2023." 2023. OECD. July 11, 2023. https://www.oecd.org/en/publications/oecd-employment-outlook-2023_08785bba-en.html.

[45] Stella, Luca, Osea Giuntella, Rania Gihleb, and Tianyi Wang. 2023. "Keeping Workers Safe in the Automation Revolution." Brookings, September 12, 2023. https://www.brookings.edu/articles/keeping-workers-safe-in-the-automation-revolution/.

[46] Newton, Casey. 2020. "Facebook Will Pay $52 Million in Settlement With Moderators Who Developed PTSD on the Job." The Verge, May 12, 2020. https://www.theverge.com/2020/5/12/21255870/facebook-content-moderator-settlement-scola-ptsd-mental-health.

[47] Bryant, Kalina. 2023. "How AI Will Impact the Next Generation Workforce." Forbes, May 31, 2023. https://www.forbes.com/sites/ kalinabryant/2023/05/31/how-ai-will-impact-the-next-generation-workforce/.

lead to discrimination in hiring, promotions, termination, pay increases, and other areas. Individuals may also experience discrimination from AI models when searching for jobs online.[48]

Shutterstock Standard License / Photo contributor Eva Corbella

Exploitation in New Value Chains - Opaque, international data enrichment value chains have limited regulations, giving rise to global labor abuses[49] like nonpayment of wages, absence of grievance mechanisms, and excessive monitoring.[50]

Misclassification - As algorithmic and remote management rise, companies increasingly outsource jobs to subcontractors.[51] Companies may

---

[48] Wall, Sheridan. 2021. "LinkedIn's Job-matching AI Was Biased. The Company's Solution? More AI." MIT Technology Review, June 25, 2021. https://www.technologyreview.com/2021/06/23/1026825/linkedin-ai-bias-ziprecruiter-monster-artificial-intelligence/.

[49] Gray, Mary L., and Siddharth Suri. Ghost Work: How to Stop Silicon Valley from Building a New Global Underclass. Boston: Houghton Mifflin Harcourt, 2019.

[50] Perrigo, Billy. 2022. "Inside Facebook's African Sweatshop." TIME, February 17, 2022. https://time.com/6147458/facebook-africa-content- moderation-employee-treatment/.

[51] Bernhardt, Annette, Lisa Kresge, Reem Suleiman, and UC Berkeley Labor Center. 2021. "Data and Algorithms at Work: The Case for Worker Technology Rights." UC Berkeley Labor

seek to outsource labor to avoid paying the full cost of employment potentially by misclassifying workers as independent contractors, or through other non-standard forms of work, preventing the workers from receiving the same workplace protections as employees.

Effects on Freedom of Association - AI could potentially weaken workers' ability to exercise their right to freedom of association and right to collective bargaining, leaving them without key advocacy mechanisms to ensure fair deployment and use of AI in the workplace. The increasing use of non-standard forms of employment could either exclude large numbers of workers from organizing and bargaining or significantly increase the legal and practical barriers to these activities. Some workplaces may use AI to monitor, and potentially act against, organizing or collective bargaining activity in the workplace. Many workers are also unaware of AI and automation technology in their workplace, limiting their power to negotiate[52] the introduction and acceptable use of AI with their employers.[53]

Global Research Opportunities:

- Evaluate existing and emerging uses of AI in the workplace internationally and employ longitudinal research to analyze how these uses impact workplaces and the labor market over time.
- Conduct sector-specific comparative studies in LMICs and HICs to determine which sectors and populations will be at the highest risk of algorithmic management, deskilling, misclassification, discrimination, and other risks of AI on workers, with a focus on vulnerable groups.
- Study AI's impact on workers and their communities, with particular focus on mental and physical health.
- Identify country-specific regulatory gaps for all workers, with special attention to non-standard workers, to exercise rights to freedom of

---

Center. https://laborcenter.berkeley.edu/wp-content/uploads/2021/11/Data-and-Algorithms-at-Work. pdf.

52 Johnston, Hannah, Chris Land-Kazlauskas, INWORK, and International Labour Organization. 2019. Organizing On-demand: Representation, Voice, and Collective Bargaining in the Gig Economy. Conditions of Work and Employment Series. https://webapps.ilo.org/wcmsp5/groups/public/–ed_protect/–protrav/–travail/documents/publication/wcms_624286.pdf.

53 Hadwiger, Felix and International Labour Organization. 2022. "Realizing the Opportunities of the Platform Economy Through Freedom of Association and Collective Bargaining." ILO Working Paper 80. International Labour Organization. https://doi.org/10.54394/VARD7939.

association and collective bargaining in the AI value chain or in the AI-impacted workplace.

- Map legal frameworks governing the deployment of algorithmic management in the workplace across countries, focused on the most protective and least protective policies.

4.5.5. Mitigating AI-Related Risks in the Global Labor Market

The following section outlines potential avenues for mitigating AI's potential negative effects on the global labor market, including value chain transparency and oversight mechanisms, policy interventions, and worker empowerment efforts.

4.5.5.1. Value Chain Transparency and Oversight

Supply Chain Tracing of AI Value Chains - Consultations with a variety of stakeholders revealed a primary research need at the nexus of labor and AI—tracing AI value chains from design to data collection, training, testing, deployment, and use. Little is known about these value chains, and research is still needed to map the business relationships and the complexities within them. Mapping these value chains will include determining how many workers are engaged and where, the types of employment involved, conditions of their work, benefits afforded (or not afforded) to them, and their access to grievance and remediation mechanisms. Additionally, there is a need for tracing the value chain downstream, beyond deployment, to the productive use of AI systems. Mapping digital systems in workplaces and companies can explore where, how, and why AI is being used, and the extent of its costs or benefits.

Enforcement Mechanisms - Ethical frameworks must be accompanied by enforcement mechanisms and accountability systems to be effective[54]. Organizations have recommended that countries identify paths to ensure all workers are protected by labor laws, including laws related to wages and hours, child labor and forced labor, human trafficking, occupational safety and health, workplace safety, and the right to organize[55]. A recent OECD report[56]

---

[54] ARTICLE 19. 2019. "Governance With Teeth: How Human Rights Can Strengthen FAT and Ethics Initiatives on Artificial Intelligence." ARTICLE 19. http://creativecommons.org/licenses/by-ncsa/2.5/legalcode.

[55] ILO, ISSA and OECD. 2023. "Providing Adequate and Sustainable Social Protection for Workers in the Gig and Platform Economy." https:// www.ilo.org/wcmsp5/groups/public/– -dgreports/ – -ddg_p/documents/publication/wcms_867535.pdf.

[56] Lane, Marguerita. 2020. "Regulating Platform Work in the Digital Age." No. 1. OECD Going Digital Toolkit Notes. OECD Publishing. https://doi. org/10.1787/181f8a7f-en.

says that countries will likely want to have specialized training for labor inspectors to ensure labor law compliance in the AI value chain. Research could determine potentially effective mechanisms and strategies for enforcing labor laws in these complex supply chains, spotlighting gaps in enforcement frameworks around the world to guide policymakers. Researchers may evaluate effective enforcement in similar supply chains.

Voluntary Commitments - Voluntary impact assessments, social impact labels, and audits can be found in various sectors to validate companies' commitments and ongoing actions to various social, environmental, and ethical causes. Some labels include Fair Trade, B Corp, GoodWeave, and Rainforest Alliance. AI auditing is a new and growing field and does not always focus on implications for workers. Incorporating labor considerations into existing or new voluntary assessments, or into requirements for ethical AI labels or certifications, could show consumers and other companies that certified AI systems are utilizing ethical labor practices in their value chain and have considered the system's impacts on the labor market and their workforce.

Corporate Reporting of AI Value Chains - Corporate reporting of the AI value chain can increase transparency, worker voice[57], and allow for more insightful research regarding corporate operations and ethical AI production and use. Corporate research could include information regarding the use of recruiters and contractors in AI value chains, and how their company mitigates risks of AI-related labor abuses, job displacement, and poor working conditions among suppliers.

Global Research Opportunities:

- Trace the value chains of AI systems and include information about the types of work involved (e.g., piece-rate or task-rate work, hourly wage work), how prevalent each type is, the number of workers engaged in this work, worker location, benefits, pay, hours worked, as well as the collective bargaining environment in the countries in which these workers are employed.
- Study the potential roles of monitoring bodies, supervisory authorities, and self-reporting in impact assessments, audits, and evaluation of the use of automated systems in the world of work.

---

[57] "Worker Voice." n.d. DOL. https://www.dol.gov/agencies/ilab/worker-voice.

- Consider how and where AI may pose unique or significant challenges to labor-focused regulatory bodies – including, for example, the enforcement impacts of business process outsourcing in AI value chains – when exploring effective labor standards and transparency requirements.
- Develop and analyze the effectiveness of impact assessments focused on ethical labor practices in AI value chains, as well as reporting mechanisms for labor transparency and accountability in AI value chains, considering varying data collection and assessment capacities among different countries. Map and evaluate existing corporate due diligence efforts in AI value chains.
- Conduct multidisciplinary research to identify procedures, systems, laws, and entities to hold AI value chain actors accountable for labor abuses. Perform comparative case studies using successful supply chain accountability systems and models from other sectors, including systems that apply to various employment models as well as work in the informal economy.

4.5.6. Policy Interventions

Social Safety Nets - To protect and support workers whose job tasks have been automated by the deployment of AI, some organizations have suggested the expansion of access to benefits such as unemployment insurance or adjustment assistance.

Decent Work in Digital Labor Platforms - The structure of digital platforms has introduced new challenges for workers, and at the same time has served to intensify existing challenges. The ILO Governing Body has included an upcoming agenda item focused on standard-setting on decent work in the platform economy. Countries including Spain, Italy, the United States, and the United Kingdom have started to develop guidance, policies, and/or legislation related to digital labor platforms[58] and worker misclassification, but there is still much work to do[59].

Education and Curriculum Development - Investing in STEM education and in education globally will help prepare the future workforce for AI-related

[58] "Cloudwork (Online Work) Principles." n.d. https://fair.work/en/fw/principles/cloudwork-principles/.

[59] International Labour Organization. n.d. "Extending social security to workers in the informal economy: Policy Resource Package." https://www.social-protection.org/gimi/Emodule.action;jsessionid=QQmVpeOYZajx06_Pu3FFCG74kzFAyx-ps-rJoD-6gX2UQ1emlzjj!-1857443667?id=65.

skills and roles, as well as the potential augmentation and displacement of jobs. Curriculum development can focus on information technology skills, computer literacy, coding, online safety, and ethical technology, as well as communication, critical thinking, teamwork, and interdisciplinary collaboration. Education systems should update curricula based on what skills are in demand to effectively prepare students for the labor market[60] (UNESCO), and should ensure accessibility of the educational infrastructure (e.g., digital textbooks, learning management systems) and curriculum content to ensure a diverse workforce.

Strengthening Collective Bargaining Rights - Collective bargaining plays a critical role in ensuring workers' voices are heard.[61] Without sufficient laws advancing collective bargaining, workers may experience unhealthy working conditions, wage theft, discrimination, harassment, and an absence of grievance and remediation mechanisms. Some stakeholders have recommended strengthening collective bargaining safeguards, to ensure workers are able to negotiate terms of AI use in the workplace and the impacts of AI-related industry changes on their jobs. To effectively bargain, experts[62] stress that workers must know which technologies are being used in the workplace and how.

LMIC-Specific Policies - Funding local research and development in the local AI industry may allow LMICs to minimize reliance on large technology companies based in high-income countries and may contribute to domestic economic growth. Additionally, for LMICs to take advantage of increased investments in STEM education and AI research and development, and to increase greater attraction of investment capital in AI research and development, they may invest in infrastructure to support these endeavors, including adequate computing power, internet access, and electricity.

---

[60] United Nations Educational, Scientific and Cultural Organization. 2022. "Recommendation on the Ethics of Artificial Intelligence." Report. United Nations Educational, Scientific and Cultural Organization. United Nations Educational, Scientific and Cultural Organization. http:// creativecommons.org/licenses/by-nc-sa/3.0/igo/.

[61] Anner, Mark, Matthew Fischer-Daly, Center for Global Workers' Rights, The Pennsylvania State University, ICF Macro, Inc., and United States Department of Labor, Bureau of International Labor Affairs. 2023. "Worker Voice: What It Is, What It Is Not, and Why It Matters." https://www. dol.gov/sites/dolgov/files/ILAB/Worker-Voice-Report-Final-3-6-24.pdf.

[62] Center for Labor and a Just Economy at Harvard Law School. 2024. "Worker Power and Voice in the AI Response." https://clje.law.harvard. edu/app/uploads/2024/01/Worker-Power-and-the-Voice-in-the-AI-Response-Report.pdf.

Global Research Opportunities:

- Assess the ability of existing policy approaches to mitigate AI-specific labor market disruptions (e.g., EU's AI Act, the Corporate Due Diligence Directive).
- Evaluate the readiness of countries' social protection systems to support workers that may be affected by AI-related disruptions and consider the feasibility of potential tax system restructuring to extend social safety nets to all affected workers.
- Develop AI tools to enhance productivity in critical sectors for LMICs (e.g., agriculture, small-scale manufacturing).
- Identify and evaluate effectiveness of proactive industry policies and practices intended to retain staff as tasks are automated and augmented.
- Review countries' privacy and intellectual property laws and explore how they may impact the use and transparency of AI in the workplace.

4.5.7. Worker Empowerment

Skills Training Programs – Upskilling programs, which help workers enhance existing skills or cultivate new skills, and reskilling programs, which aim to help workers transition to new jobs, are both valuable tools for mitigating job disruption caused by AI. Companies can support worker upskilling and reskilling by designing and implementing new training programs, with the involvement of workers, workers' organizations, and social dialogue to ensure that they are robust and effective. Research shows that workers particularly vulnerable to AI-related labor market effects may need targeted incentives to participate in these programs. Research should focus on incentivizing participation and analyzing the effectiveness of these programs in different countries and sectors[63] (OECD, "Skills Matter" 2019). Upgrading the training infrastructure and training program content is necessary to ensure accessible and inclusive upskilling opportunities. Upgrading the training infrastructure and training program content is necessary to ensure accessible and inclusive upskilling opportunities.

Data Transparency – Algorithmic management has given rise to increased collection of worker data. Workers' organizations[64] have

[63] "Skills Matter." n.d. https://www.oecd-ilibrary.org/education/skills-matter_1f029d8f-en.
[64] UNI Global Union. 2021. "Top 10 Principles For Workers' Data Privacy and Protection." https://www.dol.gov/sites/dolgov/files/ILAB/Worker- Voice-Report-Final-3-6-24.pdf.

recommended that workers should be able to access data collected about them in the workplace, and that there are processes to have data reviewed, edited, and/or deleted. Advocates also recommend that source code and AI models remain accessible, and that research prioritize the development of standards and techniques to facilitate the understanding of AI systems by workers and workers' organizations.

Collective Bargaining and Worker Voice – Collective bargaining is crucial for protecting and empowering workers during technological shifts. Workers and their representatives, especially from underserved communities, should have genuine input in the design, development, testing, training, use, and oversight of AI systems in the workplace. Doing so could help ensure workers benefit from AI and are protected from its negative effects. Worker voice improves working conditions and is associated with more effective adoption of advanced technologies.[65] Understanding how worker representation impacts labor market outcomes, working conditions, and job responsibilities is increasingly important as firms continue to adopt AI.

Global Research Opportunities:

- Determine whether worker representation in decision-making moderates or exacerbates AI's impact on working conditions, job design complexity, labor market outcomes, and mediating factors (e.g., AI literacy of worker representatives). Develop case studies in different occupations and sectors globally to determine how and where worker organizations' efforts have been effective in empowering workers in various supply chains.
- Evaluate current levels of AI literacy across countries, sectors, and demographics and identify future beneficial skills for workers in various sectors, occupations, and countries.
- Analyze the effectiveness and best practices of participatory upskilling and reskilling models across different demographics and regions, and at various levels of learning with attention to funding requirements, including tax implications, as well as scalability and applicability in LMICs.

[65] "Bringing Worker Voice Into Generative AI | MIT Sloan." 2023. MIT Sloan. December 21, 2023. https://mitsloan.mit.edu/centers-initiatives/ institute-work-and-employment-research/bringing-worker-voice-generative-ai.

- Through stakeholder consultations, develop, or evaluate existing, frameworks for achieving worker protections related to AI, including for organized workers, workers not engaged in collective bargaining, and workers engaged in platform work in the AI value chain, with attention to achieving worker protections related to data collection and use, and workers' mental and physical health concerns.
- Analyze the effectiveness of worker grievance and remediation mechanisms for algorithmic management and examine common worker and union grievances in the context of use of AI in the workplace.

Section 5: Recommended Research Practices

The practices included in this section can inform and support engagement with diverse sets of international partners. Such efforts will be most effective when tailored to the level of AI-preparedness of global AI partners. These proposed practices also provide an avenue for the implementation of the previously proposed principles that guide this research agenda. The following practices are separated by categories of global stakeholders engaged with the research landscape with a focus on research funders, research hubs, and research teams.

5.1. Research Funders

Research funders encompass organizations, institutions, or entities that provide financial support for scientific, academic, or technological research projects. They allocate resources to researchers and research institutions to facilitate the advancement of knowledge, innovation, and development in various fields. Research funders can encourage international cooperation on responsible AI research through the following:

Elevate Transparency – Transparency in AI research can include disclosing input materials, including training data sources, compute usage, hardware requirements, resource consumption, and third-party data enrichment. While research funders and publishers can introduce transparency requirements, a comprehensive approach will require broad cooperation, such as coordinating practices across international research communities and institutions.

To the extent that computing resources are supported by research funders, data on energy use, water use, and environmental impacts of the resources should be shared with researchers.

Open Funding Calls to Support International AI Research Collaboration – Funding calls are often restrictive regarding eligible countries, and individual research projects are typically carried out bilaterally. Differences between legal requirements can underlie challenges to collaboration between researchers from different countries. New mechanisms could help to support deeper collaborations in AI research with countries in LMICs, where traditional arrangements can be inadequate. Exploring new mechanisms will help to ensure AI research and development in partnership with these countries is engaged in and benefits from global advancements.

Promote Research Infrastructure Accessibility for Diverse Demographics – With the increasing size of datasets and complex computational resources required to participate in AI research, it is important to explore whether and how access to research infrastructure could be expanded. Providing state-of-the-art infrastructure across the research community (including open-source software and open datasets as appropriate) could improve access to responsible and transparent resources to support knowledge, innovation, and development in AI.

Offer Connection Opportunities – Productive collaborative research depends on researchers knowing and trusting each other. While international conferences offer some opportunities for connection, funding for focused meetings on specific topics specifically help facilitate building connections between diverse global researchers, further enhancing these collaborations. A multinational research consortium[66] allowing researchers to pair with foreign partners could simplify procedures and reduce barriers to collaboration.

Pursue Public-Private Partnerships – Public-Private Partnerships (PPPs) enable research funders to leverage the resources and expertise of the private sector through risk-sharing arrangements. These arrangements are essential in the AI space, as private sector parties have more resources to dedicate to experimentation and fundamental research and development. When properly designed and executed, PPPs can offer innovation in project design, incorporation of global expertise, and access to new sources of capital.

---

[66] Trillion Parameter Consortium (TPC). 2024. "Trillion Parameter Consortium (TPC) - Generative AI for Science and Engineering." Trillion Parameter Consortium (TPC) - Generative AI for Science and Engineering. August 9, 2024. https://tpc.dev/?r34icsym=202409.

5.2. Research Ecosystem Hubs

Conferences, journals, and professional societies provide key hubs for international engagement and the codification of AI research practices. Leading AI conferences are experimenting with mechanisms for encouraging international engagement and strengthening a focus on responsible research. For example, some conferences include a required ethics statement for submitted papers, and in a few cases, these have led to papers being removed from consideration. Research ecosystem hubs have the potential to set the basis for ethical norms for research globally and should consider the following good practices.

Incentivize Reproducibility of Research – The growing interest in AI and the rise of preprint servers, like arXiv, have improved access to recent research and enhanced the accessibility of scientific papers still awaiting peer review. However, it also poses challenges to scientific integrity. Academic journals and conferences typically select submissions that are of high quality and significance. Research ecosystem hubs should create mechanisms that incentivize the reproducibility of published research and elevate reproducibility as a global best practice to enhance scientific integrity in this space.

Foster Broadly Accepted Best Practices Around Research Publications – It is important to address the surge in paper submissions driven by differing researcher assessment methods. Differences between how countries assess the success of research via publication seems to be driving a surge in the volume of papers submitted to top academic conferences. Tying salaries and promotions to publication numbers encourages a "flood the zone" strategy and unethical behaviors like collusion rings. Promoting best practices for peer-review quality can mitigate these issues.

Coordinate and Collaborate Around AI Research Guidelines – Research is informed by researcher background, data and resources, methodology selection, planned dissemination and a multitude of other factors. International coordination and collaboration on research guidelines can assist research teams in fostering inclusive, relevant, rigorous, conflict-of-interest-free, and trustworthy AI development, global collaboration, and equitably distributed AI benefits.

Support Research Beyond Topics Prioritized by the Private Sector – Collaboration with the private sector, including through mechanisms like Cooperative Research and Development Agreements (CRADAs) with national and international partners at facilities such as DOE national laboratories, is valuable. Academic researchers are highly aware of industry interests (such as issues surrounding the maintenance of data centers). Competition for resources can lead researchers to be less engaged on research issues that expose them to diverse communities and contribute to maximizing AI's global benefit.

Nidia Dias & Google DeepMind / Better Images of AI / AI for Biodiversity / CC-BY 4.0

Provide Guidance to Navigate the Evolving Regulatory Landscape – Differences in regulatory regimes pose challenges for researchers. Professional societies and international convening bodies can guide researchers in navigating the evolving regulatory landscape and work to promote ethical standards throughout the entire research community.

5.3. Research Teams

International collaboration on AI research is, ultimately, implemented through and by research teams. The make-up of research teams will determine which perspectives and expertise are represented, which methodologies are employed, and what research resources are accessible to the team, itself. Researchers should consider the following good practices when designing a team for a research project:

Prioritize Multidisciplinary Teams – Multidisciplinary teams (including researchers in data science, computer science, and engineering, as well as those from social sciences and humanities) are key to holistically unpacking social impacts and opportunities of AI technologies. Encouraging multidisciplinary teams, while also supporting productive multidisciplinary engagements, can enhance outputs of applied research. AI used in global challenges, such as agriculture or for climate modeling, will require multidisciplinary teams for model validation and successful integration into applied workflows.

Collaborate with Local Researchers – Funds can go to researchers from various universities, organizations, and locations; however, it is essential to encourage partnership with local researchers—those situated as close as possible to the populations being studied or impacted by the results of the research. Doing so leads to organic partnerships, long-term network building, and a pooling of resources and expertise.

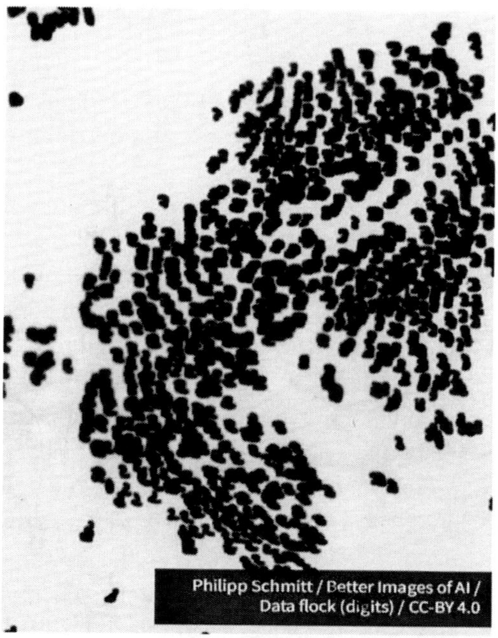

Make Use of Sociotechnical Methodologies and Research Design – It can be difficult for researchers to assess or audit AI models and tools and their impacts, particularly in settings that are novel, unfamiliar, or outside of the researchers' domestic context. Sociotechnical methods for system design and evaluation consider multiple factors outside of the technical, including human, social, and organizational, and typically deliver better value to stakeholders.

Using these methodologies helps to ensure the research considers, from inception, the context within which it will be conducted and context in which results may translate into action.

Risk Assessments – AI has significant potential to enhance the ways in which scientific research is done and to make progress on difficult research problems but also introduces potential for new risks and harms. Testing and evaluation of AI systems, techniques for quantifying, tracking, and reducing risks of harm, and studies on community impact are all areas where additional funding for research, development, experimentation, and innovation are needed. Furthermore, international research collaborations offer the opportunity to disseminate best practices, and promising advancements.

Section 6: Conclusion

The Global AI Research Agenda (GAIRA) proposes a guiding framework for research funders, policymakers, and practitioners to contribute to a balanced international AI research ecosystem where technological progress and human well-being advance hand in hand.

The recommended principles and priorities outlined in this agenda aim to align AI development with fundamental values, promote human rights and human well-being, and to help ensure responsible AI development, globally. By implementing this agenda, the international research community can foster safe, secure, and trustworthy AI development, global collaboration, and equitable access to the benefits of AI, preventing misuse and aligning AI deployment with societal values. Progress in creating this balanced ecosystem would be characterized by the effective promotion of research into the priority areas within international research networks. Doing so involves continuing conversations with global research stakeholders to maintain engagement and ensure that each research opportunity receives the necessary attention. The combined effort in each area would lead to more successful collaboration, demonstrating that the whole is greater than the sum of its parts. Given that the priorities and objectives can be too numerous for any single entity to tackle alone, this endeavor necessitates a global call to action, fostering collaboration and burden-sharing across the international research community. Ultimately, this collective effort will pave the way for a future where AI technologies will contribute positively to our global community.

Index

S

T